Lady M

About the Author

Colin Brown is the former Deputy Political Editor of the *Independent* and Political Editor of the *Sunday Telegraph* and the *Independent on Sunday*. He worked for thirty years as a lobby journalist at Westminster and is the author of five books, including *Whitehall: The Street That Shaped a Nation* (Simon and Schuster).

Lady M

The Life and Loves of Elizabeth Lamb, Viscountess Melbourne 1751–1818

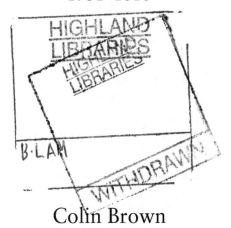

Colin Brown

AMBERLEY

To my wife and colleague, Amanda

First published 2018
This edition published 2019

Amberley Publishing
The Hill, Stroud
Gloucestershire, GL5 4EP

www.amberley-books.com

The family tree on page ix is kindly provided by Graeme Hill.

Dover House, longitudinal section, page 254, from *Survey of London: Volume 14, St
Margaret, Westminster, Part III: Whitehall II*, ed. Montagu H Cox and G Topham Forrest
(London, 1931)

Picture on page 51 courtesy Firle Place, the family seat of Nicholas Gage, 8th Viscount Gage

British Library Cataloguing in Publication Data.
A catalogue record for this book is available from the British Library.

ISBN 978 1 4456 8945 6 (paperback)
ISBN 978 1 4456 6651 8 (ebook)

Typeset in 10pt on 12pt Sabon.
Typesetting and Origination by Amberley Publishing.
Printed in the UK.

Contents

Timeline

28 July 1747	Brother Ralph Milbanke born
15 October 1751	Elizabeth Milbanke baptised
10 May 1752	John Milbanke baptised
25 October 1760	George III assumes throne
1763	Seven Years War against the French ends; Britain rules the waves, gains most of India, but close to bankruptcy
1767	Elizabeth's mother, Elizabeth Hedworth, dies
13 April 1769	Elizabeth Milbanke marries Sir Peniston Lamb
3 May 1770	Peniston Lamb born
8 June 1770	Sir Peniston and Elizabeth Lamb gain Irish title as Lord and Lady Melbourne
15 March 1779	William Lamb born
January 1781	Lord and Lady Melbourne made Viscount and Viscountess
17 April 1782	Frederick Lamb born
1770-1782	Tory Lord North administration
1775-1783	American Revolutionary War
November 1783	Lord Melbourne appointed a Gentleman of the Bedchamber to Prince of Wales
11 July 1784	George Lamb born

21 April 1787	Emily Mary Lamb born
31 August 1789	Harriet Lamb baptised
1800	Act of Union creating United Kingdom
June 1803	Harriet Lamb dies
24 January 1805	Peniston Lamb dies
3 June 1805	William Lamb marries Lady Caroline Ponsonby
1806	Nelson's funeral, Pitt's death, Whig coalition
5 February 1811	Regency begins
1812	Lord Byron affair with Lady Caroline Lamb
2 January 1815	Byron marries Lady Melbourne's niece, Annabella Milbanke
18 June 1815	Battle of Waterloo; Lady Caroline goes to Brussels to tend her brother
18 July 1815	Lord Melbourne awarded English peerage
1818	Lady Melbourne dies at Melbourne House, Whitehall, now the Scotland Office

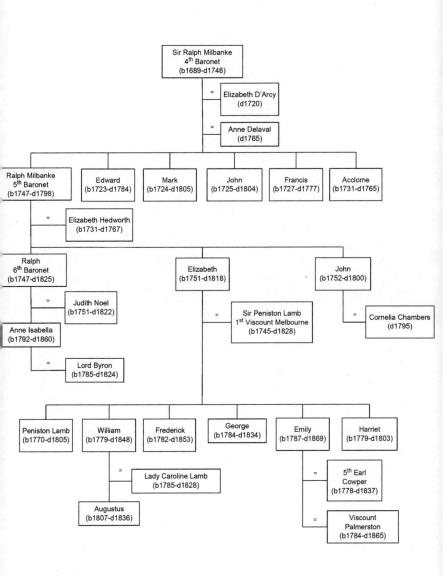

When any one braves the opinion of the World,
sooner or later they will feel the consequences of it.

Lady Melbourne, letter to Lady Caroline Lamb,
her daughter-in-law, 13 April 1810

Love is all imagination and nothing else.

Lady Melbourne to Lady Caroline Lamb, 1814

The best friend I ever had in my life, and the cleverest of women.

Byron on Lady Melbourne, 17 November 1813

Introduction

I first encountered Elizabeth, Lady Melbourne in the private suite of offices of former Deputy Prime Minister John Prescott, in the basement of a building next to Horse Guards on Whitehall.

I was researching a book on Whitehall[1] and had gone 'below stairs' at the Scotland Office, known as Dover House, where Prescott had temporary offices while he waited for the work on the Cabinet Office range along Whitehall to be completed for his Department of the Environment, Transport and the Regions.

Behind the bland Portland stone of Whitehall, I had discovered many surprises in researching my book – Wolsey's wine cellar, astonishingly still intact beneath the Ministry of Defence main building; the Tudor passage in the Cabinet Office that Henry VIII strode along with Anne Boleyn and his court on his way to play 'real' or royal tennis at his indoor court; and the Admiralty boardroom with its wind clock and amazing carvings by Grinling Gibbons.

Nothing, however, had prepared me for the surprise when I was allowed into Prescott's offices and discovered he was holding Cabinet committee meetings and working in the early days of the Blair government in what looked like the set of a Georgian costume drama. The walls were pea-green and decorated in the Etruscan style. There were gilded coronets over the doors of the interconnecting suite of rooms and French windows opening on to a pretty rose garden on Horse Guards Parade. To my untrained eye, it looked particularly feminine. I wondered aloud why Prescott was working in a Georgian lady's boudoir. Prescott, a shrewd politician despite his bluff Northern image, instantly visualised the unwanted headline: 'Scandalous cost of Prescott's Regency-style wallpaper'. He quickly told me the restoration of the rooms had nothing to do with him. It was all done by English Heritage, and had something to do with the history of the building.

I was intrigued, and decided to investigate. I found my first impression was astonishingly near the truth. They had once been the private suite of Lord and Lady Melbourne; the lady had been one of the great Whig hostesses of the Georgian period when Dover House was their private London home. Upstairs, in the airy rooms overlooking St James's Park, where the Scottish Secretary of State had her desk, Lady Melbourne hosted parties for the leading figures and great wits of the age, including Charles James Fox, the Whig leader, and his acolyte, the hilarious playwright Richard Brinsley Sheridan, who usually arrived slightly tipsy and in sparkling form.

It was at the top of the elegant staircase to the first floor that Lady Melbourne's daughter-in-law Lady Caroline Lamb met Lord Byron at a waltzing party and embarked on a wild and very public affair that scandalised even the broad-minded Georgian aristocrats who came to sup at Lady Melbourne's table. For a time it made Melbourne House the most notorious address in London.

In her prime, in the 1770s and 1780s, Lady Melbourne was described by Nathaniel Wraxall in his *Historical Memoirs of My Own Time* as 'a commanding figure exceeding the middle height, full of grace and dignity, an animated countenance, intelligent features, captivating manners and conversation: all these and many other attractions, enhanced by coquetry, met in Lady Melbourne.'

Lady Airlie, great-granddaughter of Emily Cowper, Lady Melbourne's daughter, writing a century later in her history of Whig society, said Elizabeth's 'chiselled features, her brilliant complexion and large blue eyes, with a glint of humour in them, still remain to us on the canvases of Sir Joshua Reynolds and Cosway'. In an age when hair was powdered, she wore her bright brown hair unpowdered. As she grew older, added Lady Airlie, she 'became rather large in her person, but this does not seem to have impaired her charms'. In her sixties she was still able to turn heads, including Lord Byron's.

Lady Melbourne was born not long after the Highland uprising for 'Bonnie' Prince Charlie, when the Hanoverian monarchy was still insecure. Her life spanned some of the most dramatic events in British history, including the loss of the American colonies, the wars against Revolutionary France, the rise of Napoleon and the threat of invasion, Napoleon's defeat at the Battle of Waterloo, the first Regency crisis triggered by the 'madness' of King George III and the advent of the Regency that brought her lover, the foppish Prince George, to the throne.

Prescott's rooms were the scene for many private meetings between Lady Melbourne and Byron, the man who had cuckolded her favourite son, William Lamb. Lady Melbourne and Byron became so close that they were suspected of being lovers when she was sixty-one and he was twenty-four.

They exchanged rings, and wrote many letters like lovers – Byron invariably addressed them to 'Lady M'. 'Lady M' told Lord Byron: 'You know you may come to me whenever you please and that I am always happy and delighted to see you.'[2] She was not like other women. She was not gushing or giddy like her more famous friend, Georgiana, the Duchess of Devonshire, who, a generation earlier, had created the ridiculous fashion for towering hairdos enclosing novelties such as toy ships and topped by ostrich plumes. Byron said of Lady M: 'When I do see a woman superior not only to all her own [sex] but to most of ours I worship her...'[3]

Lady M was shrewdly calculating, entertaining, 'mannish' in her attitude to sexual affairs, sympathetic without being sentimental and a good listener who was interested in what men had to say; but above all, she was discreet. She was, said her son's biographer Lord David Cecil, 'essentially a man's woman' – it was only among men she felt sure enough of her ground to be her robust self.[4] Men enjoyed laughing away an hour on her sofa; she was never touchy, difficult, shocked or low-spirited. Byron compared her conversation to champagne and valued her shrewd advice. In a letter to his publisher John Murray, he declared: 'To Lady Melbourne I write with most pleasure, and her answers – so sensible, so *tactique*...'[5] She was, he said, 'the best friend I ever had in my life, and the cleverest of women'.

She used sexual favours as a means to advance her family to rank alongside the Devonshires, the Spencers, the Ponsonbys and the Hollands. She lived by the unwritten rule that a married woman in Georgian society had a duty to produce an heir for her husband to protect his family's inheritance, but after that a woman was entitled to have affairs while her husband followed his own peccadilloes. Given the rudimentary state of birth control, Georgian wives often produced children by men who were not their husbands; they were discreetly adopted as their own.

Lady Melbourne produced six children and only one, her first son, Peniston, was by her husband, Lord Melbourne. Whether or not Lord Melbourne acquiesced in his wife's affairs is hard to prove, but he does not seem to have complained at the rich rewards her affairs brought him. Prince George, the Prince of Wales (who became the Prince Regent in 1811) was generally believed to be the father of her fourth son, also christened George, and repaid the Melbournes by putting Lord Melbourne on his private staff as a Lord of the Bedchamber and elevating them to a viscountancy.

In an age of strong women, Lady Melbourne was an influential confidante for the politicians of her day, but Lady M was much more than a Georgian agony aunt. She was a political player in her own right at a time when women not only did not have the vote, but also could not hold public office. When leading Whigs wanted to influence the Prince Regent, they came to Lady Melbourne. Lady Airlie in her history of the period, *In Whig Society*, says she was above all else a 'femme politique and her influence combined with the Duchess of Devonshire's admiration for Charles James Fox gave the political tone to the Society of Devonshire House…'

The distinguished historian, Professor L. G. Mitchell, author of a biography of Elizabeth's son, the Second Viscount Lord Melbourne, told me Lady Melbourne's influence was greatly assisted by her liaison with the Prince of Wales but it was 'founded on something yet more substantial – she was recognised as not only very beautiful but also as very intelligent. She had the sort of *esprit* that Whigs greatly valued. Her friendships with people like the Devonshires could not have survived without it…'

Lady Melbourne was often compared in her lifetime to the Marquise de Merteuil in *Les Liaisons Dangereuses*; her intrigues may seem shocking even to liberal-minded readers today. She may now be regarded as a monster who would do anything for her ambition, but she was living in an age when women had no vote and were barred from entering into politics at any official level. She could bed leaders of the Whig party but she could not sit in the public gallery of the House of Commons.

There has been a revival of interest in the Melbourne family largely due to the portrayal on television of William Lamb, the Second Viscount Melbourne, as Queen Victoria's first Prime Minister, by the handsome Rufus Sewell. Women certainly found the elder statesman attractive, as this portrait by the actress Fanny Kemble of one of his dinner parties at Brocket Hall testifies:

> I sat for some time opposite a large, crimson-covered ottoman, on which Lord Melbourne reclined, surrounded by those three enchanting Sheridan sisters, Mrs Norton, Mrs Blackwood (afterwards Lady Dufferin), and Lady St Maur (afterwards Duchess of Somerset, and always Queen of Beauty). A more remarkable collection of comely creatures, I think, could hardly be seen…[6]

But William owed his career in politics to the drive of his mother. She did not live long enough to see him became Victoria's mentor and lend the family title from a small village in the Derbyshire Dales to the state capital of Victoria in Australia.

Lady M's rise from the squire's daughter in the North Riding of Yorkshire to the pinnacle of Georgian society is an object lesson in ambition set against astonishing change both for her elite society, and the world beyond her drawing room. There have been collections of her letters to Byron, but she has never had a full biography devoted to her extraordinary life. On the 200th anniversary of her death, it seems a good time to put that right.

Colin Brown
Blackheath, 2018

I

A Marriage of Convenience

The Milbankes and the Lambs gathered in the elegant drawing room at the home of Dr Robert Lamb, the Bishop of Peterborough, in the early evening of Thursday 13 April 1769 to witness the wedding of Elizabeth Milbanke to the Bishop's nephew, Sir Peniston Lamb.

The bride was seventeen, with striking chiselled features, blue eyes and lustrous brown hair. She was wearing a dazzling set of diamonds said to be worth £30,000 – a gift from her husband. The bridegroom was twenty-four, a man-about-town, a Member of Parliament and immensely rich.

Sir Peniston had inherited more than £500,000 in cash and £500,000 in property and land[1] – around £125 million at today's prices[2] – with the baronetcy when his father, Sir Matthew Lamb, a lawyer, died a year earlier on 6 November 1768.

Sir Peniston's uncle who was to officiate at the wedding could have stepped out of the pages of a novel by Anthony Trollope. He was a wine-swilling

Elizabeth's baptism at Croft 15 October 1751. (Courtesy of North Yorks County Record Office)

The wedding register for Elizabeth's marriage to Sir Peniston Lamb.

bon viveur who liked nothing better than fox hunting with hounds at his brother's Brocket estate at Hatfield in Hertfordshire where he had been rector since 1763.

The Bishop's house in St George Street was next to the fashionable Hanover Square that was attracting the new Georgian moneyed middle classes. It was part of the fast-developing area to the east of Hyde Park known as May Fair after the scandalous annual street carnivals that had been banned only five years earlier for lowering the tone with their sideshows, bare-knuckle fights and clandestine weddings by curates prepared to tie the knot in secret for a guinea a time.

In the countdown to Elizabeth's society wedding, a special licence had to be obtained on 11 April to enable Elizabeth, who was still a minor, to marry in the Bishop's house. Two people were missing from the wedding on the Milbanke side – Elizabeth's handsome mother, Lady Elizabeth Milbanke, who had died two years earlier and her elder brother Ralph Milbanke, aged twenty-two, who may have known what sort of man his sister was about to marry.

Elizabeth missed her mother's guiding hand and her advice before her wedding but she appears willingly to have entered into her marriage vows, for better or for worse. The Bishop recorded the details in a neat hand in the marriage register:

> Sir Peniston Lamb Baronet of the Parish of St James Westminster and Elizabeth Milbanke of this Parish, a Minor, were married in the dwelling house of the Right Reverend the Lord Bishop of Peterborough in St George Street Hanover Square by and with the Consent of Sir Ralph Milbanke Baronet the natural and lawful Father of the said Minor by special Licence this thirteenth Day of April in the year One Thousand seven hundred and Sixty Nine by me.

He signed it 'Ro [Robert] Peterborough'. The bride and groom added their signatures below the Bishop's before the bride's father Sir Ralph and her younger brother John signed as witnesses. The married couple drove off in Sir Peniston's private carriage for their honeymoon at his private estate at Brocket Hall, leaving the Bishop and the guests to enjoy a wedding feast with no expense spared.

Sir Peniston's estates included the neo-classical Brocket Hall near Hatfield in Hertfordshire with good fox hunting land, and Melbourne Hall, a Renaissance-style stone pile in the rolling hills of Derbyshire and surrounded by hundreds of acres of prime farming land with copses of trees for pheasant shoots. He also had inherited a town house on the best side of Sackville Street, off the bustling West End thoroughfare of Piccadilly.

Sir Matthew's son appeared bent on frittering his fortune away as fast as possible as a carefree bachelor with the rich fun-loving friends he had made at Eton, on horse-racing, gambling, hunting, shooting, and whoring. Peniston 'indulged in all the pleasures of a pleasure-seeking age' according to the Victorian historian William McCullagh Torrens. He said Sir Peniston was 'on the whole a good-for-little indolent apathetic kindly man who never had a quarrel in his life'.[3]

His wealth dwarfed Elizabeth's dowry of £10,000 from her father, Sir Ralph Milbanke, the fifth baronet. Elizabeth had yet to be launched into London society but she brought with her something that Sir Peniston and his sister Charlotte wanted more than money – respectability.

Sir Peniston's wealth was based on 'new money'. The Lambs were seen as parvenus by the polite ladies who ruled the closely-knit incestuous world of Georgian society, known as the *bon ton*. To them, Sir Peniston was from a short line of get-rich-quick lawyers, who were little more than servants to the landed aristocracy they aspired to join. The Marchioness of Salisbury, estranged wife of James Cecil, the sixth Earl of Salisbury, had put it about with some justification that Sir Matthew Lamb had got rich by plundering the Salisbury family's estates.

Sir Peniston's father amassed his fortune in a suspiciously short period of time as a financial and legal adviser to a string of aristocratic families including the Salisburys, who owned the Jacobean Hatfield House on the hill overlooking the medieval market town of Hatfield. Sir Matthew had been their trusted legal adviser and a frequent visitor to the house built in 1611 by Robert Cecil, the first Earl of Salisbury, the Machiavellian political adviser to Queen Elizabeth I. The Marchioness must have been outraged when their upstart lawyer bought the neighbouring estate at Brocket Hall and became their neighbour.

Sir Matthew had promptly set about demolishing the old Elizabethan hall at Brocket and replacing it with his brash redbrick house done in the fashionable Palladian style to match his status. Today Brocket Hall sits proudly on a hill overlooking manicured greens and a lake in the middle of an eighteen-hole golf course owned by a Shanghai billionaire.

The Lamb baronetcy dated back only fifteen years to 1754 when Sir Peniston's father was given the title as a reward for supporting the Whig government of Henry Pelham and his brother, the Duke of Newcastle. The Milbanke title went back to the Restoration in 1660.

Elizabeth was taught at her mother's knee the Milbankes were not from ordinary farming stock. They could trace their roots to the court of Mary, Queen of Scots and a courtier called Ralph Mealbanks or Milbancke, who held the courtesy title of cupbearer at Holyrood Palace and was one of her closest attendants.

The fate of Mary Stuart – the murder of her husband Lord Darnley, her probable rape and marriage by Bothwell and her abdication – was a powerful lesson for Elizabeth about the importance of prudence with reckless lovers, especially when dealing with royalty.

Ralph Milbancke was forced to flee south across the border in the chaos after the bloody murder of Mary's alleged lover, David Rizzio, in 1566 by allies of her jealous husband. Ralph settled with his wife Dorothy in Chirton near North Shields, Northumberland and prospered from the lucrative coal trade in the Newcastle area. They passed on their wealth to their son called Mark. A grandson, also called Mark Milbancke, who was twice mayor of Newcastle, consolidated his growing riches from coal when he married Dorothy Cocke, one of three daughters, known in the local dialect as 'Cocke's canny hinnies', of another wealthy Newcastle alderman, Ralph Cocke. They were married on 4 July 1629 at the Newcastle cathedral of St Nicholas, underlining their families' local importance.

Mark Milbancke chose to back the Royalists when Newcastle was besieged in the English Civil War by Scottish forces from the north. He signed a letter by the city fathers swearing to die for the king, but he survived a bloody attack and prospered from the war. London, a Parliamentary stronghold, was desperate for coal after the execution of Charles I and Milbancke got rich shipping it south from the pits he had acquired in the North East.

Mark Milbancke was wealthy enough after the war to buy Halnaby Hall, an Elizabethan manor house, in the North Riding of Yorkshire from Sir Matthew Boynton, a Parliamentarian whose family was scarred by the war – Boynton fought for the Parliamentary side but his son died fighting for the Royalist cause at the battle of Wigan Lane.

When Cromwell died, Matthew supported the restoration of the monarchy. He sent a considerable sum to Charles II in exile on the Continent to return to England and claim the crown. Milbancke was listed among the proposed

Knights of the Royal Oak – named after the tree in which the future king hid from the Roundheads – as being worth £2,000 a year (equivalent to £275,000 a year today). He was rewarded with a knighthood, but he passed it on to his son, also called Mark, who became the first baron Milbanke in 1661.

The title was passed down through four generations to Elizabeth's grandfather, Sir Ralph Milbanke, the fourth baronet who unexpectedly inherited the title and the Halnaby estate in 1705 at the age of seventeen. He inherited it from his older brother, Sir Mark Milbanke, nineteen, who, according to family legend, died after falling from a hay cart.

Sir Ralph also inherited a passion for breeding racehorses from his father and set about turning the stable block at Halnaby Hall into one of the most prestigious stud farms in the region. An expert in the history of racing in Yorkshire, David Wilkinson, wrote that in the county, marriages often mirrored the breeding of horses.[4] It is likely this is how Sir Ralph came to marry Elizabeth D'Arcy in May 1708. They joined an extensive network of family connections in Yorkshire and for Sir Ralph, it was a marriage made in heaven; if Elizabeth D'Arcy had been a mare, she would have been a thoroughbred.

She was from a powerful Yorkshire family with deep roots in horse breeding. Elizabeth's great uncle, James D'Arcy, the MP for Richmond, was Charles II's Master of the Royal Stud at Sedbury Hall near Bedale, a short ride from Halnaby, and his son tried to keep up that tradition. James's mother was a member of the Belasyse family, whose country seat was at Newburgh Priory in Yorkshire.

Elizabeth D'Arcy's brother, Robert D'Arcy, was the third Earl of Holderness. He became Lord Lieutenant of the county, a member of the Privy Council and a senior courtier to George I. The Earls would become powerful patrons of the Milbankes.

Elizabeth D'Arcy was twenty-one and Sir Ralph was twenty when they settled down to married life at Halnaby, developing their stables as a stud. A year later, they had a daughter, Bridget, named after Elizabeth's mother, on 21 June 1709 at St Martin's church in York. Bridget later married Sir Butler Cavendish Wentworth and became known as Lady Wentworth.

The son Elizabeth and Sir Ralph hoped for never came; Elizabeth died in 1720 at the age of thirty-three without producing a Milbanke heir. Her death was a shattering blow to Sir Ralph who, at thirty-two years of age, was left a widower with a daughter, and no male heir. Within two years of his wife's death, Sir Ralph married again, this time to another heiress from the North of England, Anne Delaval.

She was the daughter of a wealthy family who had owned a country estate at Seaton Delaval in Northumberland since the Norman Conquest.

She produced the heir Sir Ralph wanted and plenty to spare. Anne and Ralph's first son was baptised Ralph like his father at the fourteenth-century family church of St Peter hard by the ancient river crossing at Croft-on-Tees on 1 June 1722. He was to become Elizabeth's father. They had five more sons in rapid succession at Halnaby Hall: Edward in 1723, Mark in 1724, John in 1725, Francis in 1727 and Acclome in 1731.[5]

The first baronet, Sir Mark Milbanke had built a fine red brick square house in the classical style on the site of the old Elizabethan house. It still had part of the Elizabethan house at its core but was faced in red brick with stone quoins, balustrading around the roof and a handsome stone entrance porch reputedly influenced by Inigo Jones, pioneer of Palladian architecture in Britain. Halnaby Hall was a home fit for a gentleman squire of fashion.

When she arrived as the mistress of Halnaby Hall, Anne wanted something more comfortable with more bedrooms for their expanding family and more room downstairs to relax. They added a new wing at Halnaby Hall to provide the latest fashionable must-have for country houses: a long, elegant drawing room and dining room with floor-to-ceiling windows, fine fireplaces and ornate mirrors in which to relax and gossip while admiring the gardens. Above the extension, they added new family bedrooms with views over their fields.

Their initials, RMA, were found in the twentieth century on a rainwater downspout with the date 1728 and they survive on a superbly crafted wrought-iron gate to the kitchen garden. It is possible Sir John Vanbrugh, who had designed the English Baroque masterpieces Blenheim Palace and Castle Howard, had a hand in the new wing. He had been commissioned by Anne's great uncle, Admiral George Delaval to build a new mansion at Seaton Delaval Hall. The Admiral died before the house was finished when unhorsed while galloping on his estate. It was left to his nephew, Captain Francis Blake Delaval, Anne's father, but it was not until 1728 – the same date as the entwined initials at Halnaby – that the Delavals moved in to their new house, which is now a National Trust property. The Trust guide to Seaton Delaval Hall says the 'Gay Delavals' had wild parties, and played outrageous tricks on their guests, including raising fake bedroom walls to expose their naked guests to view while cavorting in bed, or using hidden winches to lower a four-poster guest bed into a tank of cold water while their unsuspecting guests were in it.[6]

The Milbankes were more restrained than the Delavals but their son Ralph Milbanke, aged twenty-four, caused a family crisis when he got the daughter of his father's business associate pregnant. Elizabeth Hedworth was sixteen, the daughter by his second wife of John Hedworth, one of the main coalmine owners in Sunderland and MP for Durham for over thirty years until his death aged sixty-three.

They had a rushed marriage to avoid their child being born out of wedlock. The month before the wedding, on 31 May 1747, her father died 'in his chariot in Leicester on his journey from Bath'. The stress on Elizabeth must have been great; being heavily pregnant, she had to go ahead with the wedding on 4 July at the Hedworths' historic house, Chester Deanery in Chester-le-Street. Little more than a month later, Elizabeth gave birth to a healthy son. Their child was christened Ralph at their local church in Chester-le-Street on 20 August.

Ralph's own father died at Halnaby the following year on 28 May 1748 and was buried in the Milbanke vault. As the oldest of six brothers, Ralph, twenty-six, inherited the title as the fifth Milbanke baronet together with the Halnaby estate including the stables of the Halnaby stud, and over 2,000 acres of prime farming land in the North Riding of Yorkshire. Through his wife, he also inherited considerable wealth from the Sunderland mines.

Sir Ralph and Elizabeth went to live with their son Ralph at Halnaby and Anne, his grandmother. In 1750, they had a daughter who died three days after being born. She was buried at Croft-on-Tees but in 1751 they returned to the church by the River Tees to christen another daughter. Her exact date of birth is not known; that was not unusual – the high level of infant mortality made it more important to record the baptism than the birth to show infants were accepted into the Church before they died.

On 15 October 1751 the Milbankes rode to her christening in their private carriage the three miles from Halnaby to the church of St Peter at Croft along muddy lanes – the summer had been one of the wettest on record and the autumn saw more storms. The entry in the parish register, written in the curate's spidery hand, says simply: 'Elizabeth, daughter of Sir Ralph Milbanke Bart. and his wife, Lady Elizabeth was … baptised.'[7] Her uncle Francis became the curate there two years later. A year later they returned to christen a second son, John, on 10 May 1752.

The stone church with its squat steeple has hardly changed since Elizabeth was christened there. These days the church is locked after the theft in 1993 of a silver cup donated by Sir Ralph in 1761. I found the key at the nearby Croft Hotel by the ancient stone bridge marking the Yorkshire border with Durham.

On opening the old wooden church door, I was struck by a sight that spoke volumes about the Milbankes – the Milbanke Pew. It is a plush private family box with red velvet curtains to keep out draughts and looks as though it has been lifted out of a theatre and put down onto four stout wooden pillars at the side of the nave. The Milbanke Pew towers seven feet high over the rest of the pews, so the ordinary folk had to look up to the Milbankes as well as the Holy Cross when at prayer.

The private box is reached by a wooden staircase – the Milbankes' own stairway to heaven – with a dog gate to keep out strays. I tentatively climbed the stairs to the Milbankes' private box but was stopped by a second locked door to keep out the riff-raff. I was unable to sit where Elizabeth had gazed down on the congregation below but I noticed the hard wooden bench inside is softened with red velvet cushions. It was easy to imagine Elizabeth looking down on the folk below when her uncle Francis, the curate of Croft, preached his Sunday sermons.

Behind the Milbanke Pew is the Milbanke family tomb where successive Milbanke baronets are buried. It was created for the first Sir Mark Milbanke in 1680 with a plain block of marble surmounted by a huge helm to remind the world that came after him that he had died a knight of the realm.

Nikolaus Pesvner, the architectural critic, thought the Milbanke Pew was 'presumptuous' but he was relatively mild in his disapproval[8] in comparison with the ecclesiastical historian John Charles Cox (1843-1919), who said it was 'vulgar… the most ghastly, and almost profane pew in the kingdom, especially as comfortless-looking seats at the far back of the church were ostentatiously labelled "For the Poor". What a comment on St James ii 2, 3!'[9]

It would have been impossible for Elizabeth to leave the church without feeling the Milbankes were closer to God than ordinary mortals, unless her uncle Francis reminded the Milbankes of Matthew 19:24: 'I tell you, it is easier for a camel to go through the eye of a needle than for someone who is rich to enter the kingdom of God.' I find it hard to believe that Francis would have dared take this as his theme before the lord of the manor, even if he was his brother. Elizabeth's father was part of the growing middle classes in Georgian Britain. Despite living in rural Halnaby, he and his wife regarded themselves as fashionable people, part of the landed gentry, with powerful friends and a member of the family at the court of George II.

Elizabeth and her brothers enjoyed an idyllic childhood at their father's stud farm, with the horses on the gallops and the stables as their playground. That came to an end when her oldest brother Ralph was sent away in 1758 to be educated as a gentleman at Westminster School next to the Abbey, like his father.

Three years later, her youngest brother John was sent to Eton. Perhaps it was a sign of their growing social status that her father chose to send John there. It may also have been to toughen him up – as the second son, he would not inherit his father's estate and he was earmarked for a career as a soldier. John might have taken part in the bruising battle between the boys of the

Eton Wall Game. He remained at Eton until 1767 before joining the First Regiment of Guards.[10]

While her brothers were boarding at their public schools, Elizabeth was privately educated at home. She learned to write with elegant flowing bows to her letters. She learned to speak and write French, the language of the court, fluently. She loved music and learned to play the piano and sing. She also loved poetry and word games. In 1792, long after she had become a leading lady of London society, she had one of her word puzzles published in *The Times*:

> Form'd long ago, yet made today
> Most employed when others sleep
> What few would care to give away
> Yet none can wish to keep!

The answer to the puzzle was in the title: a bed.

As a child, she was surrounded by servants and two loving female family members, her mother Lady Elizabeth Milbanke and her grandmother, Lady Anne, who both gave the Milbankes the added cachet of their family connections.

Sir Ralph became a leading figure in Yorkshire life as a local magistrate and squire. He took his duties seriously, placing items in the local press to warn poachers on his estate they would be caught and severely punished. In 1754, when Elizabeth was three years old, he became an MP. He first stood for Scarborough on the windswept east coast of Yorkshire through the patronage of Robert D'Arcy, the fourth Earl of Holderness, who became Secretary of State for the Northern Department in the same year. Holderness later arranged for Sir Ralph to take over a seat at Richmond, a few miles from Halnaby, which was in his gift. He was to prove a valuable ally.

On 2 July 1759, the Earl of Holderness appointed Sir Ralph Colonel commanding the Richmondshire battalion of North Riding militia. The militiamen were used to enforce law and order before the regular army and the police but their duties were mainly ceremonial, marching about the county and firing volleys on the king's birthday.

The militias had proved almost useless in putting down the Jacobite rebellions of 1715 and the second uprising in 1745. The government sought to make them more professional by introducing compulsory call-up by a random ballot of names with the Militia Act of 1757. It proved hugely unpopular with the working classes who could not afford to buy an exemption like the sons of the rich. They were forced to serve in the militias for three years, often being taken away from farms where their labour was vital for their family's survival, or face imprisonment.

Sir Ralph soon found he was no longer playing at soldiers. Elizabeth's father was ordered by Holderness to march his men to the ancient market town of Hexham near the Scottish border on 9 March 1761 to confront a mob of 5,000 men protesting against the call-up. Elizabeth, aged nine, was not there but what transpired at Hexham must have been a bloody lesson in law and order that she would remember for the rest of her life.

There was a tense but peaceful stand-off between the protestors and her father's militiamen until midday when a large body of miners, between two and three hundred strong, launched an attack to break through the Richmondshire lines. Their aim was to break into the main hall where the records were kept and burn the lists of names of those being called up.

After firing warning shots, the militiamen were ordered to fire a volley directly at the protestors, causing carnage. Over forty were killed and many more were injured. Some were carried away dead in carts, others on horses. Many staggered away dying of their wounds and stained the fields with their blood. An eye-witness wrote to *The Leeds Intelligencer*:

> One poor creature, whose husband had been carried by dead a little before, came by screaming in such a manner that we heard her so far as the Abbey Gate. His name was Daniel Bowman, a labouring man, and a very inoffensive one but would go out to see what was going forward; he has left seven children. A poor woman, a widow (one Carter) with eight children and big with another going to the market to look after her son, was shot dead, and her son shot through the thigh, and they say cannot live. A woman who was come from Newcastle for a few days to see a relation and was with child, was shot through the belly as she was standing at a window.[11]

The death toll was four times greater than the atrocity at St Peter's Fields, Manchester, that became known as the Peterloo Massacre and a cause célèbre for the labour movement, yet it is forgotten today outside Hexham. Another officer gave the men the order to fire. Sir Ralph was sufficiently unperturbed to have his portrait painted in 1784 when he was sixty-three proudly wearing the uniform of the North Riding militia. His coat is red with dark blue facings and his left hand rests on his sword, which was never drawn with intent. He looks benignly to the left of the canvas, his grey hair curled over his ear. It is the sort of painting that would be hung in Halnaby Hall to recall the days when he was called to do his duty.

Elizabeth never questioned her father's role in the Hexham Massacre. She was firmly on the side of law and order when bread riots were put down by a cavalry charge under her windows in Whitehall half a century later.

It is hardly surprising that Elizabeth Milbanke grew up at Halnaby with a burning desire to make her mark in the world outside the North Riding. Her uncles broadened her horizons with their tales when they returned to Halnaby. Mark Milbanke, who was sent to join the Navy in 1736 at the age of twelve, rose to become an Admiral and colonial governor of Newfoundland. Uncle John Milbanke became rich through his marriage in 1764, when Elizabeth was thirteen, to the wealthy heiress Mary Watson-Wentworth. She was the daughter of Thomas, the first Marquess of Rockingham, who built Wentworth Woodhouse at Rotherham in Yorkshire, one of the greatest mansions in England.[12]

Acclome Milbanke was sent off to become a soldier. He joined the fifty-sixth regiment of foot from Northumberland and rose through the ranks to become a major. His regiment took part in the capture of Havana, Cuba, but he died there in 1765, possibly from malaria, when Elizabeth was fourteen.[13]

Uncle Francis Milbanke entered the Church. In a clear piece of nepotism, his brother ensured he got the living as curate of St Peter's in 1753 – a post he kept for the next twenty-five years.

Elizabeth perhaps learned her most useful lessons for life from her uncle Edward who had become a courtier when he was thirteen, long before she was born. He spent a lifetime at the court of George II, thanks to the patronage of the fourth Earl of Holderness. She may have had a yellowing copy of *The Newcastle Courier* that recorded on 8 May 1736: 'Edward, second son of Sir Ralph Milbanke of Halnaby kissed the king's hand on his being accepted as a page of honour to his majesty.'

Edward gained the royal family's trust, which Elizabeth learned was vital for a courtier – along with an ability to keep secrets. He was promoted when he was nineteen to become equerry to the king's oldest son, Prince Frederick and his German wife, Princess Augusta of Saxe-Gotha-Altenburg. Edward was an insider at the Court of St James's during a stormy period of palace politics. The artistic Prince Frederick was the heir to the throne, but his father preferred his fat, belligerent younger brother, William, the Duke of Cumberland, who became known as 'Butcher Cumberland', after he brutally crushed the Scottish highlanders, destroying their homes and attempting to destroy their culture following the Battle of Culloden in the Jacobite Rebellion of Forty-Five.

Frederick rebelled against his father – a common trait among the Hanoverians in England – but died before he inherited the crown. Despite this, Edward Milbanke was kept on as the equerry to the prince's widow, Augusta of Saxe-Gotha-Altenburg, the Dowager Princess of Wales, at

Carlton House. He was so trusted that he continued in her service after her son was crowned George III in 1760.

It was also probably through uncle Edward that her mother, Elizabeth Hedworth, was introduced to Frederick's second son, Prince Edward. She was sufficiently admired to sit for a portrait by the society artist Sir Joshua Reynolds in 1755. This was further evidence the Milbankes were making their mark in metropolitan London and rent books for the period show they occupied a house on the south side of Brook Street at number 41 in the heart of fashionable Mayfair from 1756 to 1775, later the home of the Guards Club, and a few doors down from Claridge's hotel.

During her visits to St James's Palace the young Prince Edward, who had a reputation as a womaniser, formed 'an attachment' to Elizabeth. She was eight years older than Prince Edward and in her late twenties when the liaison began. Their affair was a closely guarded family secret until it was let slip by Elizabeth's son, William Lamb, the Second Viscount Melbourne, over the dinner table to Queen Victoria in 1838 when he was her Prime Minister. The young Queen Victoria noted in her journal after discussing the Milbanke family at Windsor Castle:

> Lord M [Melbourne] told me his mother's mother was a Miss Hedworth. 'She was a very handsome woman, Lady Milbanke,' he continued. 'She was a great favourite of the Royal Family, a great favourite of Edward, Duke of York, who died abroad at Monaco; supposed to be an attachment there.'

Elizabeth Hedworth, Lady Milbanke, died suddenly in 1767 at the age of thirty-six in Bath, possibly while she was taking the spa waters for her health. Elizabeth was fifteen when the Milbanke family, Ralph, John and Elizabeth, and their grieving father watched while her uncle conducted her mother's funeral at St Peter's, Croft-on-Tees. Did they sit in the 'vulgar' Milbanke Pew for so personal a service?

A few months after her burial, Prince Edward was struck down by fever on his way to Genoa, allegedly to meet another mistress, and died in Monaco on 17 September aged twenty-eight. He was buried at Westminster Abbey.

The prince's 'attachment' to Lady Milbanke may explain why her husband Sir Ralph Milbanke never took possession of the Reynolds portrait of his late wife. Sir Ralph survived his wife by thirty-one years, and made no attempt to buy it. The painting of Lady Milbanke remained unsold in Reynolds' studio after the artist's death. However, Reynolds' accounts show that in 1773, her daughter Elizabeth bought the portrait of her mother. By then, she was making plans to move into her new mansion in Piccadilly.

2

Peniston

Sir Peniston Lamb might have stepped out of *The Rake's Progress*, Hogarth's cautionary series of etchings, and could have suffered the same fate as that poxed and penniless wastrel had his sister Charlotte not taken him in hand.

It was rumoured Sir Peniston Lamb had been living with his mistress, Harriet Powel, at his father's townhouse at 28 Sackville Street in Piccadilly and that she had called herself Harriet Lamb before he married Elizabeth Milbanke.[1]

In the year after inheriting his fortune on the death of his father, Sir Peniston had begun spending his way through his money in pursuit of pleasure, gambling at cards in the clubs of St James's, horse racing at Sandown and Goodwood on the south downs, and drinking with his riotous friends. Charlotte, who was twenty-five, a year older than her brother, did not begrudge Peniston his inheritance or need his money. She had quite enough for herself. She had married Henry Belasyse, the second Earl Fauconberg in 1766 and received £20,000 on her marriage from her father Sir Matthew Lamb.

The Belasyses were wealthy and influential figures in Yorkshire with a country seat at Newburgh Priory in the Yorkshire village of Coxwold. Henry's father, the first Earl Fauconberg, was a Lord of the Bedchamber to George II and a member of the Privy Council. When the first earl died, he bequeathed an additional £2,000 to Charlotte's husband and put £8,000 in trust for her sole use which, added to the money she had already received, amounted to £30,000 – £3.7 million today.

Charlotte did not like to see her father's inheritance frittered away by her brother's extravagance, nevertheless. She decided he needed a wife and she had someone sensible in mind. Newburgh Priory was within an easy ride of Halnaby and it is likely she met Elizabeth Milbanke socially before suggesting her as a possible wife for her brother. The Belasyses would have also known the Milbankes from their business links in the North East. The Belasyses were rooted in Durham, the town represented in Parliament for thirty-four years by Elizabeth's maternal grandfather, John Hedworth, who owned a colliery at nearby Sunderland. Their network inevitably connected through the Earl of Holderness's patronage at Westminster.

Elizabeth's father, Sir Ralph Milbanke and Charlotte's late father, Sir Matthew Lamb almost certainly knew each other from their time in the House of Commons. They overlapped at Westminster for over twenty years. Sir Ralph stepped down as the MP for Richmond in 1768 after the Earl of Holderness sold the seat, the same year Matthew died and Peniston Lamb entered the Commons as MP for the pocket borough of Ludgershall.

Elizabeth was a well-considered choice to help preserve the Lamb family fortune. She was eye-catching, well-educated and from a good family. She rode well, and was from good breeding stock. Above all, Charlotte realised Elizabeth was as shrewd as her brother Sir Peniston was foolish.

Sir Peniston was persuaded by his older sister to meet Elizabeth Milbanke, and she arranged for a number of chaperoned meetings between the two, probably in Yorkshire and later at his mansion at Brocket Hall in Hertfordshire to impress Elizabeth's father, the North Country squire, Sir Ralph. Peniston finally asked for Elizabeth's hand in marriage. Sir Ralph regarded their daughter's marriage to the rich landowning Sir Peniston as a good match. He knew Elizabeth was strong-willed enough to make up her own mind and he must have calculated that the rich bachelor would provide her with the route into Georgian society to which she aspired. Peniston was also good-looking, if a little delicate and thin-faced.

Viscount Melbourne's biographer, Torrens wrote with a heavy dose of Victorian romanticism that at twenty-three, when he inherited his father's fortune, the young baronet found himself 'a person of no small consideration. Women persuaded him that he was handsome; politicians only wanted to know what were his views; in the county [Hertfordshire] it was hoped he would reside constantly, and complete the improvements at Brocket his father had begun. Society opened its arms to so eligible a recruit and before six months, he was the suitor, slave and betrothed of one of the fairest women of the time...'

Sir Peniston broke the news he was to marry in a letter to William Fox, the family's faithful steward at Melbourne Hall: 'My wedding is fixed for next Thursday.' This sounded as though he felt his fate had been sealed by others.[2] Perhaps it had.

The day before the wedding, they visited a solicitor's office to sign the marriage settlement. It was signed by Elizabeth and Sir Peniston and was witnessed on the Milbankes' side by the bride's father, Sir Ralph and her younger brother, John, who gave his address as Wimpole Street in Marylebone.

On the Lambs' side it was witnessed by Sir Peniston's brother-in-law Lord Belasyse and two wealthy friends of Sir Peniston's father, Henry Vane the Earl of Darlington, aged forty-three, and John, the second Earl of Ashburnham, aged forty-five, a courtier to George II and Master of the Great Wardrobe to George III, who was one of his father's clients.[3]

The signature of Ralph Milbanke, Elizabeth's eldest brother, who would become the sixth baronet when their father died, was conspicuously absent from the marriage contract. I could not find his name among the signatures as a witness to any of the wedding documents. Perhaps he was too busy with the stud farm in Yorkshire to see his sister married. It is more likely that despite his fortune, Ralph objected to the man Elizabeth was about to marry. If Elizabeth had been warned about Sir Peniston's mistresses, she appears not to have let his reputation put her off.

As his part of the marriage contract, Sir Peniston agreed to provide Elizabeth with a private income of £2,000 per annum after tax – equivalent to £250,000 today. It would be raised in rents from some of Sir Peniston's estates, which he put into trust for her. These included the manors of Melton Mowbray, famous for its pies and locally produced stilton cheese; the parsonage of Melbourne with the capital messuage (house and yard); and farms in Over Haddon and Bakewell, all formerly the estates of the Coke family, who had owned Melbourne Hall for generations, before his father, Sir Matthew Lamb married into their family.

Sir Ralph Milbanke provided a dowry of £5,000 for his daughter's marriage portion, and £5,000 in cash to her husband. He also provided for a further £5,000 to be given to Elizabeth from Sir Ralph's estate when he died.

William Hogarth satirised such marriage contracts in *The Wedding Settlement* from his series of six etchings, *Marriage A-la-Mode*: the bridegroom has gout and dreams of spending his bride's dowry on a new house, while a lawyer called Silvertongue tries to persuade the bride how to invest her fortune; her two pet dogs are chained together, to symbolise the shackles of matrimony. At least Sir Peniston did not have gout.

In Richard Brinsley Sheridan's farce *The Rivals*, Lydia Languish calls the wedding contract a 'Smithfield Bargain' implying marriage has become a cattle market. A better analogy for the union of the Milbankes and the Lambs would have been the thoroughbred stud sales where both families were so much at home. Elizabeth was viewed as a thoroughbred mare, to produce an heir for Sir Peniston Lamb.

She had no problem in fulfilling that duty. She was pregnant when Sir Peniston commissioned the artist George Stubbs to produce a group portrait as a 'conversation piece' to celebrate the union of the Lambs and the Milbankes. It was to be given pride of place in the grand dining room at Brocket Hall overlooking the lake. Stubbs was already famous for his skill at painting the racehorses on which Sir Peniston and his louche friends had wagered such large sums. His landscape painting of the 'Milbankes and the Melbournes' shows Elizabeth, her father, her younger brother and her husband rather woodenly posed, with Sir Peniston on a thoroughbred. Elizabeth is seated in a small open carriage, a phaeton, drawn by a single white pony. Her auburn hair is swept up under a stylish bonnet; she wears a white shawl over a pink satin gown, which conceals her pregnancy. She wears soft grey gloves and in her right hand she carries a crop that is resting on her lap. She holds the reins in the left land, suggesting she can look after herself, despite her tender years. She is staring out of the canvas with a sideways glance, her slightly hooded blue eyes fixed on the viewer, and there is a faint smile on her lips, as if she is amused at being traded by her father, though the Countess of Airlie in her account of Whig society said her 'pouting sullen mouth' had a 'look of obstinacy'.[4]

Her father is standing beside her carriage; his arms are resting on the side of the carriage, as if he is trying to protect her in the act of giving her away. He looks a kindly soul, with soft eyes, and a sad mouth. He stares resignedly across at the two other figures in the landscape – John Milbanke, Elizabeth's younger brother, who was at the wedding; and the dashing bridegroom, Sir Peniston Lamb.

John Milbanke was seventeen at the time of his sister's marriage. He is in the centre of the canvas, but he is the least important in it. John is standing by his grey horse in a jaunty tricorn hat, a blue jacket with a long light fawn waistcoat and riding boots. He is posed casually, with his legs crossed, leaning on his horse which is nibbling at the grass, and he is completely ignoring the presence of the principal figure on the right of the painting: Sir Peniston Lamb. Sir Peniston is painted in left profile looking across at his bride-to-be and is mounted on a rich chestnut Arabian stallion – the Ferrari of its day – whose sleek lines shout thoroughbred and money. He is leaning slightly forward, his right hand casually fastened on a rein and his left hand resting on his hip, with his blue jacket gathered behind. Sir Peniston looks relaxed, but the composition looks strangely stiff and lifeless for a conversation piece. There is a small dog yapping at the horse but the stallion ignores it.

Today the painting, measuring ninety-seven cms by 147 cms, is displayed in room thirty-five at the National Gallery, having been purchased for the nation in 1975 to stop it being exported. Art students from around the world crowding in the galleries to study the canvases hardly gave it a second glance on the day I saw it, as they trooped through to the gallery next door to see the more famous *Haywain* by Constable, J M W Turner's *Fighting Temeraire* or the rearing racehorse *Whistlejacket* painted by Stubbs for its owner, the second Marquess of Rockingham for a special niche at Wentworth Woodhouse.

It is easy to understand why it is ignored. At first glance, the horses seem more animated than the humans. But that serves to underline the message more clearly than Hogarth that this is a painting about the human stud farm. It is intended as a confirmation of a binding contract about property and power. Love has nothing to do with it. Lady Melbourne once said: 'Love is all imagination and nothing else.' She was under no illusion – it was a marriage of convenience to consolidate the wealth of two families.

The Stubbs expert, Judy Egerton, who included the painting in a Stubbs exhibition she curated at the National Gallery, said: 'Underlying Stubbs' "Conversation" is the expediency of a union between new money and an old county family, no uncommon thing in English social life. Stubbs' design accords each individual character (and horse) equal rights, gracefully uniting them under the canopy of a spreading oak tree. The colouring is tender, the creaminess of the pony as finely judged as the rosy satin of his mistress's skirts. But in this "Conversation" no one is conversing; instead there are scarcely definable tensions in the air…'[5]

The wedding group has a sylvan backdrop, with a large oak tree and some rocks that were regularly used as scenery by Stubbs. Creswell Crags in Derbyshire had been used by Stubbs as a dramatic backdrop for his painting *Lord Rockingham's Arabian Stallion being led by a Groom*, and the spreading oak tree had featured in his group portrait of Captain Samuel Sharpe Pocklington with his wife and sister in 1729.[6]

Stubbs's group in the wedding picture, three men and the teenage bride, also underlined the fact that Elizabeth was setting out into a male-dominated world. But the real tensions were over a figure who was not there – absent from the wedding, Elizabeth's older brother, Ralph Milbanke, is also missing from the Stubbs composition. Ralph later married the primly moralising Judith Noel and changed his name in 1815 from Milbanke to Noel to protect her inheritance. The judgmental Judith Noel later regarded Elizabeth with disdain when she learned she had several lovers. But Judith thought Elizabeth's husband was worse. She wrote in her journal eight years after their wedding that Elizabeth was 'too good' for 'her lord and master' Sir Peniston Lamb.[7]

The Lambs' wealth did not impress people like Judith Noel, who was more interested in rank and respectability. Georgian families were highly sensitive to the relative values of titles, underpinned by good breeding. Judith took it one stage further in later life by refusing for years to socialise with both her in-laws, Elizabeth and Sir Ralph Milbanke, because of the 'scandal' surrounding their private lives.

She undoubtedly would have viewed the Lambs as socially inferior. One family history of the Milbankes says the Lambs – before marrying into their family – 'pursued the professional walks of life', meaning they were next to being tradesmen; they were certainly not gentlemen. Jane Austen picked up the point a generation later when she mocked the pretentions of the socially superior Lady Catherine de Bourgh and the silly Bingley sisters in *Pride and Prejudice* because they regarded themselves as socially superior to the Bennetts, ignoring the fact that 'their brother's fortune and their own had been acquired in trade'. In most Georgian marriages, money was a defining factor in a gentleman's or lady's prospects of marriage but money with good breeding was even better.

Sir Peniston's grandfather, Matthew Lamb, was a diligent small-town solicitor. He spent a lifetime running a respectable country legal practice in Southwell, Nottinghamshire for local landowners and businessmen. Matthew's brother, Peniston Lamb, was also a lawyer but he was in a different league. Peniston had a lucrative legal practice in London at Lincoln's Inn specialising in probate and property law for some of the wealthiest aristocrats in the country. He was paid large sums to disentangle complex legal problems in wills, property and marriage contracts for his high-class clients or to tie others in legal knots.

While Peniston was weaving his lawyerly spells for his rich clients, his brother Matthew plodded modestly through his life in the shires. He had two sons, Robert, the eldest, who entered the church and became Bishop of Peterborough, and Matthew, who was born in 1705 and followed his father into the law. Matthew was sent to work under his uncle Peniston's wing and the boy quickly learned the tricks of the legal trade in probate and conveyancing law. In 1720, Peniston Lamb became a freeman of the Royal African Company, which was set up by the Stuarts to exploit gold and then slaves in West Africa. In 1731 he sailed to the West Coast of Africa to oversee the switch in his company's trade from human cargo to gold dust and ivory.[8]

Matthew's uncle Peniston Lamb never married and when he died in 1734, he left a legacy to his nephew Robert that helped to pay for his rise in the

Church, but Peniston left the bulk of his estate, all his 'goods and Chambers in Lincoln Inn' worth around £100,000 – about £14.5 million today – to his twenty-nine year old nephew, Matthew Lamb. He also left his lucrative client list that was to prove a golden bequest for Matthew.

Under his uncle's tutelage, Matthew had become a clever land agent, legal adviser and moneylender to the members of the aristocracy he aspired to join. His uncle's clients included some of the oldest aristocratic families in England. He was skilled at unravelling legal knots in his clients' wills. Torrens wrote he immersed himself in 'pleading and demurring, weaving settlements and ravelling threads of adverse wills'.[9]

He also acted as a banker to some of his rich clients, drawing on his own increasing wealth to provide the landowning aristocrats with loans at handsome rates of interest. He thus made himself indispensable to the landed aristocracy when they were short of money. The third Duke of Marlborough was paying the colossal sum of £9,000 a year in interest on what must have been huge loans from Matthew Lamb.[10] Lord Egmont wrote: 'Lamb is very rich and is necessary to and consequently intimate with a great number of the nobility ... He can do most of any man with Lord Salisbury.'[11]

Matthew was already rich when his father died on 29 January 1735, and he took over the clients from his Southwell practice. They were mostly small landowners, shopkeepers and farmers, the backbone of his community – his father left a group of friends each a gold coin in his will. His clients included Thomas Coke, the owner of Melbourne Hall in Derbyshire, a respected former vice-chamberlain to Queen Anne, who was married to Mary Hale, a great beauty in her day.[12]

The Cokes had a daughter, Charlotte, who was born in 1710 and a son, George Lewis Coke, who was born five years later. Thomas and Mary Coke both died in 1727, when Charlotte was seventeen, and her brother was twelve, leaving them orphans. They were looked after by her mother's family in Codicote, a small village to the north of Hatfield in Hertfordshire. Matthew Lamb looked after the legal affairs for Melbourne and its estates until his death when his son took over. A year later, George came of age in 1736 and began a comprehensive plan of improvements to the hall.

George liked foreign travel and when he was away Matthew often had to deal with George's older sister Charlotte when he called at Melbourne Hall to discuss legal matters. Before long his business calls merged with pleasure; over time Matthew and Charlotte became lovers.

In 1740, they were married at the imposing twelfth-century church with a central tower by the front gates of Melbourne Hall, which is built on the scale of a small cathedral. Sir Thomas Coke laid out the gardens at Melbourne

Hall as a mini-Versailles, which he had visited in his youth. Inside the hall, the wood-panelled formal dining room was decorated with pictures of the Coke ancestors on the walls. It is said the width of the room was determined by the size of the three large portraits of George I, Queen Anne and Prince George of Denmark by Sir Godfrey Kneller. Upstairs, there were comfortable bedrooms overlooking the lawns and gardens.

A year after marrying Charlotte, Matthew decided he was rich enough to afford to buy a Parliamentary seat in the 'rotten borough' of Stockbridge in Hampshire. George was making improvements at Melbourne Hall, and Matthew and his wife moved into a town house in Red Lion Square in north London. Two years later, Charlotte gave birth to their first child, a daughter, on 1 November 1743 at the house. Parish records show she was baptised Charlotte, after her mother, on 30 November, at the church of St George the Martyr in Camden near Red Lion Square. They had a second daughter, Anne, before Charlotte finally gave birth to the son and heir that Matthew clearly hoped for. He was born on 29 January 1745 at the Lambs' house when Charlotte was thirty-five.[13]

Eleven days after his birth, they went once more to the parish church of St George the Martyr in Camden to have their baby baptised. He was christened Peniston after Matthew's generous uncle Peniston, who had started him on his way to his fortune. His name is recorded in clear handwriting in the register of baptisms on 9 February, though it is misspelled: 'Penistone, son of Matthew Lamb Esq and Charlotte his Wife.'

In 1746, with an heir and his wealth increasing, Matthew Lamb bought Brocket Hall, an Elizabethan house with a country estate in Hertfordshire neighbouring his clients, the Salisburys at Hatfield House. His grandson later admitted, as Lady Salisbury alleged, Matthew did plunder some of the Salisbury land when he was carrying out the conveyancing of Brocket Hall.

Matthew Lamb wanted a house to match his newly acquired status and hired Sir James Paine, one of the leading classical architects of the day, to demolish the old house and build a new mansion in the fashionable Palladian style on the hill overlooking the meandering river Lea. He had the river partially dammed to create a large artificial lake in front of the house.

Matthew was given a series of lucrative legal sinecures as a reward for consistently, not to say obsequiously, supporting the Pelham administration, first as solicitor to the Revenue of the Post Office in 1738 and in 1746 as legal counsel to the board of Trade. He was made a King's Counsel, which caused indignation among jealous rivals who said he 'never was an hour in Westminster Hall as a counsel in his life'.

Matthew Lamb used the patronage of one of his old clients, Earl Fitzwilliam, to exchange his Parliamentary seat in Stockbridge in 1747 for one of the two seats in the Whig stronghold which were in Fitzwilliam's gift at Peterborough, the town where his brother was the Dean and in line to become Bishop.

In 1751 Matthew's wife Charlotte received the unexpected news that her brother George Coke had died in Geneva. George left Melbourne Hall and its adjoining market town to Charlotte and her son, Peniston, who was now six years of age. Through his wife, Matthew Lamb found himself owner of Melbourne Hall where his father had been a humble solicitor.

To cap his advancement in society, in 1755, Matthew Lamb was rewarded for his unwavering loyalty to the crown with a baronetcy. It was time for another move. Red Lion Square where the Lambs had their London home was popular with lawyers, judges and King's Counsel but the moneyed classes were moving to the west end, where fine new town houses were being built in handsome squares.

In 1756, Sir Matthew and Lady Charlotte acquired the lease on a house at Twenty-eight Sackville Street, a side road off Piccadilly, from the sixty-seven-year-old Tory peer, Daniel Finch, the eighth Earl of Winchilsea. It was a terraced house, but one of the biggest properties and on the best side, the west.

Their son Peniston turned eleven that year, and was sent by his father to Eton to be subjected to the education required of gentlemen, mixing Greek and Latin with regular doses of the birch. His father paid the headmaster five guineas for the privilege, although Peniston's name was wrongly entered by Dr Barnard under his father's name, 'Matthew Lamb', in the college records.

He was not bookish and after Eton, his father did not insist on the boy wasting his time by going to university. He was allowed to follow his passions for horse racing, gambling and drinking with the friends he had made at Eton. After his father died at the age of sixty-four in 1768, Peniston seemed to be ready to quit the life of the spendthrift bachelor and try to give his life some purpose. He became an MP and a year later, he signed on as a pupil at Lincoln's Inn to become a lawyer like his late father. It did not last long.

His wife Elizabeth had found herself the chatelaine of both Brocket Hall and Melbourne Hall at the age of seventeen and with a London house to keep. In the autumn, Elizabeth's doctor confirmed she was pregnant. Betsy, as Peniston fondly called her, was due to have their first child about May.

She began applying a woman's touch to their house at Sackville Street for supper parties with some of his political contacts and the young female friends she was introduced to by Peniston's sister. On Christmas Eve Elizabeth wrote to William Fox, the steward at Melbourne Hall, saying: 'Sir Peniston desires you will send the Picture that Hangs over the Chimney in the Dining Room at Melbourne to Sackville Street by the first opportunity and begs you will see it Pack'd up very carefully. We intend sending another to supply the place.'[14]

The house was already the largest in Sackville Street with a frontage forty-five feet and a large extension at the back. Peniston had some of the ceilings richly decorated in a baroque style, probably by an Italian artisan, and made improvements to the upper floors. Betsy had Peniston commission a fine fireplace for the dining room by Sir James Paine, who had built Brocket Hall for his father.

Sackville Street was well placed for Betsy's shopping expeditions in nearby Bond Street where she bought silks for the walls. Servants could buy some goods in Sackville Street that had two apothecaries and a cheesemonger's, a tavern and a coffee house. It was also close to the Court of St James's where 'drawing room' receptions were held by King George III and Queen Charlotte, now in the tenth year of their reign.[15]

Sir Peniston's bachelor townhouse at Sackville Street, however, was not big enough for Elizabeth. Already, she was looking for a base that could match her ambition to host the most fashionable salon in London.

3

'He Must and Would See Her'

Sir Peniston Lamb began an affair with a beautiful actress and singer called Sophia Baddeley in February 1770, ten months into the marriage. Betsy was in the sixth month of her pregnancy and feeling ill with morning sickness.

Elizabeth's husband had become besotted with Sophia after seeing her perform at Ranelagh Gardens, the pleasure park in Chelsea, where she made slaves of adoring men by singing popular operatic arias for twelve pounds a week. Ranelagh was considered more respectable than the scandalous Vauxhall Gardens, south of the River Thames. The entrance charge to Ranelagh was two shillings and sixpence, more than twice what they charged at Vauxhall. 'It has totally beat Vauxhall…you can't set your foot without treading on a Prince or a Duke of Cumberland,' Horace Walpole wrote in his journal when it opened.

The leaders of polite Georgian society, princes and aristocrats, caroused at Ranelagh with their fashionably-attired female friends – in some cases their wives – under the domed roof of a huge rococo rotunda 120 feet in diameter. It was here that Sophia Baddeley sang from a stage with an orchestra to packed audiences, above the din of conversation, and customers shouting to waiters for sweetmeats and champagne.

Outside the rotunda, formal gardens were laid out in geometric patterns and dotted with fountains and water features like the gardens at the Tuileries Palace in Paris. It is now the site of the Chelsea Flower Show ground. For all its finery, Ranelagh Gardens was a place where society men and women could arrange sexual adventures; they could be seen, innocently admiring the flowers, while discreetly exchanging calling cards for assignations in the privacy of their London houses. Edward Gibbon said it was 'the most convenient place for courtships of every kind – the best market we have in England'.

Sophia's confidante, Elizabeth Steele, later wrote in her memoirs that Sophia was 'embarrassed and perplexed' by the contending passions of her suitors, when 'Peniston Lamb thrust himself forward as one of her admirers. This gentleman was about twenty-one years of age, and had been married about ten months to a very amiable woman.'

In fact, he was the same age as Sophia, who was twenty-five. His 'amiable' wife, Elizabeth, was expecting their first child in three months, but he used his wealth to buy sex from Sophia Baddeley. She was already earning good money from singing and acting and would not come cheap. She supplemented her twelve pounds for singing at Ranelagh gardens with fourteen guineas a week at the Drury Lane theatre, a total income of twenty-six pounds, equivalent today to around £3,250 per week. With bonuses from her admirers, it was enough to pay for a set of servants, and a carriage; but it was nothing compared to the small fortune that Sir Peniston was prepared to lavish on her.

Profligate men-about-town like Sir Peniston Lamb who were prepared to pay for sex could try to avoid the pox by consulting *Harris's List of Covent-Garden Ladies*, a bawdy eighteenth-century guide to the prostitutes who operated in the 'nunneries' near the Drury Lane Theatre, where stage make-up concealed the ravages of age or venereal disease.

Harris's guide included 'Miss B-nd' who was aged nineteen with auburn hair, and could be relied on to 'receive the well-formed tumid guest…and press out the last drops of the vital fluid' for any man with two guineas in his pocket. Miss B-nd would have been included in the list of 'tolerables', added Harris, 'had not the smallpox been so unkind.'[1]

Condoms, which Casanova called 'English overcoats', were used as protection against sexual diseases. They were made out of sheep gut or fish skin, secured by a red ribbon and sold at apothecaries' shops such as the one near the Melbournes' house in Sackville Street, or Half Moon Street and Orange Court, Leicester Fields. James Boswell was among their customers and boasted in his journal of going 'armoured' in pursuit of young prostitutes in 1762 in St James's Park. He also picked up a 'jolly young damsel' in the Strand and had sex with her on Westminster Bridge. There was a naval officer's daughter from Gibraltar he picked up among the prostitutes patrolling near the lawyers' inns of court at the Temple; and two pretty girls who he took in turns 'one after the other, according to their seniority' in a room at a tavern.[2]

Some ladies used a sponge soaked in brandy as a spermicide and to reduce the risk of venereal disease. Rich men such as Sir Peniston would pay thousands of pounds to keep their mistresses for their own exclusive use.

Sophia Baddeley was acutely aware that there was a fine line between being admired and being condemned as a harlot among the hypocrites of Georgian society.

Sophia had learned music from her father, Valentine Snow, who was the king's sergeant-trumpeter, and an accomplished musician – Handel wrote virtuoso parts for him – though at times he was so hard up he pawned his trumpet. His daughter was baptised in October 1744 at St Mary's, Camden and not the more upmarket St Margaret's Westminster near Horse Guards, as she later claimed. Snow trained her to sing so that she could support herself with a musical career after he had gone. She complained he was a disciplinarian and mistreated her. As soon as she got the chance, the teenage Sophia broke free by marrying an actor called Robert Baddeley at Drury Lane. Her father was a witness at the marriage.[3] Baddeley helped her to get parts at Drury Lane, including playing Ophelia. For a time she was devoted to him and they had been married for three years when, according to Steele's colourful account (probably ghost-written), Sophia was 'seduced at a party of pleasure' at Staines Bridge, where she committed 'an act that deterred her from going back to her house'. Steele probably was referring to the Three Swans at Brentford Ait, an island near Staines Bridge, between Kew and Brentford, which was a notorious meeting place for sex and drunken parties.

David Garrick, the actor manager at Drury Lane, helped her reach an amicable settlement for a separation from her husband – she agreed to underwrite her husband's debts – and she went to live with another Drury Lane Theatre actor, Charles Holland, until he died from smallpox. She attracted a chorus of admirers at the Theatre including the King's younger son, Frederick, the Duke of York, who gave her a lock of his hair, and the elderly Sir Cecil Bishop of Berkeley Square, who gave her silver plate costing £100 in return for her allowing him to have tea with her.

'Mrs Baddeley traversed the gay scenes of life, with a heart disengaged from the trammels of love,' wrote Mrs Steele. 'Among all those who laboured to gain her affections, the honourable William Hanger, second son of Lord Coleraine, was most assiduous and indefatigable and at last succeeded...'

William was neither honourable nor assiduous according to a Parliamentary guide that described him as 'a rake and a gambler'.[4] William Hanger made the mistake of introducing Mrs Baddeley to his elder brother, John, who immediately fell for her charms, and stole her from his brother. John Hanger took a handsome lodging in Dean Street, Soho, for them to live together and hired a carriage for Sophia at his own expense.[5]

John Hanger's finances could not match his promises of undying devotion. For a time, Sophia supported him, but his father heard they were living together and threatened to disown his son, cutting John off from his inheritance. John felt he had no option but to leave his lover. There was a scene worthy of a Garrick tragedy, as she pleaded in vain for John not to leave her. She threatened suicide, but Hanger abandoned her, leaving Sophia to pawn some of her jewels to pay her bills. As soon as word got out that she was no longer living with Hanger, she had approaches from a string of aristocrats such as the young Earl of Sefton; Lord Palmerston, a Lord of the Admiralty and father of the future Prime Minister; Lord March, the Duke of Queensborough; and his Grace the Duke of Northumberland.

Mrs Steele provided Sophia with a house at St James's Place, near St James's Palace, and she began her life as a courtesan, surrounded by statesmen behaving like elderly stags in the rutting season.

She was dealing with these competing lovers, 'fluctuating between gratitude and folly', when Sir Peniston Lamb thrust himself forward. He sent a note through a friend to Sophia saying that he was prepared to offer her a 'share of his fortune in exchange for the possession of her heart'. As proof of his passion, he added £300 to his letter. This was a huge sum of money for Sophia. It was equivalent in purchasing power today to over £37,000 and more than twenty times what she could earn singing at Renelagh Gardens. Sir Peniston dismissed his gift to Sophia as a mere 'bagatelle', as proof of his esteem. These were the niceties of polite society, but the bargain was clear – he was willing to pay Sophia a fortune for sex. And Sir Peniston now had even more money. His uncle Robert, Bishop of Peterborough, had died in the first week of November 1769, just seven months after officiating at Peniston and Elizabeth's wedding in his house near Hanover Square, and he had left most of his money to Peniston.

At least Bishop Lamb died the way he would have wanted, fox hunting. The Bishop, according to one journal, 'died ... being taken ill on horseback in the field while hunting: a bon viveur by which he injured his health – but much esteemed.' The report acidly added: 'His brother was the late Sir Matthew, steward and agent for the Earl of Salisbury who died very rich a little before him. Both said to be ignorant in their professions, one as a divine – the other as a lawyer.'[6]

The Bishop stipulated in his will he wanted his body to be laid beneath a plain marble slab in the chancel of Hatfield church and today his unmarked final resting place is long forgotten. His name is in the list of rectors on the wall at the church, but there is no sign of a tomb, as he wished. Robert was unmarried and in his will he left 500 guineas to his niece, Peniston's sister Charlotte, Lady Belasyse; £100 to her husband, Henry, Lord Belasyse; some small sums to his servants with his furniture and chattels; and the rest went to his nephew, Sir Peniston Lamb.[7]

Sophia Baddeley did not refuse the money offered by Sir Peniston – she rarely did – but her friend, Mrs Steele, who posed as a chaperone, accountant, agent and reluctant pimp, claimed she tried to put him off. 'Knowing his Lordship was married to a lady of great personal and acquired accomplishments, who merited all his love and attention, she recommended it to him to pay that regard to his domestic happiness, which the partner of it had every title to, and give over any thoughts of expecting success with her...'

This was pure cant, of course. Neither Sophia nor Mrs Steele had any intention of turning Sir Peniston and his money away. Sophia continued to appear to loud applause at Drury Lane with her estranged husband, Robert Baddeley, despite their separation, and King George III was so amused by her appearance with Baddeley in *The Clandestine Marriage*, a comedy co-authored by David Garrick, that he commissioned the court artist Johan Zoffany to paint her portrait. A mezzotint of the painting in the National Portrait Gallery shows Sophia in an imperious pose, with her hair elegantly swept up in the Georgian style, and long neck set off with a pearl choker.[8] Sir Joshua Reynolds produced a more flattering portrait with a print published on 10 August 1772 that is now in the British Museum collection. Mrs Baddeley is holding a small cat close to her breast and their eyes are remarkably similar, perhaps suggesting Reynolds too was captivated by her slinky, feline beauty.[9]

Sir Peniston was determined to have Sophia Baddeley to himself and he was not to be put off by his initial rebuff, said Mrs Steele. 'His passion was rather increased than abated and his liberality kept pace with it.'

Sir Peniston gave Sophia cash and paid jewellers' bills amounting to £1,370 over two weeks – equivalent to about £171,000 today. One afternoon, her friend Mrs Steele noted, he spent four hours with her and he left £200 in bank notes on the table. 'His Lordship was no sooner gone than Mrs Baddeley went to the table and took up the bank-notes...saying he ought to have left more. However, she gave it to me to place into an account, of which I always kept a regular one of all she received and paid...'[10]

Sophia's extravagance shocked even her faithful friend Mrs Steele. She spent more than three guineas a day on scented summer flowers such as moss roses and carnations. But that was a trifle compared to the sums she spent on clothes and jewels. 'I have known her go to Mr King's, the Mercer's, and lay out thirty or forty guineas for a facque [a loose dress] and coat of rich winter silk and would purchase two or three more at the same time.'

'Betsy' gave birth to a boy on 3 May 1770 at home at Sackville Street. She could have had the birth at Brocket Hall or Melbourne Hall, but Betsy decided to have her confinement in London. Richard Warren, physician to George III, lived almost next door at thirty-two Sackville Street and may have attended her.

Peniston's first son and heir was baptised Peniston after his father on 16 May in the parish of St James in Piccadilly. The register was filled out with the boy's name spelled incorrectly as Pennyston. That antique spelling would soon be dropped, and the boy would be known in the family simply as 'Pen'.

Elizabeth had no intention of breast-feeding her baby. She followed the practice of many high-society Georgian women of engaging a wet nurse to look after Peniston and returned to her social engagements. Soon the girl from the North Riding would become one of the leading hostesses of Georgian society. Her rise would be an object lesson in ambition fulfilled.

A month later, on 8 June, Sir Peniston Lamb was rewarded for his loyal, if mute, support for the North government with an Irish peerage that was posted in the *London Gazette*. Sir Peniston preferred Brocket, but when it came to his title, he chose Melbourne in memory of his mother. He would be known officially as Lord Melbourne, Baron of Kilmore in the County of Cavan, although he had never set foot in Ireland. The newly minted Lord Melbourne clearly had no shame: he chose *Virtute et Fide* (Virtue and Faith) for his motto to go with his new coat of arms.

Today, Melbourne Hall remains largely unchanged from the time that Charlotte and Matthew Lamb lived there. It is a perfect, comfortable manor house in Derbyshire stone, surrounded by the market town of Melbourne where many of the servants lived. It still has a stream by a mill that gives it its name. The Melbourne estate remains privately owned and occupied by Lord and Lady Ralph Kerr, a direct descendant of Sir John Coke, who made Melbourne Hall his home in 1629.

The hall, which is open to the public in August each year, seems to have a timeless quality about it, as if the world has passed it by, despite the distant roar of the motor-racing circuit at nearby Donington Park on race days and the package holiday flights of Thomas Cook (who was born in Melbourne) at nearby East Midlands airport.

Like his father, Sir Peniston had 'bought' his seat in the Commons in 1768 when he was twenty-one, though whether Peniston ever actually paid for it is open to doubt. George Selwyn, the MP and wit who owned the Ludgershall seat in Wiltshire where there were more sheep than voters, claimed he put it at the disposal of his friend, the Duke of Grafton, who was then Prime Minister, for the very large sum of £9,000 – around £1 million today. Grafton offered it to Sir Peniston having been assured he would be as loyal and unobtrusive as his father. Selwyn later complained he was never paid. 'Lord Melbourne... says he purchased his seat in Ludgershall. It is a falsehood. If he did, he has not paid the money he ought for it.'[11]

Grafton resigned as prime minister in January 1770 after criticism over the humiliating loss of Corsica to the French. He was replaced by the ill-fated Lord North, destined to be remembered as the Prime Minister who lost the far more important American colonies.

Lady Airlie wrote in her history of her family, *In Whig Society*, that Lord North put forward Peniston Lamb's name 'as a worthy recipient of a peerage. He was young, rich with a charming wife. He entertained largely, and would be useful person to attach to the Throne...' and keep on silently supporting his government though all its troubles.[12] Peniston continued to support the North government for the next decade until, in the complicated politics of the Georgian period, he was persuaded by his wife to switch his allegiance from the king to his son and her lover, George, the Prince of Wales in return for the honours he would bestow on both of them.

Elizabeth, Lady Melbourne was delighted to be able to share in the award of the title – even an Irish peerage – because it could be a stepping stone to an English peerage on which she had her sights firmly fixed. Lord Melbourne shared her ambition; he wrote to Fox, his steward at Melbourne: 'His Majesty having been pleased to create me a Peer of Ireland, I thought it proper to take my Title from Melbourne, it's very agreeable to me as I look upon it as a step to an English Peerage in some future time.' He added, in a reference to the birth of his son and heir, 'My Lady continues well.'

As Elizabeth made her home at Sackville Street with their baby son, her husband continued his amorous adventures with Sophia, which at times resembled a Sheridan farce. Mrs Steele reported: 'One day when I was absent, Lord Melbourne got admittance in St James's Place to drink tea with her. On my return, I found them together. She came out to me and on my remonstrating with her on the impropriety of her encouraging any gentleman's visits his Lordship, who overheard me, and fearing an attack upon him personally, threw up the parlour window and precipitately leaped out. Being too much in a hurry to take sufficient precaution about a safe landing place, he fell down the area; however, receiving no material hurt, he scrambled up again and took to his heels. His Lordship, however, as an atonement for his intrusion left banknotes on the parlour table to the amount of £200.'[13]

The next day, Lord Melbourne sent a letter to Sophia apologising for his precipitate retreat and requesting a meeting as he had something important to tell her. He asked her to meet him at Poet's Corner inside the ancient Westminster Abbey where kings and queens had been crowned since Anglo-Saxon times and where Geoffrey Chaucer was buried. It was not the most romantic of settings to woo his lover but he hoped he could meet Sophia while pretending, if he was recognised, to give her a history lesson.

Mrs Steele claims she advised Mrs Baddeley to take no notice of his letter but Sophia said it could do no harm because it was in a public place among the wax effigies of kings and queens. 'Finding her determined to go, I told her I would accompany her and remonstrate with his Lordship on the impropriety of his conduct,' said Mrs Steele. Lord Melbourne found it difficult to speak openly to Sophia with Mrs Steele standing by. 'We viewed the waxwork, and walked round the inner part of the Abbey several times; at last his Lordship requested Mrs Baddeley's private ear for three minutes.'

Mrs Steele said Lord Melbourne took Sophia on to 'the leads', usually meaning a flat lead roof. Abbey experts told me that this was probably a path in the cloisters; going on the cloister roof would have required the permission of the Dean, and climbing up a ladder was 'not a thing to do in long skirts'!

The peer wanted privacy because he had a life-changing proposition to put to Sophia: that she should give up the stage and reserve herself exclusively for him. Mrs Steele claimed she intervened and scolded Lord Melbourne for the pain he would cause his wife by his proposition to Sophia. 'He said his respect and affection for his Lady were fixed and immoveable and he would not, on any account attempt to hurt her peace of mind; it was far from his intentions but as to denying his visits to Mrs Baddeley, it was to no purpose. He must and would see her, even at the risk of his life. He had the highest regard for her, lamented the fatigues to which her profession [as an entertainer] exploited her, and should be happy to enable her to quit that profession by empowering her to live in an easier sphere of life than either a theatre, Ranelagh or any public place of entertainment would admit of.' Lord Melbourne said he would 'spend his whole fortune if necessary to defend and protect her'. He then presented Sophia with £300 in notes to close the deal. She would no longer have to work on the stage for a living.[14]

Mrs Steele said the easy money from Lord Melbourne fed Sophia's natural extravagance. 'Having almost the command of his Lordship's purse, she began to launch out into expenses she had restrained before,' said Mrs Steele. 'She went to Mr Tomkin's the Jeweller in Maiden Lane, Covent Garden, and purchased a pair of diamond ear-rings, ten diamond pins at twenty pounds each, nine rings, with plate to the amount of £920. Mr Tomkins had a diamond necklace which he valued at £450, this Mrs Baddeley set her mind on being mistress of also, though she had not money to pay for it…'

The jeweller let her take the necklace away on credit and on his next visit to her house, Lord Melbourne praised its elegance and magnificence, saying it was cheap compared to the £30,000 in diamonds he had given his wife on their wedding day and 'he must be some little judge of the value of diamonds'. Torrens wrote: 'Lord Melbourne boasted that on his marriage he had given the whole of his wife's fortune back to her in diamonds. He was very proud of her attractions and cared not what expenditure contributed to enhance the éclat of her position.'[15]. Lord Melbourne showed no qualms about the money he was showering on his mistress. He called in at Tomkin's and paid the bill for the diamond necklace and other gems Sophia had bought though she knew she did not have the funds to pay for them. Instead of complaining about her extravagance, he told Sophia if she would name it, he would buy whatever took her fancy in the jeweller's shop. Then he 'excused himself for leaving us with so much abruptness being in haste, he said, to attend his dear Betsy to the play (this being the name by which he always called his wife)'.

Mrs Steele had taken a house in the King's Road, Chelsea, and soon after their tryst at the Abbey, Lord Melbourne found Sophia there. He thought it was ideal because it was sufficiently far away from Piccadilly to enable him to visit her by hackney cab without being identified by the coat of arms of a lion with a mullet between its paws on the door of his own carriage. She told him that she felt 'more indebted to him than any man living'. She was, in effect, his own.

Charles James Fox, the Whig leader, came calling on Sophia after Lord Melbourne had gone but made no attempt to wrap his desire for sex in the niceties of romance. Mrs Steele said: 'As his professions were neither desirable nor acceptable, he was very coolly received. He took resentment at it and his resentment for Mrs Baddeley's behaviour shall not pass unnoticed...'

Lord Melbourne was welcomed with open arms, however. He bought Mrs Baddeley a cream-coloured mare that cost him sixty pounds so that they could go out riding together 'for her health' and bought a fine hunter for her companion, Mrs Steele, for fifty pounds. She could trot behind them, no doubt while they headed for the nearest heath where they could lie concealed together.

When she published Sophia's 'kiss-and-tell' memoirs, Mrs Steele spitefully included some of Peniston's letters without correction, to show 'he was not the brightest man of the age' and his education at Eton left a lot to be desired. In one he wrote: 'I send you a million kissis, remember I love you Satterday, Sunday every day...I hope you will get the horsis but I beg you will not be so ventersum, as there are bad horsis, but will get one quiet...pray destroy all letters lest anyone should find them by axcedent.'[16]

Elizabeth, with her growing network of influential friends, is likely to have heard the rumours of Peniston's liaison with Mrs Baddeley, but stoically showed no sign of being hurt by his betrayal. It was not her style. Instead, she threw herself back into the social fray and began to use her influence to show Peniston that love was a game that two could play. Lady Melbourne would play her cards with ruthless efficiency.

4

Maternal Affection and How to Create a Salon

Lord Melbourne commissioned the renowned society artist Sir Joshua Reynolds to paint a portrait of Betsy posing with Pen, his son and heir, to proclaim the establishment of the Lamb dynasty. It would hang in pride of place the grand dining room overlooking the lake in a new extension he was having built at his stately home, Brocket Hall in Hertfordshire. The painting was copied in an engraving with the title *Maternal Affection* but it was less than convincing.

Lady Melbourne was still in the first flush of motherhood when she sat for the portrait with her baby but Reynolds was in great demand and it took him three years to finish it. Elizabeth displays none of the joy of motherhood that was present in the playful Reynolds portrait of the Duchess of Devonshire clapping hands with her baby daughter Lady Georgiana Cavendish in 1784.

She poses awkwardly, looking directly out of the canvas as she lifts her baby son onto her lap from his cradle. She looks so uncomfortable that art historian Judy Egerton said her pose 'suggests that a nurse usually did this for her'.[1] Ms Egerton was right. Elizabeth had little time for the nursery and after employing a wet nurse, hired a nanny – a fierce woman from Jersey – to look after Pen so that she could return to her busy round of social engagements. Her children could never understand her affection for the nanny who stayed with the Melbournes for years.

The painting would go alongside panels depicting the theme 'Love, Time and Fecundity'. The message was clear: Lord Melbourne expected Elizabeth to produce more children to add to the Melbourne dynasty. Elizabeth, however, had no intention of devoting her life to acting as a brood mare for a man who was having an affair with an actress despite the health risks it could bring both him and his wife.

Lady Melbourne was unhappy with *Maternal Affection*. Forty years later, when the painting was exhibited in the Reynolds exhibition of 1813 at the British Institution, Lady Melbourne complained to Byron that Reynolds had made her look too old. Byron replied with flattery: 'The painter was not so much to blame as you seem to imagine by adding a few years – he foresaw you would lose nothing by them.'[2]

She was happier with another portrait of her by Reynolds commissioned by her husband in late 1770 when she was nineteen. The title of the oval canvas is *Virtute et Fide* (Virtue and Faith), the same motto her husband chose for his coat of arms. It may have been hypocritical of Elizabeth as well as her husband but Reynolds captured the reason why Lady Melbourne was so admired by the men around her. It shows Elizabeth when she still had the bloom of youth on her cheek. Her auburn hair is swept up high with a string of pearls tumbling down her neck. She looks modestly down to her right, away from the viewer. She is wearing a white dress under a light blue cape lined with ermine – a subtle reference to her newly acquired title of Lady Melbourne.

By the start of the winter social season of 1770, Elizabeth had left Pen being looked after by his nanny and immersed herself once more in the social whirl with her high-society friends. It would be unfair to suggest that Elizabeth did not care for her children; she was a devoted mother and used all her contacts to enhance their careers, but her maternal instincts were coloured by her unsentimental approach to life.

Elizabeth's relaxed attitude to motherhood shocked the Victorian writer W. M. Torrens, who wrote sourly in a biography of her second son William: 'While the joy of motherhood was new, Lady Melbourne was devoted to her first born and delighted with his praise ... Ere the winter season came again, she was ready to take part once more in the gaieties of the town.' Lady Melbourne was content, he added, 'to float on the stream of fashionable life' with ever-multiplying 'troops of young female friends'.

Masquerades and fancy dress balls were often the occasion for outrageous cross-dressing by the more adventurous ladies of the *bon ton* like Lady Melbourne, who was seen by Reynolds at a masquerade with two female friends dressed as 'pretty fellows appearing in dominoes [large cloaks with hoods] as masculine as many of the macaroni things we see everywhere'.[3]

Macaronis – named after the Italian food rich young Englishmen enjoyed on the Grand Tour – were effete male precursors of the dandies who followed Beau Brummell. Elizabeth's friends at the masquerade were Lady Margaret Fordyce, the young wife of an extremely wealthy banker who would soon go bankrupt, and Mary Panton, the Duchess of Ancaster, who, according to Horace Walpole, was the 'natural daughter of Panton, a disreputable horse jockey'. Despite being illegitimate, the Duchess of Ancaster brought with her £60,000 to the marriage and became Mistress of the Robes to Queen Charlotte for thirty-two years.

Her rich young friends from the self-appointed fashionable set drew more disapproval from the more staid, elderly aristocrats for arranging a colourful barge race on the River Thames. It ended with a ticket-only supper for 2,000 'of the quality' at Ranelagh Gardens with music by the Giardini orchestra and a 240-strong chorus.

Elizabeth, like many women of her class, conducted her own social life largely without her husband, and it is possible that she was more determined to return to the social round of balls and masquerades within months of Pen's birth because she had found out her husband was spending his days with Sophia Baddeley. Lord Melbourne told Sophia that Betsy discovered his infidelity when she read a report in a gossip column that a diamond necklace chosen by Lord Melbourne for his mistress had been delivered by mistake to his wife. Her reaction was typically restrained. She 'only smiled at the tale, and said the paper might have been better employed'.

Elizabeth, characteristically pragmatic, decided to ignore her husband's betrayal for the moment, and let him seek his amusements elsewhere. There would come a time when she too would break her marriage vows. Her determination to do nothing, at least in public, to show she was disappointed with her husband was put to the test when they encountered Mrs Baddeley at the opera house.

The day before, Sophia had confided to Mrs Steele that she was beginning to regret her affair with Lord Melbourne. 'Whenever he was with her, it took off all the pleasure she would otherwise have in his company. "But," said she, "the misfortune is, I am so deep in the mire that I am stuck fast."'[4]

Mrs Steele pressed Sophia to return to 'a more honest course of life', either returning to her profession on the stage, or in some business that Mrs Steele offered to set her up in. Mrs Steele said it would enable her to change her life and give up being an escort. Sophia said she would rather die than return to the theatre and 'she could not think of altering her situation, bad as it was, till she could not help it'.

Instead, she prepared for a Ridotto – a ball – at the Opera House where ladies were expected to wear fancy dress, without masks. 'She resolved to make up the silk she bought from Mr King and an elegant dress was made of it. It was a lilac ground with beautiful flowers scattered down it. The sleeves were puckered gauze; worn with a veil, richly trimmed with point-lace which flowed in a manner that considerably added to its beauty.'

The Opera House was crowded 'with persons of the first rank' including many of her admirers. Ladies had spared no expense to vie with each other in the beauty of their appearance, but, said Mrs Steele, no dress pleased her as much as Mrs Baddeley's, nor was any more admired.

Mrs Steele recorded how Lord and Lady Melbourne arrived 'arm in arm and walked together the whole evening, but his Lordship did not omit to give Mrs Baddeley many pleasant looks; and even Lady Melbourne bestowed a smile upon her'. Lady Melbourne was too shrewd to lose her composure at being confronted with her husband's mistress. Her knowing smile – captured in her portrait by Stubbs when she was barely eighteen – summed up her philosophy of life: 'Life is a tragedy to those who feel, and a comedy to those who think.' Elizabeth had no intention of turning her husband's folly into a tragedy. She would make a joke of his infidelity. She knew she had the measure of her Peniston: he was easily led; he may stray; but he would not leave her, especially not for a woman like Sophia Baddeley.

When Mrs Baddeley returned home with Mrs Steele from the masquerade, she told her companion she felt ill. 'She conceived for the first time in her life, she was in the way of many a married woman.' Sophia was pregnant by Lord Melbourne. She told Mrs Steele she 'wished it be kept secret until Lord Melbourne found it out himself'.

Fortunately for Lord Melbourne, he was spared the embarrassment and expense of fathering a bastard with his lover. Mrs Steele claimed Sophia had a miscarriage, 'owing to a fright in losing a favourite cat, which she had some reason to think was killed by a dog'. Whatever the truth of this unusual story – an abortion was more likely – Sophia and Mrs Steele kept up the pretence she was indisposed through illness. Lord Melbourne, still ignorant about the cause of her malady, was frequently with her and was convinced his wife had accepted his mistress. He told Sophia that his dear Betsy admired Sophia's dress at the Ridotto and said 'many civil things' about her and 'he could have kissed her dear feet for it'. When he left, he gave Sophia £100 in bank notes still unaware she had been expecting his child.

Mrs Steele describes how Mrs Baddeley, after this scare, started going to operas, the theatre and entertainments at Ranelagh and Vauxhall without Lord Melbourne, staying up until three or four in the morning before returning home to change, and then driving out in a phaeton over ten miles to breakfast with admirers at Epsom. She would fill in her days going to an exhibition or an auction, followed by an airing at Hyde Park, riding the horse Peniston had bought her; she would dress, then go to a play and on to Ranelagh; and the merry-go-round would begin again.

Elizabeth had a similar round of social engagements. A typical day for Elizabeth might start with showing off her horsemanship with a ride among friends in Hyde Park where she was judged to be one of the two best equestrian ladies, with Lady Salisbury. If she encountered her husband's lover on horseback it was never mentioned by Mrs Steele. Betsy would enjoy an afternoon shopping at Thomas King, the silk mercer in Covent Garden, or Thomas Smith, the haberdasher in New Bond Street. She dined early at Sackville Street before going out to the opera or theatre, and finally settling down to play until long after midnight at hazard, a game with dice, whist and Faro (or Pharaoh) – a card game in which large sums were won or lost at the turn of a card by the banker.

Lady Melbourne would return to Sackville Street after shopping to preside over suppers made by her cook for young Whig politicians just back from the House of Commons. Over the dinner table they would trade the latest gossip about who was up and who was down, how long the latest coalition would last, and how the war in America was going. She had quickly struck up friendships with other young rich wives of high rank whose beauty and high spirits were welcomed at entertainments; though they were frowned on by the grand dames of society.

Balls enabled women publicly to flirt with men, and in country dances – before the age of the daring waltz – gain some brief physical contact, without raising eyebrows, while swirling around the room in their elegant gowns and compulsory gloves. The rules governing balls in Georgian England were imposed as strictly as military codes of conduct. They were intended to reinforce the precedence of rank and keep out the *nouveaux riches*: 'no person concerned in *retail* trade – no theatrical nor public performer by profession' should be admitted. The italics for 'retail' signalled that other forms of trade might be permissible but shopkeepers were beyond the social pale and servants were barred. 'No servant whatever should be admitted into the vestibule or gallery on any occasion or on any pretence whatever, on ball-nights.'

Committees of ladies, bishops and old colonels presided over the balls like military tribunals. The most feared was at Almack's in King Street, St James's, where a revolving cast of high-ranking aristocratic ladies of 'the ton' sat in judgment. They banned the Duke of Wellington in 1814 – the year he returned to England a hero after the exile of Napoleon to Elba – for arriving a few minutes after midnight, the cut-off point for admission.[5]

The fearful committee of ladies who ruled Almack's door policy that year were Lady Castlereagh, Princess Esterhazy, Lady Jersey, Mrs Drummond Burrell, and Lady Cowper – Lady Melbourne's daughter, Emily. A title was an advantage but no guarantee of entry: the Iron Duke was barred again at the entrance door to Almack's years later, despite holding a voucher – the holy grail granting permission to enter the assembly-room – because he was wearing black trousers, rather than knee-breeches, which was court dress. He was told: 'Your grace cannot be admitted in trousers.' The victor of Waterloo, a great believer in rules and regulations, retreated in the face of the formidable committee of women.[6]

The committee in Bath also ruled that 'Trowsers [*sic*] or coloured pantaloons [were] not to be permitted on any account'. It is just as well the Duke did not arrive wearing Wellington boots. He would have been in breach of the rule stipulating 'no gentleman in boots or half-boots be admitted into the Ball-Rooms on ball-nights, except Officers of the Navy, or of the Army on duty, in uniform; and then without their swords'.

Almack's committee imposed their own door policy regardless of titles. 'Very often persons whose rank and fortunes entitled them to the entrée anywhere were excluded by the cliquishness of the lady patronesses for the female government of Almack's was a pure despotism and subject to all the caprices of despotic rule. It is needless to add that, like every other despotism, it was not innocent of abuses,' said one writer in the *New Monthly Magazine* who had clearly suffered the humiliation of being turned away. 'This is selection with a vengeance, the very quintessence of aristocracy. Three-fourths of nobility knock in vain for admission. Into this sanctum sanctorum, of course, the sons of commerce never think of entering on the sacred Wednesday evenings [ball nights]…' It mattered to those turned away. 'Whenever one is put but an inch out of the great circle one becomes a looker-on,' said Lady Sarah Lennox.[7]

Elizabeth and her most intimate friends were fashion leaders in their early twenties. They included Lady Mary Lennox, wife of the third Duke of Richmond and her half-sister Mrs Anne Damer, the painter and sculptor, 'one of the most gifted and accomplished women of her time'.

Writing to Lady Ossory, Horace Walpole[8] described seeing them at the French ambassador's fancy-dress ball, where the theme for women was Queen Elizabeth I. Lady Melbourne and Mrs Damer wore revealing dresses with low necklines and high lace collars to evoke the imperious style of the Virgin Queen. Walpole complained that they were crammed into an ante-room where they were forced to wait until Queen Charlotte, wife of George III, arrived late from an oratorio. The Queen was slow to leave her Lady in Waiting, Caroline Vernon, and kept everyone waiting for the ballroom to open. It was packed and the heat was as stifling as the Black Hole of Calcutta, he wrote:

> The house was all arbours and bowers, but rather more approaching to Calcutta where so many English were stewed to death. We were penned

together in the little hall till we could not breathe. The quadrilles were very pretty: Mrs Damer, Lady Sefton, Lady Melbourne and the Princess Czartoriski in blue satin with blond [lace] and *collets montes* à *la reine Elizabeth*...the men with black hats and white feathers flapping behind, danced another quadrille and then both quadrilles joined...[9]

Anne Seymour Damer was brought up at her father General Henry Conway's country seat, Park Place in Berkshire, and had a classical, 'blue-stocking' education, which was rare for most society women. Her cousin Horace Walpole encouraged Anne to develop her independence and artistic flair. Walpole acted as her guardian when her parents were out of the country, and he remained her champion for the rest of his life.

She married John Damer, the son of Lord Milton and the heir to a fortune of £30,000 in 1767. They lived a modern, extravagant life – like Elizabeth and the other young rich fashionable things – as if their days and their money would never end. It was not a happy marriage. The Damers shared the same house, but had little else in common and were rarely seen together. Damer spent his days in his London clubs, like Lord Melbourne, gaming – and losing – while he spent his nights with 'troops of women', leaving his wife to entertain herself with Lady Melbourne and their friends. Elizabeth and Anne went house-hunting together for a home in London so that Lady Melbourne could realise her ambition to become the grand society hostess, *primum inter pares*.

Peniston was preoccupied with overseeing major improvements to his late father's house at Brocket Hall. Lord Melbourne wanted something more impressive, something bigger and better to go with his title. He commissioned Sir James Paine to add a new south front to the house to provide a series of principal rooms with decorative ceilings and fine furniture supplied by Chippendale where he could entertain royalty.

There seemed to be no limit to the money Lord Melbourne was prepared to pour into his country house to make it spectacular enough to entertain their most prestigious guests, including royalty. The saloon alone cost £1,500 – roughly £187,000 today. Its walls were lined with silk, the ceilings festooned with scrollwork, and panels painted by some of the most sought-after decorators of their day including James Durno, Thomas Jones and Francis Wheatley. The state banqueting table could seat fifty-four people, and the saloon walls were decorated with new works of art telling the history of the Melbourne family. Stubbs' 'conversation piece', the 'Milbankes and the Melbournes', would dominate one wall in the banqueting room. To fill the rest of his walls, Melbourne went on a spending spree around the art studios of London.

Lord Melbourne may have been barely literate, but he had an expert eye for art. He attended the Society of Artists' exhibitions and ordered more paintings by Stubbs. He bought two by Joseph Wright of Derby – *An Academy by Lamplight* in 1769 when it was still on the artist's easel and the first version of *The Blacksmith's Shop* in 1771. He also paid 100 guineas for the first of Stubbs' enamels to be exhibited, the *Lion Attacking a Horse*. Stubbs' 'conversation piece' of the Lambs and the Milbankes was in the same exhibition and it is possible he saw the enamel work there when he went to see the painting with his wife, Elizabeth. Judy Egerton said it was 'a courageous purchase and one which must have fortified Stubbs in his determination to proceed with painting serious subjects in a medium which had hitherto been thought proper only for the pretty (or mildly erotic) decoration of snuff-boxes such as Cosway painted'.[10]

As he got older, Lord Melbourne's heart was increasingly in the country estate around Brocket where he was happy hunting, shooting and talking horse racing with his son and heir, Peniston Lamb, who grew to enjoy country pursuits just as much as his father. Elizabeth, however, had set her heart on creating a London house that would rank alongside the great houses on Piccadilly such as Devonshire House, which had not seen a Duchess since 1754 and was a ghost of its former self.

She found the perfect place, around the corner from the Melbournes' house in Sackville Street. It was an old house dating from the Restoration in 1660 and owned by sixty-five-year-old Henry Fox, the first baron Holland, who was a family friend of the Lambs and was married to the much younger Lady Caroline Lennox, daughter of the Duke of Richmond, aged forty-seven. It was in a stub of a street off the north side of Piccadilly. It had gates to close off a square in front of the house and a garden at the back with an entrance opposite Savile Row.

Lord Holland had bought the house in 1763 when he was the Paymaster General, allegedly by creaming off £50,000 a year from subsidies to foreign powers when Britain was at war with France. He denied corruption, but having been nearly bankrupted by gambling debts as a young man, he had become immensely rich from politics.[11]

Holland commissioned the fashionable neoclassical architect Robert Adam to rebuild the property. Adam drew up the designs, but Lord Holland was in failing health – he died of cancer in 1774. He had shelved Adam's plans and put the house up for sale; he needed money after he retired from Parliament to run Holland House, his stately home surrounded by 200 acres beyond Hyde Park. It was a large Jacobean mansion dating from 1605 in what is now the Holland Park area of West London. Henry Fox had been a good friend of Peniston's late father, Matthew Lamb, and they knew Fox's precocious son, Charles James Fox, the twenty-two-year-old rising star of the Whig party. Lord Holland was therefore more than happy to sell his house to Lord Melbourne, his old friend's son, but he would drive a hard bargain.

As negotiations began on buying Lord Holland's Piccadilly property, Lord Melbourne ordered an eighty-piece dinner service from the Sèvres porcelain factory in Paris. It was delivered to Lord Melbourne's Paris agent on 20 March 1771 and cost 5,197 livres and nineteen sous, about £1 million today.[12] Plates and bowls in the finest porcelain were painted with cupids, violins and bows. They were destined for the great dining room at Brocket Hall and were probably given to Betsy as a second wedding anniversary present in April. The dinner service passed down through her daughter, Lady Cowper, and remains intact at Firle Place near Lewes in East Sussex. But a dinner service, even from the finest porcelain factory in Europe, was not going to satisfy Lady Melbourne. Her ambitions were fixed on creating a new Melbourne House to match the finest houses in London.

On 1 April 1771, Lord Melbourne agreed to pay £16,500 (roughly £1 million today) for Lord Holland's Piccadilly house – £500 more than Holland had paid for it eight years before – with the intention of demolishing it, and building a new Melbourne House on the site.

Lord Melbourne engaged the king's architect Sir William Chambers to raise Melbourne House from the rubble of Lord Holland's residence. Chambers was forty-nine and at the height of his fame, having previously worked for George III on Carlton House, Buckingham House, the king's observatory in Richmond Park, and the ornamental Pagoda at Kew Garden. Chambers had also designed the gorgeous gold state coach with painted panels of cupids by Giovanni Cipriani for the king's coronation in 1760, though it was not finished until 1762 when it was used for the state opening of Parliament. It remains the star exhibit in the Royal Mews at Buckingham Palace. By hiring Sir William Chambers to build Melbourne House, the Melbournes were laying down a marker: they had arrived.

Chambers saw the commission to build Melbourne House as an opportunity to enhance his reputation and to eclipse his rival Robert Adam's very different ideas for Lord Holland's house. Chambers quickly set about ripping the old house apart. While the work continued for four years, Elizabeth's younger brother John – who was featured in her wedding portrait – fell in love with and married the architect's daughter, Cornelia. John was a Guards officer but sold his commission and married Cornelia in the Oxford Chapel at Marylebone (now St Peter, Vere Street) on 24 November 1775. Nine months later, on 20 August 1776, they had a son, christened

John Peniston Milbanke, who in 1825 would inherit the family title as the seventh Milbanke baronet. John, with the patronage of his well-connected father-in-law, became a contractor of His Majesty's Works in London.[13]

Chambers reported to Lord Melbourne in November 1771 that work was proceeding 'very briskly and very well' on his new house; the 'chamber floor' on the second floor had been nearly completed. But it would be another three to four years before the Melbournes would move in. The commission would test his skill at creating a grand house that could be used both for lavish entertainments, and as a practical family home. The first challenge was the entrance; he wanted it to be grand without being forbidding.

Chambers was disparaging about some of the entrances to houses in London, saying they resembled 'convents' with high walls and a hole for those who wished to 'creep through'. He had a much grander entrance in mind for Melbourne House. Set a hundred feet from busy Piccadilly, the house, in fashionable red brick with stone quoins, would be protected by a classical gateway, with two entrance gates set in a high wall. In the centre, the stone gateway was topped by a classical pediment lit on either side by two large lanterns.

Inside, the gates opened into the great court, 364 feet long with space for at least six carriages. There were brick pavilions on either side, containing twin coach houses, with stabling for thirteen horses on the left; on the right were kitchens and offices. Ahead there was a short flight of stone steps to the great front door. Inside, guests entered a grand hall, with a fireplace in each end wall, to be met by a porter who had a room off to the left. No expense was spared on the interior and some of the finest carpenters, plasterers and carvers who had been employed at Brocket Hall were redeployed to ornament the Piccadilly house. Thomas Chippendale was commissioned to supply large items of furniture from his workshops in St Martin's Lane as work progressed. Three principal rooms on the ground floor overlooked the lime trees and roses in the back gardens designed by Francis Wheatley, the popular portrait and landscape artist, who had been employed on the interiors at Brocket Hall.

The centrepiece of Chambers' design, reached through three open arches, was a spectacular, cantilevered 'flying' staircase in cast iron that rose up to the top of the house in a square well, lit from above by a glazed atrium. Cast iron was then in vogue for Georgian balconies and bannisters, but its use for the staircase at Melbourne House by Chambers was daring (and predated the construction of the Iron Bridge in Coalbrookdale by about five years).[14]

Like most aristocratic couples, Lord and Lady Melbourne did not share a bed but by the time they moved into Melbourne House, they slept on different floors. Lord Melbourne's bedroom was on the left of the house on the ground floor, and Lady Melbourne's bedroom was up the 'flying' great staircase on the first floor at the front of the house, overlooking the courtyard.

Chambers' annotated plans for Melbourne House are now in Sir John Soane's Museum, London.[15] They show Lord Melbourne's bedroom was entered through a small lobby and there was a dressing room where he was assisted by his butler. Both Lord and Lady Melbourne had en-suite water closets but before the advent of Victorian sewers, their pots had to be removed by the servants discreetly using the back stairs

Lord Melbourne's rooms led to his very large library at the back of the house with a floor-to-ceiling bow window overlooking the gardens. There was enough sunlight to read by but blinds were drawn to avoid the sunlight damaging the collection of leather-bound books he must rarely have read. The central room at the back of the house was the main entertaining and relaxing space, marked 'common drawing room' on Chambers' plan. It had three large windows opening over Wheatley's gardens and Savile Row.

The dining room was next door on the right. Guests could walk from the drawing room into the dining room through a line of pillars, finished by Domenico Bartoli to resemble porphyry, to take their seats at a long dining table. It was used for regular meals but was grand enough to be used for banquets at which the Prince of Wales became a regular guest. It had a large airy bay window twenty feet wide matching that of the library. Two paintings of wine and food by William Marlow were hung over an eye-catching marble chimneypiece with antique green stone by Paine. There was a spectacular example of Chippendale's art: a breathtakingly beautiful sideboard in polished inlaid wood ornamented with ormolu. Lord Melbourne paid £140 for it, making it the most expensive piece of furniture supplied by Chippendale to any of his clients. It is judged to be one of the most important pieces of furniture in the country. It was later bought by the Sitwell family for Renishaw Hall in Derbyshire and is known as the Renishaw commode.

On their way upstairs, guests could admire statues in the niches beside the flying staircase, invariably accompanied by music and the hubbub of a party going on in one of the three first-floor principal entertaining rooms. The drama of the interior was heightened also by *trompe-l'oeil* bas-reliefs of classical scenes. In the centre, two doors opened into the main drawing room where guests could enjoy the latest personal and political gossip over their champagne. The long room to the right was marked 'saloon' on Chambers' plan but was used as the ballroom, where small orchestras would play country dances and quadrilles. It became known as the round room, although it was oval-shaped and was the Melbournes' favourite entertaining space. There was a large crimson-covered seat in the bay window and an eye-catching white and coloured marble fireplace.

Lady Melbourne's 'inner sanctum', her private apartments, were across the first-floor landing. Her suite of rooms took up most of the space at the front of the house, and it was here she could entertain her most intimate friends. The rooms included her boudoir, a dressing room and a walk-in wardrobe where her maids looked after her frequent changes of dress. There was a small lobby leading to her private water closet. Chambers marked one room by the great stair as an ante-chamber leading to a state dressing room with a large bay window directly over Lord Melbourne's library on the ground floor, but this was also used as an entertaining room when the house was full of guests. The great staircase continued, spiralling upwards to the family bedrooms on the second floor and the servants' accommodation in the attic. The servants moved anonymously about the house by means of concealed servants' back stairs.

Torrens said 'large sums were lavished by Lady Melbourne with no ordinary taste and skill' on its adornment. The army of decorators and carvers hired by Chambers included Giovanni Cipriani, with whom he had collaborated on the king's gold coach, to decorate the gallery and the fifty-two-foot-long ballroom ceiling with cupids, nymphs and cherubs, classical gods and the elements, interspersed with sparkling pier glasses. Biaggio Rebecca decorated the walls with light-hearted frescos.[16]

Chambers jealously guarded his reputation and became embroiled in an extraordinary dispute with Thomas Chippendale. In August 1773, Chippendale called on Lord Melbourne's architect to show him his furniture designs in *The Director* and tell Chambers how he thought they should be displayed to best effect. The architect was furious at being told how to showcase the furniture by a mere cabinet maker. He dashed off an angry note to Lord Melbourne saying he wanted 'to be a little consulted about these matters as I am really a Very pretty Connoisseur in furniture'. He fiercely objected to Chippendale having a say in where his furniture would be placed inside Melbourne House, and complained about Chippendale's 'method of fitting up my Lady's dressing Room with Girandoles [large carved candelabra] and a Glass [mirror] out of the Centre and the Girandoles quite irregularly placed. Pictures would be much better and in the great room fewer Sophas [*sic*] and more chairs would be better than as Chippendale has designed.'[17] Chambers's pressure on Lord Melbourne worked. A year later, Melbourne meekly submitted Chippendale's designs to Chambers for his approval.

By the summer of 1773, the roof was on, the kitchen block and stables were completed and the entrance gate was in place; craftsmen were hammering away at the interior, starting at the top of the house and working down, decorating and furnishing the 'round room' on the first floor.

Chippendale supplied two elegant neo-classical cabinets veneered in holly (see page 51). They were inherited by the Melbournes' daughter, Emily Cowper, at Panshanger, passed down through the family and are now at Firle Place, where they are used to display the exquisite Melbourne Sèvres dinner service. They may have been used by the Melbournes to show off porcelain figures but William used them, partly, for books. Eight Greek and Latin lexicons signed and dated 9 September 1817 by William Lamb were discovered during conservation in 1983 when the locks to the side panels were picked. The books were covered in dust, suggesting they had not been disturbed since William put them there.[18]

Chambers had agreed to build the house for £21,300 but he was soon over budget, and Lord Melbourne – despite his vast wealth – was in arrears. The cost of the work on Melbourne House to October 1773 rose to £22,959. Lady Melbourne and her husband were forever ordering changes and they were expensive; £1,659 had been incurred for 'extra works' by 'plaisterers, painters, carvers etc' paid by Chambers. About £3,159 was then still owing by Lord Melbourne.

The architect would not accept any shoddy work, and criticised a bricklayer called Edward Gray for the 'infamous' quality of the bricks he was using for the exterior of the house.

The cost had risen further by November 1774 to about £24,632, but Chambers jotted on the back of a letter from Lord Melbourne that Lord Melbourne had paid him £25,102, leaving a balance of £470 before the architect would have to ask his client for more.

Lord Melbourne complained of the cost to Mrs Baddeley when he sat down in her house, saying he was 'tired to death with prancing about all day with his Betsy a-shopping'. Sophia said she had been shopping too, and she laid out some silks from Mr King, the silk merchant. Lord Melbourne opined that the silks were not as beautiful as Sophia, and gave her £100 to pay her bill with Mr King. He added: 'King has done well today for my Betsy has been there and bought silks to a great amount in order to hang her rooms; and when they are completed they will be very elegant.'

Mrs Steele noted: 'His Lordship declared ... upon his honour, that when the house, in Piccadilly, which he was building, was finished, and the furniture in it complete, so as to sit down in it to dinner, from a just calculation, it would cost him £100,000. "An astonishing sum!" exclaimed I. "It is a much greater sum," continued his Lordship, "than I intended, when I first began"; for Mr Chambers' the surveyor's estimate of the house and offices complete, did not exceed £30,000; but, after they had gone on some way, and had made by his orders, some few alterations, it came to twenty thousand more. So that the buildings [*sic*] of that house came to £50,000, beside the £16,000 paid for the old house and ground.'

Melbourne House certainly cost over £66,000 to complete, about £7.4 million today. Under Elizabeth's direction, it was to become for a time the most fashionable house in London. But the extraordinary cost of meeting both their ambitions would soon bring money troubles to the Melbourne household.

Lord Melbourne's artworks were displayed on the walls lined with the silk that Elizabeth had chosen at Mr King's shop in Covent Garden. Anne Damer placed a restraining hand on Elizabeth's more flamboyant flourishes. Mrs Damer moved in 1776 to a house in Sackville Street backing on to the gardens at Melbourne House and Elizabeth made arrangements to allow her friend to have a gate and a window in the wall into their garden.

Chambers dictated the design of the interior of Melbourne House right down to the door escutcheons and he had a dispute with Lord Melbourne over 'bling'. He wanted the furniture supplied by Chippendale and the mirrors to be gilded, particularly in the round room, but Lord Melbourne was against it aesthetically and also possibly because of the extra cost. Lord Melbourne wrote to Chambers saying he had stopped the gilding at Chippendale's workshops:

Upon full consideration about furnishing the round room (in which you have exceeded my utmost wish) I am more and more averse to admit any gilding whatever even in the furniture, in my opinion the Elegance of that room is from the lightness of well disposed well executed Ornaments; vastly preferable to any load of gilding we could have introduced. Therefore I am sure that carrying that Simplicity throughout, we shall succeed much better; and the novelty of a room of that sort finished without any gilding, cannot fail to Please. Therefore I wish you would consider in what manner we can colour the glass frames and Chairs, so as to correspond with that uniformity we have already so much attended to. I have stopped the gilding of any of the things for that room, at Chippendale's, altho' some few things were done, but I had rather give up that, so that we may make the room all Perfection, by which it will give me great Pleasure, and particularly as it will put your taste very superior to any in this Country.

Chambers, however, was in favour of some glitter with gold leaf. He replied to Lord Melbourne: 'It is I think clear that the Glasses and Soffas in the Niches should be gilt, for glasses without gilding are large black spots that kill the effect of every thing about them, and the dead coloured silk with which the soffas are to be covered, must have gold to relieve it; when it will suit perfectly with the room; and I am under no apprehensions that the brilliancy of the gilding will hurt the effect of the rest, but rather set its plainness off to advantage. The Chairs must of Course be gilt, but they are much too small; Arm Chairs would have answered much better.'[19]

Lord Melbourne won that battle. Visitors described the furniture as being painted white without gilding. Elizabeth ensured that the other entertaining rooms did not lack a sense of theatre. In her own dressing room, she had more wall sconces and mirrors than even Chambers wanted.

In the gallery, Elizabeth covered the walls with flowered silk framed with a carved gilt-wood border. The carved stucco ceiling was decorated in green against a red background and there were fifteen frames containing classical scenes, including Venus dressed by the Graces, the Judgement of Paris and the Triumph of Cupid. There was a large semi-circular sofa, specially designed to fit the alcove, in rich brocade and matching gilded cabriole elbow chairs. The walls of the drawing room in the centre at the back of the house were hung with crimson satin and the chimneypiece, one of several by James Paine, was of antique green marble.

Beneath the ceiling decorations on the theme of love, Elizabeth would hold court with her female friends and the leading lights of the Georgian political world, mixing a heady cocktail of Whig politics, plotting and secret pleasures, all guided by her subtle hand. 'The new wealth of the Lambs had supplied the beautiful and ambitious daughter of Sir Ralph Milbanke with the means of spreading the gilded nets of fashion,' said Torrens, with his usual barely concealed note of censure. 'And within her subtle toils a rare succession of the gaily plumaged and idly chattering birds were to be seen, caught for a little while and then let go. But Lady Melbourne was not a woman to be satisfied with a show of brilliant equipages, or the celebrity of sumptuous banquets over which the guests lingered until dawn.'[20] Her ambition, said her son's Victorian biographer, was to exchange the Irish peerage for an English one (and a seat in the House of Lords) by 'clever arts of courtiership and by those of fascination over clever men and high-born dames, epicures of quality, posts of renown, statesmen of note, and Princes of the Blood'. Torrens wondered what pain she had caused to Lord Melbourne in the process of climbing the social ladder on her back: 'What sacrifices her indolent and undemonstrative mate had silently to endure by what regrets his hours of solitude were haunted, by what jealousies his dreams were troubled, who will ever know?'

One is tempted to add, who will ever care? Lord Melbourne may not have been acquiescent in his wife's affairs at the outset, but Lady Melbourne was sufficiently strong-willed to point out to her husband that he was the first to break their marriage vows.

The tensions between them were kept private and within their marriage. Lord Melbourne eventually settled down to a grumbling acceptance of his wife's adultery in return for the honours and rewards it brought him, while he dallied with Sophia Baddeley; but his forbearance would be put to the test by the arrival of George Wyndham, the third Earl of Egremont.

Egremont was intelligent, charismatic and amusing. He was also rich – he had a very large town house in Piccadilly and owned the Petworth estate in Sussex where he displayed some of the art works collected by his father, and some of the modern painters such as William Turner, whom he sponsored. He began advising Lady Melbourne on the decorations for Melbourne House. Before long Elizabeth and the earl became the targets for scuttlebutt gossip.

One of Chippendale's magnificent cabinets, known as the Panshanger Cabinets, now at Firle Place in East Sussex, where they are used to display the Melbourne Sèvres dinner service. (Author, courtesy Firle Place, the family seat of Nicholas Gage, 8th Viscount Gage)

5

Halcyon Days at Melbourne House – and an Unmasking

The Prime Minister's son-in-law recorded in his diary a scandalous rumour that was running around the gentlemen's clubs of St James's that the Earl of Egremont had 'bought' Lady Melbourne from Lord Coleraine.

Lord Glenbervie, who was married to the daughter of Lord North, the Prime Minister, noted:

> It was a very general report and belief that … Lord Coleraine [George Hanger] sold Lady Melbourne to Lord Egremont for £13,000, that both Lady and Lord Melbourne were parties to this contract and had each a share of the money.[1]

Elizabeth's lover, George Wyndham, the third Earl of Egremont, engraving after Thomas Phillips 1810, when he was fifty-eight. (Courtesy of the National Portrait Gallery)

This was shocking even to Georgian ears but it speaks volumes for Georgian morality that it was believed by many to be true. Perhaps it was because they would believe anything about Elizabeth's former lover George Hanger, who had earned a reputation as a womaniser in the army and became equerry to the fun-loving Prince George, later the Prince Regent.

He was the youngest of three Hanger brothers who in turn inherited the title of Lord Coleraine and was shameless in his pursuit of sexual conquests, which he later claimed he 'studied' at Eton with the daughter of a seller of cabbages. He claimed some of the ladies in the Devonshire set were no different to prostitutes because they had paid for their gambling debts with sex.

In his 1802 bawdy memoirs *The Life Adventures and Opinions of Colonel George Hanger (Written by Himself)* he wrote:

> There is no great difference whether a woman receives money to intrigue or intrigues with a man to whom she has lost a sum of money too large for her finances to pay; and it is well known many modest women have liquidated their debts of honour by an honourable surrender of their persons. What female heart can gold withstand? What cat's averse to fish? ... Modest women often, to pay a debt of honour lost at cards, have honourably surrendered their persons to men equally disagreeable to them. You are tempted to the deed, to defray your necessary expenses: they have no excuse whatever; it is not even to gratify their sensual passions that they make a surrender of their persons, but only to indulge that cursed vice – gaming ... I once knew a lady so scrupulously decorous in her conduct in public that she would never give her hand to anyone but her partner in dancing but presented her elbow, who afterwards was unfortunately caught in familiar conversation with a lamplighter, one dark evening, in the house passage.

Perhaps it was true the third Earl of Egremont paid for Elizabeth to free her from a debt owed to Hanger. Lord Egremont was twenty-three, urbane, and like Elizabeth had a razor-sharp tongue. They shared a number of passions, including horse racing, farming, the Whig cause (in moderation) and the arts. He became a famous patron of the arts and she quickly appreciated his taste. She consulted him about the interiors of Melbourne House and when it was complete, he became a regular visitor to her Whig salons. In addition to sponsoring artists, who used Petworth as a college of art, he also had a stud with a string of race horses good enough to win the Oaks and the Derby five times.

Charles Greville noted in his journal after the earl's death from an old illness, an infection of the respiratory tract, 'Lord Egremont might have acted a conspicuous part in politics if he had chosen to embark on that stormy sea, and upon the rare occasions when he spoke in the House of Lords, he delivered himself with great energy and effect; but his temper, disposition and tastes were altogether incompatible with the trammels of office or the restraints of party connexions and he preferred to revel unshackled in all the enjoyments of private life, both physical and intellectual which an enormous fortune, a vigorous constitution, and literary habits placed in abundant variety before him...'

The Earl was not particularly handsome, but had that indefinable quality called charisma and a honeyed voice that charmed women and men alike. 'There was in his voice and manner, say his contemporaries, that fascination for women and even for men, which neither knew how to resist,' wrote Torrens. 'At Melbourne House, he was a constant guest and through a long course of years his friendship and sympathy were never wanting.'[2]

George Wyndham succeeded to the Egremont title in 1763 at the age of twelve and, according to Greville, he had an annual income of up to £300,000, equivalent today to over £38 million, from his various estates covering 24,000 acres. In addition to Petworth, he owned Orchard Wyndham in Somerset, Leconfield Castle and the Percy family lands in east Yorkshire, Egremont Castle in the Lake District and even the summit of England's highest mountain, Scafell Pike. He added O'Brien to his name when he inherited estates in Ireland from Percy Wyndham-O'Brien, Earl of Thomond, in 1774. In London, he inherited his father's extensive Palladian mansion at Ninety-four Piccadilly, where he kept a liveried coach steered by postilions dressed in white jackets. The house had been built by Lord Egremont's father in 1756 on the site of an inn facing Green Park between White Horse Street and Half Moon Street.

Egremont House had a half-acre garden with a Chinese gate and a Chinese pagoda laid out by Capability Brown, who had created the deer park at Petworth. To say young George Wyndham sowed his wild oats is a gross understatement. He sowed whole fields of wild oats with at least fifteen mistresses, some of whom he later accommodated at Petworth with an army of illegitimate children. When I visited Petworth, now a National Trust house open to the public, I asked how many children he had sired. 'Up to forty,' said one of the house guides. I assumed this was an exaggeration but if anything it was an underestimate.[3]

Georgiana Cavendish's disapproving mother, Countess Spencer, confidently asserted Wyndham had at least forty-three children living with their mothers at Petworth, where they 'make scenes worthy of Billingsgate or a Mad House...' Others claimed he sired over seventy offspring and only one, a daughter, was legitimate and she did not live for long.[4]

'In early life,' wrote Torrens, 'Lord Egremont professed to be no more than a man of pleasure, given to hospitality, fond of the turf, content to be a cause of war among strategic mothers. Rather shy and taciturn, many outshone him in the ballroom, none in the morning ride or garden walk.'

His youthful escapades included crashing into a bedroom at Mrs Mitchell's, a high-class brothel in Upper John Street, Soho Square, with his boisterous friends including Charles James Fox to find Viscount Bolingbroke romping with an upmarket courtesan called Liz Armistead. Liz, who spoke with a Cockney accent and counted George Cavendish, son of the fourth Duke of Devonshire, among her titled lovers, was passed around a string of aristocratic men including Frederick St John, Lord Derby, Lord Dorset and – inevitably – the lusty Prince of Wales. She found love with Fox, the future leader of the Whigs, and they married in September 1795 at Wyton near Huntingdon, but kept it secret to preserve Fox's reputation until 1802.

George Wyndham was seen by many debutantes' mothers as an ideal suitor for their daughters. He later told Lord Holland: 'There was hardly a young married lady of fashion who did not think it almost a stain upon her reputation if she was not known as having cuckolded her husband; and the only doubt was, who was to assist her in the operation.'[5]

He assisted the liberal-minded and worldly-wise Lady Melbourne in cuckolding her husband. She was in her mid-twenties but still possessed the bloom of youth, lustrous brown hair and beguiling blue eyes that had shone in the Reynolds portrait when she was nineteen. It was not just her good looks that captured the Earl of Egremont. Lady Birkenhead, who wrote an account of Georgian Piccadilly, said Lord Egremont was won over by Lady Melbourne's 'unbounded zest for life, good humour and ease in men's society'.[6]

Wyndham's women included Elizabeth Fox, the Duke of Devonshire's mistress, who later became the Duchess, and Lady Holland, by whom he had four or five children. Lady Melbourne clearly knew Wyndham's reputation, and must have known she could not capture so prolific a lover all for herself, but she was prepared to accept his advances with no emotional ties.

Having provided Lord Melbourne with an heir, Elizabeth saw nothing wrong in allowing herself to be seduced by the earl. Letters by her friends show they were seen openly together, at first in company with Lord Melbourne but later without him. They went to the theatre together in a party that included one of the Hanger brothers, and were listed by Georgiana among her guests in the Devonshires' box, with Lord Melbourne almost as an afterthought: 'We had in our Box Ly Melbourne Ly Carlisle Ld Carlisle, Ld Egremont Ld Edward Ld Melbourne Mr Storer & Mr Hanger...'[7]

Elizabeth saw no advantage in divorcing Lord Melbourne to marry Egremont. She understood the social cost of breaking up a family, and anyway, she rightly judged Wyndham was not the marrying kind. He was a moderate

Whig like Elizabeth, and they never shared the zeal of Fox, Canning and Grey and their acolytes for Thomas Paine's *Rights of Man* and the French Revolution. Elizabeth and Egremont were politically alike. They opposed Paine's 'seditious' writings but the earl never entered national politics. He obtained seats in the Commons for his younger brothers, but he was too fun-loving and (probably) self-effacing to make a political career at Westminster.

The earl hated to stand on ceremony, and in later life invited groups of people to visit his house in Sussex and leave when they wished. Guests would wander through the rooms admiring Turner's landscapes of the sun setting over the deer park alongside canvasses by Van Dyke and Constable and portraits of their society friends by Joshua Reynolds. Charles Greville, the diarist, recorded seeing Turner there, wandering around the long gallery, studying the old masters on the walls in the fading light. Petworth was, said Greville, 'like a great inn ... Everybody came when they thought fit, departed without notice or leave-taking. The house wants modern comforts and the servants are rustic and uncouth but everything is good.' Lord Egremont 'never remained for five minutes in the same place and was continually oscillating between the library and his bedroom, or wandering about the enormous house in all directions; sometimes he broke off in the middle of a conversation on some subject which appeared to interest him and disappeared and an hour after on a casual meeting would resume it just where he left off.'

Egremont was an enlightened philanthropist and caring toward his tenants; he began an emigration scheme for impoverished families from Petworth to start sheep farming and cattle rearing on land he bought near Adelaide in South Australia and in Canada.

Elizabeth and the earl shared a passion for horticulture at Petworth, with ideas which she passed on to her estate managers at Melbourne Hall, and at the earl's prompting persuaded Peniston to join investment schemes such as that for the Cromford Canal. She wrote to her steward at Melbourne Hall asking for 'twelve papers of Powders for Cows that have the Red water of the Man who lives as you go upon the Carr moor and makes Basketts...' The powders were for the two milkers she kept in Green Park, near their house in Piccadilly. In another letter, she took Fox to task over the failure properly to thin out the woodland at Melbourne Hall so that the trees would provide cover for game. But she wrote to thank Fox for supplies of meat from Melbourne: 'We are much obliged to you for the finest Mutton that ever was seen which arrived perfectly safe.'[8]

She also kept a grip on the running costs of her two country estates. She wrote to Fox, 'I beg you will hire me a Dairy Maid as soon as you can as I am obliged to part with Ruth; she has eight pounds a year ...If you can I would rather you would hire one for less than that with a promise of increasing her wages if she behaves well...I wish her to understand a Dairy & not be afraid of Work. She must also help the Confectioner in the house...'

While she kept a tight grip on the purse strings in the country, Lady Melbourne continued to spend Lord Melbourne's money as freely as his mistress, Sophia, in London. It was all bound to cause embarrassment before long. As the architects' bills for Melbourne House mounted, Mrs Baddeley appealed to Lord Melbourne to pay off her own soaring debts.

Sophia was propositioned during private parties at the notorious Three Swans on the island at Kew by a series of tradesmen wanting sex in return for wiping out her debts for clothes and jewels she had bought on credit. One merchant, who sold her expensive vases, is said to have offered Sophia £1,000 off the bill to have sex with him; she angrily refused, but she desperately needed more money to keep her creditors at bay to avoid debtors' prison. She wrote to Lord Melbourne:

My Dear Love, I am exceedingly distressed for twenty pounds and if I have it not today, it will really be of bad consequences. I think I am fully as deserving as *some folks* you are so attentive to. I dare say you know who I mean. I am sure I have no right to question you, but am sorry to think you stand in need to be constantly put in mind of your old *friends*. God bless you! I am most invariably yours, Sophia Baddeley.

Sophia was approached by another titled admirer, after she went to a puppet show, *Fantocini,* and realised she was being stared at by the Duke of Ancaster. He was in his sixties and married to Lady Melbourne's friend Mary Panton, the wealthy jockey's daughter. The next day, he called at Sophia's home in Grafton Street, where she had moved with a promise by Lord Melbourne to pay her rent. The grey-haired duke declared his love to Sophia in classical terms: 'No man can gaze on you unwounded. You are like the Basilisk whose eyes kill those whom they fix on.' Mrs Baddeley replied that his wife must be fortunate to have such a gallant husband, provided he did not think of another woman.

'I do not, except it be you and it is not in my power to avoid it,' he said. The Duke wasted no more time in putting his money on the table. 'If I could have the satisfaction to find you meet my wishes, you should be as happy as my fortune and my attention could make you.'

Sophia told him she had 'obligations' to another man, but rebuffed the elderly peer in such polite terms that he thanked her. When he left, Mrs Baddeley told Mrs Steele that in future, she would resist temptation more often, because men like the Duke of Ancaster would respect her more for saying 'no'. Scarcely had she uttered these words, however, when Lord

Melbourne arrived to spend a few hours with her. He told her he was going to Bath, or at least supposed he should, because 'his dear Betsy had talked of it' and if they did, he would be away for three weeks.

Sophia told him that if he went to Bath, she would leave London for the country. While Lord Melbourne was upstairs having sex with Mrs Baddeley, a man who Steele refers to as 'Mr P.' called, demanding money to pay some of Sophia's many debts. He wanted to know whether Lord Melbourne had been 'liberal' lately and Mrs Steele made it clear that if this anonymous caller needed more money, she would squeeze Lord Melbourne for it. After 'Mr P.' left, Lord Melbourne came downstairs, saying Sophia was suffering from a headache. 'I found her headache was a pretence to quiet Lord Melbourne who, from being in high spirits, was as noisy as he could be.'

Sophia was clearly growing bored with Lord Melbourne's 'noisy' sexual demands. She had planned to go to the seaside at Margate during Lord Melbourne's absence in Bath, but instead she went to Ranelagh, met the freebooting MP and soldier Colonel Henry Luttrell, later second Earl of Carhampton, and went off with him to Ireland, trusting that Lord Melbourne would never know. Her subterfuge was to prove her undoing.[9]

When she returned to London, the lavish expenditure on Melbourne House spurred Sophia into pressing Lord Melbourne for more money to pay off her debts. Her urgency increased when Mrs Steele was hounded by bailiffs brought in by Sophia's silk merchant, Mr King. She complained to friends that Lord Melbourne had cut her off 'without a guinea' for nine months.

'Could anyone suppose that after having led me by his bounty and the expectations he had taught me to form into expenses which I cannot answer, he should slight me as he does? Such behaviour is wicked,' she complained. 'If he loved me as he often swore he does, he would not treat me this way. If I have done anything to offend him, he ought to leave me like a gentleman, not involved as I am but free from debt and embarrassment.' Mrs Steele agreed: 'His Lordship failed in his word to me; did not make me the settlement he promised; did not pay my rent as he agreed to do; nor gave me a shilling of what Mrs Baddeley owed me, though he often assured me he would pay the whole, nor did I ever receive a present from him except the horse.'

Sophia did not know that Lord Melbourne had discovered she had gone to Ireland with Luttrell. Mrs Steele sent her debt-collector, 'Mr P.', to press Lord Melbourne for more money but he refused, saying: 'I now see the impropriety of my conduct with Mrs Baddeley and I have done with her.'[10]

As soon as word got out that Lord Melbourne had dropped her, Sophia had a queue of willing suitors wanting to call on her. Mrs Steele claimed Sophia's line of would-be lovers jostling for her affections included Lord

Delaval, the forty-six-year-old Sir John Delaval of Seaton Delaval Hall, who was related by marriage to the Milbanke family.

Sophia decided to tackle Lord Melbourne in public to embarrass him into giving her money. Her chance came at a masque held at Carlisle House on the east side of Soho Square, which had been taken over by an enterprising courtesan called Madame Cornelys, who recreated the erotic masquerades of Venice in a ninety-three-foot-long ballroom in an extension to the house. It was reached by a romantic Chinese-style bridge probably built by Chippendale, who was one of her creditors. Here she staged sensational balls and masquerades, where the rich could romp incognito behind their Venetian-style masks. Knowing that Lord Melbourne was likely to be there, Sophia made a point of going, dressed as a masked shepherdess, while Mrs Steele went in a domino, a long cloak, a man's hat with a long feather and her face covered by a mask. Sophia planned to keep her mask on the whole evening and 'attack' Lord Melbourne when she saw him. The rooms were crowded and Mrs Baddeley slipped in unrecognised behind her mask. Before long, she spotted Lord Melbourne sitting down 'with a female who had lived with him before he was married; her name was Harriet Powel though from him, she called herself Harriet Lamb and enjoyed a settlement'.

Harriet Powel was in close conversation with Lord Melbourne for some time. Sophia sat down at a little distance from them, unnoticed, but could not hear any of their conversation. At last, Harriet Powel left him and Sophia got nearer to him but did not say a word until she was within reach, when she caught hold of his arm, saying: 'Ah, rebel! Have I caught thee?'

'My God! Is it possible? What, Mrs Baddeley?' asked Lord Melbourne.

'Yes,' she said. 'It is even her.'

He pressed her not to unmask. They were surrounded by masked revellers making assignations of their own, but were oblivious to what was going on around them. A foreign minister was pleasured under the supper table by one masked lady; Mrs Steele said his family were respectable and rich because they lived near Grosvenor Square but that it was no more than he had asked Mrs Baddeley to perform at her house. Another lady who was esteemed by all those of strict virtue put her virtue behind her when she donned her mask. The son of the Dean of Exeter, dressed as a milliner, hovered close by. They overheard Lord Palmerston, father of the future Prime Minister, making a secret rendezvous for sex in an alley near his house with a lady.

The masquerade swirled round them as Lord Melbourne challenged Sophia to explain what had made her send 'Mr P.' to him to draw him into promises of more money. She told him she did no more than she thought right.

'You may possibly think so,' said Lord Melbourne. 'But I think differently.'

He asked Sophia how she had enjoyed her excursion to Ireland with her new lover. The realisation she had been found out came as a shock to Sophia, but she acted coolly, saying: 'That's not a question, my Lord, after your neglect of me that you have any right to ask. You have not acted by me as I deserve and I find a pleasure in telling you so.'

Lord Melbourne told her it was her fault, not his, that he deserted her, because if she had not gone away with Luttrell he would not have disowned her. She said that his refusal to pay her had nearly ruined 'Mr P.', who had underwritten her debts. Lord Melbourne said his own fortune was 'considerably injured' and that he did not know whether it would allow him to pay so large a sum as her debts amounted to. He told Sophia she should have cut her extravagance, not run on as she had done, for she had nearly ruined him. He refused to pay her any more money.

From that moment, Sophia began a long and tragic descent, eventually selling herself to her merchants to pay off her debts, which were estimated at over £4,000 – equivalent to more than £400,000 today. In the end, she lived with her own manservant, and died of consumption in 1786 at the age of forty-one. Harriet Powel remained a shadowy figure about whom little is known, but she and other mistresses added to the pressure on Lord Melbourne's dwindling fortune. The cost of building Melbourne House, Elizabeth's bills, and those of his mistresses began to put a severe strain on Melbourne's finances. He raised more money by remortgaging the house.

Ten years after Melbourne House was completed, there was still £3,000 owing to Chambers, secured by a bond, on which the interest was two years in arrears. Chambers remonstrated with Melbourne, who offered him a year's interest, but he still owed him the money in March 1789 when it was secured by a mortgage. The debt was still undischarged 1792, when Melbourne sold up. Yet, in spite of the cost, Melbourne declared himself pleased with the house. 'I believe few people have had better reason than myself to be pleased with so large a sum laid out,' he said.

The stables had been occupied by their horses and carriages since the spring of 1773; the designs for the screen-wall were done, and the interior work was started from the top of the house once the roof was watertight. By October 1773 most of the plasterers were out of the house, and the paving of the floor in the great hall leading to the staircase was about to begin. The Melbournes were anxious to move in. They partly moved in when the paving in the hallway was laid at the end of 1774 although the house was still a building site with the scaffolding up, workmen banging and sawing timber, and dust and dirt flying everywhere.[11]

By November 1774, like many house owners, Lord Melbourne was getting impatient with his architect because additional work was still being done.

He wrote a flattering letter to Chambers saying, 'I am sure in this you will Shew, as you have in all other parts of my works, more taste, and in every respect give me more satisfaction, than all other Architects put together could possibly have done.'[12] But his real motive was to tell Chambers he hoped the workmen would be out of the house by New Year 1775. 'I was in town for a few hours yesterday and think the Ceiling extreamley Pretty. I am afraid they will be a considerable time about it yet. I wish you to make Mr Evans determine to finish it in a month, at all Events I must beg the workmen to be out by New Year's Day.' He added that he hoped he would see 'the Yard and the Coach Houses cleared from the Dirt the Stone Masons Have made'.[13]

Elizabeth and her husband wanted to hold a spectacular 'house warming' for New Year. They would stand for no more delays; the scaffolding to the first floor was taken down, Chambers' workmen finished the 'round room', and the doors were thrown open to an invited audience of guests for morning concerts on two days to admire their creation – one of the finest private houses in London.

For Elizabeth, the daughter of a country squire from the North Riding of Yorkshire, it was a triumph. Over the five years since her marriage, Lady Melbourne had established her reputation as a clever, vivacious hostess, and her salon at Melbourne House would become one of the most fashionable places for the elite pleasure-seekers to be seen in London. Melbourne House quickly became recognised as one of the liveliest places of entertainment for the *beau monde*. The cleverest, wittiest men of Whig society stepped down from their carriages, and climbed up the steps to the front door of the Melbourne's new house off Piccadilly.

Conversation around the dinner table at Melbourne House reflected Elizabeth's personality. It was virile and challenging, but not boorish. Above all, it was fun. She knew how to get on with men, and was careful about revealing too much about herself. Lady Melbourne's 'masculine point of view' was the product of a masculine intelligence, said Lord David Cecil. 'The mental atmosphere was not fastidious. The spirit of Melbourne House offered no welcome to the new romanticism. It was plain-spoken, it laughed uproariously at fancifulness and fine feelings, it enjoyed bold opinions calculated to shock the prudish and the over-sensitive, it loved derisively to strip a character of its ideal pretentions. From mischief though, rather than from bitterness, an unflagging good humour was one of its two distinguishing attractions.'[14]

Guests at Melbourne House would enjoy a convivial supper by candlelight, before relaxing in the glittering gallery under Cipriani's cupids. The atmosphere was casual, like a gentleman's club, and unless banquets were organised, meals came and went at odd times as unexpected pleasures.

A few days after her house party in January 1775, Lady Melbourne and her coterie of friends went to the first night of the Sheridan's *The Rivals* and laughed uproariously at seeing themselves satirised on stage.

The informal mood extended to the relaxed conversations, which had the arrogance and the confidence of a club where the members are largely like-minded, though it was far from being intellectual. Elizabeth had an unusual ability to tap into a man's interests, combining feminine intuition with a man's view of the world. She would pitch herself into other people's problems, giving advice that earned the respect of men such as Lord Byron. She was capable of loving, but did not give her feelings away, and above all held to the rule that society would forgive anything, provided it was in private, and done with discretion. She had little sympathy for women who destroyed their families by giving in to their passions in a public manner; she believed a woman might have many lovers but that should be no excuse for neglecting her children or, come to that, her husband, or damaging him by outraging the accepted standards of society.

Lady Melbourne was at the peak of her powers as a society hostess when a younger star arrived who would shine for a time even brighter than Lady Melbourne: Georgiana, the Duchess of Devonshire.

6

Georgiana

William Cavendish, the fifth Duke of Devonshire, had inherited a fortune when he was only sixteen with estates that generated an estimated £60,000 a year – over £7 million today – including the honey-coloured stately home of Chatsworth in Derbyshire.

He had enjoyed the hedonistic life of a bachelor like Lord Melbourne at gaming clubs and trawling the pleasure gardens at Ranelagh for young women until he was twenty-five, when he decided the time had come to marry and produce an heir. He married Georgiana Spencer, the eldest daughter of the Earl and Countess Spencer, on 7 June 1774. There was so much excitement about the 'wedding of the year' that the date and place had to be kept secret to avoid crowds.

They were married at the parish church in Wimbledon Park near the Spencers' house, and a few days later Georgiana was presented to Queen Charlotte looking lovely at 'a drawing room' at St James's Court. She wore her wedding dress of white and gold with silver slippers, pearl drops in her hair, and a magnificent set of diamonds from the Duke, who ambled in four hours late.[1]

The excitement was passed down to the servants at Devonshire House in Piccadilly that had not seen a Duchess since the tragic death of Charlotte Cavendish from smallpox two decades earlier. Floors were polished, dust covers removed and the house was prepared for the return to its former splendour under a new chatelaine, who was still a naive seventeen-year-old.

Cavendish had been brought up to expect that his wife would supply loyalty and an heir. If he wanted romance, he could go to his mistress, a milliner called Charlotte Spencer (though no relation) who was pregnant with his illegitimate daughter, also to be called Charlotte, when he married Georgiana.

Georgiana was the same age as Lady Melbourne when she had married Sir Peniston, but they were totally different characters. Where Elizabeth was cool and calculating, Georgiana was overt and demonstrative in her affections. Lady Mary Coke wrote disapprovingly in her journal that Georgiana 'cannot walk into a room; she must come in with a hop and a jump. She seems to have unfortunate good spirits tho' I believe she is perfectly good humour'd and innocent, I don't believe she will ever be a day older.'[2]

Pitt's niece and companion, Lady Hester Stanhope, who became famous for her travels through the Middle East, caustically commented: 'As for the Duchess of D it was all "fu fu, fuh" and "what shall I do? Oh dear me! I am quite a fright!" – so much affectation that it could not be called high breeding…'[3]

Georgiana was no great conventional beauty. She admitted as much in a self-mocking verse:

> I've oft puzzled to find, why hard 'tis to trace
> The features and looks of my comical face,
> Since a moderate drawing might surely comprise
> A snub nose, a wide mouth and a pair of grey eyes.

Elizabeth was twenty-two, five years older than the Duchess, when Georgiana arrived at Devonshire House. Lady Melbourne might have more poise, but she astutely realised she could never compete with the young Duchess, who had both superior rank and a freshness that left hardened cynics grasping for superlatives about her looks.

Even the worldly-wise writer Horace Walpole in his late fifties was won over by her youthful beauty. He commented to a friend that she 'effaces all without being a beauty but her youth, figure, flowing good nature, sense and lively modesty and modest familiarity make her a phenomenon'.[4]

Knowing she could not outshine Georgiana, Elizabeth decided to make herself an indispensable ally of the Duchess, as a confidante and mentor. Keep your friends close and your rivals closer. The Duchess for her part realised the dangers of her own inexperience, and came quickly to rely on the advice from her sagacious friend Lady Melbourne, much to the annoyance of her mother, Lady Spencer.

Lady Melbourne was, said the Duchess's biographer, Amanda Foreman, 'ferociously practical and discreet, she could also be sarcastic and cutting when irritated. Georgiana was in awe of her temper…' Lady Melbourne's influence over her daughter deeply irritated Lady Spencer, and Georgiana's younger sister, Henrietta Ponsonby, Lady Duncannon – later Lady Bessborough – who was known by the family as Harriet. She so despised the prickly nature of Lady Melbourne she dubbed her 'the Thorn'. That did not deter Georgiana, who addressed her letters in the most effusive fashion to Lady Melbourne, like a young lover: '*Je t'aime mon coeur bien tendrement*, indeed, indeed, indeed, I love you dearly...'[5] She often called Lady Melbourne 'My dearest Them' for Themire, the Goddess of Justice. She was keen to win her approval in intimate notes to Elizabeth, even after some years:

> I am dead asleep my D [ea]r D[ea]r Love but [Lord] Melbourne must have a line to take to you. Do not think because I am idle that I do not love you. *Je t'aime, je t'adore, ma chere, finira qu'avec ma view.* Pray write to me, tell me that you love me and are not angry with me. I have a thousand things to say to you, *mais le moyen sans te voir* [but without the way to seeing you]? Why don't you come up. I cannot leave London this week but I hope to get a few days with you ... Bless you.[6]

Soon after she married the Duke, Georgiana became alarmed by her husband's apparent lack of affection. It had more to do with his own inhibitions than his lack of feelings for his wife. With women, he was taciturn and serious, happier discussing Shakespeare – whose works he could quote at length – than lengths of silk for dresses.

Georgiana feared she was at fault, and wrote to her domineering mother, Lady Spencer, formerly Margaret Georgiana Poyntz, for advice. Lady Spencer's father had risen from humble beginnings as the son of an upholsterer to become a privy councillor to George II and had instructed his children to be dutiful, courteous and, above all, discreet. Lady Spencer instructed her daughter to be obedient to her husband and to please him:

> Where a husband's delicacy and indulgence is so great that he will not say what he likes, the task becomes more difficult and a wife must use all possible delicacy and ingenuity in trying to find out his inclinations, and the utmost readiness in conforming to them. You have this difficult task to perform, my dearest Georgiana for the Duke of D., from a mistaken tenderness, persists in not dictating to you the things he wishes you to do, and not contradicting you in anything however disagreeable to him. This should engage you by a thousand additional motives of duty and gratitude to try to know his sentiments upon even the most trifling subjects, and especially not to enter into any engagements or form any plans without consulting him.[7]

This was the polar opposite of the more cynical advice she received from Lady Melbourne, after they became close. Amanda Foreman considered that in

Lady Spencer's eyes, Lady Melbourne 'epitomised the decadence of Georgiana's friends'. Lady Melbourne was a 'natural manager of people. She had a firm, unsentimental, even cynical view of humanity ... Once Lady Melbourne had presented [her husband] with an heir he allowed her the freedom to do and see whom she pleased.'[8] Lady Melbourne provided the comradeship that was missing in Georgiana's relationship with her mother, and their friendship was sealed in their joint escapades in fashion, the theatre – and simply having fun.

Georgian ladies – with little else to do – loved staging plays, and Georgiana and Elizabeth appeared together with Anne Damer in dramas that they staged for their friends at the Duke of Richmond's private theatre in his house in Whitehall (now the Department of Health) and Brocket Hall. These were no mere drawing room *Mansfield Park* theatricals; plays at the Duke's private theatre attracted the great figures of society to the audience, including members of the Royal family.

To celebrate their performances together, Elizabeth asked the artist Daniel Gardner to portray herself and her two friends as the three witches in *Macbeth*, which drew an inevitably caustic comment from Lady Coke:

> Has Lady Greenwich told you of the Duchess of Devonshire, Lady Melburn and Mrs Damer all being drawn in one picture in the Characters of the three Witches in Macbeth? They have chosen the Scene where they compose their Cauldron but instead of 'finger of Birth-strangled babe etc' their Cauldron is composed of roses and carnations and I daresay they think their charmes more irresistible than all the magick of the Witches.[9]

It was more than just an amusing portrait of three friends play-acting. It was how Elizabeth saw her own role in the Devonshire circle, and how she was seen by some of the leading ladies around her. Lady Melbourne saw herself as a force for good, stirring the social pot to facilitate liaisons among her friends and casting political spells for the Whigs. Her critics such as Lady Spencer and Harriet saw her influence as malevolent, and Lady Holland compared her to the scheming widow Madame de Merteuil in *Les Liaisons Dangereuses*.

The portrait in pastels was displayed in the Prince of Wales's room at Brocket Hall, which he used when he visited the Melbournes. Today it belongs to the National Portrait Gallery; the guidebook says: 'Daniel Gardner's choice of the cauldron scene from Macbeth can also be related to their shared and shadowy political machinations as leading members of the Devonshire House circle, which became a focal point for supporters of the leader of the Whigs, Charles James Fox.'

The portrait coincided in 1774 with Lady Melbourne's first political campaign with her two fellow 'witches'. In January that year, news reached

England of the attack on the East India Company's tea clippers in Boston harbour on 16 December by American colonists who tipped a precious cargo of 342 chests of tea into the water as a protest against British taxes on the commodity. Whig ladies such as Lady Sarah Lennox sympathised with the colonists while wishing to avoid British casualties. 'I pity poor Mr Penn as I do every *good* American who must suffer dreadfully in these times,' she wrote.[10]

Lord North responded by introducing more punitive measures to restore British authority in America including closing Boston harbour, taking direct control of the justice system to ensure rebels were punished, and regulating Massachusetts Bay. Lord North split opinion at home, and called a general election in 1774 to secure the authority of Parliament for his sanctions on the American colonists. Lady Melbourne joined the political campaign in support of the Whig opposition under the second Marquess of Rockingham by hosting a party for her Whig friends at Melbourne House. The general election split the nation.

The Devonshires were one of the most powerful Whig families in Britain. The dukedom was bestowed on William Cavendish, the first Duke of Devonshire, as a reward by William of Orange for signing the letter of support by leading Protestant landowners inviting William to invade Britain and depose the Catholic James II in the Glorious Revolution of 1688. The election was seen by the Whigs as a battle between enlightenment and repression by George III and his government. The Salisburys, Elizabeth's neighbours in Hertfordshire, were Tories who supported the king. The king wrote: 'The die is cast. The colonies must either submit or triumph. I do not wish to come to severer measures but we must not retreat.'

George III's repressive policy was famously denounced by Edmund Burke within days of Lady Melbourne's party at Melbourne House:

> Be content to bind America by laws of trade; you have always done it … Do not burthen them with taxes … if intemperately, unwisely, fatally, you sophisticate and poison the very source of government by urging subtle deductions, and consequences odious to those you govern, from the unlimited and illimitable nature of supreme sovereignty, you will teach them by these means to call that sovereignty itself in question … They will cast your sovereignty in your face.[11]

Lady Melbourne went to Brocket Hall to organise the local Whig campaign for the two county seats in Hertfordshire. She rode in her open landau with Mrs Brand, the wife of Thomas Brand, another Whig candidate, and entered the county town of Hertford with a band of musicians to stir up support for her Whig candidates. Agneta Yorke, widow of a former Cabinet minister, wrote: 'Lady Melbourne and Mrs Brand entered the Town in Triumph at the Head of the Melbourne Party with an open Landau filled with Musicians playing before them.'[12]

The two Whig candidates, William Plumer and Thomas Halsey, were opposed by a young Tory, the Honourable James Grimston, later Viscount Grimston, who was twenty-seven. Plumer and Halsey had the backing of all the local Whig landowners including Lord Spencer, Lord Hardwicke, Lord Howe, and George Byng of Wrotham Park, a friend of Charles James Fox. Lord Salisbury refused to back anyone, saying he would not interfere in the election.

There were 500 people eligible to vote in the seat and they were bribed with £4,000 in accommodation and entertainment to attend the hustings meeting and vote. Plumer, who was returned unanimously, said in a letter to the Duke of Portland: 'Such a scene of riot and confusion, I did never see ... Halsey and Grimston were proposed separately, and after much time and noise, the sheriff decided that Grimston had the greater show of hands.' Grimston lost in a second ballot.[13] When the dust of the hustings settled in October, Lord North was returned with an overwhelming majority, though he told the king he was uncertain about his ability to run the country.

The newly built Melbourne House became a centre for Whig opposition, a political salon with lavish parties, receptions and suppers presided over by Lady Melbourne. Every time Lord Melbourne looked in on her soirées, he found Lord Egremont by his wife's side. He may have objected but Peniston – having of course been the first to break his marriage vows with Sophia Baddeley – was too weak to intervene.

'When Lord Melbourne found Lord Egremont in constant attendance on his wife, Lord Egremont's opinion followed in preference to any other,' wrote Lady Airlie. 'The ball once rolling could only be stopped by a man of stronger character than the son of the Hertfordshire attorney possessed.'[14]

Lord Egremont was by her side when Lady Melbourne went with the Devonshires to the races at Derby in September 1775. Lord Melbourne was also part of the Devonshires' racing party, but he appears to have dropped out when the Devonshires invited their party to join them after the races at Chatsworth. No further mention of Lord Melbourne was made when Georgiana wrote to her mother. Her note, entirely in French, says: 'I got up early and we went with Lady Melbourne, Lord Egremont, Lord Cholmondeley, Lord George and Lord Frederick in a coach to the park [the Chatsworth estate]...'[15]

Lord Melbourne may have been required in London but it is possible he refused because the affair with the Earl of Egremont was so obvious. If he made any entreaties to his wife, she ignored them. Lady Melbourne stayed at Chatsworth with Lord Egremont for the rest of the week, and left Chatsworth at eight o'clock on Friday morning to go to Lady Sefton at Croxteth Hall in Lancashire before travelling on to her father, Sir Ralph Milbanke, at Halnaby Hall in Yorkshire.

She told Georgiana she was reluctant to do so because the roads were so bad and she would be 'seeing a person who is not the friendliest as you know but she had promised'. This is likely to be a reference to her father's mistress, a widow with children, who had moved in with him at Halnaby Hall following the death of Elizabeth's mother, eight years before.

The Earl of Egremont stayed another day, and left Chatsworth on Saturday with Lord Cholmondeley. The clue to the disclosure of Elizabeth's love affair comes in a letter in French from Georgiana to her mother about going to the chapel in Chatsworth on Sunday. Mr Wood, the preacher, gave a lesson 'on the clemency of our Lord for the woman caught in adultery'. She told her mother the lesson in the Bible (John 7:53–8) contained 'the famous response that he who is without fault should throw the first stone against the woman'. Georgiana added: 'We must draw the conclusion to be careful not to condemn others without being perfect ourselves.'[16]

Neither the Devonshires nor the Melbournes were particularly religious and it was extremely rare for Georgiana to quote from the Bible in her letters to her mother. Was Georgiana indirectly asking her mother not to be too judgmental about Lady Melbourne because her secret was out? If so, Lady Melbourne's week with the Earl of Egremont at Chatsworth may have proved a watershed moment in her life; the moment when Lord Melbourne tacitly accepted his wife's infidelity.

Lord and Lady Melbourne agreed not to separate or divorce despite having long-term lovers because the arrangement suited them. After his betrayal with Sophia Baddeley, Elizabeth accepted her husband's infidelities – there were rumoured to be others including Harriette Wilson, a courtesan who wrote a notorious memoir of her exploits with celebrated men such as Wellington. She claimed to have been let down by Frederick Lamb but liked his father Lord Melbourne, a broad-minded gentleman. He acquiesced in his wife's affairs because it brought him social advancement and the rewards of titles and status.

Georgiana's mother continued to press her daughter to drop Lady Melbourne. She knew Georgiana was impressionable and Elizabeth was persuasive. Lady Melbourne had shocked Georgiana with her view that it was a duty for a wife to provide a husband with an heir but that after this it was permissible to have affairs, providing one was discreet.

Lady Melbourne's 'lessons' to Georgiana appeared to have been remembered accurately when the Duchess published an anonymous novel called *The Sylph*, in which the wronged but naïve heroine is advised by Lady Besford, 'You can do what you please once you have done your duty by your husband, but not till then.'

The older, wiser 'Lady Besford' – surely drawn from Lady Melbourne – advises her to ignore her husband's infidelity and have affairs of her own: 'You do not suppose my happiness proceeds from my being married, any further than I enjoy title, rank and liberty by bearing Lord Besford's name. We do not disagree because we seldom meet. He pursues his pleasure one way, I seek mine another … My Lord kept a mistress from the moment of his marriage. What law excludes a woman from doing the same? Marriage now is a necessary kind of barter and an alliance of families – the heart is not consulted.'[17]

This was clearly bitterly drawn by the Duchess of Devonshire from her own life. The Duke had a mistress, Charlotte Spencer, when he married Georgiana. 'Lady Besford' also may have been describing Elizabeth's 'Smithfield bargain' with Sir Peniston Lamb. The passage gives 'the most intimate view of Lady Melbourne's ideas', said Jonathan David Gross, editor of her letters.[18]

Georgiana's inability to meet Lady Besford's first requirement – to produce an heir for the Duke – made her more anxious and frustrated. The Duchess of Devonshire was the toast of London, constantly in the newspapers and pursued by fashionable young men with whom she flirted. She popularised a fashion for ostrich plumes in her floppy, wide-brimmed hats. She also wore her powdered hair piled high into towering head-dresses decorated with flowers, ribbons and even fruit, all topped by nodding feathers. Lady Melbourne also wore feathers in her hair, but stopped short of the excesses of some ladies who piled their hair so high they had difficulty climbing into carriages or sleeping lying down.

Georgiana created a fashion for 'picture' hats when she posed for a celebrated portrait by Thomas Gainsborough at the height of her fame wearing a wide-brimmed hat and a knowing smile. The portrait had a chequered career; it was stolen in 1876 from Agnews, the auction house in London, by an American criminal and cut down, but in 1994 it was bought by the Chatsworth Trust at the behest of the Duke of Devonshire and returned to the house where it hangs today.

Georgiana's outrageous hairstyles were ridiculed in the popular press by the cartoonists; one by Sayer showed servants tending her hair with a long pole while another squirts a fountain of water to put out one of the feathers that has caught fire in a candelabra.

The Morning Post published a mocking guide to the attractions of the celebrity women of the *beau monde*. The Duchess of Devonshire was given high marks for beauty, her figure, elegance, wit and principles, but low marks for grace and sensibility. Lady Melbourne in contrast was given high marks for elegance, grace and principles, but low marks for wit and no marks for her figure. That was not as bad as Lady Jersey, the wayward daughter of an army chaplain, who was judged to have no sense and no principles.[19] Lady Coke reported: 'The *bon ton* are still in Town, Duchess of Devonshire, Ly Melburn, Mrs Damer etc., they have dinners, suppers, etc., and live much together.'[20]

Lady Sarah Lennox, daughter of the Duchess of Richmond, wrote from near Goodwood where her brother was building her a small new home, Halnaker House, on the racecourse:

I hear much of Ly Melbourne who is a great friend of the Dss of Richmond and comes to Goodwood every year: I find she is liked by everybody high & low & of all denominations, which I don't wonder at, for she is pleasing, sensible & desirous of pleasing, I hear, which must secure admiration.[21]

Lady Sarah disapproved of the giddy Duchess of Devonshire:

The pretty Duchess of Devonshire ... has hysteric fits in a morning & dances in the evening: she bathes, rides, dances for ten days, & lies in bed the next ten; indeed, I can't forgive her, or rather her husband, the fault of ruining her health, tho' I think she may wear ten thousand figaries [whims, or sudden impulses] on her dress without the smallest blame.

It seemed that nothing could blot their glorious Georgian lives, as long as the money did not run out. Even when it did, wealthy parents were there to help their offspring avoid the Marshalsea, the debtors' prison at Southwark. Charles Fox repeatedly called on his indulgent father, the first Lord Holland, to bail him out after running deeply into debt through cards. A few evenings before Fox moved the Repeal of the Marriage Act in February 1772 he had borrowed £10,000 to wager at whist and piquet at Brooks's in St James's Street. He was a skilful card player, but thirsted for the neck-chilling thrill of winning or losing a fortune at Faro on the turn of a single card by the banker from 'the shoe'.

Between debates in the Commons, the beetle-browed Fox fed his gambling addiction, wearing a broad-brimmed hat to protect his eyes from the candlelight. He sat up all night at Almack's playing hazard from Tuesday evening until 5 p.m. on Wednesday. He lost £12,000 and recovered it all, but by the time he rose from the card table he had lost £11,000 again. On Thursday he spoke in a debate, went to dinner after 11 p.m., then went to

White's Club where he drank and played cards until 7 a.m. the next morning, then to Almack's where he won £6,000. He took his winnings at cards to gamble on the races at Newmarket. Charles lost £10,000 while his older brother Stephen lost even more heavily, bringing the losses by the two Fox brothers in one week to £26,000 – equivalent to over £1 million today.

Their father, Lord Holland, agreed to pay off their debts, but it was a temporary respite. When Lord Holland died in 1774, he left Charles £154,000 to pay his debts, but it was all spoken for and Fox soon became as deeply in debt as before. Being in debt seemed not to trouble him and Walpole said he remained cheerful when he met him in the street as the bailiffs were removing his library of books. The Georgians were bluntly anti-Semitic about their moneylenders, many of whom were Jews, and were reluctant to pay off their debts, even when they had the money to do so. George Selwyn recorded in 1781 seeing the bailiffs loading Fox's furniture on carts outside his house in St James's Street while 'Charles, Richard and Hare [were] holding a bank of £3,000' at cards in Brooks's across the road.[22]

Sheridan, who was also frequently pursued by moneylenders, pawned his belongings but reached an agreement with his pawnbroker to borrow back the books and the plate for one night so that he could host a dinner for his guests; his dinner party on pawned plate was a success, except the pawnbroker forgot to supply the spoons.

Money in Georgian London was spent carelessly because the wealthy landowners reaped a cash harvest from their estates. They gambled because they were bored; many never had to work for a living. Lord Melbourne played Faro at Almack's with Lord Stavordale, who complained after winning £11,000 that if only he had played for higher stakes he might have won millions.

The ladies were almost as bad as the men. The Duchess of Devonshire ran up debts of more than £60,000 at cards – equivalent to their annual income from the Devonshire estates. She tried to keep the exact amount secret from her husband, who reluctantly paid off her debts against the advice of his family.[23] She never really got over her addiction to gambling; in 1802, four years before her death, her sister Lady Bessborough was still privately expressing her concern about Georgiana: 'I am in sad distress about my Sister. Sunday everything will be laid before K [the Duke of Devonshire]. He expects five or six [thousand pounds of debt] – and it comes to thirty-five [thousand pounds]! She is dreadfully agitated but if it can but be settled, I feel certain it is final and will be every thing for the happiness of both.'

Georgiana was terrified at the truth getting out, and used friends and bankers to avoid a scene with the Duke; but others in her set were complacent about their debts. Lady Melbourne seems to have avoided heavy gambling losses at cards, though she may have dabbled in shares. Horace Walpole was baffled by her carefree attitude to money:

> On Tuesday, I supped after the Opera at Mrs Meynel's with a set of the most fashionable company which, take notice, I very seldom do now, as I certainly am not of the age to mix often with young people. Lady Melbourne was standing before the fire and adjusting her feathers in the glass, says she: 'Lord! They say the stocks will blow up; that will be very comical.'
>
> These would be features for comedy if they would not be thought caricatures but today I am possessed of a genuine paper that I believe I shall leave to the Museum. It would in such a national satire as *Gulliver* be deemed too exaggerated.

The 'satire' referred to sarcastically by Walpole was a petition by the Foley brothers, Thomas and Edward, to the House of Lords for a change in the law to override their father's will so they could pay off their gambling debts.

Lord Foley had paid off £50,000 from losses at Newmarket by Thomas, his eldest son, in return for a promise to quit gambling. Within three years, Thomas owed a further £70,000. George Selwyn said in a letter to Lord Carlisle: 'Old Foley pays another £70,000 of debt and settles, I hear today, £4,000 in present upon his son and £6,000 a year more at his death.'

This generous annuity was not enough to pay off the creditors. The interest alone on their debts was £17,450 a year and they launched a campaign to allow them to plunder the whole of their legacy to pay their debts.

Lady Melbourne took up their cause but she had to contend with Horace Walpole, who said no words, no ridicule, could match the absurdity of their appeal to the Lords: 'All the Ladies Melbournes and all the Bishops' wives that kill their servants by vigils are going about town lamenting these poor orphans and soliciting the peers to redress their grievances ... Poor unfortunate children. Before thirty the eldest had spent an estate of £20,000 a year.' The younger brother, Edward, had 'dipped in the same extravagance with him' and the legislature was being asked to set aside 'a just punishment ... And if it does, it will deserve that every lad in England should waste his father's estate before his face.'

Walpole woefully predicted the end of civilisation in England: there would be mud huts in the ruins of temples; government would crumble away unless Benjamin Franklin came from America to 'new-model' the British government. 'Everybody is sensible of it, and everybody seems to think, like Lady Melbourne, that if we are blown up, it will be very comical.'

Lady Melbourne had allies to support the Foleys, including the Duchess of Devonshire, though that was a mixed blessing. The acerbic Lady Coke, a critic of Georgiana's girlish high spirits, was shocked to find the Duchess was so out of touch with reality that she seemed entertained by the distress of Thomas Foley's wife, Lady Harriet, when the bailiffs arrived at her house to seize everything she had:

> Her Grace's [Georgiana's] misfortune is a very unnatural one, that of being too happy and delighted with everything she hears and sees so the situation in which she found Lady Harriet was, in her Grace's opinion, Charming. Lady Harriet told her she had no Clothes; this was Charming above measure. She added that Bailiffs were then in the House. 'Delightful,' said her Grace. 'Lord, I am afraid we shall never have Bailiffs in Devonshire House.'[24]

Having condemned the Foleys for their recklessness from the comfort of his neo-Gothic house at Strawberry Hill, Walpole would see his cousin, Mrs Anne Damer, whom he 'loved as his own child', suffer an even worse tragedy.

Her husband John Damer and his two brothers ran up gambling debts, largely on wild bets on horse racing, totalling £70,000 and applied to their father, Lord Milton, to pay off their creditors. Lord Milton, who lived in a grand house in Park Lane, now the site of the Grosvenor House Hotel, refused. He suggested that the two older brothers should flee to France at once to escape their creditors, taking Mrs Damer with them. As the arrangements were made Mrs Damer rushed to Berkshire to say farewell to her family, but while she was away her husband took his own way out.

Walpole described the grisly details in a letter to one of his friends:

> On Thursday Mr Damer supped at the Bedford Arms in Covent Garden with four common women, a blind fiddler and no other man. At three in the morning he dismissed his seraglio, bidding each receive her guinea at the bar, and ordering Orpheus [the blind fiddler] to come up again in half an hour. When he returned he found a dead silence and smelt gunpowder. He called, the master of the house came up, and found Mr Damer sitting in his chair, dead, with a pistol by him and another in his pocket! The ball had not gone through his head nor made any report. On the table lay a scrap of paper with these words, 'The people of the house are not to blame for what has happened, which was my own act.' This was the sole tribute he paid to justice and decency![25]

Mrs Damer was unaware of her husband's suicide when she returned to London. She saw Lady Harriet Foley in her coach, and her husband Thomas, who was called Lord Balloon because he was so fat, leaning upon the coach door. They had heard about her husband's death but neither had the courage to break the news to her. Mrs Damer drove on in ignorance in her carriage, but the Foleys spotted Charles Fox on horseback and asked him to break the news to Mrs Damer.

When Fox caught up with her carriage, he too was unable to give her the grim account of what happened, but she guessed. Lady Mary Coke said that when she reached home John's brother George told her John had committed suicide. 'She was hardly in her senses and insisted upon seeing him for they did not tell her where he had shot himself till some time after.'[26]

Anne Damer's glittering career as one of the beautiful people was exploded with one gunshot. Lord Milton vindictively blamed her entirely for his son's death, saying he had killed himself because she had never loved him. His fury may have been increased by unsubstantiated rumours that his son's estrangement from his wife was due to Anne being a lesbian.[27]

Her half-sister, Lady Sarah Lennox, said John

> …was as much to blame in giving her the example of never being at home, as she was to make all her way of life opposite to his … as it's evident love was out of the question, I must give her credit for her present conduct … I believe nobody will have a right to tax her with any fault and yet she will be abused, which I take to be owing to a want of sweetness in her disposition; she is too strictly right ever to be beloved.

Lady Sarah accused Lord Milton of being brutal towards his daughter-in-law. Milton vented his fury by selling her jewels, furniture, carriages and everything he could to pay off his son's debts. He abused her for staying in his son's house. 'Upon hearing this she left it and chose to go in a hackney coach, taking only her ink-stand, a few books, her dog and her maid with her out of that fine house.'[28]

The Damers' servants were owed fourteen months' wages. She paid those in immediate want; the rest generously refused to take their back pay, and accepted no more money than they needed to get by on, said Lady Sarah. 'She walked through the house amidst them all into her hackney carriage with a firmness that is quite heroic for though she may be accused of not loving her husband, she cannot be accused of not loving her house and all her grandeur.'[29]

Mrs Damer went to stay with her mother and father, General Henry Conway and Lady Ailesbury, at their country seat at Park Place, Berkshire, to enable her to save a year's income, £2,500, to pay off more of her husband's debts. (Park Place was bought by a Russian businessman in 2011 for a reported £140 million.)

Georgiana later used the Damer tragedy in her novel. In her story, the indebted husband sells his wife to his creditor. She runs away but the husband escapes his debts by shooting himself in a cheap room at a tavern, just as Damer had done.

It was a long way from the amusing pastel portrait of the three 'good witches' or muses around the cauldron. Anne Damer retreated to Park Place to concentrate on her art, and became a celebrated sculptress. Walpole encouraged his cousin to seek solace in her art and it is possible that had this disaster not befallen her, Anne Damer would have been remembered as a socialite rather than a talented sculptress. Walpole suggested she should work in artists' studios, go to Italy to see the art treasures, and study with Dr William Cumberland Cruikshank, an anatomist. She won a series of commissions including one to model the two heads of the rivers Thames and Isis for Henley Bridge that are still there. Lady Melbourne rallied round, giving Anne some commissions for her sculptures to show her support.

Anne made her debut at the Royal Academy in 1784 with a full-size marble bust of Lady Melbourne, which Walpole said captured Elizabeth's looks to the life. Anne also modelled some amusing pieces for her friend including Lady Melbourne's two kittens in terracotta that were later carved in marble, and an osprey, the snowy-feathered fish-eating eagle, caught on Lady Melbourne's estates.[30] Lady Melbourne wrote to Georgiana:

> You can not imagine how low Spirited she has been. If ever I found her alone I was certain to find her Crying; but I hope she will be better now as she has changed the Scene for her own House was certainly the worst place she could be at...
>
> I hear Lady Harris goes to Newmarket next Tuesday and that they stay there almost all the Month, we are to be at Sir Charles Bunbury's [Lady Sarah Lennox's first husband] just before the first October meeting. I have some idea you are to be at Newmarket then pray write me word if it is so because I will endeavour to persuade Lord M [Melbourne] to Stay there till that time; if you was inclined to be compassionate you would come to Sir C B [Charles Bunbury's] too for you know how happy it would make him.[31]

Her letter also carried news that Georgiana's parents, Lord and Lady Spencer, had met Lady Melbourne's fat and jolly uncle Admiral Mark Milbanke when they unexpectedly visited his warship, HMS *Barfleur*, a ninety-gun guardship, while it was moored off Portsmouth harbour:

> I hear Lord and Lady Spencer and all the Party I saw at Brighthelmstone [Brighton] went afterwards to Portsmouth and I had an uncle there and they went on Board his ship. He came here a few Days ago and complained that there came a whole Boat full and that he did not know the name of any one of them and Baron C distressed him particularly for he asked what

War the Sailors wished for and as he [the Admiral] did not know where he came from he was afraid of telling him for fear he should hit upon his own Country – Ecrivez moi au plutot je vous en prie, adieu ma chere Duchess. [Write to me as soon as you can I pray you, goodbye my dear Duchess]

Lady Melbourne was ready to welcome Anne Damer back to society, and she returned to the laughter, music and politically charged gossip at Melbourne House. To help her get over the catastrophe, Lady Melbourne encouraged Mrs Damer to appear in some amateur productions at the Duke of Richmond's house in Whitehall. Alongside Lord Fitzgerald, Lady Buckinghamshire and her half-sister, the Duchess of Richmond she performed in two farces, *The Way to Keep Him* and *The Jealous Wife*, with Fox and Sheridan. In May 1777, less than twelve months after Damer's suicide, Lady Melbourne and her set turned out to see the first night of Sheridan's play *The School for Scandal*, which satirised his friends in the audience. They roared with laughter at *Lady Teazle* – thought by many to represent Georgiana – being berated by her husband for being a spendthrift, while *Lady Sneerwell* captured Lady Melbourne's acid tongue:

> Psha! there's no possibility of being witty without a little ill nature: the malice of a good thing is the barb that makes it stick.

In the play, Lady Sneerwell repels the attempts by Joseph Surface to seduce her, but in real life, Elizabeth was already Egremont's lover. Soon, there was gossip that Lady Melbourne was pregnant by him. Lady Coke was at a social engagement when she saw Lady Melbourne was heavily pregnant. She acidly reported the Melbournes were expecting another child despite their straightened finances: 'The Duchess of Devonshire came in … upon Lady Melburn's arm. Her Ladyship is with child which occasions great joy to my surprise, thinking as they had spent the greater part of their fortune, it was happy they had but one Child but it seems they are of different opinion.'

Lady Coke wrote in September that the Melbournes were still in London and their house open to all of the right people who remained in town, although Lady Melbourne's child was due in December: 'I hear of parties and suppers frequently; her Ladyship lies in in December.'

On 25 October Lady Coke wrote:

> The news of the day was Ly Melburn being brought to bed of twins, but as she was considerably before her time, the son died soon after it was born, but the daughter was alive and they hoped might be brought up.

She added that Lady Greenwich had been spreading gossip that Lord Egremont was the father. The gossip was confirmed by Lord Egremont's mother when she spoke to George III at court.

> Lady Greenwich is you know a little scandalous but ... Lady Egremont [Lord Egremont's mother] said something to the same effect to His Majesty in the Drawing Room [at court, at St James's], who answer'd he was sorry her Grandson was dead.[32]

In fact, Judith Noel, wife of Lady Melbourne's older brother Ralph, reported Elizabeth gave premature birth to twin girls; they were two months premature and the second twin lived for three days. *The Newcastle Courant* on 1 November reported with brutal clarity: 'The two children, of whom Lady Melbourne was delivered a few days ago, are both dead; one died immediately after it was born and the other died yesterday.'

Judith could be waspish in her letters but after staying with her sister-in-law at Brocket Hall for three days in January 1778, she had mellowed towards Elizabeth, although she would clash swords with her later on. She said: 'As to Lady Melbourne the more I know her the more I like her and think her very much too good for her *Lord & Master*.'[33] Judith said Elizabeth 'herself is as well as can be expected'. Giving birth was hazardous at the best of times. Her brother John Milbanke's wife Cornelia, daughter of Sir William Chambers, was not so fortunate. She died in 1795 giving birth to twins who also died. John poured out his grief in a marble memorial tablet at the Milbanke family church at Croft-on-Tees where she was buried:

> The grief-struck heart, the sorrow-tinged eye,
> Remembrance wakes, though lost they beauties lie,
> Two lovely babes, that heav'n in mercy gave,
> Just born to bloom, and wither in the grave...
> With me to weep, with me for years to mourn
> The best of mothers in Cornelia's urn.

Cornelia was forty-two. Elizabeth was only twenty-six when she lost her twin daughters by the Earl of Egremont. Surviving the premature birth of her twins with no ill-effects required strength, and it showed that Elizabeth was made of tough Yorkshire fibre. Within a few months, she was pregnant again.

7

Cocks Heath

Dressed in a tight red military tunic, Georgiana, the Duchess of Devonshire, cut a dashing figure as she rode with her husband at the head of the Derbyshire county militia through the streets of London.

They were riding to a vast military encampment at the hamlet of Cocks Heath on the North Downs of Kent that had been established on the orders of Lord Amherst, the head of the British armed forces, to block a threatened invasion by the French before they could reach the capital.

'The only news I cannot believe,' wrote one of Georgiana's astonished acquaintances, 'is that the Duchess of Devonshire marched through Islington at the head of the Derby militia, dressed in the uniform of that regiment.'[1]

The London Chronicle also reported she was in a military tunic but she was in the rear when they passed through on 23 June 1778: 'The Duke of Devonshire marched at their head. The whole regiment made a very noble appearance equal to any regulars whatever. If the militia of the other counties prove as good, there is no doubt but that they are a match for any force that can be brought against them. The Duchess of Devonshire followed the regiment, dressed *en militaire*, and was escorted by several attendants.'[2]

Lady Melbourne's local militia from Hertfordshire under the command of Lord Cranborne, the son of Lord Salisbury, had marched to the North Downs of Kent two weeks earlier in black boots, gaiters and red tunics with gorgets and gloves. They were among the first to arrive on 6 June, according to their order book.[3] They were followed by the Surrey regiment on 8 June, the South Hampshires and the Duke of Grafton's West Suffolks on 10 June, the West Middlesex two days later, the Duke of Devonshire's Derbyshire regiment on 25 June and the Cheshires under Lord Cholmondeley on 29 June. The South Hampshire militia commanded by Richard Worsley camped briefly at Lord Egremont's Petworth estate and it is likely the earl joined them for the ride up to Kent with Worsley's beautiful wife, Seymour, Lady Worsley. Like Georgiana, Lady Worsley wore a dashing red military tunic and red riding skirt. Lady Melbourne too rode down to Kent to the gathering throng among the fluttering county flags at the Kent encampment where she was to meet her lover, Egremont.

It took two days for the Duke and Duchess of Devonshire to ride from London to the encampment at Cocks Heath with a wagon train of carts carrying all the encumbrances of an army on the move: pots, stores, meat, bread, powder, tents for the men, and marquees for the Duke.

The Duke and Duchess of Devonshire brought with them many of the comforts of Chatsworth, the Duke's stately home in Derbyshire, including Oriental rugs, festoon curtains, fine furniture, silver plate, candelabras, and chintz sofas to recreate a stately home under canvas. Her ladyship had one more comfort – a chamber pot, carried reverently by the butler as Georgiana enthusiastically reported to her mother on 11 July 1778:

> I live entirely in camp. I have a bed in the Duke's tent which is the largest I have seen, & Betty [her maid] comes to dress me & put me to bed. The Duke has a very large tent for a dining room, it is about the size of the tents at Wimbledon [the Spencers' home], within that is the bedchamber that is still larger & has two recesses at each end, within these are the servants bedchambers dining room & kitchen … After supper there was a great confusion in the tent, for I was to undress very near in publick as my bed was brought in by some of the footmen and the others were making the D of Ds, I was very near laughing at the gravity with which Marsden brought a chamber pot into the tent.[4]

Fearing a French attack on London, Amherst appointed a seasoned warrior, Lieutenant-General William Keppel, to command the combined militia and regular armed forces camped on the rolling North Downs of Kent. The professionals, the Dragoons and regiments of hardened foot soldiers were ordered to block the most direct route from the south coast to London in mid-May, followed by the volunteers.

Wives, mistresses and prostitutes had often followed an army on the march, but great society ladies such as the Duchess and Lady Melbourne had very rarely joined the camp followers. They had been caught on a tide of national patriotism that swept the great houses of Georgian England after the French declared war on Britain in support of the Americans in the Revolutionary War. The French intervention had turned skirmishes in America into a global conflict that was soon joined by the Spanish, threatening Britain and its empire. The Duchess of Devonshire had ordered her seamstresses to create a riding tunic based on her husband's militia uniform of scarlet with green facings and the other ladies of *the ton* had followed her lead.[5] There is no record of Lady Melbourne appearing in military-style uniform (her husband appears not to have volunteered for the militias) but her presence at the camp was soon noted in Georgiana's letters to her mother.

Cocks Heath camp presented an unrivalled picturesque spectacle and drew thousands of curious tourists to witness it. 'Her Grace the Duchess of Devonshire appears every day at the head of the beauteous Amazons on Cocks Heath who are all dressed en militaire in the regimentals that distinguish the several regiments in which their Lords, etc. serve, and charm every beholder with their beauty and affability,' reported *The Morning Post*.

More than 15,000 men – half the defensive strength of Britain – were billeted in conical tents that stretched across the downs to the horizon like an encampment of American Indian tepees with smoke curling from countless camp fires. Regimental colours fluttered from flagstaffs at the head of each division where the sergeants pitched their tents. The officers' marquees were pegged out in the middle of each battalion, surrounded by the tepees of their men.

The camp was about thirty-six miles from London and ran along a ridge road about two and a half miles in length from the public house at the sign of the Cock in the village of Boughton to a copse of trees. The crash of mock battles, marching bands and the thunder of cavalry kicking up dust became so popular an attraction that a regular coach service was laid on, which took eight hours to reach Cocks Heath from the coaching taverns by London Bridge.

Eighteen battalions of infantry and four regiments of foot troops, totalling 12,850 men, encamped in one line with one regiment of dragoons on their right and a detachment of 350 men of the artillery regiment encamped in the rear of the right wing. They were supplemented by hundreds of foreign troops from German states in support of the Hanoverian monarchy.

A field officer wrote in the *London Chronicle* the 'flower of the Nobility' and the militiamen made it a magnet for sightseers. Along with the tourists came chancers, fraudsters, con artists and whores.

The Kentish Times warned its readers on 24 June 1778 the camp at Cocks Heath would bring 'all the vices of the capital to the heart of the country'; 'shoals of people' from town and country would be induced to visit this 'military raree-show'; worse, it said that instead of repelling every form of the French, it would be 'encouraging two of their most baleful productions – French wines, and French-X'.[6]

Lady Melbourne, the Duchess of Devonshire and their friends such as Lady Jersey, Mrs Crewe and Lady Claremont spent their days visiting each other's tents, gossiping and sipping tea. At night they would play cards in the larger tents, and provide dinner. The attractions of having their wives along soon waned with the officers commanding the militias.

Nine days after Georgiana wrote to her mother about the joys of glamping, the Duke of Devonshire moved Georgiana into a large house he rented on The Grove, near the park in the fashionable spa town of Tunbridge Wells, enabling the Duke and his fellow officers to get on with their soldiering and more amorous entertainments in the camp after nightfall.

Georgiana became Lady Bountiful in Tunbridge Wells, bestowing her patronage on the elegant street of Georgian shops called the Pantiles, and made celebrity appearances at balls with her friends at the assembly rooms. The Duchess wrote excitedly to her mother: 'I went to the ball at eight. I danced a minuet and four country dances ... I got vastly acquainted with all the ladies and the ball made a brilliant figure. The Duke and all his officers were there, they looked vastly smart and though there are two or three ill-looking *dogs* amongst the captains there are some very handsome ones – and a great number of young ones who will turn out very well.'

Lady Spencer after this letter clearly feared the gay mood in Tunbridge Wells was going to Georgiana's head. She warned her daughter: 'You should especially at such a place as Tunbridge keep up a civility and dignity in your behaviour to the Men of your own Set – and a courteous good-humour'd affability to the Company in general whom you are little acquainted with, whereas I suspect if you will examine your own Conduct, you put on that killing Cold look you sometimes have to those you would be *prevenante* to, and a great deal more familiarity and ease than is either necessary or proper to the Men about you.'[7]

The attractions of Tunbridge Wells began to pall as the summer nights became hotter, both for the men and their wives. By mid-July, the 'violent heat' was stifling; Georgiana complained to her mother. 'I was almost scorched at first but I went at last to Lord George [Georgiana's brother, the second Earl Spencer] in the wood where the Grenadiers were placed which was very cool.'[8]

Georgiana complained to her mother on 21 July that Tunbridge Wells was 'vile':

We went from the Pantiles to see Ly Hertford, she has an ague which becomes her as it makes her very thin. We din'd alone & went in the Evening to the ball with Ly Sefton Mrs North & the Conways, it was hot & stinking. We found Sir Charles Bunbury & Col. Crawford there, we supd at home I think this is a vile place, it is too like a town to be pleasant in summer & I liked the Camp a thousand times better. It was so much pleasanter to pass ones evenings as I did there, than I do here in a nasty room.

Lady Melbourne and Georgiana went to the camp to see the men marching and the gouty part-time officers struggling in the heat. Georgiana told her mother:

I got up very early and went to the field. The soldiers fir'd very well and I stood by the Duke and Cl Gladwin, who were near enough to have their faces smart with gun-powder, but I was not fortunate enough to have this honour. After the firing was over, Major Revel, whose gout prevents him from walking, sat on horseback to be saluted as a General. The Duke of Devonshire took his post at the head of his company and after marching about they came by Major Revel and saluted him. The D [Duke] really does it vastly well.[9]

Over dinner in the Devonshires' tent, the 'amateur' colonels, the Duke of Devonshire and Lord Cholmondeley, expressed discontent about the duties at Cocks Heath, said Georgiana:

We din'd yesterday at two. Lord Cholmondeley and Mr Henning din'd here. Lord George din'd at the General's. The General [Keppel] is indeed very severe. I have not seen him yet but he keeps up I hear an amazing state, he has a great number of attendants ... they are all afraid of him. There are several regulations with which they are discontented. They make them march and salute to quick time which is very disagreeable but the chief complaint is that so many colonels are away – the Duke of Grafton, Lord Cranborne, Lord Clive and many more ... it is very hard duty for those who are here. The Duke of Devonshire has already been three nights on piquet guard. Lord Cholmondeley, who has been here but a short time, twice. The piquet is walking around to every sentinel in the camp.

General Keppel's correspondence to Lord Amherst was quickly filled with reports of the men ignoring curfews at night and soldiers plundering wood for fires, fruit and livestock from smallholdings. There were numerous complaints of soldiers 'committing great depredations in the orchards, gardens, turnips and fruits, belonging to the poor inhabitants...' Two brothers were brutally lashed, but it did little to put a stop to the indiscipline. There were other temptations that were far more alluring than Kentish turnips. The officers and men lusted after the women who flocked to the camp.

Keppel complained to Amherst in Whitehall that it was difficult to impose a curfew on the men when they saw their officers flouting the rules: 'I fear even officers lay out of camp without leave, yet if disobedience is in them, it is not to be wondered if men follow the example of their superiors knowing that they cannot be punished for a fault their judges on court martial commit themselves.'

As night fell, Cocks Heath was lit by campfires and lanterns as the men went on their nocturnal manoeuvres. *The Morning Chronicle* reported 'the officers were in the practice of conducting their ladies, *pro nocte*, [at night] secretly into their marquees.'[10]

At first, the night-time entertainments at the camp were restrained. Lady Emily Mary, wife of James Cecil, Viscount Cranborne, opened her marquee to whist and cribbage and served supper to a large number of friends. But as the summer wore on, the men and their women became bored with camp life, and their fun descended into childish pranks. She confessed to her mother:

> Our minds have degenerated into infancy. In the beginning of the summer our evenings were passed in conversation and singing of fine songs – we then got by degrees to Macao, cribbage, whist and catches and now we are come to the point of diverting ourselves with 'Laugh and lay down' and 'I'm come a lusty wooer, my diddin, my doldin, I'm come a lusty wooer, lilly bright and shine' and ditties of that sort. As I was going to perform that wondrous feat of touching a red hot poker, she turned her head round suddenly, & set it on fire…upon these occasions I always think it right to go into something like an hysteria – I really must do something to brace my nerves.[11]

The *Cox Heath bulletin* reported: 'General Officers and Cadets, Duchesses and Demoiselles are alike exposed to the snares of beauty and are alike susceptible to the tender passion.'

The long hot nights in the open air at Cocks Heath intoxicated many young couples that summer. Georgiana's husband, the normally diffident twenty-nine-year-old William Cavendish, was easy prey for the racy Countess of Jersey among the marquees. She had inflamed the Duke's passions when she visited Chatsworth a year before with her husband, the staid and dull George Villiers, the fourth Earl of Jersey, and one of her lovers, William Fawkener.

Frances (Fanny) Villiers' back-story is quite outlandish. Her father was an army bishop-turned highwayman who was shot dead one night while attempting to hold up the mail coach at Hounslow Heath. Fanny combined 'seduction and fascination' according to Nathaniel Wraxall's memoirs of the period. Her marriage to the Earl of Jersey elevated her to the highest ranks of society. Lady Jersey's biographer, Tim Clarke, described her as 'unprincipled and malevolent, destined to become one of the most hated women in the country'.[12] Lady Jersey was 'a handsomer but wickeder woman ... little with large black eyes,' Lady Melbourne's son told Queen Victoria when he was her Prime Minister. Georgiana embraced Lady Jersey as an equal and a close friend despite the icy disdain of her mother, Countess Spencer. Lady Jersey became a lively member of the Devonshire House set, with a series of lovers who fathered some of her ten children. She had a vicious streak and was thought to have been the inspiration, with Lady Melbourne, for Sheridan's Lady Sneerwell.[13]

Georgiana discovered that while she had been touring the tents with her friends, her husband had been sharing a tent with Lady Jersey, and he made no attempt to hide the fact. Lady Jersey gloated over her success at seducing the Duke of Devonshire. On being told by Georgiana she had no bed for her in her house at Tunbridge Wells, Lady Jersey retorted: 'Then I will have a bed in your room.'

This was doubly hurtful to Georgiana whose character was without malice; the writer Fanny Burney wrote that Georgiana's beauty was in her openness – 'the expression of her smiles is so very sweet and has an ingenuousness and openness so singular that ... not the most rigid critic could deny the justice of her personal celebrity'.[14]

Unlike Lady Melbourne, who coped with her husband's infidelity by having lovers of her own, Georgiana seemed to withdraw. Her friends were alarmed that Georgiana appeared to be in thrall to Lady Jersey, reluctant to break off her friendship, or do anything to upset her. Her ally, Lady Clermont, decided to intervene and relayed the rumours of the Duke's affair with Lady Jersey to Georgiana's interfering mother, who promptly warned Lady Jersey about the consequences of pursuing the Duke, while also making it clear to the Duke that the Spencers disapproved of his behaviour. Lady Clermont could hardly claim the authority to cast the first stone, though. Georgiana told her mother:

> Lady Clermont has miscarryd, after a retard of some days, & to tell you
> the truth as it is pretty certain Mr Marsden the apothecary was the Father,

> I fear some wicked method was made use of, to procure abortion, & this is more likely as Mr Marsden might bring the drogue from his own shop...[15]

The Countess of Derby was another victim of the febrile, romantic spell over Cocks Heath. She was rated in the top three for her beauty in the *Man of Pleasure's Pocket Book*, but ruined her reputation after falling in love with the Duke of Dorset during the summer of 1778 at Cocks Heath. She ran off with the Duke, leaving her home, her husband, and her children behind to be with her lover, who dropped her soon after. She was ostracised but, following the hypocritical standards of the time, the Duke, a notorious womaniser, was welcomed back into society.

The most striking of the 'beauteous Amazons' on Cocks Heath was Seymour, Lady Worsley. She eclipsed even the amorous adventures of Lady Clermont and Lady Derby and caused a scandal that outraged even liberal-minded Georgian society. The details were revealed to the world in February 1782 when her husband Colonel Sir Richard Worsley sued Maurice George Bisset, a captain in his South Hampshire militia, for £20,000 in compensation for criminal conversation – adultery – with his wife.

Salacious reports of the hearing at the Court of the King's Bench in Westminster Hall were read avidly in London and the stately homes of the landed gentry. A maid at a bath house near Maidstone gave evidence on oath that Sir Richard, Lady Worsley and Bisset came to bathe and wash off the dust from the heat of the day at the cold bath at about noon in September. It was, she added, the end of the hop-picking season:

> Sir Richard and Mr Bissett staid at the door without while she bathed; after she had bathed, she retired into a corner to put on her shift, as Ladies usually do after bathing, and then returned to dress herself, and sat herself down on the seat ... there is a window over the door ...and from which any person who is sitting down on the seat may be seen. When she had almost finished dressing herself Sir Richard tapped at the door and said, 'Seymour! Seymour! Bisset is going to get up to look at you', or words to that affect. Looking around, she saw his face at the window; he continued there for about five minutes; [I] did not see the plaintiff on the outside but believe he must have helped the defendant up; and after Lady Worsley had dressed herself, she went out and they were all merry and laughing together.[16]

Sir Richard, an MP and powerful figure in Hampshire, who owned a stately home at Appuldurcombe on the Isle of Wight, was himself a voyeur. He encouraged his friend the first Marquess of Cholmondeley to view his wife naked to settle a bet over whether she was the 'finest proportioned woman in Europe'. Cholmondeley was used to such wagers. He once placed a bet in the wager book at Brooks's offering to pay Lord Derby 500 guineas 'whenever he fucks a woman in a balloon one thousand yards above the earth'.

They were to hide behind a screen while they spied on her washing, but unknown to Cholmondeley, Fanny agreed to help her husband win his bet by willingly posing for him naked. She gave Lord Cholmondeley his pleasure by posing on a chair as she pulled on her stockings, and then allowed him to watch her as she raised one foot on the chair to tie on her garters.

Sir Richard won his wager with Lord Cholmondeley, but he was humiliated by the outcome of the court case against Bisset. He won the case, but was awarded the derisory compensation of just one shilling on the grounds that due to his multiple affairs and his own complicity, his wife had no virtue of any value to lose.[17]

Cartoonists had a field day with the goings on at Cocks Heath. The scandal produced a new crop of crude cartoons such as *Bath of the Moderns* and *The Maidstone Whim* showing Bisset being lifted up by Sir Richard Worsley to spy on his naked wife. A bawdy cartoon called *A Trip to Cock's Heath* was hurriedly printed to cash in on the popular interest in the outrageous stories of the upper crust at the camp.[18]

It shows a group of fashionable ladies and foppish men admiring a line of phallus-shaped canon about to be fired. One gun in the distance is ejaculating a plume of smoke while the tip of another is caressed by three admiring ladies. The foremost lady is a courtesan wearing a military hat and coat (like the Duchess of Devonshire and Lady Worsley). She is carried on the shoulders of an officer, while two elderly women in the scene are evidently brothel-keepers.

When they returned to London, Worsley's friend Sir Joshua Reynolds painted Seymour's portrait wearing the red riding habit she sported at Cocks Heath. It is tight-fitting to show off her figure. Her left hand rests provocatively on her hip, her right hand holds a leather whip, and she wears a stern look on her face that suggests she would enjoy using it. The painting epitomised the temporary patriotic fervour of the *bon ton* when it was exhibited at the Royal Academy in 1780.

Not even the cool-headed and calculating Lady Melbourne was immune to the heady atmosphere of the camp at Cocks Heath that long hot summer. In late June, she and Lord Egremont pursued their tender passions freely after dark in the heat of the summer nights. By the end of July, Lady Melbourne, twenty-six, was suffering morning sickness and realised she was pregnant again.

Lady Melbourne once said: 'Never trust a man with another's secret, never trust a woman with her own.' Lady Melbourne could not keep her own secret. She confided in Georgiana when they met on a day out to see Knole House, the seat of the Sackville family near Sevenoaks. No mention was made of the father, but it was assumed it was Lord Egremont.

She pressed Georgiana to keep it secret but Georgiana wrote to her mother, Countess Spencer, on 29 July to give her the news of Lady Melbourne's pregnancy with other gossip from the camp: 'Lady Melbourne you know is in your situation and does not look well. It always makes her look thin and pale at first tho' she is so large…'

On Saturday 1 August, after window-shopping at the Pantiles, Georgiana, Lady Jersey and Lady Melbourne set out for High Rocks, a wall of crags near Tunbridge Wells linked by wooden ladders that is still a local tourist attraction. Lady Melbourne drove herself there in a phaeton, a small carriage like the one in which she posed for her wedding portrait by Stubbs. The Duchess again confided to her mother that when she got down from her carriage, Elizabeth had a fall:

> We set out for the Rocks, I drove Ly Jersey & Ly Melbourne was in her Phaeton but the road was so jumbling I thought it must be very bad for her, & she was so unlucky as to fall in getting out, but she assures me she is not hurt, you must not mention this as it is rather a secret her being with child …

Lady Melbourne, however, felt some pain in her side and feared she might suffer another miscarriage. On Monday 3 August, Georgiana added this brief note to her letter before posting it to her mother: 'Ly Melbourne left this morning, her fall has given her a pain in her side & she wish'd to consult [Doctor] Elliot about it.'[19] A decade later Sir John Elliott became physician to Elizabeth's lover Prince George, the Prince of Wales. Elliott remained close to the Melbournes and died at Brocket Hall in 1786 aged fifty.

Lady Spencer scribbled an angry reply to Georgiana urging her to drop Lady Melbourne, but her daughter refused. On 6 August, Georgiana wrote back defending Elizabeth:

> I conjure you my dearest Mama to forgive my warmth about Lady M [Melbourne] today but I do assure you that every thing I have known of her has been so right and her conduct to me so friendly and for my good that I was miserable to see her so low in your opinion – I hope you will not object to my continuing a friendship which it would be so terrible for me to break off…[20]

Safely at home in Piccadilly, Lady Melbourne was assured by her doctor that her pregnancy was not affected by the fall from her carriage. She was well enough to travel back to Tunbridge Wells where, on 13 August, the Duchess of Devonshire reported she and Lord Melbourne were part of a large party that included the notorious Lady Jersey. Lady Melbourne later returned to Brocket Hall where Elizabeth's sister-in-law, Judith Noel, found her in good health. Judith reported on 12 September 1778 Lady Melbourne was 'very agreeable *en Famille*; she is again with Child and I hope will be more carefull and have better Luck than she had last year'.

At Cocks Heath, Georgiana grew tired of the encampment as the deadening heat of summer gave way to autumn rainstorms. She was forced to wait for George III was due to review the troops, after postponing his visit until some of the controversy – and embarrassment – surrounding the camp had begun to die down.

The last two weeks of October were very wet, leaving the heath slippery and disagreeable. A huge marquee had been put up for the king's arrival. *The Kentish Gazette* reported it measured 240 feet in length and 200 feet in width; the top was 'fine canvas, beautifully painted and ornamented with military trophies'.

Georgiana told Countess Spencer: 'The ground is so squashy that they sink in every step that they take. We live entirely in the inner tent, as the flooring makes it preferable to the other ... We got to Cocks Heath to dinner, Mr Crewe, Ld Cholmondeley, Cl Dalrymple, Col'l Philipson & Mr Thorndike din'd there & we had a turtle ... they expect the king on Monday. The Duke has a fire in his tent and it is very comfortable.'[21]

The rain abated on the morning of 3 November when King George III finally arrived.[22] 'It was a great bore as we had been standing all day,' said Georgiana. The Duke of Devonshire led his men past the King at the salute, and Georgiana's discomfort in the mud was worsened by the onset of her period, which she euphemistically called 'The Prince'. It meant that, regardless of her summer flirtations, Georgiana was not with child, unlike her friend, Lady Melbourne, who continued to host parties for her friends at Melbourne House despite her pregnancy.

In December, Countess Spencer was still trying to get her daughter to drop Lady Melbourne for continuing to associate with the scandalous Lady Derby:

Lady D [Derby] insults the world with her vice – she has not only carried on her shameful connection in the most publick manner & with the highest contempt of the laws of decency and Prudence but has completed it by her most unfeeling behaviour...And if, as I am assured, she supp'd on Thursday with you & Ly J (Jersey) at Ly Melbournes she can mean nothing but to draw you in to support the triumph of Vice in which the other two have but too much reason to fear...[23]

Coxheath (it cleaned up the spelling of its name long ago) today is a sleepy dormitory town for London and the South East with a busy road that runs the length of the ridge where 15,000 soldiers once camped. There are still large open spaces where the landed gentry including Lady Melbourne went on passionate manoeuvres among the marquees at night, but the scandals that made this small hamlet the laughing stock of Georgian London are long forgotten. Few of the locals have any idea that Coxheath was once a byword for scandal or that thousands of sightseers flocked there, eager to watch the military manoeuvres and to spot celebrity ladies disporting themselves in their regimental riding habits.

There is not much to arrest the traveller in Coxheath today. The Spice Lounge, an Indian restaurant, competes for passing trade with the Phoenix Chinese Takeaway and the Coxheath Kebab and Pizza. Perhaps it is appropriate that, each June, Coxheath hosts the world championships for throwing custard pies.

There was a theatrical postscript to the story of Cocks Heath. On 30 October 1779 Lady Melbourne and Georgiana went to the premier of *The Camp*, a new musical farce by Sheridan and Garrick which proved a bigger hit than *The Rivals*, running for fifty-seven performances. Garrick caught a cold and died during the run, leading some to say he was the only casualty of the French invasion that never happened.

Lady Melbourne and the Duchess enjoyed being the butt of the jokes when they went to the first night. 'With their Ladies in their regimentals,' says one character, 'upon my conscience I believe they'd form a troop of side-saddle cavalry if there was any hopes of an invasion.'

The Duchess wrote to her mother: 'I went to the play with Ly Melbourne ... the box was quite full of men ... It was vastly good. The first act of the farce is quite charming. It occasioned peals of laughter every minute.'[24]

8

William

Elizabeth, Lady Melbourne gave birth at Melbourne House on 15 March 1779 to the baby she had conceived at Cocks Heath. The boy would become Prime Minister.

By the time the baby was carried across Piccadilly to be baptised on 11 April at the pretty Wren church of St James[1] the rumours were already circulating that the real father was the Earl of Egremont.

Lord Melbourne watched as the priest lifted the baby to the heavily decorated font with its stem depicting Adam and Eve and the serpent entwined around the Tree of Knowledge and made the sign of the cross with holy water on the child's forehead. Alongside the date, 11 April, the registrar for baptisms in Westminster wrote in a flowing hand: 'William Lamb, the son of the Rt Hon Pennyston & Elizabeth, Lord and Lady Melbourn … born 15 March.'

It should have been a proud moment for Lord Melbourne, but he almost certainly knew his second son was not his own flesh and blood. As William grew to manhood his suspicion became a conviction. Pen was fair-haired, with a delicate face and blue eyes, quite unlike William who grew tall, with a mop of dark brown hair and brilliant dark flashing eyes.[2]

The diarist Charles Greville said William was 'a very singular man, resembling in character and manner, as he did remarkably in feature his father, Lord Egremont'.[3] Greville added: 'His distinctive qualities were strong sound sense, and an innate taste for what was great and good, either in action or sentiment.'

The rumours of Lady Melbourne's scandalous affair with Lord Egremont reached Judith Noel, the priggish wife of Elizabeth's older brother, Sir Ralph Milbanke, in Seaham in the north east of England. From that moment on, she never visited Brocket Hall again and refused to discuss her sister-in-law.[4]

William's paternity was never a subject for awkward questions within the Melbourne household, either by Lord Melbourne or by William himself. The only recorded occasion it came up was when William was showing the distinguished artist Sir Edwin Landseer the pictures at Brocket Hall. The artist stopped by a portrait of the Earl of Egremont and compared his features to those of his host. 'Ah, so you've heard that story,' said William. 'But who the devil can tell who's anybody's father?'[5]

William was brought up by Lord Melbourne as his own son, but he devoted most of his love and attention to his eldest son and heir, Peniston. 'How he loved the boy, and how the young affectionate nature, cheerful and pliant and easily pleased, coiled round each fibre of paternal being,' wrote the Victorian biographer William Torrens.

His mother felt that 'if the little stranger [William] was to be prized and loved, all must come from her,' added Torrens. 'She vowed within herself devotion to the bringing-up and future destiny of her second son. Nor was it long before tiny sparks were visible of a nature very different from that which Peniston in infancy had shown.'[6]

As a child Pen loved to ride his pony in the parkland surrounding Brocket Hall. Lord Melbourne admired the way that Peniston held himself tall and proud in the saddle, bravely took his fences and was ready to take a tumble when he was following the hunt. It was often stated that Pen would have frittered away his inheritance on gambling and womanising, given the chance. A guide to the paintings from Brocket Hall says: 'Peniston was an early disappointment to his mother, taking after his father in many respects, "both moral and physical".'[7]

William laid bare the differences between himself and Pen with startling candour in an autobiographical journal that was never published:

> He was nine years older than myself. Consequently he was a man when I was a boy and there could not exist the same familiarity and intimacy between us as between Brothers who are more nearly of the same age ... He had been a good scholar ... but never having thought of Books from the time of school, his historical information was of course slight and superficial, his pursuits had been little and frivolous.[8]

But it would be wrong to suggest Pen was semi-literate like his father. He was prepared for Eton by a tutor, the Revd Thomas Marsham, curate of St Etheldreda church at Hatfield. He lodged with Marsham and his wife Elizabeth at their home, North Place, a rambling late seventeenth-century red-brick house on the Great North Road, some distance from the church on the hill at Hatfield. I found a letter in the Lamb papers at the British Library written from North Place when Pen was nine that shows he was witty, assured and very fond of his mother, an affection that was clearly returned by Lady Melbourne:

> Dear Mama, Mrs Phillips's opinion of me is amazingly flattering especially as she had most likely sipped a little too much brandy, before she threw out such an encomium. However, I will not attempt to diminish my own merits and will therefore patiently wait to be shewn to my uncles as a most civil and well-spoken school Prodigy.[9]

He told his mother Mr Marsham had been given the honour of preaching before the Sheriff at Lincoln. He would not presume to tell Mr Marsham which text to take, but he said it would not be too forward to offer his mother a text from the first book of Ecclesiastes: 'When wine is old thou shall drink it with pleasure.' Lady Melbourne would drink to that.

The most celebrated portrait of Peniston shows him indulging in his favourite pastime, racing. He proudly stands by the 1782 Derby winner Assassin with his little dog Tanner (a nickname for one of the smallest coins, the sixpence). He adopts a pose of haughty arrogance in a top hat and blue tailcoat, his right hand on the horse's reins, and his left on his hip. The horse with its shiny coat looks every inch a thoroughbred, and Peniston appears to be the proud owner. Assassin is widely described as Peniston's horse. In fact, Assassin was owned by Lord Egremont and seems to have been given to Pen by his mother's long-term lover. Assassin was foaled at Egremont's Petworth stud in 1779. The bay horse is listed in the turf register as 'the property of the Rt. Hon Earl of Egremont got by Sweetbriar out of Angelica by Snap'.[10]

Assassin raced until he was five, winning eight races, when he was retired to the Petworth stud. Unlike Lord Egremont, Assassin was never a successful sire. It is likely a proud Lord Melbourne commissioned the painting of his son by the popular sporting artist Benjamin Marshall, a follower of Stubbs, to decorate a wall at Brocket Hall. It would have hung beside the paintings of boys who were not his own.

Elizabeth and Lord Egremont continued their love affair during the most turbulent year of 1780. In June mobs roamed London burning down houses during the anti-Catholic Gordon Riots and Melbourne House was turned into a military post. But the biggest shock for Elizabeth came in July when she heard that despite his apparent devotion to her – and the birth of William – the twenty-nine-year-old Lord Egremont, the bachelor earl, was going to marry Lady Maria Waldegrave, one of three pretty nieces of Horace Walpole.

Walpole warmly welcomed the match with Lord Egremont, writing to a friend: 'He is handsome, and has between twenty and thirty thousand a year. You may imagine he was not rejected by either mother or daughter.'

A month later, in August 1780, Lord Egremont broke off the engagement, causing outrage among Lady Waldegrave's family and friends, including Walpole, who reversed his opinion of Egremont:

> Her lover is a pitiable object on whom her merit would have been deplorably thrown away ... Everybody thinks he broke off the match and condemns him ten times more than would have been the case if he had told the truth though he was guilty enough in giving provocation ... The fate of young women of quality is hard: in other countries they are shut up till their parents have bargained for without consulting them; here they are exposed to the addresses of every coxcomb that has a title or an estate to warrant his impertinence.[11]

'Old Horace' as Torrens calls Walpole, 'snarls at him in his characteristic way as "a worthless young fellow", his offence being that, having proposed to Walpole's niece, Lady Maria Waldegrave, he had seemed to grow cold, whereupon the lady's relatives in a pet threatened to break off the match, which, when he took them at their word, they much repented.'

Inevitably, Lady Melbourne was blamed for wrecking Lord Egremont's wedding plans. The Duchess of Devonshire wrote to her:

> My Dearest Dearest Themire ... I must tell you what happened to me the other night. I was dining with Mr Edward Vernon ... He is a very disagreeable foolish talking man. After having asked a thousand impertinent and ridiculous questions about everybody he said 'Was you in town when Ld E's [Egremont's] match went off?' I said no – he then said Egremont deserv'd to be hang'd and asked me what reason people gave for it and then said quite loud, 'It proves that Lady Mel is very handsome'. I looked I believe very angry and said quite gravely I couldn't possibly see what that had to do with it. Miss Curzon was sitting on the other side of him and she seemed quite astonished at the man's impertinence. Adieu my sweet love. I must go to bed – pray pray love me. I shall stay at Wimbledon when I come back and I must see you somehow – adieu my Dst Dst Themire.

Lady Mary Delany, an inveterate letter-writer in her eightieth year, also pointed the finger at Lady Melbourne: 'No reason can be assign'd as the young lady was unexceptionable by all I can hear, but the dominion he is under of a great lady (Ly M-l-b-e) who has long endeavoured to prevent any other engagement and it is suspected she has forbid the banns.'

Lady Melbourne brushed off the gossip, and Lord Melbourne's unquestioning support for Lord North was rewarded in January 1781 with a Viscountcy. Henceforth, he and his wife would be known as the Viscount and Viscountess Melbourne; it was a step up, but it was still only an Irish title. In the summer of 1781 Elizabeth conceived again, this time with her third son who was born at Melbourne House on 17 April 1782. Most of her friends assumed that like William, Frederick Lamb was fathered by the Earl of Egremont on the rebound from his aborted marriage to Lady Maria Waldegrave. Torrens noted the similarities between William and Frederick: 'As children they grew up together, for the most part at Brocket and were much attached; their features bearing marked resemblance and many of their mental qualities being equally akin.'

A month after his birth, the Melbournes gathered at St James's church Piccadilly on 14 May 1782 to see their third son christened Frederick James. Once more, the boy's father was given on the baptism register as Lord Melbourne, but no one believed he was the boy's biological father. He was christened with the same names as Frederick, the Prince of York, sparking gossip that the boy may have been of royal blood. It is possible that Elizabeth had a brief sexual fling with the seventeen-year-old Prince Frederick in August 1781 but it is unlikely; Prince Frederick was packed off around that time by his father, George III, with his four younger brothers to the University of Gottingen in Hanover to get him away from the influence of his libidinous older brother, George, the Prince of Wales, who was then nineteen.

Within a few weeks of giving birth to Frederick, Lady Melbourne was infuriated by gossip suggesting she had become Prince George's lover. She wrote to Georgiana:

> The Duke of Richmond has been here and told me you and I are rival queens and I believe if there had not been some people in the room who might have thought it odd, I should have Slap'd his Face for having such an idea.
>
> He wish'd me joy of having the Prince [of Wales] to myself. How odious people are, upon my life. I have not patience with them. ... you will perceive I am not in the best of humours, adieu my Dear Love.[12]

Elizabeth warns the Duchess of Devonshire about an outbreak of influenza in London, suggesting the letter was written in the spring. The Duke and Duchess of Devonshire had gone to Bath where the Duke was taking the water for his gout, and Georgiana was immersing herself in the spa waters in the hope of it helping her to improve her fertility and conceive the son and heir she so desperately wanted. The pressure had mounted on her to produce an heir for the Duke as her sister Harriet had given birth to two sons and her intimate friend, Elizabeth, now had three.

Lady Melbourne urged the Devonshires to stay in Bath to avoid the 'Vile and Nasty' flu epidemic. While in Bath, Georgiana had befriended Bess Foster, who became part of a triad for the next quarter-century with the Duke of Devonshire and eventually became the Duchess after Georgiana's death. Her biographer Amanda Foreman considered Bess to be a 'fake' and 'the quintessential snake in the grass' who wanted to push Georgiana out. 'It is possible they had some kind of sexual relationship with each other, but it was certainly not a traditional lesbian relationship.'[13]

Lady Melbourne's letter also shows that she had become acutely conscious of her weight gain, almost certainly after the birth of Frederick:

> Lord Melbourne is at present quite ill & nobody escapes. I have a cold in my head which I am told is a beginning but I don't intend to have it any worse tho' it might perhaps be an advantage to me as it would take off some of my Fat. I am told by some people I shall be as big as Lady Powis and by others nobody is so fat except Mrs St John. All these speeches come from Men as the Women say they don't see it by way of encouraging me I suppose to eat and drink heartily yet I may grow still fatter.[14]

She was thirty and the fashion for low-cut 'empire-line' dresses, showing off a lady's cleavage, added to the pressure on Elizabeth to get back in shape after the birth of Frederick. 'Women resorted to elaborate procedures to drive back the milk and reduce the size of the breasts,' according to Amanda Foreman. 'One remedy was to apply lint around the nipple, another was the use of hareskin treated with ointments.' Georgiana breastfed her first child, a daughter called Georgiana – 'Little G' – for nine months after her difficult birth on 12 July 1783. She rejected the pressure to engage a wet nurse by the Cavendish side of the Duke's family, who were disappointed by the birth of a daughter and believed she would be able to try again more quickly for a son and heir if she stopped breastfeeding.[15]

Elizabeth had no intention of breastfeeding her children. She employed a wet nurse for William and Frederick and was quickly back in the social swing. In June, the newspapers reported Lady Melbourne wore 'a dress of sea-green silk, trimmed with silver and numerous flowers beautifully fancied' at the celebrations for George III's birthday at court.

Prince George was slim as a teenager, when Lady Melbourne first met him. The huge scales in the Old Coffee Mill – now Messrs Berry Bros and Rudd, the wine merchants in St James's Street, where gentlemen had their weight recorded in a ledger – weighed him at a mere seven stone and eight pounds.

When he was nineteen, the Duchess of Devonshire noted he was so soft and plump he looked womanly: 'The Prince of Wales is rather tall and has a figure which though striking is not perfect. He is inclined to be too fat and looks too much like a woman in men's cloaths, but the gracefulness of his manner and his height certainly make him a pleasing figure. His face is very handsome and he is fond of dress even to a tawdry degree...'

Lady Anne Lindsay admired his hair which 'waved in profusion with all the glossy lustre of youth on it' while his eyes 'were of a clear blue, lively, full of play and intelligence ... They saw everyone, neglected no one.' Betsy Sheridan said he had 'his father's passion for knowing who and what everyone is'.[16]

The Prince of Wales had become a regular visitor to Lady Melbourne's salon in Melbourne House where he chatted and joked with the leading wits of the Whig party such as Charles James Fox and Richard Brinsley Sheridan. He had even started to frequent Brooks's, the Whig club.

Elizabeth did not let her relationship with Lord Egremont restrain her from an affair with the prince, who was due to turn twenty on 12 August 1782. She contrived the perfect way to meet the prince at Windsor, while visiting her son Peniston at Eton at regular dinners at a coaching inn called The Christopher in the town. Her husband went too, but that had never proved a problem in the past. The prince was in Windsor for a series of summer balls hosted by the king and queen at Windsor Castle for the season.

Four days before the prince's birthday, Lady Sarah Lennox, the Duke of Richmond's sister, wrote half in jest to a friend:

> Lady Melbourne loves her son so much that she goes twice a week to see him at the *Christopher* at Eton, where she and Lord Melbourne give a dinner which the Prince of Wales honours with his presence. He sups at Mr Delme's most nights after the King and Queen leave the terrass [at Windsor Castle] and he calls upon Mrs Amsted [the courtesan Elizabeth Armistead] every morning, romps with the Miss Cheshires in an evening...[17]

The prince and Lady Melbourne had plenty to chat about: Britain appeared almost ungovernable. Lord North had been forced to resign as Prime Minister in March 1782 after a vote of no confidence following the humiliating defeat by the American colonists at Yorktown; Rockingham had taken up the reins of government but had died in July; he was replaced by Lord Shelburne, who was suing for peace with the Americans; but the government remained on shaky ground. The Earl of Egremont's three-year-old bay Assassin had won the Epsom Derby in May. They could commiserate with their mutual friend Georgiana, who had given birth to a daughter a week after her sister, Harriet, had produced another boy – poor Georgiana.

By the time Elizabeth met him at The Christopher in Eton, Prince George was already sexually experienced. He had followed the practice of many aristocratic men by losing his virginity when he was sixteen to a servant girl, though in his case it was a maid of honour to his mother, Queen Charlotte of Mecklenburg-Strelitz.

A year later, George had embarked on the scandalous pursuit of wholly unsuitable escorts for which he would become infamous. His first great love was the actress Mary Robinson, with whom he fell madly in love when he saw her on stage as Perdita in *The Winter's Tale* in 1779. The Prince bombarded Mrs Robinson with passionate love letters addressed to 'Perdita' signed 'Florizel' (Perdita's lover). She agreed to give up the stage and become his mistress on the promise of £20,000 – the equivalent to over £2 million today – when he was twenty-one.[18]

His passion for Mrs Robinson was spent as soon as she surrendered to him, leaving the problem of his promise to pay her £20,000 and the return of his love letters, which he feared would be used to blackmail him. His father, refusing to dip into the royal coffers, appealed to Lord North, the Prime Minister, to help his son out of a 'shameful scrape' by his 'improper connection'. Lord North raised £5,000 to pay her off by raiding a secret government fund at the taxpayers' expense.

Prince George then fell for Countess von Hardenberg, the bored wife of a diplomat from Hanover at the Court of St James. She had already tried and failed to seduce Frederick while he was in Hanover and, having arrived in London, turned to Prince George for amusement. Initially, she refused to succumb. He was driven wild with lust for her, feigned illness and threatened suicide – his favourite tactics – until she consented 'to completing [his] happiness'. When she surrendered, George wrote to Frederick, saying he was 'in ecstasy': 'O my beloved brother,' he boasted, 'I enjoyed ... the pleasures of Elysium.'

It was difficult for a woman in Georgian society to refuse sexual favours to the heir to the throne. George relied on his position to bed a long list of women, from high-class harlots like Elizabeth Armistead to titled ladies such as Lady Campbell, daughter of the fifth Duke of Argyle, with whom he had just ended an affair when he began his liaison with Elizabeth, Lady Melbourne.

George today would be regarded as a sexual predator, but with Lady Melbourne the hunter became the hunted. Elizabeth was experienced, mature (eleven years older), and knew how to play the prince; and she may have had her husband's tacit, if unspoken, approval in becoming his mistress. The proximity to power proved a far greater aphrodisiac to Elizabeth than the prospect of the fat prince sprawled across his state bed.

Prince George was born on 12 August 1762 and subjected to strict discipline in the nursery at the Hanoverians' family home, Kew Palace, as was his brother Frederick, the Duke of York. The future King George IV suffered a repressed childhood that had turned him from being an open, cheerful child into a self-indulgent, whingeing, spoiled adolescent. Wraxall observed that George quickly became petulant – he was 'prepossessing and commonly gay though at times became suddenly overcast and sullen'.[19]

George and Frederick, who was a year younger, grew up together as brothers-in-arms against their father's strict code of behaviour. George III appointed Robert D'Arcy, Earl of Holderness, who had assisted the Milbankes through his patronage at court, as governor in charge of the princes' education. Holderness was regarded by Horace Walpole as 'a formal, dull man totally ignorant of and unversed in the world'; but then most people appeared intellectually inferior to Walpole.

George III was a polymath, but one who had the common touch – he preferred a boiled egg to a banquet and earned the nickname 'Farmer George' from his penchant for dropping in on his tenant farmers to discuss grain harvests or pig rearing. He was driven to distraction by his wayward eldest son.

George III was the first of the Hanoverian kings to be born in Britain and to speak English as a mother tongue. He won praise when he told Parliament he gloried in being English. George III never went abroad to see his lands in Hanover – the furthest south he went was a review of the fleet off the south coast of England; the furthest north he went was Worcester.

He was worried that the excesses of his son would undermine the institution of the monarchy just at the moment of greatest peril, when revolution was spreading across Europe as a threat to the network of ruling aristocratic families. At home, the House of Hanover had already faced two Jacobite rebellions and he was right to fear it could be brought down if it lost touch with public opinion when the country was financially drained by wars with the Americans and the French and facing unrest at home with riots against Catholic emancipation.

The Prince's brother Frederick pleaded with his brother in letters from Hanover not to upset their father, but George was already showing the rebellious streak that would mark his paternal relationship to the end. The king had allowed the Prince of Wales to make his debut in London society on his eighteenth birthday but refused to allow him to live outside Buckingham House. His father laid down a strict code of conduct, which Prince George ignored. He surrounded himself with louche friends such as Colonel Anthony St Leger, Charles William Windham, two rakes who, it was said, were despised by 'all good men', and Lord Chesterfield, who threw drunken parties at his house in Blackheath, backing on to the Greenwich royal park. The prince was so drunk at Chesterfield House he collapsed on a bed; the host fell down the stairs, and a dog savaged a footman.[20] Before long, his father was reading reports of the Prince of Wales engaged in drunken brawls in the gardens at Vauxhall and Ranelagh, and – his particular divertissement – driving his carriage wildly through Hyde Park.

His son's whoring and drunkenness were bad enough, but it was Prince George's political friends the king could not stomach. The king was appalled to hear that Prince George had become a regular visitor at the notorious Whig headquarters, Melbourne House, mixing happily with the politicians drawn to Lady Melbourne's relaxed salon, including Charles James Fox and his boisterous friends, Hare, Charles Grey, Grenville, Fitzpatrick, Lady Jersey's lover Fawkener, and the sparkling playwright Sheridan, who was so won over by the prince's natural charm that Sheridan's friends accused him of becoming a royal sycophant. Fox served under Rockingham and briefly joined in a coalition with his old enemy North in 1782 but he remained, in the king's eyes, a traitor, a dangerous Jacobin sympathiser who supported the French revolution and the rebellious American colonists.

Lady Melbourne was fully engaged in the political in-fighting to get the Whigs back in power after Lord North's resignation but organising the Whigs was like herding the proverbial cats. The king appointed Lord Shelburne Prime Minister, but Fox refused to serve under him. The Duke of Richmond's sister Lady Sarah Lennox wrote on 6 July, said: 'C. Fox flew out into a violent passion & resign'd. Ld John Cavendish has resign'd. It's reported the Burks [supporters of Edmund Burke] are turned out by Lord Shelburne … My br [brother] has been negotiating these three days between Lord Shelburne and the angry parties to settle matters; he has talk'd his voice quite away and sunk his spirits and health and nothing is yet fixed.'

Shelburne appointed the precociously gifted William Pitt as his Chancellor of the Exchequer at the age of twenty-three. He was known as 'Pitt the Younger' to distinguish him from his late father the Earl of Chatham who had also been Prime Minister and had helped to establish British global dominance against the French. Shelburne pursued a peace treaty in Paris with America, France and Spain but in December 1782, it became clear Shelburne could only survive with the support of North or Fox. Pitt was opposed to North for having 'precipitated Great Britain into disgrace as well as debt', so consulted Fox. Fox's father Henry had opposed Pitt's father, and Fox's 'cub' would only give his support without Shelburne. Pitt told him: 'Then we need discuss the matter no further – I did not come here to betray Lord Shelburne.'[21]

Pitt and Fox had become friendly rivals at the Commons, but now they became deadly enemies. Pitt accused Fox of being more at variance with men than with measures. On 23 February 1783 Shelburne resigned as Prime Minister after suffering another defeat in the Commons. He advised the king to send for Pitt. Acting on Shelburne's advice, the king summoned Pitt on Monday 24 February to ask him to form a government as Prime Minister, hoping that like his father he could pilot Britain out of danger; he was three months short of his twenty-fourth birthday. Lady Sarah Lennox wrote: 'Mr Pitt is young but as Lord Shelburne is only behind the curtain I presume the same administration will go on in the same manner.'[22] She underestimated Pitt like everyone else – including Fox – who would be kept out of power by him for decades. Pitt refused office, knowing he could not command a majority in the Commons. The king tried to persuade North to return to office but North would not do so without Fox, who was unacceptable to George III because Fox had supported the American rebels.

In a day of crisis talks which the king methodically logged in his journal on Sunday 23 March 1783, George III sent for North again: 'Not having heard from you since the directions I gave you yesterday, I must desire you will come instantly.'[23]

Lord North had a tense interview with the king but he refused to drop Fox. The king then reluctantly summoned Lord Portland, a moderate Whig, to form a coalition, but again failed to reach an agreement because the king refused to countenance Fox.

Towards nine o'clock that evening, the king, in exasperation, noted that he wrote to William Pitt from the Queen's House: 'Mr Pitt is desired to come here, the Duke of Portland has written an answer which ends in declining to prepare a plan for my inspection, consequently the negotiation is finally ended.'

At ten thirty-five at night, after consulting Pitt, the king sent a dismissive letter to the Duke of Portland:

> The Duke of Portland having declined drawing up the Plan of Arrangement and continuing to do so after my having this day at St James's acquainted him that I could not longer delay coming to some resolution if he did not send such a plan for my consideration this evening, I therefore take this method of acquainting him that I shall not give him any further trouble.

A copy was sent to Lord North with a final paragraph added: 'Lord North must therefore see that all Negotiation is at an end.'

Pitt wisely turned down the offer. The king refused to talk further to Fox and North because they were men 'I know I cannot trust' and their conditions for taking office made him 'a kind of slave'. George III was so depressed by the prospect of a renewed Fox-North coalition, he secretly drafted a speech announcing his plan to abdicate in favour of his wayward son, Prince George, and retire to Hanover:

> A long Experience and a serious attention to the Strange events that have successively arisen, has gradually prepared My mind to expect the time when I should be no longer of Utility to this Empire; that hour is now come; I am therefore resolved to resign My Crown and all the Dominions appertaining to it to the Prince of Wales my Eldest Son and Lawful Successor and to retire to the care of My Electoral Dominions the Original Patrimony of my Ancestors.

As the king contemplated passing his crown and his realm to his oldest son, the fun-loving heir to the throne had his heart set on another prize – Lady Melbourne. On 25 March 1783, two days after the king spent a day trying to appoint a Prime Minister, Lady Sarah Lennox wrote to Lady Susan O'Brien:

> I have no gossip to tell you but that the P. of Wales is *desperately* in love with Ly Melbourne and when she don't sit next to him at supper he is not commonly civil to his neighbours: she dances with him, something in the cow stile, but he is *en extase* with admiration at it.[24]

It is unclear what Lady Sarah meant by the 'cow style', but it conjures up an awkward picture.

The king changed his mind: he did not hand over the crown to his son. In April, a month after Lady Sarah noted the Prince of Wales's infatuation with Lady Melbourne, the government collapsed and his father had no alternative but to appoint a Fox-North coalition under the Duke of Portland who was married to Dorothy Cavendish, the Duke of Devonshire's sister – though Fox pulled the strings. Fox became Foreign Secretary and North Secretary of State for the Home Department.

Lady Melbourne's new lover planned a great twenty-first birthday party to celebrate his coming of age in August 1783 and pressed Elizabeth to give him the birthday present he wanted above all others. The king had reluctantly allowed the prince to have his own official residence at Carlton House, overlooking St James's Park and the Mall. It had been the home of his mother, Princess Augusta, the Dowager Princess of Wales, until her death in 1772. It was now rundown, and Prince George immediately commissioned Henry Holland, the architect of the hour, to carry out a complete renovation of the property in a neoclassical style. He decided that no expense should be spared on making it a magnificent palace. He had been granted a budget of £60,000 to redecorate the interior of Carlton House at the taxpayers' expense and an annual allowance of £50,000 a year to run his household. Fox had wanted to double the prince's annual allowance to £100,000 a year (about £10 million at today's prices) as a sop to the prince but it was vetoed by the Whig Prime Minister, the Duke of Portland, acting for the king, who feared it would outrage public opinion and bring 'odium' on the monarchy.

The prince was not so sensitive to public outrage and went on a wild spending spree, advised by Lady Melbourne, who helped him pick out silks for his walls and choose furniture for the state rooms in the latest chinoiserie fashion. The newspapers quickly picked up the gossip that Lady Melbourne was the latest in a scandalously long line of the young prince's mistresses. They could not write openly about their affair, but the *Morning Herald* archly reported: 'Lady Melbourne has the guidance of most of the erections on the spot...' The double-entendre was entirely intentional.

The work on Carlton House could not be finished in time for his birthday celebrations on coming of age, so he hosted a glittering party at an inn in Windsor called the White Hart. Lord and Lady Melbourne were among the many titled guests who sat down to the huge banquet to honour the Prince of Wales. Lord Melbourne later boasted that they feasted on a turtle, a present from the East India Company, weighing four hundredweight.

The prince, having attained his majority, was also free to appoint whoever he liked to his household. When the *London Gazette* was published in November 1783, it announced that he had added Lord Melbourne to his household as a Gentleman of the Bedchamber.

It can hardly be a coincidence that in the same month that her husband was made one of the closest courtiers to the Prince of Wales, Viscountess Melbourne became pregnant by the Prince of Wales. The timing suggests she wanted to be sure that before she allowed the prince to claim his birthday present, she wanted to see her reward in print. There was just one small disappointment: Elizabeth was a Viscountess, but it was an Irish title, not the English peerage she craved for herself and her family.

9

The Affectionate Brothers

While she was pregnant in 1783, Elizabeth commissioned Sir Joshua Reynolds to paint a group portrait of her three sons, Peniston, William and Frederick to hang in Brocket Hall.

The portrait shows Peniston, William and Frederick happily playing on a broken stone wall in a sylvan setting, which may have been meant to represent the Derbyshire countryside near the family's Melbourne Hall. Peniston is seated half-straddling the wall, while William, wearing a brown romper suit of sturdy cloth – ideal for playing on walls – has his left foot on a block of stone that has tumbled down and lifts up Frederick, who is no more than a toddler and wearing a dress with a pink sash. The unruly Frederick is the central figure, and looks as though he is up to mischief. He is wearing a hat in the current fashion for grand dames with ostrich plumes; it is 'the dress and attitude', said Torrens, of 'a spoilt child still an inmate of the nursery'. This was true – Reynolds later recalled that Frederick gave him 'more trouble than he liked'; the painter had to bribe the youngster into brief intervals of quiet by promises of another ride on his foot. Torrens said for all his difficulties Sir Joshua had captured his look, 'a hearty, gladsome, wayward little fellow, with a soft roguish eye and gesture full of provocation'.[1]

Pen, who was thirteen at the time, is wearing black satin knee-length breeches, white stockings and a tailcoat. His outfit looks incongruous in the rustic setting, but black knee breeches and the black tailcoat may have been used by Reynolds to signify he was at Eton; the famous top hat and tails was not the uniform then. Torrens detected on Pen's face a look of 'amusement at their gambols and of dreams less childish passing through his mind'.

The painting, measuring ninety-four inches by fifty-seven inches, is a delightful, sentimental image of childhood, 'illustrating in their varied ages the fraternal love of her children', said Torrens. It was designed to sell well as a popular print from an engraving by Sir Joshua's son, Samuel William Reynolds, under the title *The Affectionate Brothers*.

It was of course pure hokum. To be accurate, the painting should have been entitled *The Indifferent Half-brothers*. Pen and his half-brothers were never so close nor as affectionate as Reynolds portrayed them. Lady Melbourne almost certainly intended to hang it in the grand dining room at Brocket Hall alongside her Reynolds portrait of herself with Peniston when he was a baby called *Maternal Affection*.

For once, Lord Melbourne, in a rare show of anger, put his foot down and refused to give *The Affectionate Brothers* house-room at Brocket Hall. Lord Melbourne returned it to Reynolds saying it did not 'give satisfaction'. This was not an artistic objection. Torrens said: 'In conception, grace and vividness of expression, it is eminently worthy of his [Reynolds'] fame.'

Lord Melbourne clearly drew the line at having to gaze upon a painting on his wall as a permanent reminder of his wife's adultery with Lord Egremont every time he sat down to eat. It was still languishing in Sir Joshua's studio when the artist died in 1792. *The Affectionate Brothers* was bought by the fifth Earl Cowper for £800 from the trustees of Reynolds after Cowper married the brothers' sister, Emily Lamb.

Despite being pregnant again, Elizabeth threw herself into the great political drama of the moment – a general election called to decide who should govern Britain. The Fox-North coalition collapsed after being defeated in a vote in the Commons. On 19 December the king once more summoned William Pitt to St James's Palace to form a government and this time he accepted.

Pitt was still only twenty-four, making him the youngest Prime Minister in British history. Pitt was shrewd beyond his years, but got the job by default, because all the other options had been exhausted. Pitt was defeated in the Commons but refused to resign, leading to an impasse. The astonishingly young Prime Minister decided to break the political deadlock by calling a general election to decide whether Britain should be governed by Fox supported by the Prince of Wales, or Pitt supported by the king.

Elizabeth made Melbourne House a rallying point for supporters of Fox and the Prince of Wales, whose child Lady Melbourne was carrying.

It is difficult today to understand what set the Whigs and Tories apart. The terms Whigs and Tories began as insults – Tories were Irish robbers; Whigs were radical Scottish cattle drovers opposed to Catholic succession. Whigs believed in the ancient rights of Parliament over the absolute power of the monarch, secured in the 1688 Glorious Revolution, while the Tories defended the natural order of State and Church under a benign monarchy.

The ideological differences were often less important than the personalities in an era of fluid political groupings before the advent of modern political parties. Both sides were dominated by rich landowners at a time when few men had the vote, and women were barred from voting or holding any political office. Lady Melbourne and Georgiana gained their influence by rallying behind the Prince of Wales against his father.

The focus for the general election became the local battle by the Whig leader Charles James Fox to retain one of the two seats in the Parliamentary constituency of Westminster. Having dropped the idea of abdicating, George III redoubled his efforts to see the hated Fox destroyed at the ballot box. There were an estimated 12,000 men in the constituency who qualified for a vote by paying a form of property tax. It was one of the biggest electorates in the country – making it one of the most expensive to bribe.

Pitt's supporters threw everything into defeating Fox. Pitt nationally spent nearly £32,000 in electoral bribes, equivalent to over £3.5 million today, including £9,200 – £864,000 today – on the voters in Westminster.

Viscountess Melbourne and the Duchess of Devonshire acted as cheerleaders for the Whigs. Georgiana and her friends went out on the streets of London to canvass for Fox in their plumed hats. Elizabeth was prevented by her pregnancy from tramping the streets with Georgiana but she was 'no less enthusiastic' in her support for Fox, according to the newspapers. She threw open the doors of Melbourne House for the Fox campaign and it was busy with Whig grandees coming and going, carrying running tallies of how the votes were going.

Lady Salisbury, Elizabeth's rival at Hatfield, launched a counter-campaign for the Tory candidate at Westminster, Sir Cecil Wray. London had never witnessed the like before. Viscount Melbourne's biographer, Torrens, said the struggle 'became keener than ever; and the profusion of blandishments and inducements were on both sides unparalleled; for the example once set of female interference, the Countess of Salisbury and other Tory ladies sought to exert a counter-ruling influence over the electors.'

The campaign got under way on 30 March 1784. Georgiana encountered a handful of Fox's opponents in a Covent Garden pub who refused to allow her to leave until she had kissed them. The popular newspapers quickly translated Georgiana's encounter into a scandal of kisses (or gropes) for votes. Thomas Rowlandson published a cartoon on 12 April 1784 showing Georgiana in a purple coat and feathered hat embracing a fat butcher and kissing him on the lips with the caption: 'The Devonshire – or most approved method of securing votes'. A lady behind her characterised by a significant embonpoint is shouting: 'Huzzah – Fox for ever!' The hand-coloured etching was published by William Humphrey of 227 The Strand

and is now in the Royal Collection – suggesting it was bought by the Prince of Wales.[2] Prince George was a regular customer of William Humphrey's sister Hannah, whose shop at 27 St James's Street around the corner from St James's Palace displayed many of the most popular cartoons lampooning the political leaders of the day, and later the prince.

After the poll had been tallied up on the tenth day, Fox was trailing third by 318 votes. On the twentieth day of the poll, the deficit was reduced to eighty-four. The final results for the two seats were announced on 10 May: after the intervention of Georgiana's sister-in-law, the Duchess of Devonshire – and some pro-Fox bribes along the way – the Whig candidate Hood got 6,694 votes, Fox 6,233, and the Tory Wray 5,998. Fox was duly elected MP with a wafer-thin majority of 235 and was carried in a victory parade led by the Duchess of Portland and the Duchess of Devonshire in their carriages, each drawn by six horses, to Devonshire House in Piccadilly. The victor was hailed by Georgiana, 'the Grand Electress', and was presented with a victor's laurel wreath by the Prince of Wales. Nationally, Pitt could boast he had 'shot their Fox'. The general election resulted in an overwhelming Tory majority of between 120 and 180 seats for Pitt and supporters of the king. It cast Fox and his Whig friends into opposition for decades. Pitt secured his place in history as Britain's youngest Prime Minister. In contrast, Fox's political career appeared to be over at thirty-five. Fox remained out of ministerial office for over two decades until a brief spell as Foreign Secretary in the Grenville administration, close to his death in 1806.[3]

However, defeat for the Whigs did not cut off Elizabeth from power, for she retained her own influence over the Prince of Wales. Prince George was determined to celebrate Fox's return to Westminster as a two-fingered gesture to his father and threw a deliberately timed noisy party lasting from breakfast to dinner for Fox and his supporters on the lawns of Carlton House.

'In order to give piquancy to the event,' said one Victorian report, 'the Prince chose the day after the election, when all the rank, beauty, and talent of the opposition party were assembled by invitation on the lawn of his palace for the fête, precisely at the time when the King, his father, was proceeding in state down St James's Park to open the new Parliament. The wall of Carlton Gardens, and that barrier only, formed the separation between them.'

Their former enemy, Lord North, circulated among the Whig grandees, dressed like every other individual invited in his new livery of buff and blue, the Whig colours that Fox had borrowed from the American rebels. North 'beheld himself surrounded by those very persons who, scarcely fifteen months earlier, affected to regard him as an object of national execration, deserving of capital punishment'.[4]

A few days later, the prince hosted a second banquet even more magnificent than the first to antagonise his father and the king's ministers. It lasted from noon to the following morning. A 'splendid banquet was served up to the ladies, on whom, in the spirit of chivalry, his royal highness and the gentlemen present waited while they were seated at table,' one gossip columnist reported.

'It must be owned that on these occasions, for which he seemed peculiarly formed, the Prince appeared to great advantage. Louis XIV himself could scarcely have eclipsed the son of George III in a ball-room, or when doing the honours of his palace, surrounded by the pomp and attributes of luxury and royal state.'

Unfortunately, the prince drank so many bumpers of wine that he collapsed flat on his face in the middle of a quadrille and was violently sick when he was raised to his feet.

The prince had commissioned Henry Holland, the son of a London builder from Fulham who designed the Whig headquarters Brooks's Club in St James's, to turn Carlton House into a palace to rival Versailles in its glittering grandeur. Holland had become rich and famous with speculative Georgian housing estates at Cadogan Place, Hans Place and Sloane Street for the new middle class. Carlton House would be his crowning commission. The building had an enviable location, overlooking St James's Park from an elevated position on Pall Mall. It had been built of red brick for Lord Carleton in 1709 and improved for George's grandfather. William Kent, the architect who designed Horse Guards, faced it in more handsome stone.[5]

Holland erected a classical colonnade around the front of the house as a screen to shield the carriages depositing their occupants from prying eyes in the street. He also added a massive portico of six great Corinthian columns to the front entrance with a pediment carrying the prince's arms. The scale of the portico can be judged today by the towering entrance to the National Gallery on Trafalgar Square, which was transported from Carlton House.

Visitors were greeted inside a cavernous entrance hall by liveried servants who steered them towards a double staircase leading to the staterooms on the first floor. The staircase was lit from above by a glass cupola decorated with the prince's plumes and roses, which made the gilded handrails glitter in the light cascading down the stair well.

With Viscountess Melbourne's advice, he installed exotic, expensive furnishings that dazzled the eye, and restlessly kept changing them, regardless of the cost. The walls were decorated with rich damask silk made by the Spitalfields silk weavers; clocks were supplied by the fine clockmaker, Benjamin Vulliamy. In the State Room, the throne was of crimson velvet embroidered with gold. His bedroom contained a bed of crimson velvet embroidered with gold standing on a dais, in addition to four sofas, eight chairs covered in velvet and lace, and a royal commode. His friends visited him in the state bedroom in the morning while he lay almost naked in his exotic billet. Princess Lieven found him 'lying at full length in a lilac silk dressing gown, a velvet nightcap on his head, his huge bare feet [he was suffering from gout] covered with a silk net.'[6]

The Council Room was hung with tapestry from the Gobelins factory in Paris with eighteen chairs in tapestry to match. There were thirty-six matching chairs ordered for the Great Eating Room with another twenty-four chairs for the smaller Eating Room. The bills mounted steeply – £3,500 for looking glasses; silks supplied by the mercers of Pall Mall £7,800, and another £6,200 from a shop in Ludgate Hill; upholstery by Robert Campbell, a cabinet maker, at Marylebone Street cost £27,500.

The total bill for interior decoration and furniture totted up to £110,500 – around £11 million today and nearly double his entire renovation budget. That excluded the cost of the artworks he bought for his long gallery, including portraits of himself by Sir Thomas Lawrence with his head held high above a white Beau Brummel stock, to hide his double chins. The bills mounted and the prince left it to the government or his father to pay them.[7]

Today there is no trace of Carlton House. It was demolished in 1825 and the site sold off for a row of palatial houses with white stucco exteriors designed by Nash, Carlton House Terrace. The proceeds were used to pay towards the cost of transforming the Queen's House into Buckingham Palace to make it worthy of the new King George IV.

The demolition of Carlton House robbed Regent Street of its dramatic finale. John Nash designed Regent Street to finish with an architectural bang at the Regent's front door. It now ends in whimper, with a small square given over to on-street parking outside the Athenaeum Club and the statue of the Regent's brother, the Duke of York, on a column 137 feet above the traffic.

Prince George hosted daily banquets at Carlton House. The Queen's archives at Windsor show a typical menu began with a choice of spring soup, crimped cod slices, oysters and whitings for starters followed by a choice of neck of veal, chicken in a tarragon sauce, petit patties with suet, blanquettes of capon with cucumber, slices of rabbit, fillet of lamb with asparagus, or peafowl. In addition there was a sideboard of meats where guests could try saddle of mutton, 'Sir Loin' of cold beef, fillet of veal, hams, tongue, pheasant and guinea fowl.

'Prinny', as he was known by the satirists, appeared sumptuously attired like a plump bird of paradise for his introduction to the House of Lords in a costume of black velvet lined with pink satin embroidered in gold with matching pink-heeled slippers, his hair frizzed and curled. One cartoon wickedly depicted him as the 'Prince of Whales', with his fat face on the body of a whale seducing a mermaid. But that was relatively mild compared to some of the cartoons from the pen of James Gillray, whose works included 'A Voluptuary under the Horrors of Digestion'. The prince is lounging on a chair after a big meal, picking his teeth with a fork, his fat belly bursting out of his yellow waistcoat. Behind his chair is a chamber pot full of his unpaid bills; there are emptied flagons of wine peeping out from beneath the tablecloth; there are dice tossed on the floor next to debtors' notes and 'The Newmarket List', showing his passion for horseracing. His coat of arms is parodied by a crossed knife and fork and the candles are held in a wine glass and decanter. Two small pots stand on a table by his left elbow labelled 'For the Piles' and 'For a Stinking Breath'. If this tested his sense of humour it completely failed him when he saw a print showing his bloated personage with his 'Queen', the twice-widowed Maria Fitzherbert he secretly and illegally married on 15 December 1785 presiding over their Whig court. He bought the plates and had them destroyed, but prints survived.

Even his friends poked fun at his growing girth by adopting ever tighter jackets and trousers, as the second Viscount Melbourne recalled when he was dining years later with Queen Victoria. The Queen noted in her journal: 'Lord M [Melbourne] said they all tried to vex him by having their things made better and tighter than his, particularly some "leathern clothes" [leather breeches] which people wore then and which annoyed the King.'

William told the queen, 'the prince used to say to his tailor: "Why don't you make my coats fit like Paget's [Henry Paget, the Marquess of Anglesey]?" which made us laugh; as the King might well think his own figure wasn't quite as slim as Lord Anglesey's.'[8]

After the great drama of the summer was over, Elizabeth went into labour at Melbourne House. On 11 July 1784, it was officially noted in *The Times* that Viscountess Melbourne had given birth to her fourth son at Melbourne House. The infant she cradled in her arms, however, was unlike any of her three other sons. He had a shock of light red hair and this time society was in no doubt who his father was: Prince George, the Prince of Wales, and heir to the throne.

Viscount Melbourne, as the new Gentleman of the Bedchamber to the Prince of Wales, may have been cuckolded by his royal employer but showed no sign of it when he wrote to Fox, his steward at Melbourne Hall on 14 July with the glad tidings: 'Lady Melbourne was brought to bed of another Boy on Sunday last and She and the Child are as well as can be expected.'

Thomas Hill, the lawyer for the estate, hinted the Melbournes could ill afford another child when he wrote to Fox on 20 July saying: 'Lady Melbourne got a fine boy on Sunday sennight the Eleventh instant. I did not hear of it till the middle of last week and my Lady was pretty well with my

Lord and all the family. This ought to make my Lord think of Frugality, but as a Notable Noble Lord observed to me: a Great House makes a bad Figure without Suitable Living.' His words proved prophetic.[9]

On 11 August 1784, the day before his twenty-second birthday, the Prince of Wales joined Lord and Lady Melbourne by the ornate font at the church of St James in Piccadilly for the christening of their son. The prince was there as the child's godfather. He went through the responses with the curate from the Book of Common Prayer. The Prince of Wales promised to renounce Satan 'and all the spiritual forces of wickedness that rebel against God'. He renounced the evil powers of the world that corrupt and destroy the creatures of God. He was asked if he renounced the pleasures of the flesh:

'Do you renounce all sinful desires that draw you from the love of God?'

'I renounce them.'

The curate then anointed the boy's head with holy water and baptised the infant with one name: George.

Elizabeth's husband, now enjoying the new title of Viscount Melbourne, was recorded in the parish register once more as the father. He agreed without question to accept the boy as his own, though it was an open secret that his natural father was the Prince of Wales, standing by the font with adoring eyes.

He would grow into a boisterous boy, with a florid face, under a mop of unruly reddish auburn hair, unlike the other Melbourne children; his noisy high spirits were mistaken for coarseness. The artist Maria Cosway was prescient when she portrayed George Lamb as *The Infant Bacchus,* his rusty-coloured hair covered by a wreath of vine leaves. He shared his father Prince George's appetites for wine and food, and became just as obese. 'His physical bulk concealed a flawed constitution which he abused with heavy drinking, though he was no soak,' according to the Parliamentary biography of George Lamb.[10]

Fox found him 'always vulgar and noisy' though entertaining. Sydney Smith was not so entertained; after encountering George at a dinner party when he was in his forties he wrote that 'his only art in conversation seems to be to contradict plainly and plumply whatever is said upon opposite sides of the table, and then to burst out into a horse laugh and this supplies the place of wit and sense.'[11]

Emily said of her brother that his 'home and happiness' was in the theatre. George, like the other Lamb brothers, had a passion for the stage and wrote a comic opera, *Whistle for It.* He served on the management committee of the Drury Lane Theatre with Lord Byron but turned briefly to the law to earn some money before becoming an MP.

He won Fox's old Whig seat in the Westminster constituency in 1819 in a hotly contested campaign. It was so violent, according to Charles Greville, that on the day he won he was to be chaired back to Melbourne House, but he had to sneak out of the window of his campaign headquarters across a cemetery to avoid a mob.[12] He lost his seat a year later to Byron's ally John Cam Hobhouse in another bitterly fought rough-and-tumble election. His parentage was lampooned in this doggerel:

> My Good Mr Lamb
> We all Know your Dam
> But what we desire
> Is to know more of your Sire

Some considered George Lamb more immediately likable and politically more adventurous than his brother William. But that was not saying much. Many of William's friends could not tell where William stood politically; he was a very conservative Whig. William opposed an inquiry – supported by George – into the killing of protesters at Manchester known as the 'Peterloo massacre'. Greville said William was later tortured by having to support the Great Reform Bill even though he was against it. 'All his notions were aristocratic,' said Greville. 'He had no particle of sympathy for what he called progressive reform.'

In 1809, George Lamb married Caroline St Jules, Elizabeth Foster's daughter by the Duke of Devonshire, the same year she became the Duchess of Devonshire after Georgiana's death. The Duke generously gave the couple £20,000 with an annuity of £500 to his daughter for the rest of her life. She became known as 'Caro George', to distinguish her from his brother's wife, 'Caro William'. The sixth Duke of Devonshire later provided George with another seat at Dungarvan, Waterford, on the south coast of Ireland that was in his gift. William Lamb gave George and Caroline the use of Melbourne Hall in Derbyshire for the rest of their lives when he inherited the title of Viscount Melbourne from his father in 1828.[13]

The Prince of Wales maintained a friendly interest in his son's life, but his affair with Elizabeth did not last long – very few of his passions ever did. Before the christening, the Prince of Wales had already fallen madly in love with Maria Fitzherbert, twenty-eight, the daughter of a Hampshire landowner. She was a commoner and Catholic but he was so infatuated with her that he pressed Maria into a secret morganatic marriage even though it was in breach of the constitutional laws barring the heir to the throne from marrying a Papist.

Lady Melbourne was quite pragmatic about the end of her affair with the prince and she was careful to keep his friendship and influence. When their romance ended, they exchanged portraits of each other as mementoes of their lasting affection for each other. Prince George presented Lady Melbourne with a ludicrously heroic portrait of himself by Sir Joshua Reynolds. It shows the Prince of Wales in a dashing red cavalry uniform with his sword drawn standing by his charger sheltering from a storm. The prince's defiant look and martial pose are risible; he had never seen any action.

In return for the prince's gift, Elizabeth gave him a coquettish portrait of herself by Richard Cosway in the low-cut Elizabethan-style dress she had worn for the French ambassador's fancy-dress ball witnessed by Horace Walpole. The prince kept it in his private room at Carlton House until it was removed to the corridor in Windsor Castle. It is still in the Royal Collection.[14]

Elizabeth, without a flicker of irony, proudly hung the prince's life-size portrait at the far end of the state dining room at Brocket Hall where it looked directly at the Reynolds portrait of herself with Peniston as a baby called *Maternal Affection*. The prince's portrait dominated the dining room for around two hundred years until it was sold at auction and was bought by Andrew Lloyd-Webber. A copy now hangs in its place.[15] Elizabeth also hung the etching of herself, Georgiana, and Mrs Damer posing as the 'Three Witches' in a suite at Brocket Hall always allocated to prince George when he visited, as a reminder of their love affair.

Elizabeth arranged for the prince to have his own bedroom on the first floor at Brocket Hall. It was designed in the latest Chinese fashion, and the style has survived to this day. The hand-painted Chinese-style wallpaper shows exotic birds flitting across a blue sky and rose buds held in place by bamboo-like beading. The centrepiece is the prince's large red Chinese-style bed with a bedhead like a great red pagoda.

Viscountess Melbourne's bedroom could only be accessed through her husband's room until she ordered the carpenters to put in another door, opening directly onto the landing by the staircase. This had the advantage of allowing her to leave her bedroom without disturbing her husband; it also meant she could slip along the corridor to the Prince of Wales's room at the dead of night when she became the prince's mistress. Today her room overlooks the lake and the manicured eighteenth green of the golf course.

The pictures were still there fifty years later when Queen Victoria visited Brocket Hall with Prince Albert and her Prime Minister, William Lamb, the second Viscount Melbourne. She noted in her journal:

> Very soon after our arrival, we had luncheon, in a very fine large room, not generally used as a Dining room. It has a beautiful painted ceiling. At the one end there is a fine large portrait of the Pce of Wales standing beside a

horse, & at the other, of Ly Melbourne, with her eldest son, when quite an infant, — both, by Sir Joshua Reynolds. Ld Melbourne told me, that the damask on the walls, which is fine, & looks still very fresh, was bought by his father in Paris, as also the beautiful dessert service, in Sevres China. — Ld Melbourne took us round the house. There are many fine pictures in the different rooms, which it would take too long to enumerate. We went through the apartment, which used to be George IV's in which there is a fine crayon drawing, by Laurence, of Ly Melbourne, the Dss of Devonshire, & Mrs Damer, as the three Witches in Macbeth. Then we went upstairs with Ly Palmerston, where there are a number of nice airy rooms, some of them having beautiful views from the windows, but the house has a deserted look, & needs furnishing & being lived in. We then walked out, Ld M. leading me, & there were crowds of people there, who cheered loudly. Good Ld Melbourne was quite affected by it.[16]

Victoria enjoyed hearing about Lord Melbourne's family, especially his formidable mother. Victoria noted:

He said, that he thought almost every body's character was formed by their Mother, and that if the children did not turn out well, the mothers should be punished for it. I daresay his noble, fine and excellent character was formed by his mother, for she was a remarkably clever and sensible woman.[17]

Elizabeth could be accused of being calculating and mercenary, trading sex for titles but there were few other ways for a woman of talent to make her mark in a society that banned women from office. She cleverly used her feminine charms and her discretion to influence some of the great political debates of the time as a valuable go-between for the Whigs and the Prince of Wales. Lady Mary Coke noted in November 1783 that Charles James Fox 'pays her great attentions in consideration of her high favour' with the Prince of Wales. Another Whig grandee, Lord Albemarle, wrote to Lady Melbourne urging her to press the cause of Catholic emancipation on the prince. 'The chief, indeed the only point to press, if the opportunity should offer, is that of the Catholicks and to show how much the reputation and even the quiet of his future reign will depend on his conduct towards them … It would also be most useful to point out to him that if he abandons the Catholics the whole disgrace will be his.'[18]

By remaining loyal to Prince George, Elizabeth shrewdly retained him as an ally to promote her family and her sons in their careers. Writing from Brighton in the most fulsome terms, he apologised for not being able to offer

William a sinecure as warden of the Stannaries, an ancient post in the Duchy of Cornwall:

> The invariable & boundless affection (if you will allow me to speak the truth) my ever dearest Lady Melbourne which is so strongly imprinted in my Heart towards you, as well as the extreme desire I feel from the sincerity of my regard, & attachment to every Individual of your Family, would have made me most happy had it been in my power to have contrived anyhow upon the occasion of the Vacancy in the Stannaries. ... but I am & have been so cruelly situated respecting the Duchy of Cornwall that my hands are quite tied, & with sorrow to myself do I say it, must I am afraid continue so for a length of time. All this I will explain to you when we meet, as it is too long a topic for any Letter to contain. However, rest assured of this, that whilst I live I never will neglect an opportunity in which I can be of use to any of yours or I can forward any wish of yours as you well know, my ever dearest friend, or [Lord] Melbourne's. I hope that I can be depended upon and that there is no-one existing who ever <u>was is or even will be</u> so sincerely attached to you from the very bottom of their heart as yours truly affectionate George.

A few days later the Prince of Wales wrote again to Lady Melbourne in the warmest terms about another of her sons. This time he discussed ways of improving a career in the Guards for 'our dear Frederick Lamb', a phrase that raises the possibility the prince fathered not one, but two of Lady Melbourne's sons.

Lady Melbourne was never censorious about his 'marriage' to Maria Fitzherbert – unlike the Devonshires – and remained civil towards Mrs Fitzherbert even when the prince dropped her. In 1816, Lady Melbourne's judgment about Mrs Fitzherbert was validated when *The Times* reported she had been rehabilitated – Lady Melbourne attended a splendid ball and supper given by Mrs Fitzherbert at her house in Tylney Street after 'a long retirement from public life'. The Prince Regent's brothers, the Dukes of York, Clarence and Kent were there, though not the Prince Regent himself.[19]

The Prince remained Lady Melbourne's intimate friend, and attended the christenings of Lady Melbourne's two grandsons, George and Augustus. Elizabeth's fashionable friends also used her connection with the prince for their own social engagements. Whenever they wanted him to attend their parties after he became Prince Regent, it was to Lady Melbourne that they turned.

Elizabeth had her sights set on one more honour he could bestow on herself and her family – an English peerage to replace their Irish title and elevate her to the same rank as the Duchess of Devonshire.

10

Emily

At thirty-five, Viscountess Melbourne felt that her family was complete with four sons, but on 21 April 1787 she gave birth to her fifth child, a daughter, in her private suite of rooms on the first floor at Melbourne House in Piccadilly. Exactly a month later, on 21 May, she was christened Emily Mary Lamb at St James Church, Piccadilly, where her four brothers had been baptised.

Once more, the gossips speculated about the parentage of baby Emily. Her mother remained discreet, but many assumed the father was the Earl of Egremont. Certainly Emily shared her brother William's passions for the stage, theatre, and play-acting but she was closest to Frederick, with whom she grew up at Brocket Hall and Melbourne House in Piccadilly.

Her father may not have been the earl. Elizabeth had acquired a new lover: Francis Russell, the fifth Duke of Bedford, who was charming, immensely rich and a Whig. He was fourteen years younger than Elizabeth and not yet twenty when they became lovers. He was in the inner circle of the Whig party with Fox, Grenville and Lord Holland, leaving Lord Grey and Sheridan on the perimeter.

Francis had been orphaned at the age of three – his father was killed in a riding accident when he was two and his mother died the following year from consumption. He inherited Woburn Abbey and the dukedom from his grandfather at the age of six. Lady Holland wrote in her journal: 'Our parties at Devonshire House were delightfully pleasant. Lady Melbourne is uncommonly sensible and amusing though she often put me in mind of Madame de Merteuil in *Les Liaisons Dangereuses*. The Duke of Bedford is attached to her.'

'Loo', as he was called by Lady Melbourne and Georgiana, had rough manners, according to Lady Holland, but he was seen as a 'catch' by Viscountess Melbourne's Whig lady friends, not only as a sexual conquest but also as an asset for the Whig cause. He was a shrewd businessman who increased his considerable wealth by developing the Georgian squares that today bear his name and he shared Lady Melbourne's passion for agriculture, but Loo's main value was as a generous benefactor for the Whig party. He contributed £3,000 towards the costs of the Whigs' campaign to win a by-election at Westminster that went mostly on bribes to the voters. Lady Holland also noted he was 'magnificently generous to all who are in distress'.

This may well have been a knowing reference to Georgiana, for Loo gave loans to the Duchess of Devonshire to keep her creditors at bay after her losses at cards began to mount to unbridgeable sums. Correspondence lodged in the British Library reveals Georgiana used Elizabeth's friendship with Loo to arrange clandestine meetings with the young owner of Woburn, presumably to ask him to clear more debts:

'I am in a scrape about Loo, but not with Black [Charles Grey],' she writes to Elizabeth. 'This is equally addressed to you and Loo. Dear Love (That's to you) I am going to Chiswick therefore I could not see Loo last night ... as I want to see him, ask him to come to me Monday morning late...'

He was twenty-three and Elizabeth was thirty-six, but he was attracted to older women, perhaps because his mother had died when he was so young. He lived in a ménage-à-trois with Anne, Viscountess Maynard, who was in her fifties, and her husband until he began his affair with Lady Melbourne.

By the time Emily was born, Pen was away at Eton and William was at prep school with the Rev'd Marsham. Emily was born two days after Frederick's fifth birthday and George was only three. The disruptive baby girl delighted her brothers. She seemed to be all eyes and always getting into mischief and William affectionately called her 'that little devil Emily'.

Emily Lamb mixed happily with the children at Devonshire House in Piccadilly including her niece Caroline Ponsonby, daughter of Lady Duncannon, who would later marry William; and the Duke's illegitimate child by Bess Foster, Caroline St Jules, who would marry her brother George Lamb. As they grew older, William, Frederick and Emily adopted a benign contempt for Viscount Melbourne, with whom they had little in common. Emily would grow up to marry a rich landowner, Earl Cowper, and become a society hostess like her mother and take a long-term lover, Lord Palmerston (so hesitancy perhaps about the sire but no doubt about the dam).

'Emily's morals were much the same as her mother's,' said Howard Usher, the archivist at Melbourne Hall, 'and when a daughter was born [to Emily] in 1808, it was thought possible that Lord Palmerston was the father. The child was christened Emily Caroline Catherine Frances, but to avoid confusion with her mother she was always called Minnie.'[1]

When she was one year old, Emily's oldest brother Pen returned from the Continent to see his baby sister for the first time at Melbourne Hall. He brought with him his brother William. He had rescued William from his books at the Rev'd Marsham's prep school. William used to stare longingly out of the windows and wish he could be free of Latin and Greek. 'I used to think how I wish I was one of those happy fellows in the field instead of learning this consumed Latin!' If he looked out of the windows today, he would see light industrial units and the car park of a healthcare technology company.

Pen's arrival from abroad was both a surprise and a blessed relief for William. Pen left Eton in 1786 and had no pretentions about going on to university. When he left, he decided he had done with books. He wanted to go on the Grand Tour of Europe like the other sons of titled gentlemen, but the wars against the French made it difficult. Instead of studying the ruins of Rome, Lord Melbourne paid for Pen to go to the ancient Protestant court of Montbeliard on the Franco-Swiss border presided over by the Dukes of Wurttemberg. He was chaperoned by a Swiss tutor, a pastor called Mr Bignor. Pen's foreign adventures lasted less than a year.

Their hedonistic lifestyle was catching up on the Melbournes and the Devonshires, who all suffered agonies with gout. Elizabeth was only thirty-five but took to wearing a large soft shoe to ease the pain. *The Times* reported sarcastically on the Viscountess's recourse to the 'great cloth shoe'. It reported in October 1786: 'The Duchess of Devonshire in the midst of her pleasures at Chatsworth is attacked by very violent fits and Lady Melbourne has been prevented from being of the party by a severe fit of the gout. What a lesson is here for youth and beauty.'[2]

A year later, *The Times* implied she had reduced her drinking to ease her gout but Lord Melbourne had increased his intake:

> Lady Melbourne is doing all she can to keep off the gout and her Noble Lord though without designing it is deeply engaged in bringing it on. The Autumn perhaps will discover the success of their mutual endeavours. Our wishes however are strongly engaged on the side of female beauty and we have ever been in the habit of thinking a pretty foot in an elegant slipper an object of no trifling attraction.[3]

Shortly before Christmas 1787, *The Times* reported: 'We do not hear that Lady Melbourne has any reason to suspect that she shall be forced to undergo the discipline of last winter and make application to the Great Shoe. Hertfordshire air and Hertfordshire exercise may sufficiently strengthen her Ladyship's constitution to withstand the bad effects of London air and London exercise.'

Pen found his parents at Melbourne Hall when he returned to England with Mr Bignor in late 1788. He was despatched to collect William from Mr Marsham's in a carriage and they both travelled north to Melbourne Hall in Derbyshire, where their parents were preparing for a tour of stately homes in the north of England to show off their baby daughter to their family and friends.

The Melbourne family was now so large that when it set off in the late summer from Melbourne Hall a number of carriages were needed for children, nanny and servants. The first destination was Chatsworth, the magnificent neo-classical country mansion in Derbyshire, to call on the Devonshires and Elizabeth's particular friend, Georgiana. After enjoying the Devonshires' hospitality, they headed to Newburgh Priory, in North Yorkshire, to call on Lord Melbourne's sister, Charlotte, Lady Belasyse. Finally, they carried on north to Castle Howard, ancestral home in North Yorkshire of the Earls of Carlisle. There is no record of the Melbournes travelling the fifty miles further on to Elizabeth's family home at Halnaby Hall near Croft-on-Tees, where her father was living with a local married woman with a large family.

At the end of November they returned to Brocket and Pen's Swiss tutor Mr Bignor married the Swiss woman Lady Melbourne had employed for years as her children's nanny. They settled down with the family at Brocket Hall. Mr Bignor was allowed to eat 'upstairs' with the Melbourne family while his wife, as the nanny, remained firmly 'downstairs' with the servants.

Lord and Lady Melbourne returned to Melbourne House in Piccadilly before Christmas and William resumed his studies with Mr Marsham to prepare for Eton. Marsham, an Old Etonian and fellow of King's College Cambridge, was steeped in the ethos of Eton. He was a kindly soul, and spared William the rod, but left him to sit up by candlelight puzzling over problems from text books. William admitted in his private journal that he would have preferred being 'whipt' and told the answer than struggling until the solution dawned on him with the morning sun.[4]

William, who had been taken by his father to Mr Marsham's house in the autumn of 1785 when he was six years of age, so disliked his lessons he adopted the time-honoured schoolboy trick of convincing his mother he was ill to escape them.

When my father and mother were in the county their fondness naturally led them to have me with them once every week but these interruptions of study were nothing compared to those longer ones which I contrived to procure for myself by feigning sickness and thus playing upon their anxiety and affection – I soon learned all the symptoms which were considered as the most alarming, pain in the head, weight [sic] at the stomach, and had no objection to swallow my potion provided I could save myself the punishment of returning to Mr Marsham's. I have upon these occasions taken strong medicines without, as I really believe, any reason whatever.

When he was pretending to have a headache or sick stomach, he lay on his mother's couch in her rooms at Melbourne House and devoured her books.

There was in my mother's room in London a complete edition of Johnson's Poets which I [read as I] lay upon her couch during my real or feigned illnesses. I turned over the leaves of all the volumes of that collection. I read [Alexander] Pope's works with the greatest delight and eagerness and without the least fatigue. I read Dryden under more labour and effort but still with pleasure. I then tried Lucan [an epic poem on the Roman civil war] … but was unable to get through the first book…

He was helped by one of the Melbournes' footmen who was acquainted with the classics:

One of the footmen lent me one day the first volume of translations of Aristio…which left me in a fever of curiosity which, though it may have been abated, has never been satisfied … Seeing and reading plays had given me a love for the stage and the strong desire to be both an author and an actor.

By the age of eight, William was fired up by a love of literature that would burn with him through his life. He said he 'absolutely devoured every book that was put into [his] hands'. He hungrily consumed Cook's voyages; John Byron's *Narrative of the Loss of the Wager*, a shipwreck on the coast of Patagonia; Plutarch's Lives; Goldsmith's history of Rome; and a history of America. 'But of all the early books my delight was in Shakespeare, whose plays I read over and over again so that I was better acquainted with the plots, characters and incidents of them than I am at present.' Marsham 'greatly disapproved of this indulgence', but his mother encouraged him to read widely, though much of it was beyond his understanding at that age.

He stayed at Mr Marsham's for another year after their family tour of the North until in the autumn of 1789, when he was ten, William was taken by his father to Eton, his alma mater. Eton prepared the sons of the ruling landed gentry like William and Pen for running the country, as statesmen, generals, admirals or judges. But it also took in the sons of local tradesmen from Eton and Windsor, who were called Oppidans (Latin for 'belonging to a town'). They were the sons of bricklayers, coal merchants, bakers, apothecaries, poulterers, shipwrights, hosiers. They paid a reduced fee of about one guinea to the headmaster for taking in their sons and giving them an education, which was thrashed into them, if necessary, with the birch on their bare buttocks. His mother raised no objections to her favourite son going to Eton. Pen had survived, though like his father, he had taken more interest in racing form books than Homer. Eton toughened up privileged artistically-inclined boys like William Lamb for the harsh realities of life outside its walls, and, for some of them, the dangers of the Sudan, Afghanistan or China.

William was put in the house of Dr Langford, then under-master of the school, who was described by William as 'a rigid disciplinarian and disciple of Dr Barnard's, formerly head master and Provost of Eton'.

William vividly remembered his first day at school was a Saturday and he was immediately placed in the middle of the third form. A boy dropped some marbles with which he was playing and attracted the attention of the master who shook his head 'in menace of future punishment'.

William thought no more about it until the start of school on Monday morning 'when at a distance of two days ... I heard the same boy called out and saw him severely flogged – the certainty and rigour of a discipline so different from anything which I had ever witnessed inspired me with awe.'

He got used to thrashings. He later recalled that in the two years under Dr Langford's jurisdiction 'he favoured me with no more than three sound floggings which I recollect were judiciously timed and of no inconsiderable service.' William's belief that flogging could do some good has fuelled suspicions that after Eton, he became interested in flagellation. Sheridan's granddaughter, the social reformer Mrs Caroline Norton, with whom he had an affair in middle age, said in a letter to William she thought of him when she was in Rome and saw 'to my astonishment' an inlaid box in a shop of curiosities which contained a scene on 'your favourite subject of a woman whipping a child ... I had half a mind to buy it for you.'

His enthusiasm for flogging surprised Queen Victoria. She recorded in her journal sympathising with a French woman who was beaten by her husband, and how they had all laughed when Lord Melbourne said it was 'almost worthwhile for a woman to be beat, considering the exceeding pity she excites'.

A few months later, the subject of flogging came up again. The Queen recorded as saying the flogging of boys at Eton was degrading, but that view was not shared by Melbourne:

He was sometimes flogged at Eton, he told me, and that it had always an amazing effect on him; his Private Tutor used to flog him, and he said: "I don't think he flogged me enough, it would have been better if he had flogged me more". He said he was a very assiduous master, and that he (Ld.M) should have learnt more, if he hadn't always been trying to get away; he said "I liked it" (being there) "very much when my Father and Mother were in London", which, he said, they often were; but when they were only three miles off, he was always wishing to be at home; he was there three years; his eldest brother had also been there. [I] Said, flogging was so degrading; he said that never was thought so by the boys; I observed they didn't like it. "Didn't like the <u>pain</u> of it", he replied. &c.[5]

Flogging with the birch by the headmaster at Eton required the victim to take down both his trousers and his underwear, and bend over a wooden block to be struck with the birch, a practice only ended in the 1970s. William Lamb's relish for corporal punishment at Eton may been over-interpreted but his words were to take on a more sinister meaning after he married Lady Caroline Ponsonby, who claimed he corrupted her.

William also had to adjust to life without servants around him when he was at Eton. 'I never felt myself so desolate and desponding as when on the Monday at twelve o'clock after school was over I was told I might go where I would and do what I liked until dinner.' He had 'never been out of the sight of someone whose duty it was to attend upon me', and wandered lonely about Eton town 'in alarm and astonishment at the novelty of my situation'. He was given ten guineas a term by his father, and spent his pocket money on comfort food at the pastry shop, including fattening pies and sweet tarts. 'I had too much money and when I went home for the Christmas holidays, it soon appeared I had given myself a surfeit by eating without restraint.'

Eton was to supply him with a formative experience that affected him for the rest of his life: he walked away from a fight. The bookish William got in a fight with a bigger boy 'who had much longer arms and pounded amazingly'. After taking some punishment, he gave up the fight. 'I stood and reflected a little and thought to myself and then gave it up. I thought that one of the most prudent acts, but I was reckoned very dastardly for it.'

William's readiness to run away from a fight was an attitude he adopted in life in general, both in love and politics, and repeated in his marriage, much to his wife Caroline's frustration. His younger brother George, the Prince of Wales's son, was in contrast always prepared to stand up for his mother against the jibes hurled at him when he was Eton. George Lamb once knocked down Scrope Davies, Byron's friend, for calling his mother a whore.

William – despite his refusal to fight – became popular and the height of fashion by his final term; he was good at sports at Eton, particularly cricket, and put on plays including a rousing production of Sheridan's lively farce, *The*

Rivals. William's contemporaries at Eton included George Brummell, then known as 'Buck' who became famous as 'Beau', the young dandy, who would turn men's fashion into an art form, requiring two hours to dress in the morning.

When William returned to Eton in 1788, he found the school split over the Regency Question: whether King George III was mad and should be replaced by his eldest son, George, as Prince Regent. The majority of boys who had Tory fathers were implacably opposed to a Regency. Boys like William with Whig families supported the Prince of Wales, but he was in a small minority.

'I found the whole school in the greatest ferment and completely divided into two parties according to the respective connections of the boys to the Regency question,' he wrote in his journal. 'I was already a warm politician and in a minority, a small minority…'

The first signs of the king's madness began one morning at Windsor Castle in October 1788 when he complained of sharp stabbing pains in his stomach. He sent an urgent message to Sir George Baker, his doctor, asking for opium pills to kill the pain. His condition quickly worsened over the coming days and his behaviour became erratic, leading to bursts of anger at those around him, his doctor, servants, his wife, and in particular, his eldest son.

At dinner, the king grabbed George by the collar, dragged him out of his seat and threw him against a wall. The king became irritable, easily offended, and as his condition worsened, he suffered bouts of sweating that left his clothes drenched, and spoke uncontrollably, sometimes becoming so excited and agitated that he frothed at the mouth.

Baker was the physician to some of the greatest landed families in England, including the Dukes of Devonshire and Charles James Fox, and it was not long before the king's 'madness' was common knowledge among Lady Melbourne's high society friends. Viscountess Melbourne strongly supported her former lover Prince George in demanding that he should be made the Prince Regent, which was likely to herald the Whigs' return to power. The Salisburys, the Melbournes' next-door neighbours at Hatfield, supported the Tory Pitt administration, which hoped that the king would recover his senses quickly enough to stop the prince turning them out of office.

As the king's condition deteriorated, the Prince of Wales insisted on his father being removed from Windsor to the family house at Kew so that he could be hidden from public view. Seven other physicians were brought in to offer their views on the king's puzzling illness; their remedies – doses of laudanum and quinine, bleeding, blistering with hot cups on the skin, and purging – proved useless.

As the surgeons squabbled over a diagnosis, Francis Willis, an elderly clergyman and specialist in 'lunacy' with a home for the mentally ill in Lincolnshire was brought in to offer an alternative approach on 5 December

1788. Sir Simon Wessely, president of the Royal College of Psychiatrists 2014–2017, said the date is celebrated as a landmark in modern psychiatry. 'This is the first time a consultant opinion in mental disorder is summoned into the exalted world of modern medicine,' he said.[6]

Warren and most of his medical colleagues said the king would not recover his senses, but Willis patiently held out the hope that he would regain his sanity, which he had seen happen in his patients before.

Warren told the Duchess of Devonshire's mother, Lady Spencer in a letter in November, *Rex noster insanit* [the King is insane]. Pitt feared that if the King were declared mad, the Prince of Wales would bring in a new Whig administration, and he would be removed from office with no prospect of a return. Pitt began thinking of retiring from politics and taking up the law again.

Willis did not share the physicians' unanimous view that the king would never regain his senses. He set out to break the King's 'madness' with harsh discipline, including using restraints such as a straitjacket. When the king shouted obscene remarks about the Duke of Marlborough's daughter, Lady Pembroke, whom he had had lusted after for years at court, Willis stuffed the King's mouth with a handkerchief.

Queen Charlotte was furious that Prince George and Prince Frederick were using Warren's view that the king would not recover his senses to further their own ambitions. The queen heard they had made unseemly comments at Brooks's about playing cards with the 'madman'.

Fox was in Italy with Elizabeth Armistead seeking a health cure for oedema brought on by a life of heavy drinking when the news reached him of the King's incapacity. Fox immediately understood the implications, and made a 1,000-mile dash in nine days to get back to London. When he returned, looking thin and haggard, he discovered Sheridan had already ingratiated himself with the Prince of Wales and usurped Fox's position. Sheridan had used a well-worn tactic for winning the crucial vote – bribing the waverers and some of Pitt's ministers with the offer of jobs in government in return for their votes.

This provoked anger, jealousy, intrigue and feuding among the grandees as they gathered at the great houses of Whig power, Melbourne House, Holland House, Devonshire House, Brooks's Club, the Duke of Portland's mansion at Burlington House, and Carlton House. Fox was furious with Sheridan and Pitt gained strength from the fact that the Whigs began fierce in-fighting between themselves over the division of power before they had gained it.

The prince offered the post of First Lord of the Admiralty to Lord Sandwich, but Lord Portland and Fox objected. Portland, forty-three, the Duke of Devonshire's brother-in-law who was Whig Prime Minister from April to December in 1783, was the natural choice to lead a coalition of former rivals and replace Pitt as First Lord of the Treasury and Prime Minister, but he made it clear to the Prince of Wales he wanted a full apology from him for the 'very rough' way the prince had treated him during government negotiations for settling the prince's debts. Everyone seemed to be quarrelling with Sheridan. Portland refused to serve in the same cabinet as the playwright. The rising star of the Whigs, the second Earl Grey, aged twenty-four, was embarrassed when he was presented to the Prince of Wales by Sheridan at Carlton House and was offered a post as a junior minister in the Treasury. Grey was furious because he had expected to be offered the post of Chancellor of the Exchequer. The Prince asked Sheridan why Grey was being so diffident about his offer of the junior post at the Treasury. 'Sir' replied Sheridan, 'it may be diffidence or it may be ambition.'

Sheridan was right. Lady Holland noted in her journal: 'Grey is a man of violent temper and unbounded ambition.' Grey's arrogance split opinion between those who loathed him, and the few – like Georgiana – who came to love him. As the Whigs prevaricated, the debate shifted from the king's indisposition to whether Prince George was suitable to take over the Regency. The newspapers circulated rumours the prince had secretly illegally wed the twice-married Catholic, Mrs Maria Fitzherbert. A pamphlet called *The Crisis* said the public had a right to know whether the prince was 'a Papist or married to a Papist'. Sheridan – for so long a fawning, obsequious supporter of the prince – snapped when the public speculation threatened to wreck his strategy to restore the Whigs to power.[7]

The Melbournes knew all about the marriage that had taken place in a secret ceremony on 15 December 1785. Only eleven days after the marriage, the Prince spent Christmas with the Melbournes at Brocket Hall, where he could also see his baby son George Lamb.

The Prince, acting on advice by Sheridan, wrote to Portland with an olive branch: the Prince offered to 'cancel all former discontents' between the two of them. They sealed their restored friendship with a handshake when the prince paid a visit to Portland's mansion, Burlington House next door to Melbourne House. That cleared the way for Portland to become Prime Minister and the Whigs to regain power. Prince George planned to appoint his brother, Frederick, Duke of York, as Commander-in-Chief of the army. The Duke of Devonshire would be made Lord Privy Seal as a reward for Georgiana's tireless support, and it was expected he would make his 'wife', Mrs Fitzherbert, a duchess, although his ardour for her was already cooling as he realised it could damage his bid for power.

Willis's prognosis offered Pitt the hope that he could hold off the Whigs if he could play for time, which he did by tabling a motion for a Parliamentary committee to investigate the precedents for a Regency in Britain and report back. Fox smelled a rat and opposed his motion.

There were furious debates in Parliament, with Pitt and Fox in titanic clashes across the Despatch Box. The excitement around Whig salons reached fever pitch, and the prince's supporters including Lady Melbourne started sporting blue and buff striped ribbons in the Whig colours on their breasts. Georgiana went one step further by ordering Regency caps to be worn as chivalric favours for the Prince of Wales by his small army of lady friends.

This spurred Pitt to recruit a rival cheerleader for George III, the formidable Duchess of Gordon. She produced a royalist cap of red and white, and organised balls and soirées in support of the king, Pitt and the Tory cause, which proved highly popular with the public.

Lord Sydney wrote to Lord Cornwallis: 'The acrimony is beyond anything you can conceive. The ladies are as usual at the head of all animosity and are distinguished by caps, ribands and other such ensigns of party.'

Pitt was not against the idea of a Regency if the king proved too mad to rule, but he wanted to restrict the power of the Prince of Wales to appoint his own ministers, because he knew the moment George became Prince Regent, he would throw out Pitt and his ministers and replace them with Fox and his acolytes.

Fox and the Whigs demanded that the prince – as the heir to the throne – should be made Regent as a right as soon as the king was deemed unfit to continue, without reference to Parliament and without restrictions on his power. They also insisted that he should have the right to appoint anyone he liked to the Royal Household, while Pitt, realising George would pack the court with Whigs, wanted that privilege to be kept by Queen Charlotte.

The crisis came to a head on 16 December 1789 with a Parliamentary debate over Pitt's motion for a committee to kick the issue into the long grass. It would be decided by a vote in the House of Commons and the result was on a knife-edge.

The Prince of Wales, who took the vote personally, sent a nervous note to Sheridan on the eve of the Commons debate to ask if the numbers were for him or and against: 'For God's sake explain yourself – who is false? Who is staunch? Who deceives us? Pray remark will you and for Heaven's sake send me word and relieve my uneasiness.' Sheridan, having to deal with the liars who populated Parliament, was at his wits' end. He accused the Prince of having 'the most womanish mind' he had encountered.

The house was packed for the debate. Fox had not intended to speak because he was still too ill, but he intervened in a minister's speech to set out the case for allowing the prince automatically to become Regent, if the king was indefinitely indisposed.

'What must be the situation of a Regent elected by the House?' Fox demanded. 'He must be a pageant, a puppet, a creature of their own, an insult and a mocker of every maxim of Government!'

Pitt, sitting opposite Fox, realised his chance had come. He is said to have slapped his thigh, and exclaimed he would 'un-Whig the gentleman' for the rest of his days. Politically, Fox was standing on his head to support the prince. By extending the prince his unconditional support, Fox, the great reformer and 'Man of the People', was repudiating a position held by leading Whigs such as the Devonshires for a century, since the Glorious Revolution of 1688 and the subsequent Bill of Rights of 1689. They had deposed a king, James II, to assert the rights of Parliament over the monarch, and now they were throwing them away.

Pitt jumped to his feet at the despatch box, and fired back at Fox: 'To assert such a right in the Prince of Wales or any one else independent of the decision of the two houses of Parliament is … treason to the constitution of the country.'[8]

Lady Melbourne and the Duchess of Devonshire could not attend the debate – women were still barred from the public gallery of the Commons – so they waited at home nervously to hear the outcome of the vote. The Prince of Wales sat with the Duchess of Devonshire before going off to get drunk. She had a headache but stayed up until four o'clock in the morning to hear the result.

When the division was called by the Speaker, Pitt walked through the Aye lobby with his close friend William Wilberforce (who later became famous through his bill to abolish slavery), Lord George Lennox, son of the second Duke of Richmond, and the historian Nathaniel Wraxall, who later wrote an account of the period.

Viscount Melbourne, MP for Malmesbury, went through the No lobby with Fox and Sheridan, Viscount Palmerston and Lord North the former Prime Minister; the Foley brothers who had sought a change of law to clear their debts; Lord Duncannon, Harriet Spencer's husband; Horace Walpole, the writer; and Godfrey Webster, first husband of Lady Holland, a notorious rake and reckless gambler. Loo, the young fifth Duke of Bedford and Viscount Althorp, Georgiana's brother, arrived breathlessly at Devonshire House with the shattering news that the Whig opposition had been defeated by sixty-four votes, and Pitt had survived.

Pitt speedily introduced a Regency Bill as a contingency measure if the king's illness continued but it laid down restrictions on the prince's powers of patronage, if he was made Regent, to stop him replacing Pitt and the Tories with a Whig government. The queen would remain in charge of appointments to the Royal Household.

The Regency Bill was passed by the Commons on 12 February 1789, but it was not required. As Willis had predicted, after four months of manic behaviour, the king suddenly recovered his senses. He wrote tenderly to his queen: 'My dearest Charlotte I cannot but be deeply impressed by the consideration of how much you must have been affected by the long continuance of my illness. Though I do not decline to give attention to public business which may be necessary I propose to avoid all discussions that may agitate me.'

He took the advice of Pitt's physician and went off to Weymouth on the Dorset coast for a change of air, starting the fashion for sea bathing at the seaside resort; it was followed by Prince George but he went to Brighton rather than Weymouth because he could not stand his father.

George III's physicians never agreed on the cause of his illness. Specialists in the twentieth century concluded it was porphyria, which affects the nervous system causing vomiting, confusion, and seizures. Some experts have lately revised their view and believe he may have been suffering from hypomania.[9]

The Whigs descended into bickering once more. Sheridan could not blame Fox for the debacle, because he made a politically inept speech threatening action in the future if MPs did not support the Regency of Prince George. There was a popular outpouring of support for the king and queen on the streets and in theatres, and the Whigs were routinely abused or ridiculed.

On 3 December, *The Times* reported from Covent Garden theatre: 'The second appearance of their Majesties attracted an overflowing and truly brilliant audience. The royal Visitors did not enter the house till past seven o'clock when the audience with their true spirit of loyalty over due to their *Patriot King* instantaneously demanded their favourite song "God Save the King" which in the course of the evening was sung no less than six times.'[10]

Hordes of royalist supporters milled around outside Melbourne House and Devonshire House when the queen held 'a drawing room', a reception at St James's to celebrate the king's recovery. Ladies were asked to wear the message 'God Save the King' in their caps as a riposte to the Duchess of Devonshire's pro-Regent caps. The queen stood near the middle window receiving guests, one by one, but refused to speak to the Whig leaders including Fox, Sheridan, Tierney, and Grey, and she was cold towards the two princes, George and Frederick. The crush was so great, Lord Jersey reported to Lady Spencer, that ladies fainted and were reduced to tears. There was 'screaming, loss of Caps, bags, shoes and I suppose almost every part of the dress that was not quite attached strongly to the person.'

Georgiana and the Whig ladies returned exhausted and embarrassed. After a service of thanksgiving for the king's recovery at St Paul's on St George's Day, a royalist crowd joyfully unhooked Pitt's carriage from the horses in

Whitehall and pulled it into Downing Street. Pitt emerged to loud cheers. He had never been so popular, and the Whigs more downcast.

Elizabeth, Lady Melbourne, emerged from the Whig disaster largely unaffected. It had, however, a lasting impact on Georgiana, the Duchess of Devonshire. Having led from the front, she decided to retreat behind the walls of Devonshire House to avoid the abuse.

At another levee on 2 December at St James's, *The Times* reported Lord Melbourne presented his son and heir, Peniston Lamb, to the king and queen. Lady Melbourne was not listed among the guests. She was now heavily involved in her love affair with Loo, the Duke of Bedford.

In August 1789, when he was twenty-four and she was thirty-seven, Elizabeth gave birth to a second daughter at Melbourne House in Piccadilly that was widely believed to be by Loo. The parish record shows the baby was baptised Harriot Ann Lamb on 31 August 1789 at St James Piccadilly, though she became known as Harriet. The name of the father on the register once more was given as 'the Rt Hon Peniston Lord Viscount Melbourne'.

Harriet certainly resembled Loo. She was a fun-loving child and caught the eye of the painter Sir Thomas Lawrence the instant he saw her frolicking on the floor with her older sister Emily at Melbourne House. Emily later recalled she had just snatched Hariett's mop cap off her head when the door opened and their mother came in accompanied by a gentleman in black, who was very kind and said, 'Nothing can be better than that.'

Sir Thomas painted the little girls as he found them, and captured Harriet's playful look with cherry-red cheeks. They are both wearing white dresses with sashes around the waist in pink satin and Emily is still sporting her cap with a pink ribbon. It is about the only record of Harriet, apart from a letter she sent to her brother George when he was at Eton. 'Papa hears you go to school in boats,' said 'Haryot', referring to a flood. She then gave news of her dogs: 'Roy has got three beautiful puppies, which are much bigger than Nelly.' She finishes by asking George 'to write to me soon and tell me how long it is to the holidays' and signs herself 'Haryot'.

I discovered an accomplished pencil drawing of her favourite pet on a scrap of paper in the Melbourne files at Hatfield House Archive. It is the head of a family dog, a retriever or a spaniel, in profile with coloured patches shaded in. It is panting, with its tongue lolling out of its mouth, and its eyes are closed. On the reverse, is written, 'Harriet Lamb'. If it is by Harriet, it could be Nelly, her pet bitch.

II

The House Swap

Georgiana had almost despaired of ever producing an heir for the Duke of Devonshire in 1789 when the Duke took her to the Belgian health resort of Spa in the hope that its therapeutic waters would help the Duchess conceive the son they both longed for.

They were accompanied by the third person in their ménage-à-trois, Bess Foster, who had already produced an illegitimate daughter in 1785 and a son in 1788 by the Duke. After relaxing in the waters of Spa, the Devonshires went to Paris to see their friends among the French aristocracy including Marie Antoinette at Versailles.

Georgiana found the Bourbon queen sadly altered: 'Her belly quite big and no hair at all…' In September 1789 the Devonshires, unsettled by the mobs already roaming Paris streets, moved to Brussels and Georgiana became certain she was pregnant.

The duke, nicknamed *Canis* because of his dogged nature, returned to England to deal with a family crisis – Georgiana's sister, Harriet, had been caught with her lover Sheridan and her husband, Lord Duncannon, wanted a divorce. Canis stopped the divorce and returned to Brussels with Harriet and Lord Duncannon, but the Devonshire household comprising children, nannies and servants was forced to quit Brussels after being accused of spying.

Quite why the duke did not take his wife back to England at that stage is unclear. He may have decided the sea journey would risk Georgiana's pregnancy. It was an extraordinarily dangerous time for aristocrats to be touring France. The mob had stormed the Bastille on 14 July 1789 to free those accused of political crimes under Louis XVI, thus triggering the revolution with their demands for '*Liberté, égalité, fraternité*'.

Ignoring the threat, the Devonshires headed once more for Paris where they met a fleeing French nobleman who offered them his house in Passy on the outskirts of the city. They gratefully accepted. They stayed in Passy for the next eight months, as mobs roamed Paris, until on 21 May 1790, Georgiana at last gave birth to her longed-for son.

Given the extraordinary circumstances of his birth – it remains a mystery why the Devonshires decided to brave revolutionary Paris to have their child in France – it is not surprising there was gossip that the real reason for remaining abroad was that the boy was a changeling, and may have been Bess's son. Whatever the truth, the bells of churches near Chatsworth, their Derbyshire country seat, peeled with joy at the news of the birth of an heir to the estate and in August the Devonshires safely returned home with their son. He was christened William like his father with the title of Marquess of Hartington, after a village in the Peak District, granted to the first son down the Devonshire line. He became known in the family as 'Hart'.

Georgiana, thirty-three, was expected to settle down after the traumas of a difficult birth in a foreign city at the beginning of the Terror. She broke with upper class tradition and breast-fed Hart for nine months rather than using a wet nurse. With her duty to her husband done, and daily provoked by her husband's open adultery with Bess, Georgiania followed Lady Besford, the character she had based on Lady Melbourne in her romantic novel *The Sylph*: 'My Lord kept a mistress from the moment of his marriage. What law excludes a woman from doing the same?'

She took a lover and within a year, she was pregnant by him. First she toyed with John Sackville, the Duke of Dorset, a great womaniser whom she had known for thirteen years, but broke off their affair. Lady Melbourne urged Georgiana to leave him some hope because she feared a scandal if he protested too much, but for once, Georgiana rejected Elizabeth's advice. She banned him from Chatsworth:

> However good and wise your arguments are, they are not stronger than my own heart suggests to me – and I wish fairly and honestly to make you read it as I do myself. When the Duke of Dorset returned, he express'd great misery at the idea of my having without any cause on his side, spoken to him in an angry and harsh manner, especially as he was ready to give up every wish to mine, to be contented with seeing me and being on a friendly footing with me – he was particularly shocked at the idea of my forbidding him Chatsworth.

Georgiana, however, had not changed her mind; she dropped Dorset because she had another lover; she had decided to give herself to Charles Grey, the young, handsome and ambitious Whig who believed he was destined for greatness. Grey was twenty-three. His haughty looks even aroused Byron, who said Grey had the 'patrician thorough-bred look ... which I dote upon.'[1]

Georgiana knew she was playing with fire and risking everything, but like her addiction to gambling, she could not resist him. Some time in May 1791 – almost exactly a year after giving birth to 'Hart' – she became pregnant by Grey. Her pregnancy could not have come at a more inopportune moment for Georgiana. She was once more heavily in debt having given free rein to her gambling addiction by becoming, like many society women, a banker at the card game of faro. In desperation she sent a note to the third person in her marriage: 'Oh God Bess, I have gone on and lost an immense sum – I dare not tell you that it is £6,000.' In fact, it was probably ten times that sum, equivalent to the whole year's income from the Cavendish estates or around £7 million at today's prices.

She approached the society banker Thomas Coutts for a loan and received a lecture on the iniquities of gambling for her trouble, but no money: he told her to consider what she was risking 'to gratify this destructive passion ... a gamester goes on in the vain hope of recovering lost sums till he loses probably all that remains, and along with it everything which is precious.'

The Devonshires were in Bath, once more taking the waters for their gout, and staying with the Duncannons who had rented a house in Gay Street for the summer. The Duke of Devonshire returned to London, leaving Georgiana nursing her secret with her sister Harriet. The sisters planned to go to the West Country to have her baby there in seclusion.

An anonymous letter writer sent a note to the duke saying he should return to Bath to see his wife. He returned unannounced and discovered the truth. She was six months pregnant, and she could not conceal her belly beneath her skirts. He was furious and her sister, Harriet, Lady Duncannon, could hear Georgiana wailing and pleading with her husband through the wall of her room.

Georgiana threw herself on the duke's mercy. He was far from spotless. He had already had an illegitimate daughter by his first mistress, Charlotte Spencer and two children by his live-in lover, Georgiana's friend, Elizabeth Foster; but by the double-standards of the time, Georgiana was not given the liberal-minded leeway she advocated in *The Sylph*.

The duke gave Georgiana an ultimatum – she could have the baby abroad, disown Grey and have it adopted, or she could keep the baby, live with Grey, and face separation with the prospect of never seeing her other children again. Georgiana chose to give up Grey and their child as soon as it was born. Going abroad meant she had to leave behind her son, Hartington, who was only one year old. Her sister Harriet wrote a hurried note to Lady Melbourne with the news and swore her to secrecy: 'We must go abroad – immediately. Nothing else will do, neither prayers nor entreaties will alter him. He says there is no choice between this or public entire separation at home … write to me, come if you can, give us some comfort but do not betray me … on your life say not a word of it to anybody.'

Lady Melbourne received a note from Georgiana, though it avoided the unpleasant truth with a convenient lie; she said she would have to go abroad for Harriet's health. Her main concern was that Lady Melbourne should calm down Charles Grey, who she knew would be furious when he discovered she had chosen to abandon him, and their child when it was born: 'If I go, you must stem the fury of the Black Sea.'

Georgiana's interfering mother, Lady Spencer, was at Holywell, her Gothic-style country villa at St Albans. She rushed to join the family to take over the crisis. The Duke of Devonshire dithered about the final details, as he did about most decisions, but finally decided that Georgiana should go to Montpellier in the South of France directly from Bath via Southampton. She would be accompanied by her mother, Lady Spencer; Bess Foster and the duke's illegitimate daughter; Lord and Lady Duncannon whose marriage had been close to breakdown because of Harriet's affair with Sheridan, and Duncannon's six-year-old daughter, Caroline.

Georgiana avoided telling Grey of her choice and asked Lady Melbourne to act as a go-between for their letters. 'I shall make any possible use of you about Black's letters sent you when I am gone,' said Georgiana.

Lady Melbourne passed on to Grey all Georgiana's letters sent from staging posts on her way down through France. Georgiana wrote to Lady Melbourne with a Paris dateline: 'My Dearest love. We are still here. Bess has not come. This town swarms with English. Mr Stewart is the only conveyance I can find for a parcel to you containing a letter to Black. ' The parcel was delayed in the post and left Grey anxious and pining like a love-lorn teenager. When at last it arrived, he wrote to Lady Melbourne from Fallodon, his Northumberland estate: 'I can bear any scolding from you just now under the joy of this unexpected relief.'

They reached Fontainebleau on 27 November 1791 where Georgiana wrote to Lady Melbourne saying they were staying in a 'vile, vile' inn before setting off for Lyons. In December she wrote from Lyons: 'Black has been very cold and my letters from him yesterday have given me a headache which is not yet gone – why must people be harsh at such a distance? However, he is quite right.' He had turned cold because he realised she had chosen to remain under the Duke of Devonshire's protection, after being threatened with never seeing her children again. It would be two years before she would return.[2]

As the Duchess was travelling to the South of France, Lady Melbourne was entertaining the Duke of York to dinner at Melbourne House. He had recently married a German princess and he admired the size of Melbourne House. He said he was tired of his more modest house in Whitehall. It was next door to Horse Guards, and convenient for Westminster with fine views of St James's Park, but the prince said he longed for a house as grand as hers in Piccadilly.

Elizabeth, in good humour, told the duke: 'I would willingly exchange the chimes at night of St James's for those of the Abbey … I would like the opportunity of looking on the park every morning when I rise.' Torrens, the Victorian historian, said the duke told Elizabeth 'anything is possible to you.'[3]

Lord Melbourne treated the idea of an exchange of houses as a peculiar jest, said Torrens, and brushed it off as 'one of his wife's unaccountable whims' to please royalty. What may have started out as a royal joke in late 1791, soon became a serious proposition, however, as he began to see the financial advantages of the move.

Viscount Melbourne had exhausted most of his fortune in cash and had been trying to sell off land and farms in Derbyshire to pay for the privileged lifestyle the Melbournes had come to expect.

A house swap was also an attractive prospect for the Duke of York. In September he had married the rich heiress, Princess Frederica Charlotte of Prussia, niece of Frederick the Great, in Berlin, in the hope of paying off his debts at home.

They returned to London amid a great deal of rejoicing for a second wedding ceremony at Buckingham Palace. The duke needed his own palace to accommodate his wife and her retinue. York House was too small, but Melbourne House in Piccadilly appeared ideal. It was big enough for the Yorks to entertain in style and close to the court.

York House was, by the standards of Melbourne House and Devonshire House, a modest, compact town house, sandwiched between the Cabinet Office and Horse Guards in the centre of Whitehall. It had been built for a former MP, Matthew Featherstonehaugh on Crown land, previously part of Henry VIII's Palace of Whitehall near the Tudor cockpit. The house backed on to King Henry's former tiltyard and overlooked the ornamental canal at St James's Park.

Featherstonehaugh had commissioned the architect James Paine, who designed Brocket Hall for Matthew Lamb, to build a conventional flat-fronted three-storey Georgian townhouse set back from the busy main thoroughfare from Charing Cross to Westminster. It was finished in 1758.

Featherstonehaugh's mistress Emma Hart – later Nelson's mistress, Emma Hamilton – is said to have struck poses semi-naked for his friends on his dining room table in classical tableau, as she did later for admiring audiences in Naples after marrying Sir William Hamilton, the British envoy there.

After Featherstonehaugh, Lord Amherst, Commander-in-Chief of the armed forces, rented the Whitehall house from 1779 for eight years because of its convenience for Horse Guards next door. It was acquired by the Duke of York, who later succeeded Amherst as Commander-in-Chief, from Featherstonehaugh's widow on 4 December 1787.

The Duke wanted something grander than Paine's house and commissioned Henry Holland, the fashionable architect employed by the Prince of Wales at Carlton House, to create a house for him in Whitehall where he could entertain as elegantly as his brother. While he waited for Holland to finish York House, he moved into Carlton House with his elder brother George. They quickly resumed their roistering life together and began campaigning against their father, George III to make way for the Prince of Wales during the king's first bout of mental illness.

The duke was 'tall, stout, loud-voiced and jolly' and his good humour made him popular with his subordinates, particularly after wine-fuelled regimental dinners. He was brave – he fought a duel with one of his own subordinates, Charles Lennox, nephew of the Duke of Richmond, an officer in the duke's regiment the Coldstream Guards on Wimbledon Common. Lennox grazed a curl on the duke's head and the duke did not fire. Both men agreed honour had been done. Colonel Lennox later inherited the title as the Duke of Richmond and with his wife hosted the famous ball in Brussels on the eve of the Battle of Waterloo. The duke was soon able to celebrate his survival and the completion of the works at York House with a great party.

Holland's improvements were a stroke of genius. He threw a rotunda over the carriage yard and erected an elegant fan-shaped staircase up to the first floor where guests could be entertained in a ballroom and dining room with huge windows opening out on the park vista of St James's. It transformed the small house into a mini-palace. Guests who entered York House through a new portico supported on four columns on Whitehall were instantly transported into an airy entrance hall with pillars flanking the fan-shaped staircase that rose in three stages of five, ten and seven steps to the first floor entertaining rooms. There were five floors, including a deep basement for the wine cellars, and attic bedrooms for the servants, reached by narrow winding wooden staircases hidden at the sides of the house.

The Duke lived in the rooms below the new main staircase. Holland incorporated a concealed stairway from the first floor library to the duke's private suite of rooms on the ground floor, enabling him to escort women friends to his bedroom without being seen. The duke's private suite included a hot bath, a cold bath, water heater and water closet, a room for his valet, an inner dressing room and wardrobe, and the duke's bedchamber. There were three large interconnecting rooms with French windows onto a small rose garden on Horse Guards Parade. The Adam-inspired centre room was intended as an anteroom but became known after its decoration as the Etruscan Room, and was reputedly decorated by a 'celebrated French lady', though the work has been attributed to the French designer, Francoise-Joseph Belanger.

York House was Prince Frederick's home for five years. A gilded coronet was placed over the interconnecting doors by Holland. It appears to have a field-marshal's baton as well, although the prince was not promoted to field-marshal until 1795, after he left.

For Elizabeth, now entering her forties, York House offered a financial solution to her problems with the novelty of a new place to entertain her friends in Whitehall. It was only a short walk to the Houses of Parliament, and Elizabeth could continue hosting her Whig salons for political friends who could drop by on their way to and from debates at Westminster with the latest gossip or news from abroad.

The Prince of Wales, a frequent visitor to Melbourne House in Piccadilly, thought its purchase a good deal for his brother, but he was disparaging about the decorations and furniture that had suffered nearly twenty years of wear and tear. The Prince wrote to Frederick saying it was 'dirty and nasty and the furniture so worn it would be ridiculous of you to pretend to buy it as they think it totally unfit…' The exchange of houses enabled Viscount Melbourne to become mortgage-free. As it was smaller, Lady Melbourne could save on the running costs by reducing the number of the servants.

Rumours of the Melbournes' straitened circumstances had been circulating for years. Lord Melbourne was forced to raise loans to pay for the upkeep of three large properties. Unlike the Devonshires, he did not have £60,000 a year to call on from his estates. He tried to sell off several of his estates including Langsett and Bolsterstone in the moorland hills of south Yorkshire to maintain the Melbournes' lifestyle. He re-mortgaged Melbourne House in 1775 for a total £10,000 from Theodore Henry Broadhead of Soho Square within weeks of the building being completed. It was still outstanding more than fifteen years later. Chambers made several vain attempts to get Lord Melbourne to pay the interest on £3,000 he owed him for the house.

In November 1784, Lord Melbourne wrote to Chambers to apologise: 'It is not from a wish to be resolute as you term it in refusing your Capital or denying to Pay your interest. A very unexpected Draft on account of the new Parliament so much called before its time made with me money very scarce and I hope Sir you will be Content with the Payment of a Year's interest now, and the rest shall be kept back as little longer as Possible.' It was not until 1789 – fourteen years after the work was completed – that Lord Melbourne took out a further loan on the property to pay off his architect.[4]

It would be a squeeze for Elizabeth to accommodate her family at York House, as four of her six children were under ten and William was not going to stay at Eton forever. Elizabeth began planning to make York House fit for the Melbournes' arrival in Whitehall. She and Lord Melbourne would move into the Duke of York's suite of rooms 'below stairs' while her youngest children, Frederick, George, Emily and Harriet, would occupy rooms on the second floor above the entertaining rooms. (See page 254.)

The construction of the rotunda had robbed York House of its coach yard, and agreement was reached to purchase the old lottery office across the road for a coach house for the Melbournes. The lease on York House was due to expire in 1842 but an extension of 44 years was later added.

It took the lawyers months to disentangle the financial claims on both houses. His marriage to a rich Prussian princess had helped the duke to pay off some of his debts but like the Melbournes, he was living well beyond his means and had remortgaged York House a number of times to raise cash to fund his extravagant lifestyle. Two brothers, Oliver and James Farrer, gave him a new mortgage of £10,000 secured partly on York House and Oatlands, his country residence near Weybridge in Surrey, and his other estates in Surrey. He also owed several other undisclosed sums advanced to him by the two brothers. The Government increased his annual allowance by £18,000 on his marriage to £37,000 a year – the equivalent of nearly £4 million a year today – but still it was not enough.

There was a risk that the deal would become unstuck. Lady Melbourne persuaded her new lover, the Duke of Bedford, to loan the Duke of York the enormous sum of £30,000 to help him finance his side of the bargain. It is a mark of his devotion to Elizabeth that he was willing to do so, with little hope of it being repaid.

'The Melbournes I think have made an excellent bargain about their House,' Thomas Noel wrote to his sister Judith Milbanke, wife of Lady Melbourne's brother, 'and I hear have secured the payment by the D of B [Duke of Bedford] lending H.R.H. the money.'

The Duke of York celebrated the exchange with a party for the Melbournes at York House in Whitehall on 8 December and the next day the Melbournes reciprocated by hosting 'a public breakfast' at Melbourne House in Piccadilly for the Duke of York and his Duchess. They were joined by two of Elizabeth's lovers – the Prince of Wales and the Duke of Bedford with the duchess's ladies in waiting.

They were met at the door of Melbourne House by Viscount Melbourne according to *The Times*, which reported he led the royal visitors into the Breakfast Room where 'a profusion of hot and cold dishes besides teas, coffee, chocolate etc. awaited their arrival'. Lord and Lady Melbourne were so anxious to 'do honour to their Princely guest that they each brought in a dish ... The Duchess was in high spirits, much delighted with the house and entertainment – she was dressed in silk and rouged very highly'.[5]

The house exchange was finally signed on Christmas Day 1791. The contracts confirmed the Duke of York would pay Viscount Melbourne £23,571. When their debts were paid off, it left the Melbournes with a cash surplus of £10,000.

Lady Birkenhead, who studied the contracts, said: 'These documents incline one to think that the exchange of houses attributed by most writers to Lady Melbourne's anxiety to oblige Royalty, may really have been a way for the Melbournes to escape from financial difficulties with no loss of prestige.'[6]

Before she closed the door on her house in Piccadilly after sixteen years, Lady Melbourne received a letter from Georgiana, who was in Lyons in December, saying, 'I was very glad the bargain is fixed.' The duchess added: 'My Dearest Them. [Themire] Thank you for your dear letter ... you must never be angry with me and be always sure I can always explain anything that may seem wrong to you. Indeed you must know how I love you and how I think of you.' On 20 February, Georgiania gave birth to a girl, called Eliza. The Duchess may have expected to be allowed to return to England, but her husband refused to lift his ban on her return.

Meanwhile, the Melbournes moved into the new Melbourne House in Whitehall early in the New Year of 1792. With her new house half-a-mile from Parliament, Lady Melbourne could remain at the heart of Georgian affairs with no loss of prestige. Her house in Whitehall would become a favourite drop-in place for Whig politicians after late night sessions at the Houses of Parliament, particularly for the new generation of young men who would make their political debuts in the early years of the nineteenth century. She could also settle back and enjoy the middle period of her life, free of mortgages and with an extra £10,000 in the bank.

She began hosting her Whig salon in Whitehall with renewed vigour. Information gave her power in these most turbulent times. She was able to glean intelligence, as a political insider, about ministerial changes, rising and waning stars in Parliament, good speeches, bad performances, government ups and downs, which could be traded for other juicy titbits. Charles Grey, Georgiana's lover, became one of Lady Melbourne's most important sources, despite a contretemps over his support for the French revolution. Among

Lady Melbourne's correspondence is a brief note from Grey marked 'Confidential – Saturday': 'My dear Lady Melbourne, The If I wrote yesterday is now a certainty. There will be no change of Administration you will soon hear this from others, but till then don't say that you have heard it from me. Ever yrs affectionately, Grey.'

The fear that stalked Lady Melbourne's salon and her friends in the land-owning aristocracy who ruled Georgian Britain was that the growing French revolution would cross the English Channel and British Jacobins, inspired by the revolts in America and France, would seek to overthrow the ruling classes in Britain.

Lady Melbourne had never shared the enthusiasm of her more radical Whig friends for Jean Jacques Rousseau and Voltaire and did not like revolutionary talk being raised around her table. Fox had hailed the storming of the Bastille as 'the greatest event in the world'. His old friend Edmund Burke produced a counter-blast to Thomas Paine's 1791 revolutionary best-seller *Rights of Man* calling for the vote for all those who paid taxes. Burke's treatise *Reflections on the Revolution in France* became the bedrock of Tory thinking. It also led to a lasting split between Burke and Fox.

The reformists in the Whig party like Grey believed that to head off the revolution, Britain needed to concede ground to those demanding a widening of the franchise, especially in the new industrial cities that were suddenly mushrooming in the midlands and north of England. In doing so, they anticipated the Great Reform Act; but it would take another forty years to force it onto the Statute Book.

Tories and conservative Whigs believed that the only answer to mob protests, factory destroyers and political agitators like Paine was suppression. They included the Earl of Egremont, Lady Melbourne, and the Prince of Wales. Paine published the second edition of *Rights of Man* calling for the overthrow of the monarchy in 1792 and fled to France after being indicted for treason.

The headstrong Grey forced a vote to extend the franchise to more men in the belief that it would avert the threat of revolution in Britain. Grey and his fellow-Whigs were denounced as pro-French traitors. Fox supported Grey but many leading Whigs deserted them. Pitt argued reform would bring 'anarchy and confusion' from France. He won the vote in the Commons by a large margin and it split the Whigs so deeply, it seemed it would destroy the party.

On this issue, Lord Egremont decisively backed Pitt and Lady Melbourne sided with Lord Egremont, who would become so worried about the threat from France he mobilised a local militia in Sussex. The *Gentleman's*

Magazine later said: 'Always liberal in his opinions, he, nevertheless, gave his support to the illustrious William Pitt; and when it was deemed necessary to arm against the threatened aggression of France, he came forward with alacrity; and his nervous, soul-stirring eloquence, at the public meetings of the period, are not yet forgotten.'[7]

Grey forcefully and at times violently argued in favour of radical reform of the British ruling system over the dinner table when he went to Melbourne House. This earned him a rare rebuke from Lady Melbourne. She had no intention of blowing up the social pyramid that she had spent a lifetime so assiduously climbing, hauled up by royal patronage.

On 14 December 1792 – the same month that the trial of Paine *in absentia* began – one of Lady Melbourne's house guests wrote to her promising never to raise the issue of revolution at her dinner table again. Lady Melbourne thought it was important enough to copy it and keep it among her letters. It was not signed but, given the context – that year Canning began secret talks with Pitt that would lead to Canning switching his allegiance from the Whigs to the Tories – it was almost certainly from Charles Grey:

> Whatever my principles may be, you need not be afraid of my discussing them at your house. I know how ill it will be received and shall therefore avoid it however angry I may sometimes be at hearing unqualified abuse of Men whose talents and general principles I must admire particularly when it comes from those who have neither talents nor principles but are guided in all their actions solely by selfishness...
>
> You mistake me in supposing I am violent in my political opinions. At some moments I feel great apprehensions as to the effects of any change – my inclinations lead me to the reformers, my aversions strengthen these inclinations. I see too with regret Men who I always hoped would some day rescue the country from the arbitrary, the oppressive, the aristocratic Administration that now governs it, meanly playing a second part and being dupes by being the Cats paw of the very set of men their principles must make them detest (at least politically so).
>
> Seeing all this I cannot help wishing a speedy reform that will in some degree satisfy the minds of the people. I know the danger of any reform, but I cannot help looking on a present moderate one as the only means of preventing a very serious one soon.[8]

He also took a sideswipe at Lady Melbourne's long-term lover, the Earl of Egremont, who had been a lifelong opponent of Roman Catholic emancipation and opposed British appeasement towards the French revolutionaries: 'Lord Egremont's opinions do not alarm me; I think his judgment is generally good but on this subject he has always been a croaker.'

His letter is a remarkable show of audacity by Grey, given his situation: he owed a debt of gratitude to Lady Melbourne for her discretion in acting as his secret go-between with the Duchess of Devonshire while she was in exile having his baby; and he had cuckolded the Duke of Devonshire, one of the grandees of the Whig party that Grey secretly aspired one day to lead. It showed that Grey, at twenty-eight, was a man of towering self-confidence ... or breathtaking arrogance.

Grey's confidence in his own judgment was shaken a month later by an event that had shattering consequences across the capitals of Europe – the beheading of Louis XVI, the King of France, in Paris on 21 January 1793. 'Bad as I am thought, I cannot express the horror I feel at the atrocity,' Grey wrote. 'War is certain. God grant we may not all lament the consequences of it.'

His words quickly proved prophetic. In London, the Pitt government responded to the king's execution by expelling the French ambassador. The revolutionary French Convention retaliated on 1 February 1793 by declaring war on Britain. Less than a month later, at 6.30 am on 25 February, three battalions of Guards that made up a British expeditionary force to fight the revolutionary army of France paraded on Horse Guards outside Lady Melbourne's windows.

At 7 am the king came down the Mall from Buckingham Palace with the Prince of Wales and the Duke of York to review the troops. After half-an-hour on parade, they marched off to the Old Kent Road for Dover with the Duke of York at the head, and his wife in tears at his departure for war with the French.

Lady Melbourne's former house in Piccadilly fell silent after the duke left England. He was away for nearly two years commanding British forces in a muddled campaign in the Low Countries that earned him an everlasting reputation for dithering with the nursery rhyme *The Grand Old Duke of York*; 'he had ten thousand men; he marched them up to the top of the hill and marched them down again'. While he was away, his increasingly eccentric wife retreated to Oatlands, the duke's country house, with a growing menagerie of nearly forty dogs, monkeys, parrots, kangaroos and ostriches.

The Duchess of Devonshire and her party had spent months on the shores of Lake Geneva when Louis XVI was guillotined at the Place de la Revolution, followed by his queen, Marie Antoinette in October that year. The horrors of the Terror in Paris forced the Duke of Devonshire to lift his exile order on his wife. As the aristocrats of France became a hunted species, he sent a message to Georgiana telling her to return to England for her own safety.

The duchess and her entourage had arrived in Naples in April 1793 to enliven the gay parties of the Ambassador Sir William Hamilton and his wife Emma. It was mid-May before Georgiana received the Duke's summons to return. She was overcome with joy but the journey home covering over 1,100 miles skirting revolutionary France to avoid arrest by going through Switzerland, Germany and Holland would be arduous and, at times, dangerous.

Harriet's husband, Frederick, Lord Duncannon, had been forced to return to London to attend the death of his father, Lord Bessborough. Harriet thus became Lady Bessborough while she was abroad. She fell ill in Rome and it took Georgiana and her mother, Lady Spencer, until September 1793 to reach Ostend. They arrived at the northern port as the Duke of York's army was retreating to the coast, pushed back by the French at the start of his ill-starred Flanders campaign. They saw the town burning behind them as they scrambled on board a friend's yacht and sailed for England.

The Duke of Devonshire welcomed Georgiana with open arms when she landed at Dartford on 18 September and presented her with a new carriage with light blue panels and silver springs. Canis doggedly refused to adopt Eliza, her daughter by Charles Grey, as one of his own children. Lord Grey's parents agreed to bring up Eliza as their granddaughter on the family estate at Fallodon and she was given an old family surname of Courtney.

Georgiana's traumatic two years away underlined the differences between the Duchess of Devonshire and Lady Melbourne. Georgiana was completely unsure of herself, and at the mercy of whims. Her letters to her mother betray a disarming lack of self-confidence. She is constantly seeking her approval: 'You are the best mother that ever was and the dearest truest friend and if I had lost every other blessing through my imprudence and folly I should still think myself happy that I could see you and be loved by you.'[9]

In contrast to the Duchess, Lady Melbourne was the senior partner in her marriage to Peniston Lamb and refused to allow their numerous affairs to threaten their relationship. No matter how complex the Melbournes' love lives became, her priority was to hold her family and its property together. Her son's biographer, Lord David Cecil, said even in the most 'vertiginous complications of intrigue and dissipation', Lady Melbourne could be relied on to remain dignified, collected – and reasonable; 'her philosophy taught her that the world must be kept going.'[10]

Lady Melbourne's former house in Piccadilly was sold in 1802 by the Duke of York and Albany to pay off more of his debts. His banker, Thomas Coutts, began pressing the duke to repay his mortgage on the property of £22,000. He also had an outstanding mortgage of £38,000 with the Farrer brothers, bringing his mortgage debt to a total £60,000 – equivalent to £4.8 million today.

An enterprising young builder called Alexander Copland agreed to pay £37,000 in stages, providing he could get enough subscribers. A board of trustees commissioned the ubiquitous Henry Holland to convert Lady Melbourne's former house into eighteen spacious bachelor apartments, known as 'sets', connected by a covered walkway called the Ropewalk.

The property was renamed 'Albany' after the duke to give it more cachet. It was intended that the sets would be managed like a hotel, with a kitchen, extensive wine cellars, hot and cold baths, and a live-in maître-d'hôtel to oversee the communal dining room – Lady Melbourne's great dining room on the first floor. Shops were incorporated in the scheme by Holland and the shop windows were framed by six eagles on pillars, modelled in Coade stone, to reflect a fashion in Georgian London for everything French, in spite of the war.[11]

From the outset, Lady Melbourne's former house quickly attracted a long list of VIP tenants and Albany remains a prestigious address today. When I approached the front door for an interior photograph the porter was firm. 'The members don't like you taking photographs.' The message was clear – I should push off.

The first tenants included the Romantic poet Lord Byron who was later to fall under Lady Melbourne's spell. Byron rented set 2A – Lord Melbourne's former library on the ground floor overlooking the gardens to the left of the main staircase – from Lord Althorp and he lived there during the most turbulent period of his life with his faithful valet Fletcher and Mrs Mule, a wizened old maid. He wrote to Lady Melbourne: 'I am in *my* and *your* Albany rooms. I think you should have been included in the lease.'[12]

She replied with sadness, saying Melbourne House in Piccadilly was 'where most of my happiest days were pass'd – whilst I lived in that House, no Misfortune reach'd me, and I should not have disliked to be an appendage to the Lease to live in it again'.[13]Misfortune soon would come calling at her home in Whitehall.

12

Tragedy

Lord and Lady Melbourne watched in dismay as her former lover the Prince of Wales swayed and staggered at the altar beside his bride Caroline of Brunswick at their wedding in the Chapel Royal at St James's on 8 April 1795. It was obvious the prince was drunk.

Prince George had fortified himself for his ordeal by gulping down large tumblers of brandy before the ceremony. He had taken an instant dislike to his twenty-six-year-old bride when he had met her three days earlier; he objected to her coarse manners, and her even more unrefined approach to personal hygiene.

His friend Lord Malmesbury, an experienced diplomat who had been sent to bring her to England, did not have the nerve to tell the prince the truth: she lacked the ladylike graces expected of a queen of England, and personal hygiene left something to be desired – he observed her stockings were 'never well washed or changed enough'.

Caroline was equally unimpressed by her first meeting with the thirty-two-year-old prince when she arrived at St James's Palace: 'I find him very stout and by no means as handsome as his portrait.' She also felt discomfited by the presence of the prince's mistress, Lady Jersey, who, it was rumoured, had chosen Caroline as her lover's bride because she knew she would not be a rival.

Lady Jersey sneered at Caroline over a pre-nuptial dinner. Caroline was feisty, funny and extrovert but courtiers were appalled by Caroline's uncouth conversation 'rattling, affected raillery and wit and throwing out coarse vulgar hints about Lady Jersey who was present'.

The prince had to be physically supported by two of his closest friends, Elizabeth's latest lover, the Duke of Bedford, and the Duke of Roxburghe. The slightly built Duke of Bedford had difficulty in stopping the prince falling over as the Archbishop of Canterbury worked haltingly through the service. Lady Melbourne's son William later told Queen Victoria: 'The Prince was like a man doing a thing in desperation. It was like Macheath going to his execution and he was quite drunk.'

The witnesses included Lady Jersey and Lord Melbourne, who was there in his role as part of the prince's household. Three months later, Lord Melbourne was relieved of his duties when the prince was forced to economise after Parliament refused to increase his allowance. Lady Melbourne wrote to the prince in July on her husband's behalf – he had a diplomatic illness that preventing him putting pen to paper. She pledged their undying loyalty and offered her husband's services in the future 'without any other consideration than the pleasure he shall receive from being useful to your Royal Highness…' It may have sounded obsequious but it was to pay dividends.[1]

The prince was forced to economise after his Treasurer, Colonel Hotham carried out an audit of the prince's expenditure and was horrified to discover his debts amounted to £269,878 6s 7d although his income was only £12,500 a quarter. His stables alone cost £31,000 a year, interest on his loans amounted to more than £25,000. The prince could not stop spending. He lavished huge sums on Carlton House – he blew £2,166 on new table linen, and £3,419 on chandeliers.

Not content with his excessive spending on Carlton House, he commissioned Henry Holland to enlarge his Marine Pavilion, a former farmhouse on the Steyne at Brighthelmstone, with two new wings. Holland designed them in the restrained neoclassical style, but when George became Prince Regent, he paid John Nash to turn the pavilion into a Mughal fantasy palace with domes and minarets.

He paid £50,000 to allow Mrs Fitzherbert her own private household. And there was his wardrobe. He ran up huge bills with his tailor John Weston of 27 Old Bond Street. Today he would be classed as a shopaholic – in one month, he ordered more than sixty waistcoats of various designs and colours from the same tailor. His business was a mixed blessing for his tailors as he rarely paid his bills.

At his wedding reception in the Queen's apartments in St James's Palace, he continued drinking brandy and when he retired to the royal bridal suite, the groom slumped senseless by the fireplace where he remained asleep during his wedding night. He managed to assert his conjugal rights later, but he complained his bride was not a virgin: 'Her manners were not those of a novice. In taking those liberties, natural on these occasions, she said, "Ah mon dieu qu'il est gros!" and how should she know this without a previous means of comparison?'[2]

It was not a time for princely extravagance. The war against the French was going badly – in April, the Duke of York and his army were forced to evacuate from Bremen; a Royal Navy squadron under Cornwallis had to withdraw against a superior French force off Brittany; there were food shortages and bread riots at home and Pitt was so desperate for money to finance the war in May he introduced a tax on hair powder – it hit the rich, except for the royal family and their servants, who were exempt.

In October 1795, George III's state coach was attacked on his way from St James's Palace to the House of Lords with Lords Onslow and Westmoreland. Gillray dashed off a cartoon called *The Republican – Attack* published by Hannah Humphreys at her shop that had moved to Old Bond Street depicting a man in a Jacobin red cap with a blunderbuss firing at the king. The mob – all easily identified as leading Whigs including Fox and Sheridan who are carrying clubs – wave a banner proclaiming 'Peace or Bread'. Pitt is driving the carriage onward with Tories as coachmen including his friend Dundas.

The *St James Chronicle* reported: 'On his way to the House, particularly in Parliament-street, his Majesty was assailed by hootings and hissings which came from groups, evidently stationed at certain distances for the purpose, who were in their cry of "No war, No Pitt". Some were unruly; a few appear to have been mischievously inclined as several stones and other articles were flung, nine of which were perceived to reach the King's carriage, in which two of the glass panels were broke...' *The Tomahawk or Censor General*, a right-wing publication, said it was 'no doubt an adjourned meeting of the *London Corresponding Society*', regarded as a subversive gang.

Whig MPs such as the Marquess of Lansdowne claimed it was all got up by Pitt and the Duke of Portland, then Home Secretary, to justify suppressive measures including the suspension of Habeas Corpus, the ancient right of prisoners to be produced in a court of law and tougher laws on sedition, banning meetings of more than fifty people. Pitt introduced a bill to widen sedition to include advocacy of a change of government. It meant 'no pamphlets, no petitions, no meetings, no reform', wrote historian Simon Schama.[3]

The Prince of Wales, despite collapsing on his wedding night, still managed to get Caroline pregnant. Nine months later on 7 January 1796, the prince was able to break the news to his mother that the Princess 'after a terrible hard labour for above twelve hours' had given birth to 'an immense girl', who was christened Princess Charlotte.

A year after Charlotte's birth, George deserted his wife and Caroline and went to live at Montagu House, next to Lord Chesterfield's house, at Blackheath, backing onto the former royal hunting park at Greenwich. She courted scandal and there were wild allegations about her sexual exploits with a string of men including politician George Canning, the painter Thomas Lawrence and seafarers such as Henry Hood, son of the naval hero Lord Hood. A so-called 'delicate investigation' headed by four statesmen including the Prime Minister Lord Grenville was set up in secret to prove her infidelity but was abandoned after it found no hard evidence. She wanted to go home to Brunswick but it had been overrun by the French, and her father killed. She was forced to remain in England until Napoleon's defeat in 1814 when she fled to the Continent as soon as peace with France was declared. The following year the Prince Regent ordered Montagu House to be demolished. All that remains today of her house are the steps to her walk-in bath.

Elizabeth transferred her own ambitions to her favourite son, William. Torrens wrote: 'Lady Melbourne's aspirations for distinction and influence renewed their youth as she gazed upon her favourite son. Accustomed to flattery, and too quick-witted to be deceived thereby, she probably gave little heed to looks and words of admiration of which he was the object, from daughters who longed to dance with him and fathers who liked being asked to dine.'[4]

She encouraged William's lofty view of himself by telling him he possessed a poetic genius. She had moulded William to expect more from life, and to be ambitious but, despite his promising start, he seemed indolent and not fired up by the prospect of the career in politics she had wanted for him. In October 1796, William left Eton and after a brief stay at Melbourne House, went off with Lord Melbourne and his preceptor Rev'd Marsham in the autumn to sign on at Trinity College Cambridge as Fellow Commoner, which entitled him to wear a gown, knee breeches, and a hat instead of an academic cap, and to dine at the fellows' table. William's ego was boosted when he won the declamation prize for a speech at the end of the Michaelmas term in 1798 in the chapel of Trinity on the theme 'The progressive improvements of mankind'. It espoused the optimistic Whig doctrine that Man and virtue will grow … gradually: 'Crime is a curse only to the period in which it is successful; but virtue whether successful or otherwise blesses not only its own age but remotest posterity.'[5]

William's speech was quoted admiringly in the Commons four years later by his political hero Charles James Fox in a eulogy to the memory of his friend and generous Whig financial supporter, Francis Russell, the Duke of Bedford, following his unexpected death. But before that, William had already allowed flattery to go to his head.

He paid a premium at Cambridge to play the part of the dilettante son of a nobleman, without the necessity of going to lectures, and he admitted he spent his time 'boating, fighting with bargees, riding, walking, shooting and fishing,' in addition to drinking and gambling. He joined the bloods – the Bullingdon Club of its day – an elite group of rich young men bent on getting drunk and causing mayhem in the town for their own amusement. It was difficult, he said later, to find a person 'more completely conceited. Presumptuous and self-confident, who had a greater contempt for most of the rest of mankind.'

When William returned to London from Cambridge in 1799, Lady Holland invited him to dinner after hearing he was a 'rising genius' but found him 'pleasant but supercilious'. He treated three of her friends with contempt for being anti-Jacobin, 'an affectation he has caught from ye Duke of Bedford'. He had also adopted a ridiculous upper-class inability to sound his 'Rs'. Georgiana's daughter, Harriet Cavendish complained he was very drunk at a party at Melbourne House and he talked to her 'in a loud voice the whole time of the danger of a young woman believing in weligion and pwactising mowality'. He lounged on a sofa rather than joining in the dancing.

William 'wore an air of carelessness', said Torrens, 'and how he looked and what he said was his earliest affectation and it stuck by him to the last for nobody ever happened to have coats that fitted better, books more full of ideas or worthier of being remembered, and in conversation, words more nicely chosen and heavily shotted with meaning. But from the outset, some vague and unaccountable wish to be thought indolent and idle appears to have had a witchery for him.'

Lady Granville thought his brother Frederick Lamb was even worse. 'He sees life in the most degrading light and he simplifies the thing by thinking all men rogues and all women ***.'

William and Frederick swaggered through parties with Tom Sheridan, the playwright's son, and Lord Charles Kinnaird at the houses of the rich, displaying their contempt for the older generation, showing off, playing drunk, acting like rich spoiled brats. William bragged, 'A woman is exactly like a mare; very good to ride, but apt to kick in harness.'[6]

Lady Melbourne became anxious about her sons, particularly William, and his lack of ambition for a career in politics or anything else. She decided that William needed taking in hand. First, he needed to find a career to provide an income, because what was left of the Lamb family fortune would all go to Pen.

Lord Melbourne had already given Pen, as his cherished son and heir, a generous annual allowance of £5,000 on his twenty-first birthday. This was more than enough to enable Pen to live an independent life in London. In 1793, his father also gifted Pen his seat at Newport on the Isle of Wight.

Elizabeth, 'Lady M', etching by Braun Clement after John Hoppner. (© National Portrait Gallery)

Halnaby Hall, the Milbankes' home, where Elizabeth was born. (Courtesy North Yorks County Record Office)

The Milbanke family pew at Croft. (Author)

Above: The Milbankes and the Melbournes by George Stubbs, *c.* 1769. To the left can be seen Elizabeth as a young bride of eighteen with her father, Sir Ralph Milbanke; on horseback to the right is young Sir Peniston. (© The National Gallery)

Right: Elizabeth when she was twenty-one, by Richard Cosway. She gave a copy to her lover, George, the Prince of Wales. (Royal Collection Trust © Her Majesty Queen Elizabeth II 2016)

Melbourne Hall, Derbyshire – Elizabeth took a keen interest in agriculture. (Author)

Dining room at Melbourne Hall. (Author)

Elizabeth preferred Brocket Hall, the Lambs' country house in Hertfordshire with landscaped grounds and bridge. (Author)

Ballroom at Brocket Hall; the Prince of Wales gave Elizabeth the portrait that dominates the room. (Courtesy Brocket Hall)

The Chinese room at Brocket Hall, where the Prince of Wales stayed. (Courtesy Brocket Hall)

Melbourne House
Piccadilly, now luxury flats
called the Albany. (Author)

Sophia Baddeley, courtesan
and Peniston's lover. (© the
British Museum)

A rival chatelaine; Georgiana, Duchess of Devonshire by Gainsborough. (© Devonshire Collection, Chatsworth. Reproduced by permission of Chatsworth Settlement Trustees. Source Chatsworth Photo Library 4356595)

Left: *Maternal Affection* – Lady M with baby Peniston by Joshua Reynolds. (© the British Museum)

Below: His Royal Highness George Prince of Wales presented this portrait of himself to Elizabeth as a love token. It was hung at Brocket Hall in the dining room. (Royal Collection Trust © Her Majesty Queen Elizabeth II 2016)

Right: Lady in scarlet – the
scandalous Lady Worsley as she
appeared at Cocks Heath by
Sir Joshua Reynolds. (Reproduced
by kind permission of the Trustees
of the seventh Earl of Harewood
Will Trust and the Trustees of the
Harewood House Trust)

Below: 'A Trip to Cock's Heath',
military camp; a bawdy satire.
This is where Elizabeth may have
conceived her son, William. (Etching
28 October 1778 © British Museum
1851.0901.9)

Left: Prince George as he looked when he was Prince of Wales, by Sir Joshua Reynolds. (© Tate Images)

Below: York House, Whitehall, as it looked when it was exchanged by the Duke of York with the Melbournes.

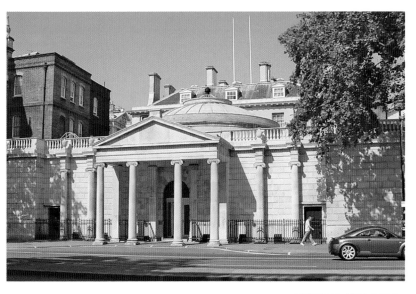

Above: Melbourne House, Whitehall, as it looks today. (Author)

Right: The Melbournes' ground floor apartments, decorated in Regency style. (© Jaime Turner)

Below: The ground floor apartments of Lord and Lady Melbourne as they may have looked when Elizabeth entertained Byron there. (© Jaime Turner)

The Duke of York's coronet and field marshal's baton over the doors. (© Jaime Turner)

Peniston Lamb with powdered hair, shortly before he died.

William Lamb, later
Prime Minister Second
Viscount Melbourne,
was handsome, but
weak; portrait by
Sir Thomas Lawrence.
(© National Portrait
Gallery)

The waif-like Lady
Caroline Lamb, dressed
as a pageboy with
cropped hair, earned
Elizabeth's wrath for her
affairs. (© Devonshire
Collection. Reproduced
by permission of the
Chatsworth Settlement
Trustees)

Above: The grand staircase inside Melbourne House – Byron stumbled on the stairs at his first visit and considered it an 'omen'. (© Jaime Turner)

Left: Lord Byron – 'mad, bad and dangerous to know' – who had an affair with Caroline Lamb in 1812. (LOC)

Top right: Could this be Lady Caroline's room? Alcove for a bed and walk-in wardrobe to the left. (© Jaime Turner)

Right: St Etheldreda's Church, Hatfield, where Lady Melbourne is buried. (Author)

Below right: Gates at Halnaby – all that is left of the hall. (Author)

Below: The Three Witches from Macbeth (Elizabeth Lamb, Viscountess Melbourne; Georgiana, Duchess of Devonshire; Anne Seymour Damer) by Daniel Gardner, gouache and chalk, 1775. (Accepted in lieu of tax by H.M. Government and allocated to the Gallery, 2011. Courtesy of the National Portrait Gallery)

Above: Sketch of child reputedly by Lady Caroline Lamb at Melbourne Hall. 'Mais tout y meurt.' (Author)

Below left: *The Affectionate Brothers*, 1783–85 (oil on canvas), by Joshua Reynolds (1734–92) – Lord Melbourne refused to buy it, perhaps because the two younger boys were not his. (Firle Place collection, Sussex, Bridgeman Images)

Below right: Second Viscount Melbourne, painting at Melbourne Hall. (Author)

'Lord Melbourne was a Whig disposed to rally to government in wartime and his heir [Pen], who made no mark in Parliament, was a silent supporter,' says one Parliamentary guide. '[Pen] Lamb's critics claimed that he had neglected Parliament while in it, was fonder of racing, opera and theatricals, was "only known at the Pic Nic and at Boodle's" and once asked how many quarter sessions there were in a year.'[7]

Pen gave up his seat in 1796. He briefly returned to Parliament in 1802 when he allowed himself to be used by his mother's political rival, the Marquess of Salisbury, to stop a former Foxite Whig being re-elected in the Marquess's Hertfordshire fiefdom. Pen was a 'capital' shot and was more interested in pursuing his married mistress, Sophia Musters, a noted equestrian he met at Lewes races, than politics.

Having paid for Pen's seat, Lord Melbourne refused to purchase a second seat for William. Lady Melbourne toyed with the idea of sending William to follow her uncle into the Church. This sounded to her friends a most unlikely prospect – the Lambs were not religious – but the Church was then seen as a living rather than a calling. Lord Egremont, however, would not hear of William taking the cloth.

William would have preferred to spend time on a Grand Tour after Eton and Cambridge, but that option was closed by the revolutionary wars against the French. Instead, he decided on a get-rich-quick career in the law following the example of his paternal grandfather Matthew Lamb. He had shown you could become rich as a lawyer, if you were clever. This came as another disappointment to Lady Melbourne, but she reluctantly saw the law could be a stepping-stone to the political career she really wanted for her son.

The Duke of Bedford convinced Elizabeth that William needed the rigour of Professor John Millar's radical lectures at Glasgow University to fire him up with reformist zeal. William was persuaded by his mother to spend two years on a diet of radical Whiggery at Glasgow University to finish his studies before reading for the bar, and to take Frederick with him to ease the pain of being alone in Scotland. She recruited the help of Lord Lauderdale, who wrote to Professor Millar:

> There is a young man who wishes much to reside in your house next winter. He is a younger son of Lord Melbourne's. He has a reputation and I believe really possesses uncommon talents. He means to go to the English Bar with a view to follow the law as a profession. He is the only person I have ever yet recommended to you of whom I think I could with any safety say that you will have real comfort and satisfaction in having him as a pupil. I wish you to write me a letter such as I may show to them stating whether you

can have room for him the time he must be at Glasgow etc. It is the Duke of Bedford who has applied to me about it.[8]

Professor Millar found room in his house for William and his seventeen-year-old brother Frederick.[9] William complained about the weather – it was constantly raining and everyone had coughs – and the grime, saying it was the dirtiest city he had ever seen. After lectures, William and Frederick were surprised to discover social life in Glasgow was as genteel as Eton and Cambridge. William reported back to his mother: 'We drink healths at dinner, hand around the cake at tea and put our spoons into our cups when we desire to have no more; exactly in the same manner we used to behave at Eton and Cambridge.'

The only exclusive custom and a 'devilish good' one that he thought ought to be adopted at Melbourne House was allowing the ladies to remain with the men at the table after dinner while the whisky bottle was sent round. It was, he said, 'very comfortable and very exhilarating and affords an opportunity for many jokes'.[10]

William and Frederick, fuelled by Millar's radical lectures, were full of youthful enthusiasm for the French and Napoleon, then the First Consul, excusing the revolution and exulting in French victories against Britain's Continental allies in letters to their mother.

William was outraged in 1800 when Pitt refused peace overtures by Napoleon, believing the government wanted to use the emergency to clamp down on dissent. 'Bonaparte laid a snare for us,' he said in a letter to his mother. 'If any can produce any sensation on this panic-struck, prejudiced British people this desperate measure, together with the hardness of the season, the dearness of corn and the distress of trade seem calamities severe enough to excite in their minds a little inquiry … I wish the French may be able to defend themselves from their enemies abroad and at home.' The time might not be far off, he said, when ministers would be 'devilishly glad' to be able to disown Pitt as mad. 'If the enthusiasm of the French can be roused for one more effort they will gain their point.'[11]

He was disparaging about her lover, the Duke of Bedford's speech in the Lords on the government's failure to grasp Bonaparte's peace offer as 'weak and querulous' and he said Lord Holland's speech was 'nothing at all – unless they can say something more plain and decisive they had better hold their tongues.'

During a vacation from his Glasgow studies in May 1800, William returned to London so full of Millar's pro-Bonapartist views (and arrogance), he alarmed Lord Egremont, who, showing fatherly concern, told Lady Melbourne he thought it would be dreadful if William turned into a doctrinaire prig.[12]

She passed on Lord Egremont's concern, and William agreed: 'I daresay Lord Egremont is right enough about the disputatious disposition of those men who have been so unfortunate as to have been at Millar's, but this I take to be the case through the whole university as much as Millar's...'

William conceded a few weeks later: 'Lord Egremont is very good and not the less so because he is in some measure right. You did not tell him, I suppose, that I say so.' The truth is he had already lost faith in Millar when the professor said he would rather have an invasion and Britain led by Napoleon than another Tory government. William marvelled at how such clever men could be so silly.

During his vacation in May, there was an event that brought the young iconoclast closer to the English crown. Lady Melbourne was hosting a dinner party for the Prince of Wales at Melbourne House when news reached them that another assassination attempt had been made on the king. A former Guards officer with a grievance called Hatfield fired a pistol at George III as he entered his box at the Theatre Royal in Drury Lane. The king had survived, and the officer had been taken into custody.

Lady Melbourne suggested the prince should go to his father, but he was reluctant to leave. He was enjoying a hearty dinner in convivial company with his loyal friends, and insisted on continuing with his supper. He brushed aside her suggestions he should attend his father, but Lady Melbourne insisted, ordered his carriage to the door in Whitehall and told William to accompany the prince.

She bundled the prince away to the theatre, where his father had stayed as if nothing had happened. When Prince George arrived, he found his brother, Frederick, Duke of York, already there and realised that he would have been pilloried if he had not gone to make sure his father was unharmed.

'After tendering their congratulations to His Majesty on his narrow escape, they withdrew to the apartment where the offender was in custody, and remained during the preliminary examination of witnesses who saw him present and fire the pistol,' said William Torrens. 'Hatfield recognised the Duke (of York) under whom he had served and said he was a good fellow.'[13]

The prince returned to Melbourne House before midnight, full of gratitude for Lady Melbourne persuading him to go. William also came out of the episode with a stronger bond with the prince although that was a mixed blessing: 'He was thenceforth more frequently included in the invitations to Carlton House and became unluckily an early partaker in its revelries,' said Torrens.

Very few weeks passed when William did not walk across the Mall from Melbourne House to dine at Carlton House with the Prince of Wales, said Lord David Cecil.

He sat, an observant young man, listening to his royal host as, hour by hour, he poured forth the kaleidoscopic effusions of his preposterous egotism; now abusing his parents, now bragging of his amorous conquests, now courting the applause of the company by his vivid mimicry of Mr Pitt or Lord North, now soliciting their sympathy by sentimental laments on the unexampled misery of his lot. It was very entertaining; it was also very instructive. At Carlton House William got his first lessons in an art that was to be the instrument of his greatest success in later life, the art of getting on with royal personages. Lady Melbourne carried his instructions a step further; she showed him how to manage them for their good.[14]

William returned to Glasgow and parted company with Millar in 1801. By the time William entered the Commons in November 1806, he was anti-Bonaparte and in 1816 supported the suspension of the Habeas Corpus Act.[15]

Lady Melbourne arranged for William to be enrolled at Lincoln's Inn for his pupillage by Henry Addington, the son of Pitt's physician who had just become Prime Minister, but made sure his terms coincided with Parliamentary sittings so he could study law while keeping in touch at Westminster. He was taught by a Mr Roberts in the Special Pleaders' office until he was called to the Bar with chambers at 4 Pump Court. He went on the Northern circuit in January 1805 as a Special Pleader, but preparing briefs for prosecuting villains in Manchester and Liverpool courts from some dusty legal office was hardly the career Lady Melbourne had in mind for her favourite son.

His mother hinted at her disappointment about her son's choice of career, in a letter to Lady Holland who had inquired about her sons:

> His intention is to put himself immediately under a Special Pleader and to study from morning till night for a year which is not a very agreeable prospect tho' it may turn out very useful. I am extremely obliged to you for thinking of my young men and for all your kindness to them and altho' I have the highest opinion of your skill, yet I believe even you would find bringing them to what is call'd polish a very arduous under-taking.[16]

William revealed in his journal that while he scratched away at his law books, he fell under the spell of a scheming, money-grabbing mistress: 'I had fallen into the power of a lady of no very strict virtue and was entirely devoted to her. Morning, noon and night I was at her house or pining after the moment when I should be there. All my hours were passed in attending upon her, in flattering her vanity by exposing myself in public with her, in gratifying her fancies and obeying her caprices.'

He did not name her but it could have been the courtesan, Harriette Wilson, who claimed to have had both William and Frederick – and possibly Lord Melbourne – among her lovers. William's siren demanded he should spend the summer with her at Brighthelmstone among the fashionable set who surrounded the Prince of Wales. Instead, William was persuaded by his Old Etonian friend Charles Kinnaird to go to Scotland for a holiday grouse shooting at Kinnaird's estate on the River Tay in Perthshire. 'I had not reached Edinburgh before the chain which had wound so tightly around me in London that I could stir neither hand nor foot began to relax its folds, and ten days of shooting upon the moors [provided] the most efficacious remedy for love.'

Elizabeth, now in her fiftieth year, entered a golden age as a society hostess with the Prince of Wales one of her most frequent guests both at Melbourne House in Whitehall and Brocket Hall. Despite her thickening waistline and her occasional bouts of pain from gout, she could still stir the blood of the older stags in the Georgian clubs; but her passion was for Loo, the Duke of Bedford.

It came as a double blow when she heard Loo was engaged to be married and that his bride-to-be was Georgiana, youngest daughter of Lady Gordon, a stalwart Tory. Not only was she going to lose a lover, but also the Whigs would be losing a source of financial support to a Tory rival.

The formidable Duchess of Gordon presided over Gordon Castle in Morayshire and helped to found the Gordon Highlanders with her husband, Alexander, the fourth Duke of Gordon. The duchess had proved herself a doughty fighter for Pitt in the 1784 general election, and was adept at fixing marriages for her five daughters – her eldest daughter Charlotte married the Duke of Richmond, Susan married the Duke of Manchester and Louisa married the Marquess of Cornwallis. Her triumph in stealing the duke from the arms of Lady Melbourne for her youngest daughter was a coup of which Lady Melbourne would have been proud, if the roles had been reversed.

Elizabeth shrugged off Loo's failure to tell her he was going to marry; she recognised that at thirty-seven he needed to produce a son and heir and told Georgiana, the Duchess of Devonshire, 'if he has taken a fancy *tout est dit*...' The duchess was not so relaxed. She wrote to Lady Melbourne, to 'vent' her anger:

> Indeed we are all undone; no possible event could have so thoroughly have overturned the habit of our society as this ... I think I am more hurt at his having seemed to act out of his own good character – with regard to you (tho' I have no doubt that it was from the fear of hurting you) it was unlike him

but he has acted strangely towards the girl … If he has a mind to secede can he now with honour? Good God how could he? What is so extraordinary and so unlike him to have spoken to her before he knew he was free…[17]

The Duchess took it as an affront that the future chatelaine of Woburn Abbey, the Duke of Bedford's stately pile, would be a Scot. 'What a futurity for Loo to be surrounded with plotting, shabby Scotts men,' she wrote indignantly to Lady Melbourne. 'The very amiabilite that some time arises from the grotesque originality of Scotch people is in a line very different from what one should have thought would be Loo's election for the Mistress of Wooburn (sic).'

Georgiana's distress was self-interested. Loo had secretly loaned the Duchess large sums of money to put off creditors for her gambling debts. She had asked him for a loan of £6,000 to 'wipe out all her debts' but he knew it was a lie – her debts were vastly more than that – and he turned her down. She privately admitted in her letter written from her mother's house in St Albans that Loo had hardened his attitude towards her. 'Alas when he only sees me … he can make no allowances.'

Georgiana apologised to Lady Melbourne for being out of sorts at a Masquerade where Lady Melbourne clearly lost her temper with her. 'You can have no idea how sorry I was to have vex'd you at the Masquerade,' she writes. 'But I wish to acquit myself about Black (Charles Grey) because the truth was that I was worried to death about something else the whole night.'

It is almost certain Georgiana was preoccupied by her money worries: 'I am very sorry that Loo has taken anything wrong. I love him so dearly and think him (independent of gratitude) so delightful that I cannot bear his taking anything ill … Once more God Bless you Dearest. Make Loo come to me again as he us'd – as for the Gordons, as pretty as the girl is, I cannot conceive that the old objections are not as much in force as ever.' She added: 'For God's sake burn this letter. I would not for worlds appear impertinent to Loo.'

Their private anxieties about Loo were overtaken when he fell ill with a strangulated hernia. When she heard of his illness, the Duchess of Devonshire began a distraught letter to Lady Melbourne:

I cannot go to bed without writing to you tho my head is very bad. Oh my Love – how anxious and agitated I feel about our dear Loo … My dearest Love I cannot express what I feel and suffer for him and how terrible it is to have no means of intelligence. Do not think I am selfish enough to think of my own anxiety only. I do indeed feel yours from my very heart.[18]

The next day, she finished her letter, folded it up and sent it off. Lady Melbourne, at home in Whitehall, read:

> I was so overcome with shock that they have never given me the detail'd account. I cannot at all calm myself and I own I see everything in the most gloomy way: may heaven preserve him but I fear the danger is still very great … My dearest Love – How shall we meet? Will it be in misery or reliev'd from this terrible misfortune? Believe me no one can feel for you or love you more tenderly than I do. God bless you dear dear Love. I cannot write…[19]

Loo appeared to rally. He bore 'a frightful operation' to repair the hernia 'with heroic fortitude' but the shock of the operation and probably infection, given the rudimentary standards of clinical hygiene, proved too great and on 2 March 1802 he died.

Lady Gordon was not to be out-done by death. The Gordons including Georgiana had joined the exodus of English aristocrats from London to Paris to enjoy the short-lived peace secured with Bonaparte by Addington in 1802 with the Treaty of Amiens.

Loo had written a deathbed letter to Georgiana and asked his brother John Russell to deliver it to his fiancée in Paris. John, whose wife had died a year before, followed his brother's dying wish, went to Paris, met Lady Georgiana, and – encouraged by Lady Gordon – fell in love with his brother's fiancée. The new Duke of Bedford married Georgiana completing the coup for the Duchess of Gordon. 'Even death seemed unable to defeat her matrimonial purpose,' wrote Lady Airlie.[20]

Peace with the French with the Treaty of Amiens in 1802 opened up the Continent to the bottled-up British for the first time in a decade. Whig figures such as Fox and Lady Melbourne's high society friends including Elizabeth Foster, Harriet, Lady Bessborough, her husband Frederick Ponsonby, their sons John and Willy, and her strikingly odd daughter, 'Caro' Ponsonby, then aged seventeen, seized the opportunity to return to Paris to enjoy the thrill of a city under Bonaparte and renew acquaintances with the few aristocrats who had survived the guillotine.

Lady Melbourne did not follow the stampede of elegantly dressed ladies to Paris – there is no evidence she ever went abroad – but she collected all the gossip in letters from her friends there. Lady Bessborough wrote to Lady Melbourne saying that Lady Georgiana Gordon was already out of mourning for Loo. Harriet would attend a party hosted by Lady Gordon for her daughter's sake, but she complained about encountering the lower orders at the theatre:

I shall go to her in an evening sometimes for Caro's sake. Paris is going to be very gay; hitherto it has been like a new world ...Talleyrand and I believe Berthier are going to open their houses – but even there I am told the society will consist of foreigners and some Bankers and Avocats wives... Nothing can be more extraordinary than the look of the Theatres as in the boxes next you you see Women who appear to be the lowest kind of tradespeople – the Men worse still – and in coming out, even of the Opera, you are surrounded by men whom you would only see at the Hustings.

Another of her friends, George Robinson tells Lady Melbourne that *le petit bon homme* – Napoleon – is 'very sore about English newspapers' ridiculing him. Another correspondent informs her that Bonaparte's taste for the English had improved the dress of French women; there were fewer who exposed their nipples in the Parisian style with daring low cut dresses, though some English women still did so: 'They are not near so uncovered as they were – unluckily some English women chuse to dress in the extreme also.'

In London Lady Melbourne attended a fete at Ranelagh Gardens to celebrate the peace with the Duchess of Devonshire and the Prince of Wales who stayed until 2am. It was hosted by the Pic Nic Society (so-called because they originally provided their own snacks for their events). A guard of 100 soldiers of the Coldstream regiment were stationed around the gardens, on the lawn and in front of Ranelagh House 'to prevent improper persons from obstructing the Company in getting out of their carriages'.

The Times reported: 'The *Pic Nic Society* gave their promised Fete in honour of the Peace last Friday night at Ranelagh. It was conducted with uncommon order and propriety and to the attractions of a Ball and superb Supper were added the splendid novelties of a night balloon and an artificial comet which produced a grand effect.'[21]

The Duchess of Devonshire had become reclusive since losing the sight in one eye. Her husband was also suffering from painful gout in his knees and feet. She wrote to Lady Melbourne at Christmas saying she was shut up in 'melancholy' Hardwick Hall, the former home of the Elizabethan grand dame the Countess of Shrewsbury, 'Bess of Hardwick', near Chatsworth. Caro, her sister's daughter, 'calls this purgatory and Chatsworth Paradise and we do wander about like uneasy souls,' said Georgiana.

Lady Melbourne's carefree life became troubled when her youngest daughter, Harriet, the fun-loving child whose impish face had caught the eye of Sir Thomas Lawrence, developed a persistent cough and hot sweats. These were the worrying first symptoms of the Georgian curse, tuberculosis. Fearing the worst, her mother desperately sought a cure from the doctors.

It is estimated that one in three of the deaths in London in the eighteenth century were due to tuberculosis, also known as scrofula or 'The White Death' because its victims were deathly pale. Today it can be treated by antibiotics and is mainly associated with poverty and rough sleepers, but in Georgian London with pools of infection in the teeming alleyways, fed by workers moving from the land to the town, there was no effective cure apart from rest, and for those who could afford it, the dry air around the Mediterranean coasts. Lady Melbourne's doctors advised her to take her daughter abroad to a drier climate for her health. She failed to act and soon it was too late – the peace with the French broke down in May 1803 making travel to the Continent too risky. Harriet's condition gradually worsened and she died a month later at the age of fourteen.

On 13 June, Elizabeth and the Melbourne family rode in their carriages behind the horse-drawn hearse from Brocket Hall to the church on the hill at Hatfield. Lady Melbourne dressed in black watched her child's coffin carried into the church of St Etheldreda and laid to rest in the family tomb. Harriet's death filled her eldest brother Pen with dread; he was suffering from a persistent cough, like his dead sister, and general tiredness. Two weeks after his sister was buried, Pen sat down with a lawyer and witnesses on 29 June 1803 and solemnly signed his last will and testament.

A miniature portrait by John Smart shows Peniston with a thin delicate face, blue eyes, and almost feminine beauty. He is wearing a blue coat, white waistcoat, frilled chemise, a white stock tightly tied at the neck in the fashion led by Beau Brummel, with his hair powdered white. He looks as fragile as a figure in porcelain. He seemed to recover in 1803 for a short time but his symptoms returned in another form in September 1804 and in January 1805 he became gradually weaker. His mother was distraught at the danger to her son. His doctor, Sir Walter Farquhar, had expressed concern when the symptoms first showed. Lady Melbourne confided her fears in a letter in January 1805 to her third son, Frederick.

Dst F. I have just received yr Letter & am so persuaded of your kindness yet I should not hesitate a moment in desiring [you] to come if I thought it necessary which thank God it is not at present, & preclude any such necessity – I am alarm'd & frightened more than I ever tell & every move & alteration of his countenance has an effect upon me that I cannot describe.[22]

Frederick and his mother were close; he was someone to whom she felt able to unburden her feelings. After studying with William at Glasgow and at Trinity College, Cambridge, Frederick joined the Yorkshire East Riding regiment and served as aide-de-camp to General Colin McKenzie but Lady Melbourne used her influence with the Prince of Wales to get Frederick a career as a diplomat. She continued to worry about his safety on foreign missions and later pressed the Prince of Wales, when he became Regent, to intervene to stop Frederick going to Sicily in 1812 before Napoleon was defeated because she feared it would be dangerous.

She said she was at home alone in Whitehall except for Emily and did not need to tell Frederick what a state of nervousness she was in. 'I do not think I am apt to deceive myself,' she added. 'My thoughts are often too gloomy for this & and I am convinced yet he has no complaint that may not arise from debility … I wish I could be certain of that fact.'

She took some comfort from the fact that Pen was not suffering from the burning fever like Harriet, and she fancied his countenance looked better and more like himself. 'I am now writing after he is gone to bed & am more anxious for tomorrow than I can describe & so I am every night. Two or three days more in the way he has pass'd the two last would be a great comfort for if I see amendment I don't care how gradual it is.'

She continued writing the letter over another day or two, her hopes being raised one day, and dashed the next:

Yesterday was a nervous day but this Morng I am in much better Spirits. Pearson [George Pearson, a physician and chemist], Farquhar and Grant met here and he is gone back to Brocket Hall and George [Lamb] with him. They think that he has no appearance of any other complaint except Frustrated Nerves – but this to a degree you can have no idea of – Pearson's opinion was very favourable and I think Pen return'd much better satisfied – They gave him doses of Opium to calm his Nerves – he got on Horseback Yesterday before we set out and is now with the idea of the greatest delights in riding.

A few days after her letter, Pen's condition worsened. He was emaciated by tuberculosis and Lady Melbourne boldly invited Pen's mistress Mrs Sophia Musters to his bedside to comfort him. Sophia was a beauty with portraits by Reynolds and Romney and had also caught the lecherous eye of the Prince of Wales. She was married and twelve years Pen's senior but they were devoted to each other.

Pen died in Mrs Musters' arms on 24 January 1805. He was thirty-four. He was buried on 1 February at the church of St Etheldreda, Hatfield, where he had watched the body of his sister Harriet being laid to rest two years before. Lord Melbourne was shattered by grief to see his son and heir buried there. Lady Bessborough, never one to waste a grisly story, wrote to Lord

Granville about the autopsy on Pen: 'I am just come home very much out of spirits. The Melbournes were in a shocking state with the details of poor Pen's having been open'd. Without a single symptom of it, his Lungs were completely decay'd and Farquhar [the doctor] says he thinks Emily is in a very precarious state.' In fact, Emily lived to the age of seventy-two.

William was in Manchester when he was summoned back to London by his mother with the news that his brother had died. He was shocked by Pen's death, and confided in his memoir the final illness had brought the brothers closer:

> We had begun to grow much closer together and particularly from the beginning of his illness he seemed to delight in my society and repose in me great confidence. I was deeply struck with his death which the disposition and ignorance of youth rendered to me almost unexpected.[23]

But he was unsentimental. Pen had become dissolute after he left Eton, William wrote in his journal. 'From that time, he lived wholly amidst the amusements and dissipation of the world.'

Viscount Melbourne, devastated by Pen's death, sank deeper into drink as he entered old age. He had invested all his hopes in his eldest son as his heir, and now he was helpless to stop what remained of his fortune and his title being devolved on the boy he knew was not of his blood. He could not stop William inheriting everything after he had gone – but the Viscount was not above petty spite. He had to give William, as his legal heir, an annual allowance, but cut the sum he had given to Pen from £5,000 to £2,000 per annum. Even so, William privately felt released by Pen's death. It had transformed William's prospects as the second son in a humdrum legal office into one of the most eligible bachelors in London as the heir to the Melbourne title and the – albeit dwindling – Melbourne estates. His first inclination was to give up 'the tedium of the law' to concentrate on studying the classics, with a view to becoming a great writer. He confided in his journal: 'I very shortly resolved upon quitting the bar. I was now Heir to a considerable property and perhaps it would not have been entirely becoming to have continued in the profession.'

'But this plan was never carried into effect,' he added. He was in love. 'A passion which I had long cherished but had repressed while prudence forbade the indulgence of it now that it felt all obstacles removed out of its way, broke forth and became master.'

William Lamb was now ready to propose marriage to his childhood sweetheart, the strange, skeletal daughter of Lord and Lady Bessborough they called Caro.

13

Two Weddings and a Funeral

Elizabeth, Viscountess Melbourne was recuperating from her son Pen's death in the bracing sea air of Brighton when she heard news that lifted her spirits. There were to be two weddings in the family after the funeral.

The Prince of Wales had generously put his Marine Pavilion, his army of servants, his chefs and his stables in Brighton at Lady Melbourne's disposal to spend some time by the seaside, away from the bustle of St James's, to grieve for her son. The Duchess of Devonshire wrote to Lady Melbourne: 'I quite love the Prince for his good nature in lending you his House & I am sure air and quiet will do you more good than the constant exertion you were forced to here. Everybody is anxious about you and enquiring about you...'

Lady Melbourne was accompanied by her daughter Emily, but Lord Melbourne, who was mortified by the loss of his heir, found his own way of seeking solace elsewhere. He was not in Brighton.

Henry Holland had transformed the Pavilion from a farmhouse into a handsome villa with two wings in the shape of a letter 'E'. Through April, Elizabeth was able to go for walks in mourning dress with Emily along the fashionable promenade called the Steyne or to go for rides when the weather allowed.

While his mother was still in mourning in Brighton, Pen's death had freed William to propose to his childhood sweetheart, Lord and Lady Bessborough's daughter, Caroline Ponsonby. William sent Caroline an ardent letter of love on May Day:

I have loved you for four years, loved you deeply, dearly, faithfully – so faithfully that my love has withstood my firm determination to conquer it when honour forbade my declaring myself – has withstood all that absence, variety of objects, my own endeavours to seek and like others, or to occupy my mind with fix'd attention to my profession, could do to shake it.

Caroline was enraptured by his words; she showed the letter to her mother, threw her arms around her neck and said she loved William 'more than anyone in the world apart from you'.

Caroline's mother Harriet was far from delighted at the prospect of having the woman she called 'The Thorn' as her daughter's mother-in-law. On 2 May, a day after William's proposal, Harriet wrote to her former lover, Lord Granville, describing her dilemma:

> I have long foreseen and endeavoured to avoid what has just happened – Wm Lamb's proposing to her but she likes him too much for me to do more than entreat a little further acquaintance on both sides and not having this declared immediately which precludes all possibility of retreat.[1]

Lady Bessborough conceded William had a 'thousand good qualities, is very clever which is absolutely necessary for her, and above all, she has preferred him from childhood and is now so much in love with him that before his speaking, I dread its affecting her health'. She added:

> But on the other hand, I dislike the connection extremely. I dislike his manners and still more his principles and his creed, or rather no creed. Yet to her his behaviour has been honourable and his letter is beautiful.

William was twenty-six and Caroline nineteen. Elizabeth knew that Caroline had been highly strung and given to tantrums when she was growing up; she had played with Lady Melbourne's other children at Devonshire House, at the Melbourne's Brocket Hall and at Lord Egremont's estate at Petworth where Egremont took a fatherly interest in William. Caroline's parents had been so worried they had consulted some of the leading medical practitioners to see if she was mad. They could find nothing wrong. They had hoped she would grow out of it, but Elizabeth knew there were still concerns. She was prepared to subordinate any doubts there may have been about Caroline's mental stability for the personal and political advantages the match would bring her family.

By marrying Caroline Ponsonby, William was cementing a bridge between the Lambs and the Devonshires, one of the greatest Whig households in the country. It was the fulfilment of one of Lady Melbourne's greatest ambitions. William's marriage into the highest ranks in Georgian society would neutralise any lasting snobbery regarding the parvenu Lambs.

Elizabeth was excitedly arranging to leave Brighton to prepare for the marriage when she received a letter from Peter, the fifth Earl Cowper, asking permission to visit her and Emily in Brighton. He was well liked by the Melbourne family and Lady Melbourne had been hoping for more than a year that he would propose to her daughter.[2] Emily had already rejected a proposal of marriage two years earlier from Charles Kinnaird, the heir to a Scottish estate and William's close friend. It was Kinnaird who took her brother grouse shooting on the Scottish moors when he was trying to disentangle himself from a demanding lover in London. Lady Melbourne had entertained Kinnaird at Brocket Hall and he felt he had a right to think his proposal would be welcome; when Emily rejected him, he refused to take Emily's 'no' for an answer.

Emily described the excruciating embarrassment of Kinnaird's second attempt in a letter to her brother Frederick who had warned Emily that Kinnaird might propose to her:

> This morning he [Kinnaird] sent to beg a conference with Mama and *one more* with me. This was acceded to but with considerable nervousness on my part. It began worse than yesterday's with a great many oaths on his part taking heaven and earth to witness that he could love only me. I endeavour'd to compose him and to explain his case, namely that I would love if I could but that I could not and that my friendship he should have…I tell nobody for I think it is acting dishonourably towards him and Mama says she knows nothing about it.

There was a good reason for Elizabeth playing dumb over Kinnaird, according to Lady Airlie, Emily's great-granddaughter: 'It is possible that Lady Melbourne had always had other intentions for her daughter.' Lady Melbourne had identified Earl Cowper as a more promising suitor for Emily's hand. Georgiana had first recommended the attractive young earl to Elizabeth four years earlier writing gushingly that he was 'understanding … cultivated and yet unassuming so that you must draw him out to know what he knows … I defy him not to be lov'd – as to person, the Duke and all the young ladies have given it in his favour even thinking him handsomer than Lord Granville.'

This was high praise indeed; her sister Harriet had loved Granville Leveson-Gower 'passionately for seventeen years' and had two children by him before he married Georgiana's daughter, Harriet, known as 'Harrio'.

To add to his charms, Earl Cowper was a Whig. The 'Whig circle' had pounced on him. Since then, Lady Melbourne had patiently encouraged him to lose his shyness and seek Emily's hand. Earl Cowper was twenty-seven and rich. Lady Airlie described him as 'a man of much personal beauty and the owner of great possessions'. These included Panshanger, a country mansion near Hertford and a short ride away from Brocket Hall. The match was a great coup for Viscountess Melbourne.

Lady Melbourne replied telling Lord Cowper he was welcome to visit them at the prince's house by the sea at his earliest opportunity. Elizabeth, who had been in regular contact with the earl, treated him like a son and before he left there was an understanding that he and Emily were to marry.

The prospect of two marriages in the family acted like a tonic on Lady Melbourne. After weeks of calm, the prince's marine house became a scene of hectic packing. She called for the carriages to be prepared for their departure from Brighton. She would travel on to Brocket Hall rather than stay in Whitehall, where her husband was still coming to terms with Pen's death.

A few days after her departure from Brighton, Earl Cowper wrote a conspiratorial letter to Lady Melbourne at Brocket Hall discussing the legal arrangements for the wedding with Emily:

> I shall be extremely happy to come to Brocket on Friday and stay till Monday when I think the whole may be declared. Pray do not mention it before we meet ... I shall certainly get it all arranged before we go to town; you must not go to Devonshire House tomorrow night or I know very well that your looks will betray you ... Pray burn this. Yrs. Most affectly Cowper.

He was barely able to contain his excitement when he wrote to Emily the next night:

> Pray is it a dream or not? For as I am quite alone here I am so distrustful of my own thoughts that I cannot decide which. I shall not therefore be easy till our meeting at Brocket tomorrow ... The last thing I remember with certainty is that you promised at Devonshire House to carry a bottle of Champagne in your pocket to Mrs —'s ball by way of encouragement to me to dance & as that ceremony has not taken place I feel half persuaded that there has been some good reason to prevent it ... Good bye my dearest Emily till we meet & believe me always Yours most affectionly Cowper.

Emily sent a note to her mother to thank her for arranging the match: 'It is owing to you dearest Mama that I can thus sign my name inside this pledge of happiness "Emily Cowper".' She drew a wedding ring with her new name inside it. Their wedding was scheduled for Melbourne House in July, but first Lady Melbourne had to prepare for William's wedding to Caroline.

As the news of the twin weddings began to spread, Elizabeth Foster, the Duke of Devonshire's mistress, wrote to her son Augustus: 'Caroline Ponsonby is to be married to William Lamb, now an elder brother. It is to be next week and Lord Cowper's marriage is declared with Emily Lamb and they are all to be here tonight. These are certainly two as pretty marriages as possible. The Melbournes, as the Queen good naturedly said, wanted this consolation after their trying misfortunes and they are happy with it.'[3]

Caroline had always been rebellious and given to histrionics. Her mother had had an intense love affair with Sheridan and there is still speculation that the fiery playwright was Caroline's father – which may explain a lot.[4] Caroline later admitted drawing rooms and looking glasses, the usual accessories of refined society ladies, were abhorrent to her. She grew up as a tomboy: 'I preferred washing a dog or polishing a piece of Derbyshire spar [a semi-precious stone] or breaking a horse if they would let me.'

She attributed her later foibles to her upbringing, but exaggerated the extent to which she was allowed to run wild. When Caroline was six, she had been dragged off to France by her mother, Harriet, as part of the Devonshire party accompanying Georgiana while she secretly had her baby by Charles Grey. It was a hugely eventful trip for such an impressionable child. Her mother had suffered from spasms, a stroke, and sometimes coughed up blood, the result, it was thought, of a suicide attempt when she lost up to £50,000 with her sister on the stock exchange.

Her father Frederick, Lord Duncannon, inherited the Bessborough title while they were in Italy when his father died and she became Lady Caroline. He had to return to London and it was soon after that her mother began an affair with a dashing officer, Granville Leveson-Gower, the first Earl Granville, who was twenty-one, twelve years younger than Harriet. It became a life-long love affair – she loved him 'to idolatry' – but the immediate effect on Caro was that it further reduced her mother's attentiveness just when her daughter craved it.

They travelled through Florence and Siena to Rome where Harriet suffered a recurrence of her mysterious illness with the symptoms of coughing, sometimes with blood, that were shocking to Caroline. It delayed the Bessboroughs' return to England until August 1794, a year after Georgiana's return. When they arrived home, Caroline's tantrums seemed to have worsened.

Caroline later claimed she was allowed to run wild in Italy but that is regarded today as part of the fantasy world she created around herself; her mother's physician, Dr Drew, travelled with them, and acted as Caroline's tutor. Her long-suffering grandmother Lady Spencer also imposed discipline on the child, sometimes slapping her or confining her to her room when she was naughty, which was frequently.

Caroline contracted intestinal worms when the family crossed the Alps into Italy and nearly died from fever; she was skeletal by the time she returned to England at the age of eight giving her a boyish appearance that she kept for the rest of her life.

Lord David Cecil, William's biographer, and youngest son of the fourth Marquess of Salisbury speculated that Caroline's waiflike looks – a *Sprite*, an elf with blonde curls – appealed to William's 'particular taste both for little girls and for entertaining characters'.

She had a childlike voice, with a slight lisp affected as part of the 'Devonshire House drawl', an idiosyncratic way of pronouncing words such as yaller for yellow and 'Harryot' for Harriet that helped to further exclude the outside world from the rarefied life inside the Devonshires' social bubble.

Her grandmother suspected she was suffering from an underlying illness and sought an opinion from Dr Drew, her family doctor, but he dismissed this theory. She said: 'We had a sad day again with Caroline. The irritation of this dear child's temper must be from illness – Dr Drew persists in it that it is only obstinacy and that harsh means must be used but from all I can observe they only irritate and make her more obstinate while the perpetual crying they occasion shakes her delicate frame and makes her pale as death … I must try what encouragement and indulgence will do but her perverseness is beyond what can be described or conceived.'

Dr Drew gave the child increasing amounts of laudanum – drops of liquid opium – for her hysterical episodes to calm her down.[5] Two years later, Lady Spencer sought a second opinion from Dr Pelham Warren, the son of Richard Warren, George III's physician, who had died eight years earlier.

'At ten years old I was taken to my godmother, Lady Spencer's, [in St Albans] where the housekeeper in hoop and ruffles reigned over seventy servants and attended the ladies in the drawing-room,' Caroline recalled.

'All my childhood I was a trouble, not a pleasure; and my temper was so wayward that Lady Spencer got Dr Warren to examine me. He said I was neither to learn anything nor see anyone for fear the violent passions and strong whims found in me should lead to madness.'[6]

Caroline blamed Dr Warren for learning nothing until she was fifteen, when she got to know William on visits to Brocket. William, who was twenty-one, later wrote in his autobiography that was when he fell in love with Caroline. William and Caro shared a mutual love of plays and poetry, and they would walk for hours through the grounds at Brocket or rest against a tree in the shade of its limbs while William read poetry in a singing fashion to Caroline and they discussed their ambition to put on plays.

Georgiana's daughter Harrio noted: 'William Lamb and Caro Ponsonby seem mutually captivated. When the rest were at games etc., William was in a corner reading and explaining poetry to Car and in the morning, reading tales of wonder together on the *tither tother* [a love seat].' When they left, said Harrio, 'she roared all the way from Brocket to Roehampton [the Spencers' home]'.[7]

Their engagement was a devastating blow to Lord Hartington, Georgiana's son known as 'Hart', who had nursed a love for Caroline from his childhood. He was so overcome when he found out she was engaged to William Lamb he went into shock and threw a fit. The family physician, Walter Farquhar had to be called to give him a sedative. Hart never quite got over the disappointment, and never married.

Lady Bessborough reluctantly gave her consent for William to marry Caroline because Caroline wanted it. Their interview in a corridor behind the private box at the Drury Lane theatre turned out to be more of a farce than the play. 'We met him at Dy. Lane,' Lady Bessborough told Lord Granville. 'I never saw anything so warm and animated as his manner towards her and of course he soon succeeded in obtaining every promise he wished. I had not seen him to speak to and he follow'd me into the passage. I was very nervous and on telling him I knew Lord B. [Bessborough] join'd with me in leaving everything to Caro's decision, he answered: "And that decision is in my favour, thank heaven!" and so saying, threw his arms round me and kiss'd me. At that very moment I look'd up and saw the Pope [Tory minister George Canning][8] and Mr Hammond before me in the utmost astonishment. W., frighten'd at their appearance, started back and ran downstairs.'

Lady Bessborough was worried that having seen her being kissed and embraced, Canning would wrongly assume she was having an affair with William Lamb. She was desperate to correct that misunderstanding, and ran after Canning to tell him the truth.

'No words can paint to you my confusion, but unable to bear the Pope's mortifying conjectures even till all was declar'd, I flew after him and calling him out, told him the cause of what he saw.'

Lady Bessborough said: 'He touch'd me to that degree with his kindness that I could not resist pressing his hand to my lips. (I hope it was not wrong?).' Canning passed on the news that Lady Bessborough's daughter Caroline Ponsonby was to be married to William Lamb, and before long it was in the newspapers.

Lady Melbourne's servants at Melbourne Hall could not believe it when they read the news that Master William was to marry. On 27 May 1805 Lady Melbourne wrote to Henry Fox, her steward at Melbourne House to confirm the reports:

> Mr Fox – I find Hassard [the agent at Brocket] did not believe the paragraph he saw in the papers about Williams Marriage – it is fact & I believe they will be married on Monday next. The Lady is Lady Caroline Ponsonby, daughter to Lord Bessborough. Emily is also going to be married to Lord Cowper & we are extremely happy at both matches.

Her letters were normally countersigned 'Melbourne' to qualify for the concession to peers of the realm whose mail was delivered free of charge. This letter was stamped 'Free' and countersigned 'Egremont', showing Lord Egremont was with Elizabeth when it was sent and underlining his fatherly interest.[9] The mothers-in-law called a temporary cessation of hostilities for a glittering pre-wedding party hosted on 2 June by Harriet's sister Georgiana at Devonshire House. The two grand dames appeared as friends as the bride was showered with presents.

Elizabeth Foster broke the news to her son, Augustus, another secret admirer of Caroline, who was in America:

> Caroline Ponsonby is to be married tomorrow. She looks prettier than ever I saw her. Sometimes she is very nervous, but in general she appears to be very happy. W Lamb seems quite devoted to her. They supped here last night and she received her presents and gave some. Lord Morpeth [George Howard, sixth earl of Carlisle who had married Georgiana's daughter 'Little G'] gave her a beautiful aqua marina clasp. I gave her a little pearl cross with a small diamond in the middle. Caroline gives a hair bracelet with an amethyst clasp. Lord Melbourne gave her a beautiful set of amethysts and Lady M a diamond wreath. The Duke of Devonshire gives her a wedding gown and the Duchess a beautiful veil. Harriet gives her a beautiful burnt topaz cross … what a comfort to have her so near, and yet what a trial to poor Lady Bessborough.[10]

Lady Bessborough's 'trial' was having to accept 'The Thorn' into her family. Lady Melbourne's 'wreath' was a sparkling tiara of floral diamonds '*en tremblant*' that shimmered when the bride walked. William gave Harriet a portrait of his bride-to-be that was such a beautiful likeness that it won her over.

Shortly before eight o'clock the next evening, William and Caroline and their families gathered for the wedding ceremony in the drawing room of the Bessborough's grand London residence at 2 Cavendish Square – today rebuilt as prestige offices – in the fashionable Georgian square north of Oxford Street.

The parish register for St Mary, Marylebone, still bears the record of their wedding, number 1156, in Rev. James Preedy's handwriting.[11] The bride's father, Lord Bessborough, and her uncle, the second Earl Spencer, Georgiana's brother, signed as witnesses. William's signature is free flowing; Lady Caroline's is small and neat.

Lady Caroline wore the white wedding gown with fine lace sleeves and neck, which had been given her by the Duke of Devonshire, with a single string of pearls. Georgiana, Caroline's aunt, thought the lace high up around her neck gave her something of an 'Eastern' appearance. The diamonds of the mothers-in-law, Lady Melbourne and Lady Bessborough, sparkled with the refracted light from the great candelabras.

The bride spoke her marriage vows, to honour and obey in sickness and in health, firmly without a hitch but as the ceremony drew to its close with a kiss with William, Caroline began to weep. Lady Caroline was then seized by an unaccountable fit of rage with the Rev. Preedy, 'a drunken old clergyman' from Hatfield, tore her gown and fainted. William swept her up and carried her from the room. She had still not recovered her composure an hour later, when they were seen off by their families in their carriage for a fortnight's honeymoon at Brocket Hall.

The little drama was an early taste of Caroline's histrionics that would dog William's marriage. Caroline claimed she was overwhelmed by the reality of her new life, being taken away from her mother, and her childhood home. She had surprised her mother by the vehemence of her love for her when, staying at Manresa, the Bessboroughs' house in the 'country' in Roehampton on the weekend before they were married, she sharply told William: 'My dear William judge what my love must be when I can leave such a mother as this for you…'

Augustus Foster mourned her marriage. 'I cannot fancy Caroline married,' he wrote to his mother Bess Foster on 30 July 1805 from Washington where he was secretary of the legation. 'I cannot be glad of it. How changed she must be – the delicate Ariel, the Little Fairy Queen, become a wife and soon perhaps a mother … It is the first death of a woman.'[12]

Augustus was right. Apart from the separation from her family, Caro, '*The Fairie Queen*', professed herself shocked by William's sexual demands on their wedding night at Brocket Hall. Lady Bessborough planned to visit her a few days after the couple had started their honeymoon but Caroline initially was too indisposed to see her mother. 'Poor little Caro has been ill, and would see nobody not even me until today. I am just going,' Lady Bessborough wrote to a friend. Lady Bessborough wanted to comfort her 'nervous indisposition and soothe the discomfort and shock of losing her virginity', according to Lady Caroline's biographer, Paul Douglass.[13]

Caroline later claimed in a letter to Lady Melbourne that William had corrupted her: he had 'amused himself with instructing me in things I need never have heard or known – & the disgust that I at first felt for the world's wickedness I till then had never even heard of'. It is unclear what she was hinting at, but there is speculation that it may have been sadomasochism and flagellation that had fired William's imagination since his days at Eton, or anal sex.

Lady Bessborough sympathised with Caroline: 'Really being married is a state of great suffering to a girl in every way. I do think it very hard that men should always have *beau jeu* on all occasions and that all pain, *Morale et Physique*, should be reserved for us.' She was unaware of the 'disgusting' demands allegedly made by William on her daughter.[14] Caroline was still suffering from nervous exhaustion, when her grandmother, Lady Spencer, came to visit her at Brocket a few days later. Lady Spencer was kept waiting an hour to allow Caroline's nerves to settle and when she did at last come into the drawing room, 'she desired to see me alone and began panting and throwing herself in a chair'.

Caroline overcame the shock of marriage, and walked arm-in-arm with William through the gardens and lawns of Brocket Hall running down to the lake, as far as the picturesque stone bridge where they could look back at the house bathed in June sunshine. Such periods of calm were rare. Caroline in fact enjoyed the sexual charge of a full-blooded, fiery love affair with her husband; she would throw crockery along with her tantrums; and for the first three years of their married life, Caroline revelled in her stormy marriage to William. She later admitted she needed the excitement of their rows and their passionate reconciliations.

When they returned from their honeymoon, William and Lady Caroline Lamb were allowed to entertain their friends in the drawing room and dining room on the first floor of Melbourne House. Their bedroom was on the second floor overlooking the park. Caroline decorated their private rooms with the cherubs she fell in love with in Italy as a child, and drew more cherubs in her journal. She also ordered a scarlet and sepia livery for her pages, running up tailor's bills that they could ill-afford.

In the Lamb papers at the British Library are notes that Caroline sent from her room to her mother-in-law via her servants: 'My Dearest Lady

Melbourne, I have not been down to you this morning for a sort of conscience that I did not please you by my conduct last night – now as I never promised perfection I can only stop when I find myself wrong. Therefore be merciful … I asked Lord Melbourne to tell you I was going to dine early.'[15]

I discovered all Caro's cherubs had been painted out by the civil service when I climbed the narrow wooden staircase to the second floor of Melbourne House in search of her bedroom. Even so, Lady Caroline Lamb's room was unmistakable. It has views overlooking St James's Park with a door connecting it to another room with a fireplace that could have been their sitting room or William's bedroom. Her bedroom has an alcove ten feet wide and eight feet deep, wide enough to accommodate a queen-sized bed. To the right of the alcove is a door leading to a long narrow cupboard that may once have been a walk-in wardrobe where Caro kept her gowns. It was being used to store files and there was a desk in the alcove where her bed would have been. I asked a young civil servant if she ever felt a sense of Caroline in the room. She told me she once heard rustling, as if from a lady arranging a dress. 'It was so loud that I stepped out into the corridor. I thought someone had a lady's dress on and it was rustling but there was no sign of anyone,' she told me.[16]

Caroline was possessive; she was reluctant to let William out of her sight, and for a time they were lost in each other, even when they visited friends. They were a star couple, in demand for weekend parties in the country or dinners in London. They were invited into Lady Holland's box at the theatre where they talked 'considerably louder than the actors', and went to masquerades in fancy dress.

The courtesan Harriette Wilson thought William looked 'so stupid' dressed in an Italian outfit at a masquerade that it was clear Lady Caroline had insisted on her husband 'showing himself beautiful to gratify her vanity'. They enjoyed escaping from the backbiting in London with long breaks in the countryside, hosting shooting parties at Melbourne Hall, and hunting at Brocket Hall.

They were guests of Lord Abercorn at his stately home at Bentley Priory, where they strolled in the grounds, read the classics, and put on an amateur production of *The Rivals*. Harrio, who noted their closeness before they married, described William and Caro reading out of the same book and sharing the same chair while the Aberdeens 'played at spillikins with their arms round one another's necks' and the Hinchinbrookes sat on a couch 'very civil and simpering'.

On a typical day at home in Whitehall, they would stay in bed until about ten-thirty am, breakfast, read something informative such as

Thomas Newton's book on the prophesies of the Bible, William would rehearse his lines for a play, then he would go for a walk while Caroline got dressed. They would go for a drive in a carriage, and read Shakespeare in the afternoon before dressing for dinner at six pm and in the evening they talked, played cards, amused themselves until supper at ten-thirty and bed at eleven.

Lady Bessborough perceptively observed that William needed to 'conquer his shyness and Laziness' when she described being at Brocket Hall with the newly-weds. 'We are out all morning and in the evening William reads to us while she and I draw,' she reported to Lord Granville. 'I hope from my heart they will be happy, and I think they promise to be so; he is delightful and his manner to me every thing I could wish, but as Harrio says, it is not enough for a man and woman to like one another and marry but they must also marry Father and Mother, Brothers and Sisters on both sides…I like William of all things, but I could dispense with some of his entours [entourage, a sharp reference to his mother, Lady Melbourne] – but this I must not even whisper.'

The mothers-in-law quickly resumed hostilities. On 12 June Lady Bessborough described the joy in the servants' quarters over the marriage at her town house at Cavendish Square but complained about 'The Thorn' to Lord Granville:

> I am writing to you to the sound of the fiddles and tabours of a ball which is still going on for Caro's marriage; first l'Office and now the Servants' Hall are footing it away in honour of her, and I conclude getting very drunk as I heard my health this moment drank with three loud cheers.
>
> All this gaiety does not make me feel the House less forlorn without her, but she is so happy it would be very selfish not to feel so also.
>
> Last night, I went to White Hall but some how or other I am not comfortable. The *Thorn* [Lady Melbourne] tho' she seem'd delighted with the marriage has throughout had a degree of sharpness towards me that is very unpleasant.
>
> Yesterday, after various very unpleasant *cuts*, she told me she hoped the Daughter would turn out better than the Mother, or William might have to repent of his choice … This was said half joke, half earnest but there are subjects too sore to bear a joke … I felt hurt and possibly could have retorted but check'd myself, however; and only said I hoped and believ'd she would prove much better – 'especially (I added) with the help of your advice' (I would not say example)…
>
> Whether it is a plan of subduing me or, as my Sister [Georgiana] thinks, a little jealously from fancying William pays me more attention than her (which is far from the truth), I do not know but it is uncomfortable.[17]

A month after William's wedding, Emily was married to Earl Cowper on Saturday 20 July in the wonderfully light and airy first-floor drawing room at Melbourne House. The guests included the Prince of Wales and Emily's brother William with his new wife, Lady Caroline Lamb. The ceremony took place in the evening, and as soon as it was over, Lady Melbourne conducted the bride to her carriage and the newly married Cowpers were waved off from Horse Guards Parade.

The newspapers reported:

> On Saturday evening were married by special licence, at Lord Melbourne's house, at Whitehall, Lord Cowper to the Hon. Miss Lamb, his Lordship's youngest daughter. The Bride-Maids were Lady Harriet Cavendish and Miss Wyndham; his Lordship gave her away. The ceremony was performed by the Rev. Mr Kates. Among the company were: His Royal Highness the Prince of Wales, Sir George and Lady Wombwell, Mr and Lady C. Lamb, Mr and Mrs Henry Cowper, Mr Spencer, Mr Henry Cowper.
>
> The Bride was very elegantly dressed. Immediately after the ceremony, Lady Melbourne conducted the Bride to her carriage and took leave of her in a very tender and affectionate manner. The happy pair drove off with great speed for his Lordship's seat in Herts [Panshanger] where they intend passing the honey moon.

As dusk fell over St James's Park and twinkling candles illuminated her house, Lady Melbourne must have felt a huge sense of satisfaction at her success in arranging two weddings.

While the newly married Lambs and Cowpers were absorbed in their lives, the rest of the country was gripped by the fear of a French invasion by Bonaparte and his forces; following the collapse of the peace there were rumours that 'Boney' had been seen on the north coast of France where an invasion force was being assembled. William had been made a major in the Hertfordshire Volunteer Infantry the year before.

As a show of defiance, the king reviewed a display of regiments of the Loyal London Volunteers in Hyde Park and on 12 June the Royal Family including the Prince of Wales's wife Caroline turned out in force at a 'drawing room' at St James's Court. Bells were rung in the morning; at noon the Hyde Park and Tower guns were fired; and at night the theatres, public offices and the shops of the king's tradesmen were lit up. 'Feathers never were worn in greater profusion,' said one newspaper report.

In the first week of November news reached London of a great naval victory on Monday 21 October. A British fleet under the command of

Vice-Admiral Horatio Nelson had defeated the combined fleets of France and Spain off Cape Trafalgar, a headland in south west Spain. The news did not reach London until around 6 November when a special edition of the *London Gazette* reported it had 'pleased the Almighty Disposer of all events to grant his Majesty's arms a complete and glorious victory'. Jubilation was tempered by the news that Nelson had been killed at his moment of triumph, shot by a sniper from the rigging of the French man-of-war, *Redoubtable*, as he paced the deck of his flagship, HMS *Victory*.

Lady Melbourne sent her agent Fox at Melbourne Hall in Derbyshire a copy of the *Gazette* announcing the news. 'I think you will like to read an account of this glorious victory which has caused great rejoicings here although a gloom is thrown over the whole by the loss of Lord Nelson which must be sincerely and deservedly regretted by the whole nation.'[18]

Victory at Trafalgar had lifted the threat of a French invasion but Nelson's death cast a pall over Melbourne House and Whitehall. Lady Melbourne found her home after the New Year celebrations was enveloped by preparations for Nelson's state funeral. Nelson's coffin, hewn from the mast of the *L'Orient*, the French flagship that blew up at the Battle of the Nile, was carried solemnly from a naval barge at Whitehall Steps to the Admiralty building, two hundred yards from Melbourne House as a band played the Death March. The next morning, 9 January 1806, the funeral cortège assembled beneath Lady Melbourne's windows on Horse Guards Parade. Nelson's coffin was carried on a massive carriage carved to look like the prow and stern of the *Victory*. The procession was so long, the head reached St Paul's before the tail left Horse Guards.

Lady Bessborough watched it pass by from a vantage point in a house at Charing Cross. 'The moment the Car appear'd which bore the body you could have heard a pin fall and without any order to do so, they all took off their hats. I cannot tell you the effect this simple action produc'd ... Meanwhile the dead march was play'd in soft tones and the pauses fill'd with cannon and the roll of the muffled drums.'[19]

Troops lining the route included Lady Bessborough's son, Captain Frederick Cavendish Ponsonby of the Sixtieth Regiment of Foot, who soon would be in the thick of the fighting with Wellington's army as it battled to eject the French from Portugal and Spain.

Elizabeth Foster was also moved by the procession. 'You cannot conceive how knocked up I feel,' she wrote to her son. 'We are going – Fred, Caro and I – to Brocket tomorrow for a few days. I think it will do us good.'[20]

Nelson's funeral was to be the overture to a year of sorrow for the nation, and Lady Melbourne. On 23 January the Prime Minister, William Pitt, suddenly died at Downing Street, around the corner from Melbourne House. Pitt had been sick with gout when he saw Nelson off for the last time from Downing Street but his death shocked the nation. The Melbournes had been his political opponents for decades but William was moved to tears by the loss.

Lady Bessborough wrote to Lord Granville: 'Everyone feels it: the shock, the regret is general. When W Lamb came in and told me he had seen Farquhar who could only say, "All is over", the tears were in his eyes too as he spoke; and as I had drawn my veil over my face, he said: "Do not be asham'd of Crying; that heart must be callous indeed which could hear of the extinction of such a man unmov'd".' His physician, Sir Walter Farquhar said he was emaciated, unable to stomach food or drink and died 'of old age at forty-six as much as if he had been ninety'.

Farquhar blamed the pressure of work – Pitt's pulse rose from 80 to 120 every time he received a 'green box' of Cabinet papers – coupled with Napoleon's shattering defeat of the Russian and Austrian armies at Austerlitz on 2 December 1805, which left him seemingly invincible on the mainland of Continental Europe.

The real cause of his death, like many contemporaries, was liver failure caused by years of heavy drinking. Hogarth's riotous print *Gin Lane* showed the dangers of gin to the poor, but the rich also slowly drank themselves to death on brandy, port and claret, partly because water was potentially lethal. It was not until 1854 that Dr John Snow identified a public water pump in Soho as the source of a cholera outbreak.

Pitt's doctor, Anthony Addington, father of Henry, later the Whig Prime Minister, recommended drinking port for his health at university. He took the advice too much to heart; he regularly drank at least three bottles of port wine – wine fortified by brandy – at a single sitting and sometimes got through six bottles in a day, though the bottles were smaller than they are now.

In February 1806 the Melbournes were once more hit by a family tragedy. William had at last found a seat through his friend Kinnaird at Leominster and was campaigning there when he was recalled to London. Caroline had written anxiously to her married cousin 'Little G', Georgiana, the Duchess of Devonshire's daughter, whether 'it is bad for you to sleep with your husband in the most significant sense of the word while pregnant'. When William arrived home, he found she had had a miscarriage that left her downcast.

There was a silver lining to all the dark clouds over Melbourne House. Pitt's death forced George III to accept the hated Whigs in office for the first time in twenty-three years to avert a constitutional crisis. Lady Melbourne's friends were back in power. On 11 February, the king appointed a coalition government with the Whig William Wyndham Grenville as Prime Minister. It became known as the 'Ministry of All the Talents' although it was dominated by the Whigs.

Lady Melbourne and the Duchess of Devonshire were overjoyed. The ailing duchess despite her disabilities threw open the doors of Devonshire House and hosted balls and receptions to celebrate the appointment of her friends and former lovers to high office. Fox, who stood for everything the king most despised, was made Foreign Secretary to pursue peace with Napoleon; Charles Grey, who had fathered Georgiana's daughter Eliza, was put in charge of the Admiralty; and Sheridan was appointed Treasurer of the Navy.

Gillray lampooned them in a cartoon *Making Decent*. It depicted the Cabinet preparing for office: Sheridan is washing his hands; Fox with the permanent five o'clock shadow is shaving; Grey, wearing the naval uniform of the First Lord of the Admiralty, is brushing his teeth in a mirror with the Prince of Wales feathers on the top of the frame; Vansittart is puffing clouds of powder over Sidmouth's wig; and in the centre, Grenville is yanking up his trousers over an enormous backside, making the joke that it was a 'broad bottomed' coalition.[21]

It was to be Georgiana's last hurrah. She was still only forty-eight but Georgiana was a victim of the Georgian lifestyle; her body was a ruin of its former fashionable self, as Lady Holland acidly commented: 'Her figure is corpulent, her complexion coarse, one eye gone, and her neck immense. How frail is the tenure of beauty!'

A month after celebrating the return of her friends to power, Georgiana, the most celebrated beauty of her day became jaundiced and died at 3.30 am on 30 March. It was discovered she had died from an abscess on the liver, brought on by years of heavy drinking.

Her death was a body blow to Lady Melbourne who had been her intimate friend for over thirty years and had shared her dramas, her frolics with fashion, her political intrigues, and sometimes her lovers. 'Lady Melbourne was first and foremost a femme politique and her influence, combined with the Duchess of Devonshire's admiration for Charles James Fox, gave political tone to the Society of Devonshire House,' said Lady Airlie.[22]

Georgiana's death came as a blessed relief from her suffering. Her grief-stricken sister, Harriet told Lord Granville: 'Anything so horrible, so killing, as her three days' agony no human being ever witnessed. I saw it all, held her thro' all her struggles, saw her expire and since have again and again kiss'd her cold lips and press'd her lifeless body to my heart – and yet I am alive...'

There was one enduring bright spot for Lady Melbourne amid the gloom that year: on 26 June 1806, her daughter Emily presented Elizabeth with her first grandchild. Lady Cowper gave birth to a healthy young son. Parish records show the boy was christened on 23 August 1806 at St George's Church, Hanover Square, around the corner from Lord Cowper's fine town house. He was baptised George Augustus Frederick in honour of the Prince of Wales who stood as his godfather. His birth, however, increased the pressure on Caroline to produce an heir for William.

Three weeks later, Melbourne House was plunged into mourning again. On 13 September 1806, the great champion of the Whigs, Charles James Fox, Pitt's greatest rival, who had campaigned in the streets with Georgiana and Lady Melbourne, died. He was an alcoholic and suffered from oedema, retention of water on his legs, known to the Georgians as dropsy. Lady Bessborough, who tearfully visited Fox shortly before he died, said: 'His face and hands are dreadfully drawn and emaciated, his complexion sallow beyond measure, his bosom sunk – and then all at once a body and Legs so enormous that it looks like the things with which they dress up Falstaff.' Fox died of liver failure. He was fifty-seven.

Once more the 'Great and the Good' of Whig society turned out for the funeral, this time at Westminster Abbey. The *fin de siècle* air that descended on Whitehall was palpable. 'This dreadful year is to be mark'd by the loss of all that is brilliant, great, or noble,' wrote Lady Bessborough.[23]

The Duke of Richmond wrote tenderly to Lady Melbourne: 'Pray let me know how you go on, for with all Your Philosophy and your sense you have a Heart that must suffer dreadfully on such occasions and makes the best Health feel its consequences.'[24]

In one fraught year, Lady Melbourne had lost her closest society friend, her political hero, and a grandchild. Lady Melbourne, however, refused to be downcast. Her maxim was stoical: 'You must in this life allow yourself to be as little depressed as possible and support everything with as much fortitude as you can muster.'[25]

She continued to visit her friend Bess, the duke's mistress, at Devonshire House, though she hid her thinning hair with a turban when she played chess with Emily and Georgiana's daughter, Harrio. She was not melancholy because she still had ambitious plans for her own family – and William's political career to think about.

14

Scandal

The boy stood up and slipped out of the public gallery of the House of Commons as the cheers were still ringing around the chamber in acclamation of William Lamb, who had just made his maiden speech.

He quickly descended the flight of steps to the members' lobby and walked briskly through the ancient Westminster Hall into the cold November air. He pulled down the brim of his hat and drew his large coat around his throat as he crossed Palace Yard into Parliament Street, threading a path through the hackney carriages and headed towards Whitehall. He dashed across the street dodging the carriages on their way to the West End and strode past Downing Street to the small-pillared portico that marked the entrance to Melbourne House, next to Horse Guards. He darted inside.

Once inside the door, the boy startled Hazard, the Melbourne's faithful Butler, by throwing off his hat and coat before bounding up the stairs to the Lambs' private apartments. Hazard went upstairs to the dining room where a reception was being held and discreetly informed Viscountess Melbourne that Lady Caroline Lamb had returned.

The Viscountess was hosting a supper party in honour of her son William's maiden speech at the House of Commons and she was furious.

William had been given the signal honour of making the loyal address to King George III at the Opening of Parliament on Friday 19 November 1806. It had been arranged by the Leader of the House, Lady Melbourne's old friend Charles Grey, Viscount Howick, a former lover of Georgiana, the Duchess of Devonshire.

She had invited a few old family friends and leading ladies of Georgian society, including Lady Elizabeth Foster, who was to become the new Duchess of Devonshire, for a small celebration. Lady Melbourne had mingled with her guests, surrounded by a convivial hum of conversation until she realised Caroline, William's troublesome wife, was not there. She assumed the wilful Caroline was having one of her tantrums in her room and asked her butler and his staff to find her and bring her down. He returned to say that she was nowhere to be found.

Lady Caroline had wanted to see her husband deliver his speech, but as a woman, she was barred from doing so. She could have paid for a ticket to sit in the ventilator room, an uncomfortable closed space above the chamber inside a false ceiling installed by Wren. It was directly above the central chandelier and unbearably hot from the dozens of candles that burned below; it was also impossible to see speakers, unless ladies strained their necks. Even then, they could only see the MPs' feet.

There was only one way she could witness her husband's Parliamentary debut: by dressing up as a man. With her short hair, she could easily pass for a boy and asked her brother Willy, who was nineteen and shared her love of the outrageous, to lend her some clothes to carry out her *coup de théâtre*. He gave her his hat and overcoat, a shirt and some breeches to wear.

She had gone into the Commons with Willy and his friend, Mr Ross, and sat on the edge of her seat in the public gallery nervously looking down on the government benches to see William deliver his maiden speech, hoping that she would not be discovered before he addressed the House.

The House was packed for the opening of Parliament and she had admitted to being 'frightened to death' with nerves. She knew his speech by heart. They had rehearsed it together in their rooms on the second floor of Melbourne House. It was not the brilliant show of rhetorical fireworks that his mother may have wished for. It was a workmanlike defence of his Whig friends who were in government.

He deftly reconciled the change in Whig policy from suing for peace with Napoleon Bonaparte to supporting the war; peace had been an honourable policy, he said, but Bonaparte did not want it, since inflicting the crushing defeat on the Austrians at the Battle of Austerlitz a year before. Now Britain was forced to confront Bonaparte in war. William's words were similar to those used by Winston Churchill when Britain faced destruction 134 years later, in spirit at least, if not oratorical impact:

It is not without the utmost awe and inquietude that we can behold the period, so long menaced, at length arrived: a period when the power of the enemy is predominant and unlimited over the greater part of Europe, and when Great Britain, with the exception of two powerful allies, is left unsupported and compelled to rely for its security on those resources, on which, I am confident, we might rely implicitly—the natural courage and the unparalleled spirit of the people.[1]

He was expected to avoid controversy in the 'loyal' address to the king but William's speech nevertheless signalled his own gradual shift from the reforming zeal of some of his oldest Whig friends towards the more moderate policies of Pitt's followers. For Caro, it did not matter if it was conventional, or pedestrian. What mattered to her was they had done it together; she wanted to share in his momentary flash of fame.

Caroline was jubilant at her own audacity, having flouted the stuffy rules of the Commons to see her husband make his debut. Her mother-in-law confronted her with a face like thunder. Caroline told Lady Melbourne she had been at Lady Holland's. Her mother-in-law knew it was a lie but decided to let the matter rest, for now; if William did not mind his wife's antics, nor could she. She would allow William to try to control his odd, wayward wife his own way for the time being. She knew Caroline was highly strung and feared a confrontation would push her over the edge.

Lady Elizabeth Foster recorded the drama in her diary:

> There was great anxiety. Caroline Lamb was missing! We guessed she had been to the House of Commons but she pretended she went to Holland House. She was not come back to Whitehall and Lady Melb. was angry; however, she said that if William did not disapprove, she would say nothing more. It came out that W Ponsonby [Caroline's brother] had got her some of his clothes and with the help of Mr Ross had gone with her to the House of Commons – her delight was extreme, as was her agitation – but gave no sign of it.[2]

Caroline's mood swings from high spirits to despair had alarmed the Lamb family and her friends. She had been depressed by the loss of her baby at the start of the year, but a month after dashing from the Commons, she had started to suffer morning sickness. Her doctors told her she was expecting again, and the baby conceived around Christmas was due in August 1807.

She feared she would suffer another miscarriage because she was physically too weak to have children. Caroline complained of feeling ill through her pregnancy and as her time approached, she took to her bed at Melbourne House. Her cousin, Lady Harriet Granville, Harrio, said she was 'very weak and full of pains and fatigue'.

Caroline's anxious mother, Harriet, Lady Bessborough, moved into Melbourne House to be with Caroline when she began her labour. She wrote to Lord Granville: 'All to day I have pass'd in extreme anxiety for my dear

Caro; she is ill but so slow and lingering I know not what to think. She and all of them insisted on my going to sup at Emily's [Lady Melbourne's daughter]. It was dull; a majority of women, Frederick Lamb making love to Miss Long, Lord H to Miss Drummond, and that frightful Lord Monson to pretty little Lady Emily Saville. Mr Hill was the only Disengaged Man I knew to speak to.'

The next day, 29 August 1807, Harriet reported to Lord Granville: 'Caroline has given birth to a very fine boy. I am too happy and too tired to write more to night but you I am sure will be glad of any thing that makes me so.'[3]

It was a quick birth but painful because the baby was so big. William was overjoyed to be a father. He wrote to his friend Lady Holland that his son was 'very large for so small a woman which quality of the child made the labour very hard and painful, tho' it was very short lasting'.

Lady Melbourne made sure the baptism of William's son was one of the society events of the year. She invited a small but glittering gathering of titled friends led by the Prince of Wales to a colourful christening party at Melbourne House on 13 October 1807. The house was decked out with fairy lights for the occasion. The party in the drawing room overlooking St James's Park started at five o'clock in the afternoon, and went on until the small hours.

'You will see an account of our christening in the newspapers,' Harriet told Lord Glanville, who was on a diplomatic mission in St Petersburg, Russia. 'The entrance look'd like an illuminated temple, quite beautiful, and Caro's fine apartment prevented all crowd or heat … I will not tell you how pretty the child look'd, nor how fine we were all dress'd, nor what the Prince said, and Caro said and I said – were you a woman I should certainly impart, but reckon you are disqualified by your Sex from tasting. I must however tell you of Mr Sheridan's ingenuity.'[4]

Sheridan had started to pester Harriet with whom he had had an affair twenty years earlier. She was hostile when he asked Harriet if he might come to the christening because she suspected he would make a scene and tried to put him off, saying it was up to Lady Melbourne to issue invitations. She warned Lady Melbourne not to invite him and pressed her daughter Caroline not to give him an invitation. Lady Melbourne refused his request, saying the christening party was only for family and that if she began to admit strangers there was no end to the people who would wish to attend.

Sheridan devised a cunning way of gatecrashing the party. He was no longer a minister; the Ministry of All the Talents collapsed over the refusal of George III to accept Irish emancipation and the Whigs were out of office again. But he used his friendship with the Prince of Wales to get through the door of

Melbourne House without an invitation. He followed the prince inside. Harriet described what happened in one of her regular letters to Lord Granville: 'When we all dress'd expecting the Prince, the 'double battants' [doors] were thrown open with great fracas and in enter'd Mr Sheridan, announcing the Prince, and himself as the attendant he had chosen to accompany him.'[5]

As he had posed as the prince's aide, there was nothing Viscountess Melbourne or Lady Bessborough could do to eject Sheridan. The Reverend James Preedy – the same 'drunken old clergyman' who had officiated at Caroline and William's wedding – baptised the baby boy George Augustus Frederick, in honour of the Prince of Wales, who stood as the child's godfather.[6]

The boy's two redoubtable grandmothers looked on with Harriet's mother, Lady Spencer, the child's great grandmother. Then they sat down to dinner and Sheridan grabbed a chair opposite Harriet and her daughter, Caroline. The newspapers reported: 'At half past seven the company sat down to an elegant dinner. His Royal Highness the Prince of Wales sat at the head of the table, Viscountess Melbourne on his right and Viscount Melbourne on his left. The Duke of Devonshire, Earl and Countess Cowper, Earl and Countess of Bessborough, Viscount Duncannon, Lady Elizabeth Foster, the Right Hon R B Sheridan, the Hon W Ponsonby and Mr Crowle were present.'

After dinner, they played a word game to amuse themselves. Sheridan hurriedly scribbled six lines and handed the paper to Caro, to write a witty reply. It was headed 'Motto by the Revd. Mr Purdy [Sheridan appears to have got the curate's name wrong] to George Augustus Frederick Lamb':

> Grant Heav'n, sweet Babe, thou mayst inherit
> What nature only can impart
> Thy Father's manly sense and spirit,
> They Mother's grave and gentle Heart
> And when to Manhood's hopes and duties grown
> Be thou a Prop to thy great Sponsor's throne.

The tribute to the boy's 'great sponsor', the Prince of Wales, was calculated to gain some hearty cheers for Sheridan's lines. Caroline refused to play, saying she was too ill, and left the table. Her mother tried to compose a witty response for her:

> May he who wrote ye verse impart
> To the sweet Baby whom he blesses
> As shrewd a head, a better heart
> And talents he alone possesses.

Lady Bessborough admitted her lines were 'very bad' but said she had not a moment to compose them. Sheridan read them aloud but changed the last couplet to read:

> A wiser head, as pure a heart
> And greater wealth than he possesses.

It was long after midnight that the Prince of Wales called for his carriage though he complained he was suffering from a headache and pain in his eye, no doubt from an earlier hangover. Bess Foster, who married the Duke of Devonshire two years later, recorded: 'The fatigue was great to us all.'[7]

Sheridan continued to pester Harriet after the christening of her grandson. She told Lord Granville in a letter in November he had turned up unannounced at Brocket Hall when she paid a visit to Caroline, William and her grandchild Augustus. Lady Bessborough had timed her arrival carefully so that she avoided Lady Melbourne, who had already returned to London.

'As we drove up to the door, a Barouche and four drove up too. I ran up to Caro asking what company they could have. "None," she said, "for all the servants are gone with Ly. M [Melbourne] and we only stayed because it was fine and you coming".'[8]

Sheridan stepped out of the carriage. Harriet was irritated, but he wheedled his way into staying a couple of nights and entertained Caroline, William, and Lord and Lady Bessborough with a tour-de-force of his wit. Harriet begged Caro and William not to let him stay another night, but Sheridan remained as an unwanted houseguest, chasing Harriet in and out of rooms, up and down stairs, even into Augustus's nursery, where 'he threw himself on his knees before me'.

Eventually Sheridan was persuaded to leave, but continued to pursue Harriet when he was drunk. Sheridan was in his cups at a party at Melbourne House in Whitehall on 7 April 1808. Augustus's nanny, Miss Berry wrote in her diary: 'An immense assembly. We came away at half-past twelve and walked beyond the Admiralty to the carriage. Many of the company were not away till near three and the Prince of Wales and a very few persons supped below stairs in Lady Melbourne's apartment, and were not gone till past six. Sheridan of the number, was completely drunk.'[9]

Sheridan's pursuit of her mother was the least of Caroline's worries. Augustus had started to have convulsions at the age of nine months, when he began teething. Caroline was horrified; her doctors assured her his convulsions were not unusual. She also had the growing realisation that Augustus was not like other children, and handicapped in some way; he stared into space; he learned to read but physically found it tiring to write. He suffered from epileptic fits, and was treated with quack cures – leeches and magnetic massages on the head.[10]

By the age of six, Augustus appeared backward compared to other boys his age, and given to screaming fits that led occasionally to seizures. He also had trouble breathing. A doctor was summoned to make a thorough examination of the boy and he concluded that Augustus 'has no defect that he can perceive in mind or body … These screams are nothing but temper'.

William hired a tutor to teach Augustus Greek and Latin but it was a vain struggle and Caroline began to feel she was to blame in some way. In 1816, when he was nine, Caroline wrote to Lady Melbourne: 'You will not wonder Dearest Lady Melbourne that I should feel almost heart broken about Augustus. I usually am dispirited. I never know what to do. He has had 4 attacks today, 2 very very severe ones … he is to take one of Evans powders tonight … I have been ill myself but I believe it is greatly [increased] by anxiety about My Boy.'[11]

Augustus may have been autistic, but that is far from clear. He was at first kept in the nursery with his nanny, Miss Berry, in an attic room at the top of Melbourne House. Later he was removed to a cottage with another nanny, Miss Webster, at Brompton. His aunt Lady Emily Cowper described going with Lord Melbourne to see him there: 'He is a little better … because he is kept very quiet and almost starved … the moment he gets the least into health they [fits] return bad again … His head was covered with the marks of Leeches.'[12]

Augustus appeared to his family to stop mental development at the age of seven or eight and his nanny complained when he was a big teenager he would tumble her to the floor and sit on her. Emily wrote unkindly, 'I went to the play last night to see Frankenstein and the huge creature without any sense put us in mind of Augustus.'[13]

Caroline at times appeared to be in denial about Augustus, insisting he was cured, when she found she was pregnant again, before sinking once more into depression about him. Caroline's mother and her sister were worried her health would not support another pregnancy; they thought she looked 'very thin'. Their fears were proved right.

In the cold winter of 1809, after it had snowed, she went into labour and gave birth to a daughter, who was too premature to survive in a world without incubators. She lived through the night, but died the next morning as she was cradled by Harriet at Caro's bedside.

When Doctor Farquhar arrived, there was nothing he could do for the infant, but he examined Caroline and pronounced she would survive the strain of her premature birth. However, the trauma of losing a second child had a lasting impact on Caroline; she felt depressed and inadequate.

The blows to Caroline's already fragile state of mind may have contributed to her increasingly unpredictable behaviour. A sketch by Caroline at Melbourne Hall shows a baby in a graveyard with a church in the background and the heart-rending caption: *mais tout y meurt* – but everything dies there.

William, too, appeared cold towards her, and avoided the emotional pain by absorbing himself in his own political world at Westminster. Caroline flew into rages when he insisted on leaving her behind to go to the Commons, and they quarrelled over their finances. Caroline felt trapped by the unromantic, unfeeling, unsympathetic Lambs. She had written to her cousin Hart, who had loved her, bidding him farewell as his fairy queen after her wedding. Now she turned to others for emotional support.

She told Lady Holland that when she went to the Isle of Wight she put on boys' shoe buckles, a red Emery [short-haired] wig and a boarding school frock 'so that I looked like a boy dressed up for a girl & in that character told everyone that I personated Lady Caroline Lamb...' When she returned to London, she went to balls and masquerades. She 'jumped like a Harlequin, laughed heartily and had no mercy on any one.' She ignored 'those whose malice, more abundant than their wit, treated me Cavalierly.'

Having tired of these 'juvenile freaks', she dipped behind a curtain and adopted another disguise in a gown and a cassock – as the clergyman Sydney Smith, who had become a celebrity in London society as a wit and preacher.

She was clearly heading for a fall, and it came swiftly, when she began an affair with Sir Godfrey Vassall Webster, Lady Holland's son by her first husband. A Parliamentary guide said Sir Godfrey was like his father – 'one of the greatest blackguards in London'.[14]

Caroline depicted him in her novel *Glenarvon* as a cold, arrogant rake, who was preoccupied with horses and gambling. He stayed up all night so often playing cards he claimed to his associates he had breakfasted on fifteen consecutive mornings before going to bed. One contemporary said: 'He is young, indeed, well-born and well-looking, but in every other respect a more complete contrast to William Lamb cannot be imagined.' Perhaps that was his attraction for Caro.[15]

Lady Holland, daughter of a Jamaican plantation owner, had married Sir Godfrey Webster at the age of sixteen. They had five children including Godfrey, before she had an affair with Henry Fox, nephew of Charles James Fox, in Naples in 1794. She married Fox, the third Baron Holland, in 1797 two days after divorcing Webster and presided over a Whig salon at Holland House amid the fields of Kensington to eclipse both Lady Melbourne and the Duchess of Devonshire for a younger generation. It was on the west side of Hyde Park and a pleasant ride away from Whitehall for Caroline.

Celebrated politicians, writers and intellectuals who went to Lady Holland's dinner parties including Lord Grey and Talleyrand were expected to fall into line with her whims. She shifted her guests' dinner places after each course, and interrupted conversations with her own outspoken views, which included staunch support for Napoleon, even after he was exiled to St Helena following his defeat at the Battle of Waterloo. Macaulay, the Whig historian, described being put in his place by Lady Holland tapping her fan on the table and saying 'Now Macaulay we have had enough of this, give us something else.' Few stood up to her, except Sydney Smith who, on being told to ring the bell, said: 'Oh yes! And shall I sweep the room?'[16]

Lady Melbourne's son, William, later told Queen Victoria she was 'very handsome though very large and she has a vulgar mouth; she used always to say "A vulgar, ordinary mouth I have".'[17]

Caroline's public romance with Lady Holland's son, Webster, enraged Lady Melbourne who put an ultimatum in writing to her: she could drop Webster and be forgiven, loved and confided in by her family, or, she could carry on with her scandalous liaison with Webster and be ostracised.

A mother-in-law's wrath – an angry letter from Lady Melbourne to Lady Caroline Lamb over her flirting with Webster. (Mss 45546 f16 copyright British Library Board)

On 14 March 1810, Caroline replied to her mother-in-law with a rambling, contradictory and in parts incoherent letter promising she would abandon Webster:

> My dearest Lady Melbourne,
> I must indeed have a heart of iron if it was not most deeply wounded and affected by your letter and conversation, by my Mother's sorrow and by the unparalleled kindness and patience of my friends – and you make me this offer; shall I again be received, be loved, be confided in by you all. God knows and my heart the sacrifice is greater than it should be but I will make it. By this very post I write to Sir Godfrey. I tell him the same to you and my resolution is as irrevocable as it is painful yet you may trust me. I may possibly never see him again. I leave that to him but leave him also the choice....
>
> I solemnly on my knees call God to witness that (unless ill) I return here on Tuesday and consent neither to write to nor see Sir Godfrey any more but in Public by accident as a common acquaintance. I even go further. I will avoid him.
>
> I will write no more. No indeed, indeed I will not. It shall end here. You say you will forgive me. I will consent to everything. Never let his name be mentioned.[18]

She then goes on to excuse herself by accusing William of corrupting her 'childlike innocence' with 'disgusting' sexual demands:

> Those principles which I came to William with – that horror of vice, of deceit of anything that was the least improper, that Religion I believed in then without a doubt and with what William pleased to call superstitious enthusiasms – merited praise and ought to have been cherished. They were safeguards to a character like mine and the almost childlike innocence and inexperience I had preserved till then.
>
> All at once this was thrown off and William himself taught me to regard without horror all the forms of restraints I had lain so much stress on ... He called me Prudish and said I was strait-laced – amused himself with instructing me in things I had never heard of or known – and the disgust I at first felt to the world's wickedness I till then had never even heard of – in a very short time gave way to a general laxity of principles which little by little unperceived by you all has been undermining the few virtues I ever possessed.

Caro blames William's lack of passion for her transgression:

> William's love for me is such that he is almost blind to my faults yet that
> first ardour that romantic passion which we both experienced was far too
> violent to last – contrary to the general opinion on this subject it has lasted
> far longer on his side than mine with its enthusiasm also its inconveniences.
> My temper is calm. We never quarrel; never shake the House with storms
> of passion as we did for the first three years. I can command myself now
> and he rejoices in the change yet he looks not for the cause; gratitude
> affection even love remain in my heart but those feelings which carry with
> them such a charm and existing so many years unabated had lately been on
> the decline – forgive me Lady Melbourne for telling you all this – I would
> wish to account for a conduct which appears to me as inconceivable as it is
> without excuse.
>
> To your strong mind all I have said will appear very foolish, yet remember
> I write with full confidence in your compassion…

Despite the obvious turmoil in her mind, her handwriting is small and
neat, written carefully like a child. She signed herself 'Yours most gratefully
<u>un</u>dutifully and affectionately Caroline Lamb.'

All her promises and protestations notwithstanding, Lady Caroline was
seen at a ball openly flirting with Webster again on 12 April 1810. Lady
Melbourne was incandescent with fury and wrote to her the next day one
of the most withering letters from a mother-in-law it is possible to conceive.
It is among her correspondence in the Lamb archive at the British Library
and Lady Melbourne's venom has lost none of its sting; the pages burn with
indignation:

> I only write you a few lines for the purpose of preventing your coming to
> me loaded with falsehood & flattery under the impression that it will have
> any effect – which I most solemnly assure you it will not – I see you have no
> shame nor compunction for your past conduct every action every impulse
> of your mind is directed by Sir Godfrey Webster – I lament it, but as I can
> do no good I shall withdraw myself and suffer no more croaking upon
> your hurt – Your behaviour last night was disgraceful in its appearances
> and so disgusting from its motives that it is quite impossible it should ever
> be effaced from my mind.
>
> When any one braves the opinion of the World, sooner or later they will
> feel the consequences of it and although at first people may have excused

your forming friendships with all those who are censured for their conduct, from your youth and inexperience, yet when they see you continue to single them out and to overlook all the decencys [sic] imposed by Society – they will look upon you as belonging to the same class.[19]

Lady Melbourne, writing with long flowing loops that arch backwards from her 'ds', accuses Caroline of forming an attachment to a French courtesan, who was shunned by respectable society, and her husband, 'because they are friends of Sir Godfrey Webster':

> Had you been sincere in your promises of amendment or wished to make any return to William for his kindness – you would have discarded and driven from your presence any persons or things that would remind you of the unworthy Object for whose sake you had run such risks & exposed yourself so much – but on the contrary you seem to delight in everything that recalls him to you – & to honour those disgraceful feelings which have caused so much unhappiness to those who ought to be dearest to you.
>
> A Married Woman should consider that by such levity she not only compromises her own honour and character but also that of her Husband – but you seek only to please yourself. You think you can blind your Husband and cajole your friends.
>
> Only one word more *let me alone. I will have no* more conversations with you upon this hateful Subject. I repeat it – let me alone & and do not drive me to explain the meaning of the cold civility that will henceforward pass between us.

Caroline wrote to Lady Melbourne a few days later:

> Sir G Webster says he will rather die than leave England without speaking to me alone. I would rather quarrel with my whole family, lose my reputation and have my heart broke than not do it … If I may see him tomorrow and if you will not tell my mother … what passed tonight I will be as gentle as a lamb.
>
> I will try to conquer feelings which are now too strong for my reason to command. I will put myself in yours and my mother's hands and be guided by you but if I am twice to despair I will deceive you all. I speak not as a menace. I care not for what may be thought or said … None of you shall ever know till too late to what you have reduced me.[20]

She wanted to keep two gifts from Webster, a puppy and a bracelet carrying a lock of his hair. Lady Melbourne must have wondered about Caroline's sanity when she said the puppy had gone mad while she was with Augustus and she thought it was as an act of God:

A sudden terror came into my head as I looked on my little blossoming Augustus that I might be punished for my conduct because of what I neglected – your kindness, my mother's, my husband, my own husband – all around me…

I am very superstitious …This morning the dog – the beautiful little puppy – playing and running about me snapped at the child [Augustus] but did not bite him. It raised my fears. Great God I thought if this dog should go mad and bite William's child what would become of me. I went into the garden and took a long walk. The dog suddenly dropped before me in a fit foaming at the mouth. It turned my heart sick. I trembled all over. I took it home. I pray that I might be forgiven – then it was I tore my bracelet off and wrote to William … They say the dog is mad.[21]

On my knees I have written to William to tell him not any falsehoods, not as you say any stories to conceal my guilt – the whole disgraceful truth.

I have told him I have deceived him. I have trusted entirely to his mercy and generosity, yet as I have not said any of you know anything about it, do not mention it to him. But my dearest Lady Melbourne, write and tell me you forgive me.

Some question whether Caroline consummated her affair with Webster. In telling William 'the whole disgraceful truth' and admitting she 'deceived' William, she left little doubt that her relationship with Webster was sexual.

It may seem the height of hypocrisy in Lady Melbourne that having frequently committed adultery herself, she could criticise her daughter-in-law for her infidelity. But Caroline's 'crime' in Lady Melbourne's eyes was her determination to flout the rules of society in public. The key observation is that 'by such levity she not only compromises her own honour and character *but also that of her Husband*'. She also alienated Webster's influential mother, Lady Holland, for bringing scandal on her family too.

Caroline was beyond the reach of such moral codes. She was bored with her wealth, by the hypocrisy of her mother-in-law and the Devonshire House set and alienated from the unfeeling Lambs and the Melbournes. Caroline, above all, was bored with William. She could not help herself. She felt trapped like an exotic bird in a gilded cage: she complained at being surrounded by a family that prized candour and facts above romantic fantasies; that spoke in loud voices; that had raised cynicism to an art form. William lost his passion and became dull prose, while Caroline longed for poetry.

She later poured out her feelings as the heroine in her novel *Glenarvon*:

> What talents she had were of a sort they could not appreciate; and all the defects were those which they most despised. The refinement, the romance, the sentiment she had imbibed appeared in their eyes assumed and unnatural; her strict opinions perfectly ridiculous; her enthusiasm absolute insanity; and the violence of her temper, if contradicted or opposed, the pettishness of a spoiled and wayward child.

She may have publicly flirted with Webster to fire William's passion, but that tactic could never have worked. He was too placid for such tricks; he expected the affair with Webster to burn itself out, and other men to act as honourably as he would. He naively told Lady Elizabeth Foster that 'if he felt a growing passion for his friend's wife he would fly to the further end of the earth to resist the danger'.[22]

Bess Foster's son Augustus, who had secretly admired Caroline, thought William Lamb should share the blame. He wrote to his mother: 'I must say I think her husband is a great deal to blame, for, had he studied a little more Shakespeare's *Taming of the Shrew*, he might have checked her at least so as to prevent such dreadful and shameful excesses in a disposition not naturally wicked.'[23]

Caroline dramatically swore on her knees before God to Lady Melbourne she would never repeat her betrayal of her husband and his family, but she was about to do it all again, this time with a lion of English Romanticism: George Gordon Byron, the sixth Baron Byron.

15

Byron

The sixth baron Byron literally stumbled into the lives of the Melbournes in 1812 when Lady Caroline Lamb was hosting a morning dancing party in the first-floor drawing room at Melbourne House in Whitehall.

Lord Byron, whose left leg was one-and-a-half inches longer than the right,[1] tripped on the red carpet on his way up the grand staircase to the reception. 'I remember in going upstairs I stumbled and remarked to Moore [Thomas Moore, Byron's friend and biographer], who accompanied me, that it was a bad omen. I ought to have taken the warning.'[2]

When Byron reached the top of the stairs he was welcomed by Caroline with open arms. A small orchestra was playing a lilting melody in triple time beyond the twin doors of the drawing room, where her friends Emily, 'Hart' and Lady Jersey were practising their steps for the latest craze from Vienna.

Byron, like the waltz, had taken London by storm. His epic poem *Childe Harold's Pilgrimage* had made him an overnight literary star among the ladies of Georgian society like Lady Caroline, with its combination of despair, contempt and modern political satire. 'I awoke one morning and found myself famous,' he said.

It is difficult to over-estimate the impact his verses had on the small enclosed society that had a hand in running the country. Everyone was versifying, politicians and their mistresses, young men and their adoring girlfriends, all turned everyday events into poetical offerings to impress their friends. Lady Melbourne's correspondence is full of bad verse from her sons and their lovers, though she rarely resorted to couplets herself.

For Caroline it was like having a rock star arriving at her house party; she was the Regency equivalent of a groupie. She guided the poet into the ballroom to introduce him to an adoring audience of middle-aged and younger ladies, and their jealous, sceptical men.

Lady Melbourne's society friends who strained their necks to see the poet included Lady Jersey, Lady Holland, Lady Kinnaird and Mrs George Lamb, the Duke of Devonshire's illegitimate daughter, Caroline St Jules, who had married Lady Melbourne's son George by the Prince of Wales.

Byron had a high forehead, a mane of black curly hair, and wore a very narrow white Sarsnet cravat with the shirt collar falling over it. He was closely observed by Caroline's niece, Annabella Milbanke, who sat along the side of the ballroom hardly noticed by anyone, except the poet who claimed she caught his eye. 'His face was void of colour, he wore no whiskers. His eyes were grey fringed with long black lashes; and his air was imposing, but rather supercilious,' Annabella wrote to her mother.

> His mouth continually betrays the acrimony of his spirit. I should judge him sincere and independent – sincere at least in society as far as he can be whilst dissimulating the violence of his scorn. He very often hides his mouth with his hand when speaking. He professed himself partial to Music … It appeared to me that he tried to control his natural sarcasm and vehemence as much as he could in order not to offend but at times his lips thickened with disdain, and his eyes rolled impatiently. Indeed the scene was calculated to shew human absurdities. There was the listless gaiety which so surely bespeaks the absence of enjoyment. Waltzing in vain attempted to give animation.[3]

Caroline wanted to meet Byron immediately after reading an advance copy of *Childe Harold's Pilgrimage* by Samuel Rogers who was used by his publisher John Murray to promote the book by word of mouth among opinion-formers in Georgian high society.

'I heard nothing of him till one day Rogers (for he, Moore and Spencer were all my lovers and wrote me up to the skies – I was in the clouds) said, "You should know the new poet," and he offered me the MS of *Childe Harold* to read. I read it and that was enough,' Caroline later recalled.[4]

Caroline asked Rogers for an introduction to the poet, but he was swamped by similar requests. 'Rogers said, "He has a club-foot, and bites his nails." I said, "If he was as ugly as Aesop I must know him."'

'Hart', the Duke of Devonshire's son, wanted dancing parties but had banned entertainment from the Devonshires' London house in July 1811 for a year of mourning for his late father, so helped to throw them at Melbourne House instead. Caroline said: 'So we had them in the great drawing-room at

Whitehall. All the *bon ton* assembled there continually. There was nothing so fashionable.'[5]

Years later Caroline recalled to a journalist:

> You may imagine what forty or fifty people dancing from 12 in the morning until near dinner time all young gay and noisy were – in the evenings we either had opposition suppers or went out to Balls and routs – was the life I then led when Moore and Rogers introduced Byron to me...
>
> What you say of his falling upstairs and of Miss Milbanke is all true. Lord Byron three days after this brought me a rose and carnation and used the very words I mentioned in *Glenarvon* – with a half-sarcastic smile saying: 'Your Ladyship I am told likes all that is new and rare for a moment.' I have them still.[6]

Caroline was unaware Byron hated the new dance largely because, with his shortened left leg, he could not waltz elegantly. He wrote a satirical poem *The Waltz* anonymously to condemn it. The dance which now appears so graceful seemed shocking to older Georgian eyes and came to symbolise both the elegance and the decadence associated with the new age of the Regency, presided over by the dissolute Prince George. It allowed partners to get close and personal for the first time; country-dances had never been so 'voluptuous', Byron complained. It brought out a rare bout of prudery in the poet:

> Waltz – Waltz – alone both arms and legs demands,
> Liberal of feet – and lavish of her hands;
> Hands which may freely range in public sight,
> Where ne'er before – but – pray "put out the light".

Byron put an unerring finger on its sexual attraction:

> To You, ye single gentlemen, who seek
> Torments for life, or pleasures for a week
> As Love or Hymen your endeavours guide
> To gain your own, or snatch another's bride...

And he described how loose Regency gowns enabled men to seek their pleasure of ladies without the obstacle of laced corsets:

> No treacherous powder bids Conjecture quake
> No stiff-starched stays make meddling fingers ache.

Byron also mocked the appeal of the waltz because of its novelty, like the new Prince Regent. The Regency period officially began on 5 February 1811 when Prince George took over the reins of power from his father. The king had been pushed into a final bout of madness by the death of his beloved youngest daughter, Princess Amelia from tuberculosis on 2 November 1810. The next day, he was strapped in a straitjacket and Prince George began measuring up for a new outfit to match his newly exalted position.

Lady Melbourne and her Whig friends expected the prince to replace the Tory Spencer Perceval's government with a Whig administration when he became Regent. The Whigs were so confident they had already shared out the Cabinet posts, amid the usual bickering: Grenville would be Prime Minister for a second term; and Charles Grey, Lord Howick, would be Foreign Secretary. However, they were bitterly disappointed when the Prince Regent refused, despite Lady Melbourne's best efforts to persuade the prince to stand by his Whig allies.[7]

The Regency has often been called the Age of Elegance, but it was in truth the Age of Unrest. There were riots in London at the rising price of bread and there were violent protests in the countryside at ingenious machines that were taking the jobs of skilled weavers and spinners. The poor were being driven off the fields by landowners using enclosure Acts and forced to scratch a living in the industrial towns that were growing across the north. The 'peasant poet' John Clare cried out for the lost common land in these lines from *The Fallen Elm*: 'Thus came enclosure – ruin was its guide…'

Lord Byron used his maiden speech in the House of Lords on 27 February 1812 to denounce a bill that made frame breaking a capital offence. He defended Nottinghamshire weavers, who claimed to follow King Ludd and were known as Luddites. They were facing the death penalty for breaking weaving frames. Byron saluted them in a song:

> As the Liberty lads o'er the sea
> Bought their freedom, and cheaply, with blood
> So we boys we will die fighting or live free
> And down with all kings but King Ludd!

Byron warned the wealthy aristocrats in the Lords whose textile mills were being targeted, the protestors they proposed to hang were 'the mob that labour in your fields and in your houses – that man your navy and recruit your army – that have enabled you to defy all the world and can also defy you when neglect and calamity have driven them to despair. You may call the people a mob but do not forget that a mob too often speaks the sentiments of the people.'

His words fell on deaf ears. The law was passed. Caroline agreed with Byron but got little sympathy from Lady Melbourne or William Lamb who voted with the Tories for increasingly repressive measures against the troublemakers.

The Prince Regent ignored public appeals for help and appeared determined to outdo Louis XVI in his careless extravagance. The Prince Regent brought back Lord Melbourne to the post of Lord of the Bedchamber and celebrated his inauguration in June 1812 with a lavish fete at Carlton House. Lord and Lady Melbourne were among 2,000 guests invited to attend the Prince's party of the decade.

The Prince Regent was dressed for the occasion in the uniform of a field marshal, a rank from which his father had always disbarred him, with the Order of the Garter and a glittering aigrette. No expense was spared. Marquees were erected on the gardens of Carlton House for a sumptuous banquet. Small gold and silvery fish swam in an artificial stream that ran along the centre of the top table in the prince's Gothic conservatory.

Carlton House was open to the public and on the last day the crush was so great ladies fainted. 'Four females were found on their backs in a lifeless state on the ground with their clothes almost completely torn off,' said one account. *The Morning Chronicle* reported: 'The number of stray shoes in the court yard was so great they filled a large tub from which the shoeless ladies were invited to select their lost property.'[8]

When they got inside Carlton House, guests marvelled at the magnificence of the décor. With Lady Melbourne's guidance, the Prince Regent splashed out huge sums on refurbishing at Carlton House in a style fit for the new age of the Regency – £260,000 on furniture, £49,000 on upholstery, £23,000 on plate. He spent £60,000 on a silver-gilt dinner service to rival one supplied to the Emperor Napoleon by the Sèvres factory in France; it is still in use for royal banquets today.

Outside in the streets of London, there were bread riots. Byron's reflections on wasted youth, the disillusionment of a generation with revolutionary wars and imperialists, set against the backdrop of exotic foreign travel, glowering summits, cascades, ruins, all overlaid by Romantic pessimism chimed precisely with Caro's own fashionable passion for tragic verse.

Byron's scepticism about the glory of war also echoed perfectly Caroline's view after hearing her brother Frederick Cavendish Ponsonby, a hero of

Talavera, castigating the Spanish for failing to support British forces in the action. Byron's anti-war message in *Childe Harold* struck home:

> Three hosts combine to offer sacrifice
> Three tongues prefer strange orisons on high;
> Three gaudy standards flout the pale blue skies
> The shouts are France, Spain, Albion, Victory!
> The foe, the victim, and the fond ally
> That fights for all but ever fights in vain
> Are met – as if at home they could not die –
> To feed the crow on Talavera's plain
> And fertilize the field that each pretends to gain
> There shall they rot – Ambition's honour'd fools'
> Yes, Honour decks the turf that wraps their clay!
> Vain Sophistry![9]

His epic tale was based on Byron's travels through the wilder parts of Portugal, Spain, Albania, Greece and Turkey with John Cam Hobhouse, who he had met at university. Byron offered a far more intoxicating drug than anything the crass Sir Godfrey Webster could give Caroline. His natural melancholy mixed with lordly disdain for convention, the hypocrisy of society, and his lonely raptures found an echo deep in Caroline's heart. Said Torrens:

The fascination wrought upon her susceptible and credulous fancy by his account of his youth and foreign adventures, his dark hints at the hidden griefs, the sorrows of his loneliness, the pain of early disappointments, and his real or pretended indifference to passing success; the ever changing beauty of his features and the glittering splendour of his verse; and all these laid with a look and tone of ineffable gallantry at her feet by one whose nobility dated from the Conquest, fairly bewildered her.[10]

Caroline wrote anonymously to the poet on 9 March six days after reading the first two cantos of *Childe Harold*. She said his book was 'beautiful' but cautioned him not to throw his talents away in gloom and regrets for the past 'and above all live here in your own Country which will be proud of you'. Who better to guide the inexperienced author than herself? He was twenty-four and she was twenty-seven.

Within forty-eight hours, she unmasked herself and sent him another letter, this time signed, with her own lines:

> Oh that like Childe Harold I had power
> With master hand to strike the thrilling Lyre
> To sing of Courts and Camps and Ladies Bower
> And cheer the sameness of each passing hour…

She told him to leave a reply for her at Hookhams bookshop in Old Bond Street and when that failed, she went to meet him at a ball hosted by Lady Westmoreland who had met Byron in Italy and introduced him to London society; but he was surrounded by female admirers and she turned on her heel and left. His curiosity was aroused by this and he conspired with Lady Holland to meet her at Holland House.

'I was sitting with Lord and Lady Holland when he was announced,' she recalled. 'Lady Holland said, "I must present Lord Byron to you." Lord Byron said, "That offer was made to you before; may I ask why you rejected it?" He begged permission to come and see me.'

He did so the next day at Melbourne House. 'Rogers and Moore were standing by me; I was on the sofa. I had just come in from riding; I was filthy and heated.'

There was an immediate frisson of sexual attraction between Caroline in her tight riding jacket, still hot and dusty from her ride, and the cool, pale-faced Romantic poet. 'When Lord Byron was announced, I flew out of the room to wash myself. When I returned, Rogers said, "Lord Byron you are a happy man. Lady Caroline has been sitting here in all her dirt with us, but when you were announced she flew to beautify herself."'

Caroline confided in her journal: 'That beautiful pale face is my fate.' Perhaps her face was his fate; she was boyish, with blonde curls so reminiscent of John Edelston, a choirboy with whom he fell in love at Cambridge. Byron's cool demeanour was a pose. He adopted the lordly air of the socially detached aristocrat as a front. 'No one could have been less detached,' said Lord David Cecil. 'By nature acutely sensitive to the opinion of others, his confidence had been early undermined by his lame leg, his bullying drunken mother and the poverty-stricken and provincial circumstances of his childhood. A gnawing, resentful mistrust of all men, and more especially of women, warred continuously in his breast with an obsessing desire to make an impression on anyone by any means. There was nothing he would not do to score a hit or avoid a humiliation.'[11]

Byron had a love-hate relationship with his mother, the Scottish heiress Lady Catherine Gordon, after his father, a soldier called 'Mad Jack' Byron, had deserted her. He became very close – too close – to his half-sister Augusta who was born five years earlier to Byron's father and his first wife, the former Marchioness of Carmarthen.

Lord Byron told Caroline he wished to come and see her again at eight o'clock when she was alone. That was her dinner hour, and she agreed. 'From that moment, for more than nine months, he almost lived at Melbourne House,' said Lady Caroline.

Caroline tried to reconcile her love for her husband William with her infatuation for Byron in some lines she sent the poet: 'Strong love I feel for one I shall not name – What I should feel for thee could never be the same – But Admiration interest is free – And that *Childe Harold* may receive from me.'

Admiration was never going to be enough for the headstrong Caroline. Despite all the tortured protestations to Lady Melbourne after her affair with Sir Godfrey Webster that she would change her ways and play the faithful wife to William – 'the one I shall not name' – she was set on a passionate love affair with Byron.

Through the summer of 1812, Caroline and Byron flaunted their affair across the ballrooms and drawing rooms of London. Caroline was constantly by his side; they spent hours upstairs together at Melbourne House. Caroline's androgynous looks appealed to Byron. She became notorious for dressing as a boy in a plumed hat and tight scarlet breeches with a scarlet and silver-laced hussar jacket. She disguised herself as one of her own pages to visit Byron incognito at his private rooms in St James's Street where they could indulge their passions.

Caroline liked to affirm her love affairs with heated rows, and they had fiery lovers' tiffs. They rowed about Caroline's love of waltzing, which she claimed he banned; and they rowed about Byron going to watch the public execution of John Bellingham, the deranged tradesman who assassinated the Prime Minister Spencer Perceval with a pistol in the Commons. Caroline was against capital punishment and was appalled he should have witnessed the hanging.

They argued and patched things up by making love. Byron told his biographer, Thomas Medwin: 'One was made up in a very odd way and without any verbal explanation. She will remember it.' It was unclear what Byron was hinting at, but it led to speculation he had broken a taboo by forcing her to have anal sex.[12] By the time the summer of 1812 was over, the love affair had burned itself out, at least as far as Byron was concerned, and he wanted to find a way to end it. Being pursued by Caroline, he said, was like being 'pursued by a skeleton'. Torrens said the reason for their break-up was that they were too alike. She would upbraid Byron for being like the rest of his sex, 'too self-engrossed' but that charge could be applied equally to Caroline.

It was said of Byron his 'overweening egotism' needed to be gratified by special recognition in the glittering throng but Caroline also liked to show off. She prided herself on her writing and believed she was a collaborator, not a follower of Byron; she so closely associated herself with her hero, she convinced herself they were twin souls; but her verse never matched Byron's. Her voice was light and musical and compared to Byron's grandiloquence, said Torrens, Caroline's verse was like the 'tinkling of lyric bells'.

Her passion for Byron was unquenchable: 'Byron loved me as never woman was loved ... we went about everywhere together and were at last invited always as if we had been married. It was a strange scene but it was not vanity misled me. I grew to love him better than virtue, Religion ... He broke my heart & still I love him.' Caroline would not let him go so easily as he wished.

Hobhouse was in Byron's rooms at 8 St James's Street when Caroline arrived disguised in a great coat over a page's outfit. She said she had come to elope with Byron and when Hobhouse objected, she melodramatically tried to seize a court sword that was lying on a sofa and said 'blood will be spent'. She was persuaded to go, and left feeling more confused and broken than ever. She later blamed Byron for destroying her happiness. Until he stumbled into her life, she said she had been 'the happiest and gayest of human beings I do believe without exception – *I had married for love* and love the most romantic and ardent ... My husband and I were so fond of each other that false as I too soon proved he never would part with me.'

She was conveniently forgetting she had already had an affair with Sir Godfrey Webster when she was introduced to Byron.

A fortnight after bursting into his rooms, Caroline sent Byron a love letter on 9 August 1812 with a contribution for the collection of locks of hair she knew he kept from his former lovers.

Caroline's donation to his collection of lovers' locks was like none of his other trophies – she sent him some curls of her pubic hair. They were bloodied because she had cut herself by trimming too close with her scissors. She attached a letter asking Byron to send her some of his hair, but not 'those hairs':

I ask'd you not to send blood but Yet do – because if it means love I like to have it. I cut the hair too close and bled much more than you need – do not you the same o pray put not scissors points near where *quei capelli* [those hairs] grow – sooner take it from the arm or wrist – pray be careful & Byron, tell me why a few conversations with the Queen Mothers [Lady Melbourne and Lady Bessborough] always change you.[13]

She added a note in lovers' code declaring she was his wife: 'Caroline Byron – next to Thyrsa Dearest & most faithful – God bless you own love – *ricordati di Biondetta* [remember Biondetta] from your wild Antelope.'

'*Biondetta*' was a reference to Cazotte's *Le diable amoureux, the Devil in Love*, in which a Spanish nobleman is seduced by the Devil disguised as *Biondetta*, a fair-haired female dressed as a page. It was a theme to which she frequently returned in her 'commonplace book' of jottings and thoughts, now held in the John Murray Archive.

Byron and Caroline exchanged many notes about Dante's *Inferno* and this may have had a sinister meaning for her disenchanted lover: 'Remember Biondetta – she turned into a Devil.' Caroline pledged: 'I will kneel and be torn from your feet before I will give you up – or sooner be parted with.'

Caroline again broke into Byron's rooms and scrawled 'Remember Me!' in the flyleaf of one of Byron's books. He retorted in verse with a famous put-down:

> Remember thee! Aye, doubt it not.
> Thy husband too shall think of thee!
> By neither shalt thou be forgot,
> Thou false to him, thou fiend to me…

In 1812, William Lamb saw his life and his political career in ruins along with his marriage. William was undoubtedly suffering from depression brought on by the stress of his wife's scandalous affairs and the daily gossiping behind his back at the Commons, but it would be wrong to blame it all on Byron. Even before Byron tripped into their lives, William complained about being overcome by a strange lethargy which he said unmanned him when he came to speak in the Commons chamber: 'I can walk in the shrubbery here at Brocket Hall and reason and enlarge upon almost any topic but in the House of Commons, whether it be from apprehension or heat, or long waiting, or the tediousness of much of what I hear, a torpor of all my faculties almost always comes upon me, and I feel as if I had neither ideas nor opinion even upon the subjects which interest me most deeply.'[14]

He had all the attributes to be a rising political star, but something held him back. He had started out with the generous support of Charles James Fox but proceeded to squander his contacts in the Whig party that had been so assiduously built up by his mother. She was dismayed by his carelessness about his political career.

She was indignant when he refused to put himself forward for the Hertford vacancy caused by Pen's death and she was furious when it was snapped up by Cecil's Tory candidate, Baker. Lord Melbourne had stumped up 2,000 guineas for William to take Lord Kinnaird's seat at Leominster in 1805 but he quickly had to find another at Haddington Burghs at the election in 1806. A year later, Lord Melbourne purchased an Irish seat at Portarlington for William that cost him £5,000. It lasted until 1812 when a general election was called following the assassination of Spencer Perceval.

William had expected high office to come to him, but had alienated many of his mother's friends. He could not ask Lord Melbourne for more money and he failed through a combination of his own vanity and lack of funds to find a seat. Lady Melbourne, Lady Holland and William's mother-in-law, Lady Bessborough, urgently pressed the Whig grandees to find William a seat at Peterborough where the Lambs had influence or St Albans, Lady Spencer's home; but it was in vain. In February 1812, he turned down the offer by the Prince of Wales of a place as a Treasury minister his mother had clearly engineered. Lord Grey, an intimate friend of his mother for years, did nothing for him, believing William was a Canningite, leading William to accuse Grey of having a 'sly suspicious' attitude towards him.

Part of William's problem, politically and romantically, was that he was too tolerant both towards his wife and his politics. He was so excessively moderate his allies did not know what he stood for. He set out his moderate creed to his mother: 'Toleration is the only good and first principle, and toleration for every opinion that can possibly be formed.'

When he lost his seat, it brought him close to despair. William wrote to his mother in September 1812 that losing his Commons seat was killing him: 'It is actually cutting my throat – it is depriving me of the great object of my life at the moment…'

He was writing from Lismore, the Duke of Devonshire's stately home in Ireland, where he had gone with Caroline for some respite from the publicity surrounding her affair with Byron. His letter reveals Lord Melbourne had already been forced to sell more of his estates to fund their expenditure. William complained: 'I have no money. I am embarrassed to a certain degree by circumstances which I am willing to explain. My income is insufficient … I cannot expect my Father to bear the whole burthen [and] I do not know whether I could justify to myself the suffering a further debt to be accumulated upon my account, which must in the end lead to serious embarrassment and to the further dismemberment of the property.' He added: 'These are the opinions which have led me to form a resolution which I do not name too strongly when I call it my public ruin.' The candle had burned low, and his letter ends in a whimper: 'I write in the dark so cannot add any more at present. Yours ever affectedly and affectionately, Wm Lamb.' William added a warning in a postscript to his mother urging her not to trust the Irish post on the subject of Caroline. 'Pray be cautious how far you put anything upon paper about it. Word of mouth is better.'[15]

Lady Melbourne passed his letter to Lady Holland, who had asked whether there was anything that could be done for William. Lady Melbourne told her: 'Now my opinion is that this is *nonsense*.'

It came as a bitter double-blow to Lady Melbourne to see all her hopes for her favourite son – his marriage and his political career – being ruined by his own indolence. Even the Prince of Wales appeared to have abandoned the Whigs. And she still had the problem of Caroline.

16

Lady M's Unlikely Lover

Caro was in a black mood when her mother called at Melbourne House in Whitehall on a hot Wednesday, 12 August 1812, to collect her for a family trip to the Bessborough estates in Ireland. In Caro's tortured mind, she had convinced herself her lover Lord Byron was ready to elope with her and she was distraught at being taken away from him.

Lord Melbourne, who never understood this highly-strung irritant in his household, lost his temper with Caroline when he encountered her in the drawing room on the first floor of Melbourne House. He had wished for a long time he could throw her out of his house; now he gave vent to his feelings. Caroline screamed back at Lord Melbourne saying she would go to Byron. Lord Melbourne bitterly retorted Byron would not have her. Her mother, Harriet, Lady Bessborough was appalled. 'She answered so rudely, so disrespectfully, that I was frightened,' said Lady Bessborough.

Lady Bessborough ran down the wide semi-circular staircase to call Lady Melbourne who was in the Melbournes' suite of rooms below stairs. 'We returned instantly together, but met Lord Melbourne on the stair, pale as death and screaming to the Porter to stop Caroline. It was in vain. She had disappeared in a moment, too quick for the servants who ran out after her to guess which way she had turned.'[1]

Lady Bessborough drove up and down Parliament Street anxiously searching the streets in vain for her daughter but they returned to Melbourne House convinced that once her anger had subsided Caro would return.

Lord Melbourne then admitted that Caroline had shouted she would go off with Lord Byron. Melbourne angrily told her to go to Byron and be damned, adding Byron would not take her. That is when she ran out of the house.

Armed with that information, Lady Melbourne and Lady Bessborough took Lady Melbourne's carriage to Lord Byron's rooms at 8 St James's Street.

'We went, Lady Melbourne and I, immediately there but found him as much astonished and as much frightened when we heard it as we were. He promised to restore her if she was to be found and kept his word. Meanwhile I drove or walked to every place I could think possible she should be at,' said Lady Bessborough.

Lady Bessborough sent an anguished note to her lover Lord Granville: 'Oh G., Caroline is gone. It is too horrible. She is not with Lord Byron, but where she is God knows.'

Later that night, she sent another longer note to Granville telling the whole dramatic story. She had promised to dine at nine pm with 'Hart' at Devonshire House. He was now the Duke of Devonshire, having succeeded his father in 1811. Harriet was quite exhausted, but hoped 'as he had seen her in the morning he might give me some idea to find her'. Hart, who had been secretly in love with Caro, disappointed his aunt. He had no idea where she was.

While they were dining, they received a note from Byron saying he had discovered where Caroline had gone and was following her. He said Caro had handed a note to Byron's servant with instructions to inform him that she had left a letter for him at her family home, 2 Cavendish Square. It was attached to a packet of letters to her mother explaining her reasons for running away. Byron dashed to Cavendish Square and found a letter from Caroline saying she was planning to go to Portsmouth and embark on the first vessel that sailed, wherever it might take her. Caroline may have thought that by taking the initiative she could force Byron to elope with her – otherwise, why would she have left him the letter?

Byron still did not know exactly where she was but found out Caroline had run up Pall Mall at noon, when it was busy, and stopped a Hackney carriage. Lord Byron tracked down the driver. 'Lord Byron, by following, threatening and bribing the Hackney coachman, at length prevailed upon him to carry him to where she was,' said Lady Bessborough.

Byron learned Caroline had ordered the driver to take her through the first turnpike out of London, where the cobbles ended, beyond Hyde Park to Holland House. There she borrowed twenty guineas on a fine opal ring she frequently wore to pay for her escape. The Hackney carriage driver then took her to a chemist's shop in nearby Kensington. The coachman took Byron to the chemist's shop in Kensington, where he found Caroline was hiding pending her flight to the coast. She had told the owners that she was running away from friends and would never return to them. Byron forced his way in, telling the owners he was her brother and took her back by carriage to her mother's house at Cavendish Square.

Lady Bessborough was so traumatised she could hardly speak and said she was mortified to admit that it was more by Byron's persuasion than hers that Caroline was induced to return home with her to the Melbourne House in Whitehall.

'I went in before her and William most kindly promised to receive and forgive her. The Melbournes too, were very good, and she seemed much touched by their reception. But how long will it last?'

The stress on Caroline's mother was so great that Lady Bessborough had a seizure in the coach on her return to Cavendish Square. Mrs Peterson, Lady Bessborough's maid, was so appalled, she wrote immediately to Lady Melbourne to tell her that when Lady Bessborough's carriage arrived they found her ladyship 'at the bottom of the carriage in a fit' and it was with 'great difficulty the footmen got her out'. She almost certainly had suffered a mild stroke. Her maid said: 'Oh Madam think of my Horror when I saw her poor mouth all on one side and her face as cold as marble – we was all distracted – she continued senseless for a length of time. We got Mr Walker [a doctor] and thank God she by degrees got better.'[2]

The trauma of the day's events left Lady Bessborough coughing up blood from an old throat condition that had alarmed her family in the past. She thought she must have broken a little vein in her throat and was so downcast, she wanted to die. She told Granville: 'Why was it not a large one? I do no good to any one, and am grown rather a burthen than pleasure to all those I love most.'

Mrs Peterson was so indignant she wrote to Lady Caroline and accused her of 'cruel and unnatural' behaviour towards her mother: 'Surely you do not wish to be the Death of your Mother … Even her footmen cryed out Shame on you for alas you have exposed yourself to all London you are the talk of every Groom and footman about the Town. A few months ago it was Sir Godfrey & now another has turned your Head and made you forget what a Husband you have what an angel Child besides making you torture all your kind relations & friends in the most cruel manner.'

With her servants turning against Caroline, Lady Bessborough dreaded that the story would get out. 'What an escape!' Lady Bessborough exclaimed in her letter to Lord Granville. 'She had taken a place in a stage [a stagecoach]. G. Dear G., all this will end ill; if it does not to her, it will to me.'

When the dust settled, Lady Bessborough bravely went on with her mission to take Caroline to Ireland with Lord Bessborough and William despite her own illness.

In London, Lord Byron discovered he had a supporter from the most unlikely source – the mother of the man he had cuckolded, Lady Melbourne. Her motive was the same as Byron's: she wanted to break Caroline's obsession with Byron to save William's marriage, and would do anything to achieve it. Byron and Lady Melbourne began an exchange of letters that has left a remarkably detailed and intimate picture of their life and times – and their intrigues together. Invariably, Byron addressed her in his letters as 'Lady M'.

Byron produced an unexpected late flowering of Lady Melbourne's sexual life. She was sixty-one but still capable of arousing the twenty-four-year-old poet. She was suffering gout and rheumatism in her knees, but they exchanged notes like lovers in the first flush of youthful passion; they went to the theatre together; he flirted outrageously: 'Why won't you go off with me? I am sure our elopement would cause a 'greater sensation' … than any event since Eve ran away with the Apple.'

In September 1812, while Caro was away with the Bessboroughs, Lord Byron joined the Melbournes, the Jerseys, the Cowpers and the Hollands for a convivial week at Cheltenham, the elegant spa town that had become a fashionable watering hole.

Lord Byron, who was a guest of Lord and Lady Holland, stayed on when the others left and on 13 September he wrote a confessional letter to Lady M. He complained Cheltenham was a 'desart' without her. Then he told Lady Melbourne that Lady Bessborough was to blame for the affair with Caroline:

> Poor Lady Bessborough! … I must let you into one little secret – her folly half did this. At the commencement she piqued that 'vanity' (which it would be the vainest thing in the world to deny) by telling me she was certain I was not beloved 'that I was only led on for the sake of &c.,' This raised a devil between us … I made no answer but determined not to pursue for pursuit it was not – but to sit still and in a week after I was convinced – not that [Caroline] loved me for I do not believe in the existence of what is called Love – but that any other man in my situation would have believed that he was loved.

He told Lady M if she would help him play his part he could be free of Caroline by December because he had taken a fancy to another member of her family, Annabella Milbanke. Anne Isabella Milbanke, known by the family as Annabella, was Lady Melbourne's niece. She was the twenty-year-old daughter of Lady Melbourne's brother Sir Ralph Milbanke, the sixth baronet, and his feisty wife Judith Noel, daughter of Sir Edward Noel of Kirkby Mallory in the Midlands, the first Viscount Wentworth.

Now, my dear Lady M., you are all out as to my real sentiments. I was, am and shall be, I fear, attached to another, one to whom I have never said much, but have never lost sight of, and the whole of this interlude has been the result of circumstances which it may be too late to regret…there was and is one whom I wished to marry, had not this affair intervened… As I have said so much, I may as well say all. The woman I mean is Miss Milbanke…

Now, my dear Lady M., I am completely in your power.[3]

From that moment on, they became co-conspirators to destroy Caroline's love for the poet by encouraging the match between Annabella and Lord Byron. But in forming their conspiracy, as improbable as it seemed, they lit the flame for their own affair.

In September 1812, just a month after receiving Caroline's cutting of her pubic hair, Byron told her mother-in-law he admired her 'as much as ever you were admired'.

In reply, Lady M tells Byron it would be a 'catastrophe' were they to become *de facto* lovers (though she does not rule it out):

You say, "I admire you certainly as much as ever you were admired" & a great deal more I assure than ever I was admired in ye same way. I may have been beloved – but Love is not admiration – Lovers admire of course without knowing why – Yours therefore is much <u>more flattering</u> as I said the other day – but you quite astonished me when I found your usual playfulness chang'd into such a formal <u>tirade</u> –I have hardly yet recover'd my Surprise – now I have told you every thing and have shewn myself to you. I can not see why you should wish that you had not known me – it can not lead to any regrets, unless circumstances should not stop it entirely our Friendship will be very pleasant to both as any sentiment must be where all is sunshine – and Where love does not introduce itself there can be no jealousies, torments and quarrels – & should this catastrophe take place, it will at least to me, always be a pleasing recollection, that we should have been good friends.

He insisted she was not like other women; she was supreme among her sex. Lady Melbourne's letter shows the wisdom of her years in its caution, but it also betrays how she was won over by his flattery:

What high flown compliments you have paid me, for Heavens sake lower me to my proper level, or I shall be quite alarm'd when I see you again.

I shall neither dare Speak before you, nor to you and as to talking my usual nonsense that must be quite out of the question, as I shall soon drop from this Pinnacle where you have placed me – do let me down easily that I may not break my Bones by a sudden fall; what can you have in yr Head, 'Men of distinguished abilities' *ce sont des Hommes comme les autres* [they are Men like the others] and I am a Woman, *comme les autres* [like the others], Superior in nothing – I happen fortunately to be gifted with a fund of good Nature and cheerfulness, and very great Spirits – and have a little more tact than my Neighbours, and people call me pleasant because I am always inclined in conversation to enter into the Subjects that seem most adapted to the taste of those with whom I happen to be – when they are not too high for aspiration.[4]

This was the same day that William wrote his letter of despair to his mother from Ireland. She reacted to Byron's letter like a coquettish young girl and showed little sympathy for her son's self-indulgence.

Lady M became enamoured with Lord Byron, despite all his faults, or perhaps because of them. Caroline claims she coined the description 'mad, bad and dangerous to know' about Byron but he was also fun, gay and disarmingly witty. He and Lady M shared a cynical view of the world, and formed a conspiratorial bond in scheming to end Caroline's pursuit of Byron.

Lady Melbourne assured Byron in her letter on 29 September 1812 she would give him the 'earliest intelligence in my power' of Caroline's return from Ireland. She added: 'I think you attach too much blame to yourself – she was no Novice and tho' I give her credit for being what one must believe, every Heroine of a Romance to be, yet she knew to be upon her guard & can not be looked upon as the Victim of a designing man.'

This was music to Byron's ears. She added a word of advice as a friend: he should ditch Caroline before launching his assault on Annabella: 'Do you think you can manage both her and C. [Caroline] – impossible!'

As she folded her letter to send it, Lady Melbourne's servant brought her two letters from Caroline in Ireland. Lady Melbourne added a postscript to Byron saying Caroline was playing her false by trying to act upon her feelings 'to make me tell her something about you. *This I shall not do* ... She desires me to tell her whether I have heard from you since I left Cheltenham. Perhaps she may have ask'd you the same question – let us be in the same story. I shall give her no answer till I hear from you or see you, therefore decide what we shall say.'

Lady M said she did not wish to hurt Caroline, but she could not be reasoned with while she was 'in this consistent state of imbalance ... if she thought her friends cared less she would be more likely to take some other Fancy – the result of all this seems to me that ye best thing you can do is <u>to marry</u> & that in fact you can get out of this Scrape by no other means'.[5]

Lady Melbourne's critics particularly in the Noel family believe her actions towards Annabella from this moment on show Lady Melbourne to have been a monster. Biographer Malcolm Elwin in his meticulous life of Annabella defends Lady Melbourne against the charge of being as bad as Mistress Overdone, the bawd in Shakespeare's *Measure for Measure*, saying it was reasonable for Annabella's aunt to inquire if she felt inclined to accept Byron after he declared his preference for her.[6] I would not be so kind to Lady Melbourne. She conspired with Byron to encourage his marriage to Annabella despite knowing all that she did about Byron. Her motive was to protect her own son; it had little to do with Annabella or her happiness. That is why Annabella concluded with some justification she had been infamously wronged by her aunt.

Lady Melbourne kept out of the way of the younger generation who were now invited to Melbourne House by her sons by going 'below stairs', occupying the ground-floor rooms with her husband. On 6 November 1812 Byron wrote to Lady M asking for permission to visit her in her inner sanctum: 'I presume that I may have access to the lower regions of Melbourne House from which my ascent [to Lady Caroline's rooms] has long excluded me.'[7]

It was around this time that Byron and Elizabeth exchanged rings like lovers – Byron wrote to 'Dear Lady M': 'You have long ago forgotten a certain ring [for] which I am still in your debt and I hope you will not reject the only thing I ever dared to present you, nor violate the conditions on which I accepted your own by refusing this.'[8]

Byron hinted to John Murray, his publisher, that he had been tempted but never consummated his love for Lady Melbourne: 'To Lady Melbourne I write with most pleasure – and her answers, so sensible, so *tactique* – I never met with half her talent. If she had been a few years a younger, what a fool she would have made of me had she thought it worth her while – and I should have lost a most valuable and agreeable friend.'

Caroline later wrote a despairing letter to Byron that suggests she believed he and Lady Melbourne *were* lovers:

> How many angry looks from Lady M. how many frowns will be my fate – & perhaps from you – the mouth will be turned with its corners to the ground – however I cannot be worse off as someone said when they were in the Pillory ... Think of my situation how extraordinary! – My mother

in Law actually in the place I held – her ring instead of mine – her letters instead of mine – her heart – but do you believe whether she or any others feel for you what I felt … I literally saw nothing but your ear for a whole hour one night – it is perfectly unlike any ear in nature & … requires a Chapter to itself.[9]

Annabella's mother, Judith Noel later claimed Lord Byron boasted of being Lady Melbourne's lover at the same time as Caroline Lamb:

If Lord B is to be believed, he was at that time carrying on a criminal connection with Lady M. as well as with Lady C. L. [Caroline Lamb]…

Ld – [Byron said] that in 1813 he had absolute criminal Connection with an old Lady at the same time as with her Daughter in Law – that 'She absolutely proposed it to him and that he said, 'She [was] so old he hardly knew how to set about it.' Lord B told this also to his Sister – this explains much, which was before inexplicable … it has been said and believed in that diabolical Set the Lady lives in – but with that set it is not reprobated – can too great caution be used to such a Woman?

What an infamous Woman She is – if the Lord [Byron] is to be believed, She sent for him to the House in W [Whitehall] expressly to visit Lady C L [Caroline Lamb] and each Lady knew the conduct of the other. I request You will buy and read the Book entitled Les Liaisons Dangereuses … You will there find the Viscountess depicted exactly in La Marquise.

Lady Noel's aim by this time was to blacken Byron's reputation in a court case to seek a legal separation from Byron for her daughter, Annabella, and custody of a child, and it suited her to tar Lady Melbourne's name with the same brush as Byron – but that did not make her assertions untrue.

Murray said Lady Melbourne's letters, which he kept in his archives, show the 'powerful influence' she had over Byron. Byron admits this in his letter to 'My Dear Lady M' on 23 December 1812: 'You know I have obeyed you in everything – in my suit to the Princess of Parallelograms [Annabella was a mathematician], my breach with little *Mania* [Caroline] … You have been my director, and are still, for I do not know anything you could not make me do, or undo.'[10]

Lady Melbourne guided Byron with the benefit of her years of experience about love:

You say you are Suspicious and unreasonable when you are in Love – when a Man is unreasonable, it is quite *impossible* not to deceive him because

210

no one will expose themselves to be quarrel'd with and Scolded when they can avoid it by some little Subterfuge … I believe much the best way is to confide in the person you love, you have much the best chance – if you meet with an honourable person she will love you ten times better for the confidence you repose in her – and if a bad one it don't much Signify, she will deceive you, do what you will. There is my creed.

Byron took Lady M at her word and assured her that he may have lied to Caroline, but he had only told the truth to Lady M: 'Lady Caroline is suspicious of our counter-plots, and I am obliged to be as treacherous as Talleyrand but remember that treachery is truth to you.'

Shortly before Christmas in 1812, he told Lady M he intended to return what he sarcastically called Caroline's 'brilliant documents' to her: 'My Dear Ldy M … This I will do on my return to *you* and *you* only, or Ldy Bessborough, save and except one box full which I must for certain reasons burn in your presence, so pray have a good fire, and fireguard, on my next visit.' He did not say what the letters to be burned contained.[11]

He informed Lady Melbourne as part of his plan for escaping from Caroline, he had started an affair with Lady Oxford, the obliging wife of Edward Harley, the fifth Earl of Oxford, who had so many children by other lovers they were known as the 'Harleian Miscellany'.

'I mean (entre nous, my dear Machieavel) to play off Ldy O [Oxford] against her.' When Caroline heard of their affair, she wrote a letter to Lady Oxford with a series of 'unanswerable' questions. Exasperated, Lord Byron wrote to Lady Melbourne: 'Is she mad or mischievous only?' It was a question that went to the heart of the 'Caroline problem'.

Having added Lady Oxford to his conquests, he sent Caroline a dismissive letter under Lady Oxford's seal – a coronet with her initials – that was calculated to wound her. She instantly recognised Lady Oxford's seal. 'It destroyed me, I lost my brain, I was bled, leeched,' Caroline said. The leech, however – though an unkind description perhaps – was Caroline; she would not let go of Byron.

Before Christmas 1812, Caroline assembled all her letters from Byron and his miniature portrait and threw them on a bonfire at Brocket Hall, shouting incantations around the pyre with local village children as they burned. This event convinced Byron she was mad, but she was not mad enough to destroy the originals; she burned copies.

A month later, Caroline struck again. She forged Byron's signature on a letter authorising John Murray, Byron's publisher, to give her the original 'Newstead miniature' painting of Byron from his office at Albemarle Street.

Byron was upset at losing the painting – he had wanted to give it to Lady Oxford – but he was more alarmed at Caroline's ability to forge his signature and mimic his writing style, complete with blots, a talent she had learned as a teenager to amuse her family.

He wrote indignantly to Lady Melbourne: 'Why she herself should say that she forged my name to obtain it I cannot tell – but by her letter of yesterday … she expressly avows this in her wild way and Delphine language …Will you recover my effigy if you can?'

As the price of the miniature's return, Caroline demanded a lock of Byron's hair. Byron was reluctant but Lady Melbourne wrote to Byron the next day 25 March 1813 scolding him: 'Really by yr reluctance to have yr Hair touched or to part with any of it – I am tempted to think there is some particular charm to it.'

Byron acquiesced but instead of his own dark curls, Byron sent her a lock of hair from Lady Oxford, which Lady Melbourne found uproariously funny. It secured the return of the miniature.

Lady Caroline had one more melodramatic gesture to make. She slashed her wrists at Lady Heathcote's ball on 5 July 1813 when goaded by Byron and spattered her dress with blood. According to her own account, he had made her promise never to waltz, but Lady Heathcote asked her to begin the dance:

> …I bitterly answered – 'Oh yes! I am in a merry humour.' I did so – but whispered to Lord Byron, 'I conclude I may waltz *now*.' He answered sarcastically 'With everybody in turn – you always did it better than anyone. I shall have pleasure in seeing you.' I did so – you may judge with what feelings. After this, feeling ill, I went into a small inner room where supper was prepared. Lord Byron and Lady Rancliffe entered. After seeing me he said: 'I have been admiring your dexterity.' I clasped a knife, not intending anything. 'Do my dear,' he said. 'But if you mean to act a Roman's part, mind which way you strike with your knife – be it at your own heart, not mine – you have struck there already.' 'Byron,' I said, and ran away with the knife.'[12]

Both Caroline and Byron later tried to play down the incident after it was reported in the newspapers. 'I never stabbed myself. It is false,' said Caroline. 'Lady Rancliffe and Lady Tankerville screamed and said I would; people pulled to get it from me; I was terrified; my hand got cut and the blood came over my gown.'[13]

Everyone seemed to be there except her husband William, who had not gone with Caroline to the ball. Lady Melbourne had called for help from her son Frederick Lamb to help restrain Caroline. Her behaviour scandalised the ageing ladies of the *bon ton* and Lady M condemned Caroline in a letter to Byron:

> She must have gone to Ly. H (Heathcote's) determined to pique you by her waltzing & when she found that fail'd, in her passion she wish'd to expose you, not feeling how much worse it was for herself ... I was able to send for Frederick [Lamb, her third son] whom I knew could hold her & I could not by myself & indeed I must do Ly. B [Bessborough] the justice to say that her representation of her violence in these paroxysms was not at all exaggerated.
>
> I could not have believed it possible for any one to carry absurdity to such a pitch. I call it so for I am convinced she knows perfectly what she is about all the time, but she has no idea of controlling her fury... She broke a Glass & Scratched herself as you call it with the broken pieces – Ly O [Ossulstone] & Ly H [Heathcote] – screamed instead of taking it from her & I had just left off holding her for 2 minutes – she had a pair of Scissors in her hand when I went up with which she was Wounding herself but not deeply – pray if you answer her Letters do not let her find out I have written you word of all this ... I cannot described how fatigued I was yesterday. I must finish. Yrs ever. EM[14]

Lady Melbourne added: 'She is now like a Barrel of Gunpowder and takes fire with the most trifling spark...'

17

Honeymoon in Hell

Lord Byron suddenly started out of his sleep in a sweat in the four-poster bed at Halnaby Hall and cried out: 'Good God, I am surely in hell!'

He was, in fact, on his honeymoon. Byron had dreamt the ruddy glow cast by a burning taper through the crimson curtains of the four-poster bed was the fires of hell.[1]

Byron married Annabella Milbanke at eleven am on 2 January 1815 in the drawing room of the Milbankes' house in Seaham on the northeast coast of England. His friend Sir John Hobhouse was his best man.

Annabella was dressed plainly in a white muslin gown trimmed with lace at the bottom with a white muslin jacket, and her head was bare. Hobhouse noted in his journal she sat as firm as a rock and during the whole ceremony looked steadily at Byron. She repeated the words of the service audibly and well. Byron stumbled when he was required to say, 'I, George Gordon.' When he came to the words 'with all my worldly goods I thee endow' he looked at Hobhouse with a telling half-smile.

There was no wedding reception and ominously dark clouds were gathering with the threat of snow when they climbed into their carriage to take them the forty-three miles to Halnaby Hall for their honeymoon. The hall had been put at their disposal for three weeks by Annabella's parents, Judith Noel and Sir Ralph Milbanke, the sixth baronet, who inherited the Halnaby estate with the title from his father in 1793.

Byron's mood darkened like the icy weather before the carriage moved off. 'As soon as we got into the carriage his countenance changed to gloom and defiance,' said Annabella. 'He began singing in a wild manner as he usually does when angry.'

Byron claimed he was 'vexed by my wife's prudery' because a lady's maid sat between himself and his bride in the carriage for the entire journey. He scarcely spoke to Annabella until they passed Durham, when they heard the 'joy bells' ringing to celebrate their wedding. He spoke bitterly about 'our happiness' and told her that one of his great objects in marrying her was to triumph over the others who wanted to marry her.

They stopped at a coaching inn at Rushyford, ten miles south of Durham where Byron told his wife: 'I wonder how much longer I shall be able to keep up the part I have been playing…' Before they reached Halnaby 'he began to reveal his hatred of my Mother and told me some unfavourable things which Lady Melbourne had asserted of her character.'

It was already dark when the carriage drew up outside Halnaby Hall after their seven-hour journey. Byron jumped out of the carriage and strode into the grand entrance hall, leaving his bride in the freezing cold to walk to the house alone. It snowed heavily and they were forced to hunker down for days, increasing the claustrophobic atmosphere inside the hall where Bell's aunt Elizabeth, Lady M, had been born sixty-three years before.

On their wedding night, Annabella said Byron asked her with 'an appearance of aversion if I meant to sleep in the same bed with him – said he hated sleeping with any woman, but I might do as I chose. He told me insultingly that "one animal of the kind was as good to him as another", provided she was young.'

They had separate rooms along the corridor on the first floor of Halnaby Hall. Byron was late getting up and Annabella went to see him in the library. In a tone of cold sarcasm, he said: 'It's too late now – it's done – you should have thought of it sooner … You were determined not to marry a man in whose family there was insanity.' He had heard from Lady Melbourne this was one of her requirements for a husband.

Byron had first noticed Annabella three years earlier when he walked into the drawing room at Melbourne House where people were waltzing at Caroline's fateful morning party.

'On entering the room I observed a young lady, more simply dressed than the rest of the assembly sitting alone upon a sofa,' said Byron. 'I took her for a humble companion and asked [Moore] if I was right in my conjecture? "She is a great heiress," he said in a whisper that became lower as he proceeded; "you had better marry her and repair the old place, Newstead".' She was no dazzling beauty though Byron thought there was 'something piquant and what we term pretty in Miss Milbanke'.

Her features were feminine, though not regular. She had the fairest skin imaginable. Her figure was perfect for her height, and there was a simplicity, a retired modesty about her, which was very characteristic and formed a happy contrast to the cold artificial formality and studied stiffness which was called fashion. She interested me exceedingly ... It was a fatal day.

He asked Caroline who she was. He learned that she was Lady Melbourne's niece, Annabella Milbanke. She was a month off her twentieth birthday and had turned down a string of suitors since her arrival in London for the season in 1810 including Lord Wellington's brother-in-law Major General Edward Pakenham.

She was in London visiting her cousins with the permission of her prudish mother, Lady Judith (Noel) Milbanke, Lady Melbourne's sister-in-law. Annabella may have been the country cousin to the Melbournes but she was not in awe of William Lamb, or his wife; she was amused at Caroline's 'attempted quotations' from Byron's *Julius Caesar* and disapproved of William's manners. She told her mother she had been invited by Lady Caroline to a party but assured Lady Milbanke that she would cut Lady Holland if they were introduced.

'If I am asked to be introduced to Lady Holland's acquaintance, I shall certainly decline.' She noted Lady Holland's 'countenance says that she is capable of determined malice' though she found Lady Melbourne 'was *very* kind and seemed really anxious to promote my wishes but nobody appears more *sincerely* friendly than Mrs Lamb (wife of George Lamb). Indeed I think her too kind-hearted to be *quite fashionable*'.

Caroline invited Annabella to her morning party where she noted she 'saw Lord Byron for the first time'. She had begun to read *Childe Harold* having heard everyone at Melbourne House talking about it and was just as intrigued as the other ladies by Byron's appearance in the room, which she carefully noted in her journal. Annabella did not speak to him directly 'for all the women were absurdly courting him and trying to *deserve* the lash of his Satire' and she was 'not desirous of a place in his lays'.

The next day, Annabella wrote a perceptive letter to Lady Milbanke: 'Yesterday I went to a morning party at Lady Caroline Lamb's where my curiosity was much gratified by seeing Lord Byron, the object at present of universal attention. Lady C [Caroline] has of course seized on him, notwithstanding the reluctance he manifests to be shackled by her. What a shining situation she will have in his next satire! His poem sufficiently proves that he can feel nobly but he has discouraged his own goodness. His features are well formed – his upper lip is drawn towards the nose with an expression of impatient disgust. His eye is restlessly thoughtful.'

Presciently, she added: 'I cannot worship talents that are unconnected with the love of man, nor be captivated by that Genius which is barren in blessings. So I made no offering at the shrine of *Childe Harold*, though I shall not refuse the acquaintance if it comes my way.'

Over the coming days, she warmed to Byron when they met at social gatherings with the Lamb family. She spent three days at Brocket Hall with Lady Melbourne, Lord and Lady Cowper, William and Lady Caroline Lamb, Elizabeth Foster, who had become the Duchess of Devonshire and Mrs George Lamb, known by the family as 'Caro George' to distinguish her from 'Caro William'. She thought 'Caro George', who became a close friend, 'more sensible than ever' but 'Caro William' did 'not do justice to her understanding. She conceals its power under the Childish manner which she either indulges or affects.'

Annabella told her mother she spoke to Byron, 'the comet of this year', at Lady Gosford's assembly where he 'shone with his customary glory'. She was irritated that William Bankes, a suitor whom she had already rebuffed, treated her 'as his property' and put Byron off.

'He certainly is very shy, and in consequence of our acquaintance did not proceed that night,' she confided in her mother. The next night, she met Byron again at another supper party hosted by Emily, Lady Cowper and had 'some very pleasing conversation' with him. She noted that there was still a softer side lacking in his character that could win her over. 'Lord Byron is certainly very interesting, but he wants that calm benevolence which could only touch my heart.' She joked: 'I am just going to a morning party at Lady Caroline Lamb's. My Cousins cannot live without me.'

She added: 'He is sincerely repentant for the evil he has done, though he has not resolution (without aid) to adopt a new course of conduct & feeling.' She added: 'Lord Byron is without exception of young or old more agreeable in conversation than any person I ever knew … He really is most truly an object of compassion … I think of him that he is a very bad, very good man.'[2]

Judith Milbanke was alarmed by her daughter's growing fondness for the notorious poet. She was so disturbed she asked Lady Melbourne, whom she heartily disliked, to intervene on her behalf and warn off Annabella from becoming attached to Byron. Lady Melbourne genuinely appears to have tried to do Judith's bidding, for Annabella told her mother: 'Lady Caroline has been very ill. She has desired to see me today and I am going in consequence to Whitehall. I shall then exert my eloquence to prove to Lady Melbourne there is no danger in my meeting Lord Byron.'

Annabella, whom Byron called Bell, was the polar opposite of Lady Caroline Lamb. She was not given to shows of emotional fireworks; she had an analytical mind and a love for mathematics, giving rise to Byron's rather endearing soubriquet for her quoted earlier, the 'Princess of Parallelograms'. So what attracted Byron to Bell?

He admitted he was not 'in love' with her but he was attracted by her intelligence and her rank: 'I admire her because she is a clever woman, an amiable woman, and of high blood, for I have still a few Norman and Scotch inherited prejudices on the last score. As to *Love*, that is done in a week...'

Perhaps a greater allure was Annabella's supposed fortune, whispered in his ear by his friend Moore when Byron first saw her. He needed independent means because, despite his fame and phenomenal sales, he was almost permanently in debt. Byron refused for years to take any income from his publisher because it was beneath his aristocratic principles to be paid like a hack writer.

A year before he married Bell, Byron boasted to his half-sister Augusta: 'I shall marry, if I can find any thing inclined to barter money for rank within six months; after which I shall return to my friends the Turks.'

There were rumours his debts amounted to £25,000, which he denied. He confidently assured Lady Melbourne the sale of his inherited estate in Rochdale and Newstead Abbey that alone would raise £140,000 would allow Annabella and himself to be 'as independent as half the peerage'.[3]

If Byron's interest in Annabella was purely mercenary, however, he was to be disappointed. Her parents were never rich. Her mother complained about being 'as poor as Job' when they inherited Halnaby Hall from Lady Melbourne's father.[4] Byron later complained the world had said he married Annabella for her fortune, but 'all I ever received ... was £10,000'. This was the equivalent today £668,000 but the sale of Newstead Abbey fell through, and he was hampered by a law suit over his attempt to sell his property in Rochdale, which he reckoned had cost him at least £14,000. While they were on their honeymoon, Lady Melbourne found a house for them to rent in London; it was at 13 Piccadilly Terrace and owned by the Duchess of Devonshire; it cost £700 a year, which they could ill-afford. They each had a carriage and staff to pay for. Byron said that they soon spent what money they had.

Lady Melbourne had tried to put Annabella off Byron, but when she failed to heed her warning, her aunt no longer felt obliged to act as her protector. After receiving his letter from Cheltenham on 13 September 1812, she did everything she could to facilitate the match: 'Poor Annabella. Her innocent Eyes will have to contend with the Black and probably experienced ones of your Innamorata [lover]; recollect in the mean time how much they will improve *if* she *should* be in love with you.'[5]

There was just one problem. Byron said he had heard Annabella was already engaged to another suitor called George Eden. 'Before I become a candidate for the distinguished honour of Nepotism to your Ladyship, it will be as well for me to know that your Niece is not already disposed of to a better bidder; if not I should like it of all things, were it only for the pleasure of calling you Aunt!'

He also posed the question: 'does Annabella Waltz?' He admitted it might seem an odd question, but 'it was very essential point with me' – he did not want to suffer the same humiliation about playing the wallflower at balls with Annabella as he had with Caroline. 'I wish somebody would say at once that I wish to propose to her but I have great doubts of her – it rests with <u>herself</u> entirely…'[6]

Lady M did as she was asked. Posing as a neutral go-between, Lady Melbourne wrote to Annabella to press Byron's case. Annabella gave her reply to Lady Melbourne in a letter on 12 October: it was 'no'. She thanked her aunt for the 'strong testimony in his favour' but said she believed he 'never will be the object of that strong affection which would make me happy in domestic life.'

Byron wrote to Lady M: 'I should have very much liked to be your relation. Tell A that I am more proud of her rejection than I can ever be of another's acceptance … This sounds rather equivocal but if she takes it in the sense I mean it & you don't blunder it in the delivery with one of your wicked laughs it will do for want of anything better.'

Byron told Lady M: 'My principal inducement was the tie to yourself which I confess would have delighted me. I congratulate A [Annabella] and myself on our mutual escape. That would have been but a cold collation, and I prefer hot dinners.'[7] Byron told Lady M he was inclined to go back to a hot-blooded Italian opera singer who reminded him of the women he had in Venice although she gorged on chicken wings, sweetbreads, custards, peaches and port wine. 'A woman should never be seen eating or drinking unless it be lobster salad and champagne.'

Lady Melbourne was not to be put off so easily. Her whole philosophy about marriage was that love had little to do with it. From a purely pragmatic point of view, Byron seemed to her a prime catch for Annabella. She wrote again to Annabella from Whitehall on 21 October 1812 to change her mind by subtly playing on her vanity:

Dear Annabella,
I have this day received an Answer from Lord Byron … he desires me to say how much obliged he is to you for the candour & fairness with which

you have told him your Sentiments – that altho' unfavourable to his hopes, or more properly to his Wishes, for hopes he declares he had not, your conduct on this occasion has increased the high opinion he had before entertain'd of your abilities, & excellent qualities & increases the regret he feels at your decision, as well as his admiration for your character.[8]

Annabella went up to London to see Lady Melbourne about Byron. Playing the wise old aunt, Lady Melbourne urged her to accept his assurances and to meet him 'without any awkwardness'. But she also pricked Annabella's conscience by posing the question – if she could turn down Byron, what sort of husband did she want?

Annabella went away and in her analytical way, put down her thoughts on paper, a practice she called 'collecting my sentiments'. She wrote to Lady Melbourne on 25 October 1812[9] with a list of her requirements. It was headed 'AIM's (Anne Isabella Milbanke's) husband':

> He must have consistent principles of Duty governing strong and *generous* feelings and reducing them under the command of Reason –
>
> Genius is not in my opinion *necessary*, though desirable, *if united* with what I have just mentioned –
>
> I require freedom from suspicion and from *habitual* ill humour also an equal tenor of affection towards me, not that violent attachment which is susceptible of sudden increase or diminution *from trifles…*
>
> Rank is indifferent to me – Good connections I think an important advantage –
>
> I do not regard beauty but am influenced by the manners of a gentleman without which I scarcely think that any one could attract me…
>
> I would not enter into a family where there was a strong tendency to Insanity.

Annabella's exacting standards were inherited from her even more prissy mother Judith Noel. Lady Milbanke strongly disapproved of Lady Melbourne and refused to visit Halnaby Hall for twenty-one years while Elizabeth's father, Sir Ralph Milbanke, the fifth baronet, was alive because of the 'scandal' – he was living with a married woman, a Mrs Ridley, which she said, meant 'his household could not be visited by a woman of reputation'.[10]

Sir Ralph's will led to a bitter family feud when he died on 8 January 1793 and left £5,000 to his mistress and her six children. Elizabeth's brother John was furious. He was made an executor of the will, but had been left little or nothing, and in a fit of pique refused to carry it out.

Elizabeth got nothing from the will. Judith – perhaps in the knowledge that her husband, as the eldest son, was going to inherit the estate and the title –sympathised with Mrs Ridley, writing: 'That Brute John Milbanke wants to seize the £5,000 left to Mrs Ridley and her six Children as he fancies there is some flaw which enables him to do so, but I hope & believe it is safely theirs.'

John Milbanke desperately needed the money. He was already suffering with an illness that proved fatal. His son, John Peniston Milbanke, and his second wife, Elizabeth Fenwick, were heavily in debt and in 1799 Lady Melbourne intervened on her brother's behalf by writing to a creditor to ask for more time for John P to pay off his debts. She said John was too ill to write for himself. Her brother died at Dawlish in Devon a year later. She persuaded Lord Melbourne to pay £1,000 to settle the debt.[11]

Judith Milbanke lost no time in establishing herself as the Lady of Halnaby Manor as soon as Elizabeth's father was dead. They left Seaham, the house they built by the coast, and spent the summer at Halnaby Hall entertaining the landed gentry from the East Riding, and ended their season with a brilliant ball and supper for 187 people at the Hall.

She had avoided Lady Melbourne's society for years, ever since hearing the rumours that her second son William was fathered by Lord Egremont. She refused to relent even though, as a great Whig lady, Lady Melbourne would have been useful to her husband when he became an MP in 1791. Ralph wrote to his sister soon after becoming an MP to try to heal the rift. He complained that she had shown 'coolness' towards his wife. Lady Melbourne wrote from Brocket Hall vehemently denying any coldness on her part. Judith replied, accusing Elizabeth of being two-faced:

> I readily allow nothing in your outward manner to me gave room for the Assertion [of being cold towards her]. But your disapprobation of things you have supposed or been informed I was capable of has been too frequently expressed and too strongly marked for it not from various quarters to have come round to my knowledge ... had You under these impressions taxed me openly and upbraided me ever so warmly, it could not have hurt me like the insinuations you have dropped to others.[12]

Given their soured relations, Judith Milbanke must have resented Lady Melbourne's interference in her daughter's future. Lady Melbourne did not let that discourage her; perhaps the fact that Judith clearly disapproved of her spurred her on to promote the match.

Viscountess Melbourne returned Annabella's list of requirements for a husband with her own comments, and gave her niece some pithy advice on the 'lottery of marriage'. She agreed with Annabella on some points:

> A good looking Man is often preferable to a beautiful one – I am strongly of the same opinion as the manners of a Gentleman without which no person can be agreeable or ought to be tolerated with a view to making him your husband…
>
> Genius – certainly not necessary but very agreeable as it serves to lighten the Weight and sometimes dullness that is often attendant upon good sense and reason when not join'd to cheerfulness and other pleasant qualities…
>
> The great requisites to me would be good Sense, good Nature and cheerfulness…surely that is the sort of Man with whom you may hope to pass your life happily and whom you must like.

With all these requisites, said Lady Melbourne, a 'man has my free leave to be obstinate, perverse, morose, sulky and ill-natured…'

Lady Melbourne had one last acid word of advice. 'On the whole it appears to me that it is almost impossible while you remain on the Stilts on which you are mounted you should ever find a person worthy to be your husband. Marriage after all we can say or do must be a sort of Lottery … A man possessed of such a Character as you have drawn would marry you from reason, and not from Love – which you will not say is what you would wish or like.'[13]

The barb in Lady Melbourne's letter stung Annabella. She replied, point-by-point, before adding: 'After so full an explanation, you will perhaps take off my stilts, and allow that I am only on tiptoe.'

Annabella was tiptoeing to disaster. And Lady M was complicit in pointing the way.[14]

Though she could not complain she had not been warned. Annabella had dinner with a friend of her mother's Mrs Gally Knight, with an estate near Byron's Newstead Abbey, who told her some anecdotes that 'gave me much concern as they indicated feelings dreadfully perverted'. He could not resist a challenge. He bragged to Lady Melbourne he had made love in the billiard room to Lady Frances Wedderburn-Webster because her husband, one of his best friends, had said she could be trusted.

A year passed after Annabella rejected Byron's proposal before Lady Melbourne managed to rekindle their romance. She suggested another meeting with her niece. Byron agreed: 'I shall be very happy to encounter A… I saw you last night but I was literally jammed in between a cursed card-table and an elbow chair, so that I could not rise but in the most ungainly of all possible postures, and you are the last person before whom I would appear more awkward in my devoirs than I naturally am.'

There was a more awkward problem. Lady Melbourne almost certainly knew by now Byron was already engaged in an incestuous affair with his twenty-nine-year-old half-sister, Augusta Leigh, who was married and lived at Six Mile Bottom near Newmarket in Cambridgeshire. Her third daughter, Elizabeth Medora Leigh, was born on 15 April 1814 and Byron dropped heavy hints he was the father. In a letter to Lady M when the child was born, he said: 'It is not an "Ape" and if it is, it must be my fault.'

Lady Melbourne kept her suspicions about Byron's incestuous love affair with his half-sister secret from Annabella. She later tried to justify her silence by accusing Annabella of 'the grossest deceit' by pretending to be engaged to George Eden to avoid Byron's proposal. In a letter to Byron on 30 April 1814, Lady Melbourne said:

> When people try to impose upon me I have great pleasure in imposing upon them; it always produces some fun – as to her [Annabella] I do not feel myself the least bound to give her any advice. When I did she would not take it, & since that time she has endeavour'd to conceal all her feelings upon the subject from me.

Lady Melbourne then refers to the knowledge which Byron has entrusted to her, which appears to confirm that she knew about his incestuous affair with Augusta.

> To say you are not to blame would be absurd but for my Life I cannot blame you half so much as any other person would and this is not from partiality but from a knowledge of your circumstances and of your character – You have been led into it and never allowed to escape from the Nets that first entangled you...

Lady Melbourne said that Annabella, an only child, 'has been Spoiled & allowed to do exactly what she liked from Childhood – & like most persons, who reason much, she bewilders and deceives herself...'[15]

On 10 June, she wrote again to Byron:

> I am shock'd at some of the things you sd to me last Night, & think the easy manner in which two people have accustom'd themselves to consider their Situation quite *terrible* – but I shall not say more at present, as I see it is so

useless. I can not reproach myself with having omitted any thing in my power to prevent the mischief and calamitys that must happen, I fear – but I will not croak or prophesy misfortunes – tho I am very melancholy. Yrs ever. EM

Her failure to tell Annabella about her suspicions exposes Lady Melbourne to the charge that she was just as much a scheming monster as the fictional character *Madame de Merteuil* in *Les Liaisons Dangereuses* with whom she was frequently compared. In her defence, incest was judged less of a sin in Georgian society than it is today.

Annabella had penned a typically priggish letter to Byron when they were engaged saying: 'My regard for your welfare did not arise from blindness to your errors; I was interested by the strength and generosity of your feelings and I honoured you for that pure sense of moral rectitude which could not be perverted, though perhaps tried by the practice of Vice.'

She was not aware then that his 'vices' included incest. Suspicions began to dawn on Annabella the day after their wedding when Byron received a letter from Augusta at their honeymoon retreat. It affected Byron strangely, she said. He read Augusta's opening line aloud to her: 'Dearest, first and best of human beings…' Then, almost triumphantly, he said: 'There – what do you think of that?'

Her suspicions suddenly arose, 'if transient as lightning, not less blasting', at the violence of Byron's reaction when Annabella mentioned she had been reading Dryden's *Don Sebastian* and alluded to an incestuous union of half-brother and sister through ignorance of their parentage.

'His terror and rage were excessive … He took up his dagger which with his pistols lay on the table and left the room. I heard him violently close the door of his own room in the long gallery and, I thought, lock it.'

During the three weeks they were on honeymoon at Halnaby Hall, Byron showed Annabella a letter from Lady Melbourne written before they were engaged in which she tried to dissuade him from the commission of some 'atrocious crime' saying it was worse than anything she had ever heard or known of. 'It is a crime for which there is no salvation in this world whatever there may be in the next.'

Lady Melbourne had remonstrated with him 'on the cruelty of depriving of all future peace or happiness a woman who had hitherto, whether deservedly or not, preserved a good reputation – that he must always consider himself as the cause of her misery … that he was "on the brink of a precipice and if you do not retreat, you are lost for ever".'

Annabella confided in her maid that Lady Melbourne was referring to a plan by Byron to elope with his sister to Sicily before his marriage. Byron told

Annabella that he had taken Lady Melbourne's advice *in part*, but not *altogether*. Annabella believed he was admitting he had committed incest with Augusta when he stayed with her at her home in Six Mile Bottom.

He walked up and down the long gallery at Halnaby Hall 'like a Maniac' and in his doom-laden mood discussed making a will, said Annabella. 'He told me he had two natural children whom he should provide for. At this and many other times he has told me he had another Wife – one of his expressions was "I have another wife *somewhere*." When I laughed at this, he said, "You may find it true". He continually endeavoured to make me jealous of his sister, lamenting my presence and her absence, saying "Nobody understands me but Augusta" – "I shall never love anybody as well as her".'

Over the days that followed at Halnaby Hall, locked in by the freezing temperatures outside, Byron's mood gave way to remorse and he repeatedly referred to being cursed. 'He endeavoured to make me believe him guilty of atrocious crimes ... "I am a villain – I could convince you of it in three words".' He said, "Had you married me two years ago you would have saved me from that which I never can get over."'

Annabella said this implied 'a dreadful load of criminality he had incurred in that interval' including making his half-sister pregnant. She told Harriet Beecher Stowe, the American author of *Uncle Tom's Cabin*, on her deathbed: 'Mrs Stowe he was guilty of incest with his sister!'[16]

Five days after the wedding, Byron wrote to Lady Melbourne but said nothing about the gloom at Halnaby Hall, except he had caught a cold: 'Bell & I go on extremely well so far without any other company than our own selves as yet. I got a wife and a cold on the same day, but have got rid of the last pretty speedily.' The implication is clear.

Annabella gave birth to Byron's daughter, Augusta Ada, at home at 13 Piccadilly Terrace at 1 pm on Sunday 10 December 1815. The baby was fine, but Annabella was in turmoil. She claimed Byron had told her about two months before her confinement he had taken a mistress and had continually taunted her with it; on the day before she went into labour he asked her 'with the strongest expression of aversion and disgust, if I chose to live with him any more.'[17]

Within two months of Ada's birth, 'Bell' left Byron and demanded a separation on the grounds of his cruelty and adultery. Their daughter inherited Annabella's analytical genius, and went on to become the outstanding mathematician, Ada Lovelace, a pioneer of modern computing with Charles Babbage.

All trace of Halnaby Hall where the Byrons spent their 'honeymoon in hell' today has gone. The house was one of many minor stately homes that were demolished in 1952 to avoid the punitive death duties introduced by the 1945 Attlee Labour government to raise money for its sweeping welfare reforms – and seen by some as an act of class hatred. Death taxes amounted to an eye-watering eighty per cent of the capital value of the Duke of Devonshire's estate at Chatsworth in Derbyshire. He raised the money, but many owners did not. It is estimated up to 200 of the minor 'stately homes of England' – too minor to be adopted by the National Trust – have been pulled down since the Second World War through a combination of death duties and the soaring cost of running large houses.

Halnaby Hall with 15,543 acres was sold at auction in 1952 and stripped bare of ceilings, wooden decorations and stone. The remains were finally blown up with dynamite. The red bricks from the once elegant hall went as hard core for road building. Some Yorkshire pubs are rumoured to have ornately carved ceilings from Halnaby Hall.

Fittings from bedroom number four, where Byron and Annabella spent their honeymoon, went under the hammer for small sums. Lot 308 – two sliding sash windows went for £7; Lot 312 – the cast iron fireplace from Byron's room with carved wood mantelpiece and a Satyr relief, basket of flowers and grape and vine carvings, raised 240 guineas; Lot 310 – seventy-one feet of wood panelling thirty-five inches high from Byron's bedroom fetched £13; and Lot 207 – curtain rods from Byron's room were knocked down for £1.

Lot 528, described as 'The stately stone staircase with ornamented balustrading and moulded mahogany handrail to the galleried landing' comprising thirty five-feet-three-inches wide steps rising in four flights with three quarter landings, went for £120.

A local couple, Lawrence and Eva Banner bought the site of the hall in 1960 with the stables and remains of the seventeenth-century servants' quarters. Eva recalled seeing the ruins 'looking like a bombsite' in her privately published history of the hall, and the Milbanke family, *Halnaby People*.[18]

'The building was stripped of its treasures and the coup de grace was delivered by explosives. All that remained was a pile of brick rubble used for hard-core with giant oak beams incongruously pointing at varying angles to the sky,' she said.

The large gatehouses, the handsome Georgian stable block, parts of the kitchen garden and hothouses, and the servants' quarters survived. The stables, which went under the hammer for £2,000, are now a luxurious bed and breakfast where I stayed when I went in search of Elizabeth's birthplace. The site where the hall stood for three centuries is now lush green pasture with not a brick to be seen. The place where one of the great political hostesses of the Georgian age was born was occupied by two longhorn cattle chewing the cud.

18

The Monster and the Weasel

Frederick Lamb arrived breathlessly at Melbourne House at about half-past eight on Monday evening 27 March 1815 with the latest dramatic news from France. He had fled Paris just ten hours before Napoleon Bonaparte arrived.

He had remained there longer than he intended to collect papers to the value of £20,000 belonging to the Bourbons, the French Royal family, who had been ousted once more by *le petit Caporal*. Frederick was at the Congress of Vienna as part of the British diplomatic delegation under Lord Castlereagh when they heard the shocking news that Bonaparte had escaped from exile on the isle of Elba. The Emperor had issued a call to arms when he landed unopposed in the South of France with a small force. He had marched on Paris through the mountains, gathering an army as he went. Marshal Michel Ney, who had been sent to stop him, joined Napoleon's force with his men.

Frederick had spent a fortnight in Paris before rushing to the coast. As alarm spread through London, *The Times* reported on 29 March 1815:

Mr Lamb proceeded from Paris to Lille; from that place he made across the country to Ostend where he secured a packet [a ship] for Mrs Fitzherbert [the Prince Regent's 'wife'] for Monday, she being afraid to venture on account of the boisterous weather. The Honourable Gentleman [Frederick Lamb] ventured in an open boat from Ostend accompanied by Colonel Tench with dispatches from Brussels ... Yesterday the Honourable Gentleman attended the Prince Regent at Carlton House by his Royal Highness's command and was honoured with an interview from twelve o'clock until two.

The Duke of Wellington, who had been appointed commander-in-chief of the allied forces by the Congress, calmly gathered his forces at Brussels and waited to be joined by the reliable old ally General Gebhard Blücher and the Prussian army. While he waited, Wellington scouted out a ridge with a reverse slope to hide his men from Napoleon's 'daughters', his thirty-pound cannon. He found what he was looking for at a place called Mont St Jean, nine miles south of Brussels, where he intended to stop Napoleon's advance; he then rode back to the capital to carry on with his social engagements.

As Wellington prepared for the decisive battle that would decide European history for the next hundred years, red coats were deployed at Westminster to protect MPs going into the Commons to vote on a bill known as the Corn Law. It was hated because it artificially kept the price of corn, and bread, high to support the farmers – including wealthy landowners like the Melbournes and the Devonshires – at the expense of the poor.

Lady Melbourne wrote to her recently married niece Lady Byron in April 1815 saying she had been house hunting for them while they were away on their honeymoon. She had found a house to rent on Piccadilly. It was owned by Bess Foster, the Duchess of Devonshire, and had four mostly light and airy bedrooms. She detailed all its advantages – she enclosed a sketch of the room plan – but neglected one detail: the cost. It would prove too high for Byron. In passing, Lady Melbourne said while she was writing, a mob had been charged outside her windows by cavalry on Horse Guards Parade:

> It was necessary to have ye assistance of the Military and about a dozen of the Horse Guards galloped *at* the people and dispersed them. Two men were rode over but not injured & this passing close to my windows made it impossible not to break off writing & it was with great difficulty I could finish my letter ... Last night the Mob made many attempts on different houses but found them all guarded and no mischief was I believe done.
>
> Today it rains hard, which will probably prevent their assembling in great Numbers and the Town is full of Military so I conclude the Ministers think themselves tolerably Safe – they were very much frightened and not without reason for this Mob seems to be extremely savage and much more in earnest than any I ever remember. They tear up Iron rails & force open the door of the House & if they get in as they did at Mr Robinson's they throw all the furniture out of ye Windows in to the Street where it is broken to pieces or carried away [Robinson, a strong supporter of the corn laws, called in some soldiers who shot and killed a young woman] – Mr Yorks house and Mr Darnlys have suffered considerably – Lord

Eldon – for ye honour of ye North – shew'd great courage – there is a private communication from his House to ye Museum Garden thro' which he went to get some soldiers who were on guard there & returned with them and took two of the rioters himself.[1]

She added a postscript saying she had been wrong – at night, the mob had attacked and damaged the homes of Lord Bathurst, the Secretary for War, Lord King, Lord Mansfield and Sir William Rowley. The mob also smashed the windows at Mr Ponsonby's house at 19 Curzon Street, tore up the railings outside the Earl of Derby's house, and the plant hunter Joseph Banks in Soho Square had his parlour door smashed and his valuable papers strewn around the street.[2]

Like her lover Lord Egremont, Elizabeth supported the Corn Law, but wisely did not advertise the fact – those who openly supported the bill had their homes trashed by the protestors: windows were smashed in Lord Castlereagh's house in St James's Square while he was deciding the fate of Europe at Vienna. Lady Melbourne had little sympathy for the rioters. In a letter to Frederick, Lady Melbourne said she did not want to bore him with the detail but she had studied a previous Corn Bill, the effects of the War, two bad harvests and the fall in the currency, and it had worked 'to the advantage of both growers and consumers'.

The Corn Law 'tumults' were similar to the anti-Poll Tax riots in London in 1989 by protestors who felt they had no other way of expressing their anger. But with the fear of revolution stalking the aristocratic rulers of Britain, the government under Lord Liverpool – perhaps the most underrated of British Prime Ministers – responded with a range of repressive measures. They were supported by William Lamb and his mother, who had been given a brutal lesson in putting down rebellion by her father's militia at the Hexham Massacre when she was nine.

The violent suppression of the protests culminated in the Peterloo Massacre in Manchester in 1819 when Percy Bysshe Shelley, Byron's close friend, famously castigated Castlereagh, the Leader of the House of Commons, who defended government policy, in his poem *The Mask of Anarchy* with this couplet: 'I met Murder on the Way – he had a mask like Castlereagh.'

Some protestors in March 1815 were clearly intent on the overthrow of the monarchy. Lady Melbourne noted in her letter to Annabella they threw 'a loaf steeped in blood and tied up in crepe' – a symbol of the French revolution – into the garden at Carlton House. 'This has caused some mirth and must have been done by some person as a Joke – but which I have no doubt would be taken very Seriously.'

In Brussels, the Duke of Wellington tried to avoid panic among the titled tourists who came to enjoy the spectacle of their soldiers fighting the French by giving the impression he was unconcerned at the threat to the city from Bonaparte. On Thursday, 15 June, the Duke of Wellington attended a society ball with his senior officers and many of the high society ladies who had been attracted to the excitement of war like moths to a flame. It was hosted by Charles Lennox, the fourth Duke of Richmond, nephew of the third Duke of Richmond who was a close friend of the Melbournes, and his wife, Charlotte, Lady Richmond. It was held in a converted coach house, decked out with bunting and colours, at the back of the house they had rented in central Brussels. It would become known as the most famous ball in history.

The Scottish Highlanders danced reels to the sound of bagpipes and the lovely Lady Frances Wedderburn-Webster, with whom Byron had flirted a year before, sat next to the Duke of Wellington. She was heavily pregnant. The child was born in Paris in August and christened Charles Byron.[3] Wellington was so besotted with her, he took the time to scribble notes to her concerning her safety immediately before and after the battle.

Wellington was still at the ball when he received reports that Bonaparte had stolen twenty-four hours on him by force-marching his army across the Belgium border. Wellington exclaimed: 'Napoleon has humbugged me by God.' Officers who were immediately ordered to their posts included Caroline's brother Colonel Frederick Cavendish Ponsonby, the cavalry officer who had fought with distinction at Talavera through the Peninsular campaign. Three days later, on 18 June – a Sunday – on the slopes at Mont St Jean, Frederick Ponsonby courageously led the Twelfth Light Dragoons in a charge against the French but was slashed in both arms and knocked from his horse by a sabre blow to his head.

Frederick's survival is one of the most remarkable to emerge from the battle. 'I was thrown senseless on my face to the ground. Recovering, I raised myself a little to look round, being I believe at that time in a condition to get up and run away, when a Lancer passing exclaimed: Tu n'es pas mort, coquin [you're not dead scoundrel] and struck his lance through my back. My head dropped, the blood gushed into my mouth, a difficulty of breathing came on. I thought all was over…'[4]

He was ridden over by allied Prussian cavalry and robbed by retreating infantrymen; a French officer gave him a sip of brandy before leaving him for dead. Miraculously, he survived the night on the battlefield despite being wounded seven times and was found by a British soldier, barely alive among the dead, dying and robbed on the slopes of Mont St Jean.

Caroline, who was partying on the Isle of Wight, at first heard her brother had been killed; but then she had news that he had survived and was recovering with terrible injuries in a hospital in Brussels. Caroline rushed to his bedside with William. They arrived in Brussels on 6 July and for a time she tended Frederick's wounds until he was stronger.

Her mother, Lady Bessborough, arrived two days later, having hurried from Schaffhausen in northern Switzerland, where she had been en-route to England. She had intended to winter in the South of France with her husband during the peace, but had been caught out by Bonaparte's escape and had been forced to flee to Italy.

Caroline seemed strangely detached from the real horror. It is estimated nearly 50,000 men were killed or wounded, with casualties almost even on both sides. She wrote to Lady Melbourne: 'The great amusement at Bruxelles indeed the only one except visiting the sick is to make large parties and go to the field of Battle & pick up a skull or grape shot or an old shoe or a letter & bring it home. William has been there. I shall not go – unless when Fred gets better and goes with me ... It is rather a love making moment, the half wounded Officers reclining with pretty ladies visiting them.'[5]

Caroline could not resist finishing with some lines on the poignancy of Lady Richmond's 'fatal' ball, though she was not there: 'There never was such a ball – so fine and so sad. All the young men who appeared there shot dead a few days later.'

Byron was also drawn to the battlefield when he left England for good. In 1816, Byron fled Britain and joined the tourists who travelled to the battlefield and bought some souvenirs that he sent back to his publisher John Murray.

He added a third canto to *Childe Harold* about the battle and the ball that preceded it:

> Ah! Then and there was hurrying to and fro
> And gathering tears and tremblings of distress
> And cheeks all pale, which but an hour ago
> Blushed at the praise of their own loveliness
> And there were sudden partings, such as press
> The life from out young hearts and chocking sighs
> Which ne'er might be repeated; who could guess
> If ever more should meet those mutual eyes
> Since upon night so sweet such awful morn could rise...

Byron was moved by the banality of the battlefield; it had already been turned back to cornfields fed by blood by the time he visited:

> Stop! – for thy tread is on an Empire's dust!
> An Earthquake's spoil is sepulchred below!
> Is the spot mark'd with no colossal bust?
> Nor column trophied for triumphant show?
> None but the moral's truth tells simpler so,
> As the ground was before, then let it be
> How the red rain hath made the harvest grow!
> And is this all the world has gain'd by thee
> Thou first and last of fields! King-making Victory?[6]

I found Byron's souvenirs from Waterloo are still held at the publisher's offices in Albemarle Street wrapped in tissue paper in small boxes – a large ball of grapeshot, stained perhaps with a soldier's blood; a couple of muddy leather French cockades; and a highly-polished brass badge bearing an imperial eagle with the number 55 cut out of the plate signifying it was taken from a tunic in Napoleon's fifty-fifth regiment. They had the something of the same shock effect in Regency London as a Nazi swastika has now.

By August, Frederick was strong enough to return to England. Wellington's military secretary, Lord FitzRoy Somerset, later Lord Raglan, the hapless allied commander in the Crimea War, acidly remarked Ponsonby was 'in dread of Caro's sisterly persecutions but she was soon prevailed upon to prefer parading about the town at all hours'.

Relieved of looking after her brother, Caroline went with William to join the parade of fashionable men and women who had flocked to Paris where Wellington, as head of the army of occupation, ruled supreme. Caro became one of his small band of ardent female admirers.

Her cousin, Harrio Cavendish, reported: 'Nothing is agissant ['acting', going on] but Caroline William in a purple riding habit tormenting everybody, but I am convinced primed for an attack on the Duke of Wellington … I have no doubt that she will to a certain extent succeed as no dose of flattery is too strong for him to swallow or her to administer. Poor William hides in one small room while she assembles lovers and tradespeople in another.'

Caroline was still prepared to play the drama queen over her love for Byron. At a dinner at Lord Holland's house in Paris, it was mentioned Byron was coming to Paris. Caroline, who was with William, shocked the guests by saying in that case, she would extend her stay.

When they returned to their hotel, Mr and Mrs Kemble, who had been at the dinner, saw across the court yard Caroline in her room, with her arm around William's neck apparently in a loving embrace. They saw her suddenly 'flying round the room, seizing and flinging on the floor cups, saucers, plates – the whole cabaret, vases, candlesticks, her poor husband pursuing and attempting to restrain his mad moiety...' In fact, Byron did not go to Paris.[7]

William calmly closed the curtains, and waited patiently until her rage subsided. He complacently stood by while Caroline flirted with lovers in Paris including a rich adventurer, Michael Bruce; but Caroline was aiming higher. She was soon seen monopolising the Duke of Wellington at a party, and was thought to have succeeded in her campaign to bed him. She returned to England with a personal trophy – the Duke's cloak he wore in the battle, still spattered with mud from the battlefield. It was sold in 2015 at auction by Sotheby's for £47,500.

William told Queen Victoria that he had started to go grey in Paris with the stress. He said he got three women to pull out the grey hairs but gave up because it was too painful. Victoria disapproved of his vanity – she thought he dyed his hair too black and teased him about grooming his bushy black eyebrows.

When she returned to Melbourne House, Lady Melbourne and Caroline's mother were convinced Caroline was deranged. The last straw came when she hurled a ball at a page that had been throwing squibs in the fire; it hit him so hard it drew blood. She panicked, rushed into the hallway and cried: 'I've murdered the page!' It was a flesh wound, but it convinced the Lambs she was mad. 'The servants and the people in the street caught the sound and it was soon spread about. William Lamb would not live with me. All his family united in insisting on our separation,' said Caroline.

The incident united the Lambs in pressing William to seek a separation from Caroline. William appeared acquiescent. In February 1816 the rumours of a separation had reached Byron, whose own marriage was in trouble; he wrote to Lady Melbourne asking if the rumours about a 'wicked scandal' were true. She replied: 'It may or may not be a "wicked scandal" but as far as I am concerned it is not true.'

It was not entirely a lie, though she was being economical with the truth. Lady Melbourne was against a legal separation between Caroline and William if it could be avoided, because it could lead to a legal battle in open court and further scandal for the Melbourne family. Lady Melbourne preferred another, more discreet option – declaring Caroline 'insane', which was one of the grounds for divorce in Regency Britain.[8]

It was enthusiastically supported by her daughter, Lady Emily Cowper and son Frederick and from Caroline's own family by her aunt, Lavinia Spencer, wife of George John Spencer, Lord Althorp. The sticking point was William, who still nursed a deep affection for Caroline and was reluctant to agree to have her declared insane. He bowed to pressure from his mother, sister and brother to allow a doctor called Moore to see if Caroline was insane.[9] Caroline was determined to fight it. She fired off a furious letter to Lady Melbourne that bristles with hurt and indignation:

> I heard with surprise the means which you propose – in the first observe that nothing but absolute force shall induce me to consent. In the next, observe that from this I know – I entirely (renounce) all intercourse with an Aunt [Lavinia Spencer] who can so coldly and casually attempt what Lord [Westmoreland] unfortunately attempted against his wife – thank God I have friends to support me. Whatever means are taken they shall be taken publicly – Wm Lamb has promised to agree to no private attempts to pronounce the mother of his child insane. The Boys Parents and himself will stand by me. I cannot feel but utterly disgusted at Mr Moore's conduct. However you proceed if it is your pleasure only remember that I utterly deny any authority you may choose to claim whilst I live … For fear you should misrepresent this letter as you have others I have taken copies of it and sent a copy of each to those friends who remain to support me. Yours no longer as dutiful and affectionate, Caroline Lamb.[10]

Faced with her threat of public exposure, William held back. Caroline later told a friend Moore had 'proved me mad'. His diagnosis is missing from the archives but in the Lamb archives at Hertford is a diagnosis by Dr Goddard of 54 Conduit Street about Caroline's mental state presented to William on 19 October 1825 following her descent into heavy drinking. Goddard said she had a 'predisposition to the high form of insanity which shows itself at certain times and particularly so when exposed to any excitement':

> I consider that her Ladyship with kind treatment and occasional restraint might recover or at any rate become calm and rational. But there are friends who must be removed from her; measures must be taken to make her take less wine, and some situation must be chosen where she can be governed with every appearance of governing herself. Lady Caroline is very suspicious and therefore I have only had time to write these few lines.[11]

He also found worrying evidence of oedema on her stomach from her heavy drinking that ultimately caused her death. In 2016, I asked a leading psychiatrist, Dr James Stone, clinical senior lecturer in psychiatry at King's College, London, whether Lady Caroline Lamb would be diagnosed as mentally ill today. Caroline was not 'mad'.

Dr Stone told me: 'Some of her behaviours are more suggestive of histrionic personality disorder, characterised by theatricality, exaggerated expression of emotions, suggestibility, continual seeking of excitement and being the centre of attention. Alternatively, and rather more speculatively, it is possible that she may have had some aspects of a pervasive developmental disorder (Asperger's syndrome). She appeared to have difficulty in understanding social conventions at times, and as a child, her behaviour was noted to be particularly difficult to cope with.' (See Annexe).

Lady Melbourne and her family pursued the only course left open to them – a legal separation between William and Caroline, allowing Caroline to live at Brocket Hall with Augustus, which Caroline had promised not to fight. Lady Melbourne went to Brocket Hall to make sure Caroline signed a separation agreement. William went upstairs to persuade his wife to sign. Downstairs, Lady Melbourne, her children, and her lawyers waited, and waited. His brother George Lamb went to find out what had caused the delay. Emily Eden, the daughter of a prominent Whig politician, wrote: 'George writes me word ... Lady Melbourne set out one morning from London to try and arrange matters and on her arrival she found the happy couple at breakfast and Lady Caroline drawling out "William some more muffins?" – and everything made up.'[12] Caroline won, but she was still not satisfied. She sent a bitter note to Lady Melbourne to justify her actions:

> I cannot go to bed without wishing you goodnight. As you are not at home God Bless you Dear Lady Melbourne, act by me as your own heart tells you is fitting, if severely I will try to bear it ... half my friends cut me, all my acquaintances are offended, I most certainly said not one thing malignant of any of my acquaintances except Lady Holland ... Lady Holland has behaved very [badly] towards me many times and shabbily towards Wm [William] but there all enmity ends.'[13]

The enmity did not end, however. She declared that Emily would remain her enemy for life, and reneged on her promises about signing the documents for a legal separation: 'As to any promises I may have been forced to make when a strait waistcoat and a Mad Doctor are held forth to view – they cannot expect I should think them binding.'

Lord Melbourne was furious at the failure to deal with Caroline and once more lost his temper with her when she returned with the Lamb family to Melbourne House in Whitehall. He ordered her to leave and abused Lady Bessborough. That sent Caroline over the edge again, as it had done four years earlier.

Unknown to the Melbournes, she had been writing feverishly over the past few weeks a novel ridiculing her family and friends under a thinly veiled guise of fiction. John Murray had refused to publish, realising the storm it would cause among his elite clients.

Now, in a fit of fury at Lord Melbourne, she secretly sent the manuscript of her hastily written Gothic novel *Glenarvon* to Henry Colburn, a small publisher who was prepared to take a risk (as small publishers often are).

Caroline recalled: 'I had been ordered out of the House in no gentle language; my mother was spoke to with the most barbarous roughness in my presence ... I was proved mad. Mr Moore assured me I was so ... I appealed to a few but my letters were not even answered. I went to Roehampton (her family home). Lady Jersey to the extreme annoyance of my father, turned her back on me ... William returned and a dreadful scene passed between Lord M [Melbourne] and Mama [Lady Bessborough]. That night I sent the novel.'[14]

It paid off handsomely for Colburn, going into four reprints and establishing him as a publisher, but it was a disaster for Caroline. She upset all sides with her satire including the Devonshires, who believed part of the plot about a child being a changeling was a deliberate attempt to raise old rumours that Hartington, the Duke's heir, had actually been Bess's child and illegitimate. Lord Holland cut her dead, and Lady Jersey invoked the ultimate sanction – she struck her name off the Almack's list. Emily got Caroline reinstated 'in Lady Jersey's teeth' but that took several years.

Lady Melbourne only read the first volume and found it

> ...so disagreeable to me that I don't feel as if I had the courage to proceed. I never can excuse the falsehoods she tells about William and the account she gives of a society in which she had lived from her childhood. She knew them perfectly, unfortunately they did not know her, and William the least of all, and to this hour she has the art of deceiving him as to her real character.

Lady Melbourne revived the plan for a legal separation. Her fresh determination to act may have been energised by an extraordinary letter from

Lord Egremont that had survived the burning of his private papers by his heir. It lies in a miscellaneous file of Lamb papers among the Salisbury archives at Hatfield House. In a rare flash of anger, he accused Lady Melbourne of failing to protect 'poor William' from his own lack of willpower.

His letter is full of fatherly concern for her two sons, William and Frederick, and should dispel all doubts that Egremont was their real father. It is datelined 'Petworth Thursday' and mentions a court case from July 1816 that shows it must have been written in the summer of that year.

Lord Egremont begins mundanely enough by offering help to Lady Melbourne to get a reliable horse. She appears to have asked him for a horse from his stable, but he says these days he rides nothing bigger than a pony (like the viscountess, he is sixty-four) and his thoroughbred three-year-olds are 'neither strong enough nor old enough' for her to ride. He suggests she gets a horse from the Dragoons who have 'very steady safe good horses used to Troops and fire which is always a good thing.'

He talks about Lady Melbourne staying with him in Brighton while Lord and Lady Cowper (Emily, Lady Melbourne's daughter, also believed to have been fathered by Egremont) are taking a house at Worthing. 'I will have two rooms ready for you ... please give me a day or two ... the housekeeper is gone to London and she comes to us at Brighton on Friday.'

He says it is better for Frederick to earn promotion with Castlereagh at the resumed Vienna Congress rather than relying on the royal patronage of the Prince Regent: 'Between ourselves it is much more to his credit to owe his promotion to Lord Castlereagh's good opinion.'

Then he turns to the subject of their son William:

But for poor William and it really is afflicting to see him chained to that little nasty infamous mad woman and not only for his happiness, his conduct also, for it not only depresses him in his own estimation and exertions but it lowers his character in the world who see him submitting patiently to be the talk of the town for such a little detestable weasel when it is well known that with the least attention sufficient proof might have been had last spring to emancipate him from her for ever and I really thought that you and Lord M [Melbourne] and George and Lord and Lady Cowper and all the rational brains of the Family ought to join in stating it to him fully and strongly and so put an end to that foolish reserve of his which has hitherto been her preservation. If he had communicated openly with Frederick or any sensible person it would have been done long ago. I hope you will not sacrifice your son to any regard for that affected old Baggage [Lady Bessborough] the mother of the Monster. I am sure you have done

enough … [to] take such an incumbrance off her hands … But having given
her a thorough trial – fair chance – you have done everything for her and
may now think of nothing but your son.[15]

Lord Egremont believed that Lady Melbourne had missed an opportunity in
the summer of 1815 to rid William of 'the Monster'. He was also right to have
concerns about their son. William Lamb characteristically appeared overwhelmed
by indolence after being cuckolded by Byron. He was convinced that Caroline's
passion for Byron would burn itself out, and Byron did not truly love his wife.
Caroline complained later: 'He cared nothing for my morals. I might flirt and
go about with whom I pleased. He was privy to my affair with Lord Byron, and
laughed at it. His indolence rendered him insensible to everything.'[16]

   William was doubly humiliated, because he knew nothing of his wife's
novel until the morning it was published on 9 May 1816. He told her:
'Caroline, I have stood your friend till now – I even think you ill-used; but
if it is true this Novel is published – and as they say against us all – I will
never see you more.' He was heard muttering: 'I wish I was dead. I wish
I was dead.' This was a turning point for Caroline and the Lambs. Having
failed to declare her mad, they renewed their efforts to persuade William
to seek a legal separation. Caroline hit back in a long and rambling letter
attacking Lord Melbourne for threatening to turn Caroline and William out
of Melbourne House. She preyed on Lady Melbourne's maternal instincts:

> William has a fancy that he should die soon of an illness like Fox. I attribute
> all this to anxiety of mind and vexation. It was at this occurrence I urged
> you to delay talking of changes for unless Lord Melbourne wishes us to
> take a House now – there can be, it seems to me, no use to enter upon this
> subject just at present. But as I know he imputes the basest motive to me …
> tell him that he need be under no sort of [doubt] he has the power to turn
> us out tomorrow if he chooses and as George [Lamb] Emily [Cowper] the
> Prince [Regent] Lord Egremont and all his friends advise it, I hope he would
> be happier when he has given William the greatest pain he can inflict. As to
> me whom he likes to wound and to punish – he knows me but little.[17]

Lord Melbourne, she added, had told her that her own friends had gone
against her, that no-one received her for social engagements any more, that
she was 'scorned by all'.

   She tries to twist the knife: 'He [Lord Melbourne] acts in a manner to bring
this to pass. But I [would] care not were it not that I can see William's health
and spirits decline … The time may come and that soon when you will regret

your severity ... after you have turned William out of your house to gratify the malevolence of those who hate me.'

She includes Emily, Lady Cowper, in that list with a curse: 'Perhaps Lady Cowper now triumphant in the thought of having mortified one she despises and hates may herself suffer. Her child may be taken from her and a thousand afflictions may visit her ... I do not wish or hope or expect to move you, neither does William. My arts are not employed in aggravating his sorrow but in soothing – I write with asperity because I see that he suffers ... Lord Melbourne [will] in his latter years lament too late his severity, however just.'

She says the publishers of *Glenarvon* have sold 1,500 copies and want a new second edition. She adds with a threat to do more damage by following up *Glenarvon* with a 'tell-all' autobiography:

> I will now do nothing more that can harm William but when you turn us
> out of doors which Lord Melbourne has pledged himself to do, I find ...
> I owe it to all to publish ... a full refutation of all the calumnies that have
> been spread against me and my infamous book – and comment about Lord
> Byron's conduct for the last few years.[18]

Lady Melbourne opted for a compromise. Talk of a legal separation was shelved for now; there was a further medical inquiry into her sanity, but Caroline was sent off to the relative peace of Brocket Hall where she remained with Augustus, almost in contented exile, until her death from alcohol in 1828 at the age of forty-two.

In the midst of her own family crisis over a separation for Caroline and William, Lady Melbourne heard rumours that Annabella was also seeking a legal separation from Lord Byron.

Annabella and her mother did not trust Lady Melbourne an inch. Documents in the Lovelace archive at the Bodleian Library in Oxford are thick with charge and counter-charge against the villainous Byron – but the controlling demon in the background is Lady Melbourne.

Annabella needed evidence and met Caroline in secret at George Lamb's house. Minutes of the meeting show Caroline said Lord Byron had given her various intimations 'of a criminal intercourse' with Augusta after his sister came to live with him at Bennet Street, St James's, in 1813.

Byron had told her: 'There is a woman I love so passionately – she is with child by me and if a daughter, it shall be called *Medora*...' Caroline had refused to believe Byron had committed incest until he showed her his letters from Augusta saying: 'Oh B. if we loved one another as we did in childhood – then it was innocent.'

Caroline claimed she refused to have 'intimate' relations with Byron after that. 'The last time we parted for ever as he pressed his lips on mine (it was in the Albany) he said, "poor Caro, if every one hates me, you, I see will never change – No, not with ill usage!" & I said "yes, I am changed and shall come near you no more." For then he showed me letters & told me things I cannot repeat, & all my attachment went. This was our last parting scene – well I remember it. It had an effect upon me not to be conceived – three years I had worshipped him.'[19]

Caroline told Annabella that Byron had also confessed to 'the practice of unnatural crime' – sodomy – with a page called Robert Rushton and three 'schoolfellows whom he had thus perverted'. He had practised it 'unrestrictedly' in Turkey. This gave Annabella all the ammunition she needed.

Caroline warned her:

Do you remember that you have to oppose 2 of the greatest Hypocrites & most corrupted wretches that were ever suffered to Exist on this earth [Lady Melbourne and Byron] ... I request you to take most particular care what you say to Lady M – you may ruin me if you chuse by shewing any one on earth this letter but you will ruin yourself if you are not extremely guarded. Take a high tone. Seem sure of everything but tell her nothing – & for God sake do not name me. I think it perfectly useless to trust her ... pray take care – above all let her not imagine What you know.[20]

Lady Noel and her daughter agreed to do all they could to keep Lady Melbourne out of the affair. Annabella's father Sir Ralph Noel (he changed his name from Milbanke to comply with an inheritance by his wife) drafted a letter to Byron's lawyers claiming that Annabella had been forced from her home with Byron because of 'fears for her personal safety', which Byron hotly denied. Lady Noel told her daughter she had bought a pair of pistols for defence, should there be an attempt to kidnap her granddaughter, Ada.

In a letter dated 2 February 1816, Ralph Noel wrote to Byron:

However painful it may be to me, I find myself compelled by every feeling as a Parent and as a Man to address your Lordship on a subject which I hardly suppose will be any surprise to you – Very recently circumstances have come to my knowledge which convince that with your opinions it cannot tend to your happiness to continue to live with Lady Byron.

Noel suggested separation. A note on the letter says it was returned unread by Byron's sister, Mrs Leigh.

On 17 March 1816, Annabella wrote to her mother: 'I have just signed my name after Lord Byron's to an article of Separation ... I am so glad the whole has been managed without Lady M's interference. She is frightened out of her senses on finding from Mrs George Lamb that I knew her misdeeds towards me ... I have now the fairest reasons for cutting her altogether, and I don't know what good she can ever do me.'

Lady Noel wrote back two days later saying: 'I think it *incumbent* on You to *break* with her entirely – not from *resentment* so much as to enable You and Your Friends to *contradict* the *Lies* and aspersions She has held out lately.'

On 25 April 1816, a month before Caroline produced *Glenarvon*, the rumours circulating of Byron's incest, sodomy and homosexual encounters forced Byron to flee to the Continent. 'I was accused of every monstrous vice by public rumour ... I was advised not to go to the theatres lest I should be hissed nor to do my duty in Parliament lest I be insulted on the way,' he complained. The rumours followed him across the English Channel. In Switzerland, 'in the shadow of the Alps and by the blue depth of the lakes – I was pursued and breathed upon by the same blight. So I went a little farther and settled myself by the waves of the Adriatic like the stag at bay who betakes him to the waters.'[21] It took years for William Lamb to stir himself into anger against Byron. It was a mark of William's good nature that when he did, he was outraged at Byron's callous treatment of his wife.

Queen Victoria noted in her journal William told her Byron 'behaved like a demon to Lady Byron; the abominations he said and did are hardly to be believed':

He said his [Byron's] mind and heart were quite crooked and perverted. He married Lady Byron out of pique, Lord Melbourne said; she had refused him, I think twice and he was determined to marry her. 'He married her for her money,' he added, 'and he told her almost immediately after he married her that now he had her, he would break her heart'. He said Lady Byron fell a sacrifice to her love of literature and her vanity about that. She admired his writings and that a man who wrote so well 'must be right at bottom'. 'And she suffered dreadfully, poor thing!' he added with great feeling. He said she was an excellent person: 'stiff, demure and dogmatical and accustomed to be the idol at home'. But that she was not the person calculated to suit him (Byron).

I observed that I thought Byron was very fond of his child; Lord Melbourne answered that he did not think he <u>really</u> was. He said that he made a sensation like a 'meteor' in the world; so young, and writing such poems; he was very handsome; his brow and eyes and hair beautiful; the lower part of the face rather too large; and 'with that lame, all which excited an interest'. Lady Byron, like the rest was attracted by this.

I observed that a bad spirit pervaded all his writings. Lord Melbourne said: 'Yes a misanthropic, bitter feeling pervaded all his writings.' Southey said, Lord Melbourne told me (which Lord Byron did not at all like), 'that his writings were of the Satanic School'. Lord Melbourne added: 'He (Ld Byron) was quite the Poet of the Devil.'[22]

Lady Melbourne had been forced to deal with the twin crises in her family – the marriage disasters of the Byrons and the Lambs – but she must have felt her family's fortunes had turned a corner: William was returned to Parliament and she had the satisfaction of knowing that she had achieved her greatest goal.

On 18 July 1815, a month after Wellington's great victory at Waterloo, the *London Gazette* announced (along with a list of promotions for Wellington's officers) the Prince Regent had been pleased to grant 'the Right Honourable Peniston, Viscount Melbourne, by the name, style and title of Baron Melbourne, of Melbourne, in the county of Derby.'

At last, Elizabeth had gained an English hereditary title with an automatic seat in the House of Lords for her husband. That secured the Melbournes their place among the highest ranks of Georgian society. There was just one snag. In order to claim it, Lord Melbourne had to pay £600 for his peerage to be registered with the Kings of Arms and he did not have the money. 'The call for as much as £600 fees for my patent of Peerage has distressed me at present,' Lord Melbourne told his steward at Melbourne Hall. He ordered the steward to cut down some trees and sell off some timber from the estate to pay for his peerage. She may have helped her husband spend most of his fortune, but Viscountess Melbourne had at last achieved her crowning ambition.[23]

19

The Last Word

Lady Melbourne became addicted to opium in her sixties, which was to contribute to her end. She always had a robust physique but she suffered from bouts of rheumatism in her knees and her legs, for which she sought relief from a range of quack medicines. Her chief relief came from laudanum, the Georgian cure-all, containing potent amounts of opium.

She complained in January 1815 in a letter to Byron that she had been laid upon her couch for three or four days by a violent headache – perhaps migraine – which had returned after eight years. 'It is a sort of Nervous Head ache which affects the sight and sometimes you see half a face and sometimes two faces – I see you laugh!'[1]

She still rode great distances, and as late as October 1817 wrote to 'Dearest Fred', her third son, asking him to look out for a horse for her to ride. 'I should not like to ride so tall a horse; it is very uncomfortable & I have always rode low horses. Jersey was the tallest I ever had … being rough is the only fault I have with my Mare – she really carries me very well.' She asks him to look out for a 'clever strong Active low horse' for her, providing it is 'safe & good tempered' and tells him she intends to ride over to Panshanger to stay with her daughter Emily and her husband, Lord Cowper for three or four days.

> I mean to ride as much as I can for I have not been quite well lately. My stomach has been out of sorts and I expect that it will cure me, I have also got a good deal of Rheumatism in my knee which makes me think of you as you always complain of it. I believe it always comes whenever there has been a Strain … God help you. Lord Melbourne would send his love but is fast Asleep upon the opposite Couch.[2]

She tried not to complain to her family but on 16 January wrote again to Frederick saying she asked Sir Walter Farquhar for medicine for her pain but found he was ill and instead had seen Dr Richard Warren, the Prince Regent's physician, '& am now under the influence of some of his large doses'. Warren was giving her greater doses of opium than Farquhar, because her body had become tolerant to the drug.

'He says my complaint is Bilious & Rheumatism upon strain'd & weakened Musciles – I was cupp'd on my knee at Brocket but the only use I have as you found from it has been such Soreness and tenderness that I can hardly tell whether I have any pain in it or not, the other being so much more troublesome.'

On 23 January, she wrote again to Frederick saying 'the Rheumatism continues & the pain is not to be endured. I have better Nights and the pain is greater in the day when I don't move, but then I get the fidgets & must move, although the consequence is an Acute pain in my knee or Thigh or down my leg.'

By 17 February, she complained to 'Dearest Fred': 'I can not get rid of these pains – I have been tired by ingesting – all sorts of things. I think I told you of this Indian Oil, then the tinctuary of laudanum then the plants ground, next I shall try the Spirits of Wine.'

William wrote to Frederick that he was sorry to say that their mother was suffering a very painful illness 'which although it is attended by no present danger, cannot, considering all the circumstances, not make one very uneasy – her stomach has been much destroyed and a great deal of illness and very acute and very frequent pain from Rheumatism from the knee, upwards and downwards. This suffering … made her look very ill when she was at Brocket. She has come to town to see Warren. Her stomach has improved but the pain still continues and she looks much worn and distressed by it.'

He added: 'Since I wrote the above, Caroline has been to see Warren…he assures her that there is no danger and that a considerable amendment has taken place. She suffers very much – I trust he is right.'[3]

On 13 March she wrote once more to Frederick: 'I am in great pain and go into a Warm Bath twice a day … my pain is in my thigh, my knees and down my Leg & into my Foot … God Bless you Dearest Fred. If I could write a word that I was released from the pain I should be very happy.'

Given more of Dr Warren's 'large doses' of laudanum to kill the pain, which may have been sciatica triggered by a tumour, she had seizures and slipped into a coma. All her family were at her bedside apart from Frederick, who was abroad on a diplomatic mission. William wrote on 28 March from Melbourne House in Whitehall to Frederick telling him to come home because their mother was dying. He told his brothers her doctors including

Warren thought, considering her confinement, her pain and her age, the end could not far away.

For two or three nights she had been awake until four or five o'clock in the morning because of the pain, before she fell asleep, but she was 'worn out' by the distress. She had very deep-seated inflammation about the hip joint; some cases had been treated successfully by bleeding of the parts that were inflamed, said William, but in their mother's case, 'nothing of that kind can now be attempted'. He added: 'The calamity, the greatest which could befall us, is one that I have always anticipated.'

On 3 April, Lord Melbourne wrote to Fox at Melbourne Hall: 'I can give you nothing but the most unfavourable account of Lady M.' The same day, William wrote again to Frederick:

> The fact is that since I wrote before her decline has been more rapid than the physicians expected … Her pulse is feverish; she has passed the last six or seven nights in the most disturbed and restless manner, subject to pain and nervous irritation almost worse than pain, which will not suffer her to remain in bed for five or ten minutes together … Since three o'clock in the day yesterday she has taken very little sustenance, not more than two or three spoonfuls of wine and some portions of a draught … You must be aware this cannot be of long continuance … Emily has been indefatigable in her attentions but is a good deal worn out – she is far gone with child … My father is as might be expected most disconcerted and it is impossible not to reflect with pain that this is the most distressing and miserable part of what he has to undergo – Adieu.[4]

Elizabeth died in the bedroom on the ground floor of Melbourne House on 6 April 1818. She was sixty-six. She had dominated the social scene for over four decades and her passing was a landmark in the history of the Georgian period. Queen Victoria noted in her journal:

> The Duke of Sutherland told me the other night that Lord Melbourne's mother (whom he knew) was a very agreeable sensible clever woman and that Lord Melbourne was very like her as to features. Lady Melbourne was very large latterly. Lord Melbourne's father, on the contrary, the Duke said, was very far from agreeable or clever; he was a short fat man and not like any of his children.[5]

It is said Viscountess Melbourne rallied before she died and gave her sons and daughter the last offerings of her worldly advice – she told William to achieve greatness, and urged Emily to stay constant, not to Lord Cowper, her husband, but to her lover, Lord Palmerston. William Lamb wrote to Fox to inform the estate workers and servants at Melbourne Hall: 'I have to inform you of the melancholy event of Lady Melbourne's decease, which took place this morning – her end was tranquil & free from pain, but the suffering of her illness has been great – you will communicate this sad intelligence to Mr Middleton [the vicar] & all at Melbourne.'[6]

Lord Melbourne – deprived of the support of the woman who had directed his life – wrote: 'Thank God my health is pretty good considering I suffer such an irreparable loss.'

The Prince Regent assured Emily Lady Cowper that he had visited Lady Melbourne every day on her deathbed and she expired in his arms. Lady Cowper knew it was a lie.[7]

Largely thanks to her affair with the Prince Regent, Lady Melbourne had achieved her goal of gaining a place for her family at the highest level in English society through the Melbourne title, but in many other respects she may have reflected in those lucid moments on her death bed that her life had ended in failure: her beloved son William's political career was a disappointment and his marriage a disaster; Frederick was a disgruntled diplomat; George would never become the leading playwright or actor he wanted to be; Emily had inherited her mother's gift for entertaining, but her marriage to Earl Cowper was another source of dissatisfaction.

As she lay dying, she could not know that William would become Queen Victoria's favourite Prime Minister; that after Cowper's death Emily would marry the great Victorian statesman, Lord Palmerston, and that the dynasty she had founded would be remembered forever over 10,400 miles away in the name of a city in the state of Victoria, Australia: Melbourne.

Her body was carried back to Brocket Hall and buried in the Melbourne vault inside St Etheldreda's Church, Hatfield, next to Hatfield House, the home of her political rivals, the Salisburys. The chief mourners were Earl Cowper, William and George Lamb. Frederick did not return to England in time to see his mother alive, and was unable to see her buried. The burial

Register of burial of Viscountess Melbourne. (Courtesy Hertfordshire Archives and Libraries (HALS))

record says simply: Elizabeth Viscountess Melbourne, buried Hatfield 14 April, aged 66, F. I. Faithful, Curate.'[8]

Anyone expecting today to find a marble tomb or monument marking the last resting place of Lady M and her son, who was twice Prime Minister, will be disappointed. There is a Salisbury chapel containing the ornate tomb of Robert Cecil, with his effigy on top showing how he was in life, and a skeleton underneath, as a reminder to parishioners that the high and mighty first Lord Salisbury left the world as he came into it, with nothing.

In contrast to the Cecils and the Salisburys, there is nothing to show Lady Melbourne is buried here. The entrance to the Melbourne vault disappeared from view when the nave was rebuilt in 1870. A guide book to the church says the 'vault was well nigh forgotten until it was recovered by the late Clerk, who remembered the interment; the entrance is immediately beneath the pulpit.' The only sign the Melbournes are buried at Hatfield is a brass plate to the Second Viscount Melbourne on a pillar behind the pulpit.

Byron said of her:

Lady M who might have been my mother excited an interest in my feelings that few young women have been able to awaken. She was a charming person – a sort of modern Aspasia, uniting the energy of a man's mind with the delicacy and tenderness of a woman's. She wrote and spoke admirably, because she felt admirably. Envy, malice, hatred or uncharitableness found no place in her feelings. She had all of the philosophy, save its moroseness, and all of nature, save its defects and general faiblesse ... I have often thought that, with a little more youth, Lady M might have turned my head, at all events she often turned my heart, by bringing me back to mild feelings when the demon passion was strong within me. Her mind and heart were as fresh as if only sixteen summers had flown over her, instead of four times that number.[9]

William can have the last word. In old age, as he reflected on his mother's life, he said: 'My mother was a most remarkable woman, not merely clever and engaging but the most sagacious woman I knew. She kept me straight as long as she lived ... A remarkable woman, and devoted mother, and excellent wife – but not chaste, not chaste.' Elizabeth, Lady M, would have concurred.

Annexe by Dr James Stone

There are a number of features of Lady Caroline Lamb's history that have been suggested to be indicative of mental illness. These include her rapid mood swings and incessant questioning as a child, and her tempers and social disinhibition as an adult. Her behaviour was often at odds with accepted etiquette, and she made no attempt to hide her affairs, which were seen by her family and acquaintances as scandalous. Her affair with Byron was characterised by an intensity that was all-consuming. On one occasion she cut herself with a knife – although it was not clear whether she intended to do this. In addition, she wrote to his publisher by forging his handwriting and requested a miniature of him. She also set fire to Byron's papers in a bonfire.

These factors have led to the speculation that she might have had a diagnosis of bipolar affective disorder, however there appears little evidence to support this diagnosis according to current diagnostic criteria. There were no long periods of intractable depression, as far as can be ascertained from what has been written, and the episodes of disinhibition appear relatively short-lived and impulsive. Some of her behaviours are more suggestive of histrionic personality disorder, characterised by theatricality, exaggerated expression of emotions, suggestibility, continual seeking of excitement and being the centre of attention. Alternatively, and rather more speculatively, it is possible that she may have had some aspects of a pervasive developmental disorder (Asperger's syndrome). She appeared to have difficulty in understanding social conventions at times, and as a child, her behaviour was noted to be particularly difficult to cope with. For example, she had frequent uncontrollable tempers, and she became easily distressed when her carers did not answer her questions in ways that she wanted them to. In later life, this also manifested in her apparent naivety when dealing with her peers. This diagnosis appears less likely when considered in the context of her abilities in social situations in her later life – apparently finding socialising and forming friendships easy – although these were often considered outside normal behaviour for someone of her station, and on some occasions 'beyond the pale'. Whether this was because Lady Caroline was unable to understand the expectations of society, or on the other hand, that she did understand them but decided to ignore them is a matter for conjecture. It is worthy of note, however, that females with Asperger's syndrome are often much more objectively able to cope in social situations than their male counterparts.

Lastly I should highlight the fact that it is exceptionally difficult to construct a robust psychiatric formulation based entirely on historical notes and so these suggestions should be taken entirely as speculation, and not as a formal statement of her likely diagnosis. Indeed, it is perfectly possible that Lady Caroline Lamb did not have any formal psychiatric diagnosis, and her behaviour merely represented that of a free thinker who did not wish to conform to societal norms. It remains a matter of speculation whether today she would be classified as having a mental illness

Dr James Stone, Clinical Senior Lecturer in Psychiatry, King's College London Institute of Psychiatry, Psychology and Neuroscience, Honorary Consultant Psychiatrist, South London and Maudsley NHS Trust

Postscript

The first Viscount Melbourne, Elizabeth's husband, sank into heavy drinking and senility following his wife's death. He died in 1828 aged eighty-three and his remains joined his wife in the family vault at Hatfield Church. His hereditary title went to his second son, William, although Peniston almost certainly was not his biological father.

William Lamb, the second Viscount Melbourne became Queen Victoria's first Prime Minister, when she was only eighteen. She doted on him. He served as Prime Minister from March to November 1834 under William IV and then from 1835 to 1841. He never married again after his wife Caroline's death, but he had at least two mistresses including Sheridan's daughter, Mrs Caroline Norton, whose husband sued Lord Melbourne for 'criminal conversation' with his wife, but lost. He died aged sixty-nine at Brocket Hall on 24 November 1848 after a stroke and was buried in the Melbourne vault at St Etheldreda Church, Hatfield. The city of Melbourne in Australia was named after him.

Lady Caroline Lamb never became Lady Melbourne, dying before William inherited the title from his father. She spent her last years at Brocket Hall with her father-in-law and son, Augustus, after signing the deed of separation in 1825. The year before Caroline was riding across the estate in a carriage with William in front on a horse when William met a funeral procession at the turnpike and asked whose funeral it was. It was Byron's. He had died at Missolonghi, Greece, from a fever and his body was being carried in a black funeral carriage to its final resting place in Hucknall near Newstead Abbey. 'He was very much affected and shocked,' Caroline recalled. 'I of course was not told.' When she did find out, 'it made me very ill again.' On 2 October 1827 her doctor wrote to William saying that because of the presence of fluid gathered and felt on her abdomen, and other disease, 'I have apprehensions of the greatest danger.' He added a note dictated by Caroline: 'My dearest William, I really feel better.' She died on 25 January 1828 as a result of oedema, fluid retention, after years of heavy drinking and laudanum abuse. She was forty-two. She was buried in the churchyard at St Etheldreda's Church, Hatfield. Her son **Augustus** died in 1836 aged twenty-nine.

Frederick Lamb, third Viscount Melbourne, and the last of the Melbournes, inherited the family title when his brother William died. He was in the diplomatic service in posts in Sicily and Vienna as the British Ambassador and married Alexandrina, who was thirty years younger than him. He later became Lord Beauvale but died childless aged seventy in 1853 and the Melbourne title expired. Brocket Hall then passed to the Cowper family.

Emily Lamb, Countess Cowper and Lady Palmerston took over from her mother as a great society hostess in the Victorian era. She had her mother's gift for practical politics, and her sexual drive – while married to Earl Cowper, she had a long affair with Lord Palmerston, Foreign Secretary and Prime Minister. She married Palmerston in 1839 after her husband's death. 'Pam' was known as 'Lord Cupid' because of his sexual conquests. Visitors to the snooker room at Brocket Hall are today told that Palmerston is said to have died here – having sex with a maid on the snooker table in 1865. He was given a state funeral and buried in the north transept at Westminster Abbey. Emily died in 1869 aged eighty-two and was buried with Palmerston.

George Gordon, Lord Byron never returned to England after fleeing to the Continent in 1816. He died from fever on 19 April 1824 aged thirty-six at Missolonghi, Aetolia, then part of the Ottoman Empire, now mainland Greece. He was buried at the church of St Mary Magdalene, Hucknall, near Newstead Abbey, his ancestral home. His wife, Annabella 'Bell' Noel Byron, divorced him in 1816 and lived until 1860 when she died aged sixty-seven from breast cancer. She is buried at Kensal Green Cemetery, London. Their daughter, Ada, Countess Lovelace, collaborated with Charles Burbage on the development of the first computer.

Melbourne House, Whitehall was sold after the first Viscount Melbourne died in 1828 to Agar Ellis, an MP who was made Lord Dover in 1831. It then became known as Dover House and its notoriety largely forgotten. In 1885, it was acquired by the government and offered to Gladstone in 1886 as his residence instead of Number Ten when he was Prime Minister but he turned it down for being too grand – he said it would require him 'to receive' guests. It was allocated to Scottish ministers and remains the London office of the Scotland Office today. It has five floors including the basement and is unique in Whitehall for having no lift.

Melbourne House Piccadilly remains largely intact, though it was turned into luxury bachelor flats known as 'sets' and renamed Albany after it was sold by the Duke of York and Albany in 1802. A two-bed flat there today can sell for £7 million. Residents have included Lord Byron in set 2A, and several Prime Ministers including Sir Edward Heath, William Gladstone and Lord Melbourne, who was born there and for a time lived in one of the apartments.

George Wyndham, third Earl of Egremont, believed to be the father of William Lamb and probably Emily and Frederick Lamb, died in 1837 – from inflammation of the trachea – without an heir, and the title passed to his nephew, George, on whose death in 1845 it became extinct. In 1947 Petworth House was passed with a large endowment to the National Trust. It is partly occupied by the writer Lord Max Egremont, son of John Wyndham who was created a Baron in 1963 and revived the Egremont title.

Prince George, the Prince Regent – probably the father of George Lamb – set the style for the Regency period, commissioning Regent Street and spending lavishly on Buckingham Palace and Brighton Pavilion. He plunged the monarchy into a series of controversies after Lady Melbourne's death. He tried to divorce Queen Caroline by introducing a Pains and Penalties Bill in Parliament over allegations of her adultery with a string of lovers at her house in Blackheath, South East London. Caroline was in Italy where she was rumoured to have taken a lover, but returned to defend herself in a public show trial in the House of Lords. The bill was abandoned before a vote in the Commons, and it backfired on the Prince Regent, making Caroline more popular than ever. His father died in 1820 and on 19 July 1821 George barred Caroline from his coronation as George IV at Westminster Abbey, leaving her demanding entry at the great West door. She died within a month, on 7 August 1821, conveniently for George. He died in 1830 aged sixty-seven and was buried – unmourned by most – at St George's Chapel, Windsor Castle.

George Lamb, playwright and Whig MP. When his brother William went to the Home Office, George went with him as a home office minister in Lord Grey's administration until his death in 1834, aged forty-nine. He married Caroline St Jules, the Duke of Devonshire's illegitimate daughter by Bess Foster but they had no children.

The Milbanke Title was held by Lady Melbourne's older brother, Ralph, the sixth baronet, until his death on 19 March 1825 at the age of seventy-seven though from 1815 he changed his name to Noel. It continued until 24 November 1947 when it died out with Sir Ralph, the twelfth baronet, an adventurer who shot himself aged forty-two in his flat in Mayfair.

Select Bibliography

Byron's Corbeau Blanc, Jonathan David Gross, Liverpool University Press, Liverpool 1997.

Lord Byron's Wife, Malcolm Elwin, Macdonald and Co, London 1962.

The Countess, the Scandalous Life of Frances, Lady Jersey, Tim Clarke, Amberley 2016.

Georgiana, the Duchess of Devonshire, Amanda Foreman, HarperCollins, London 1998.

Lady Caroline Lamb, A Biography, Paul Douglass, Palgrave Macmillan, London 2004.

Memoirs of William, Second Viscount Melbourne, edited by W. M. Torrens, Macmillan and Co, London 1878.

In Whig Society, Lady Airlie, Hodder and Stoughton, London 1921.

The Life and Letters of Lady Sarah Lennox, John Murray, London 1902.

Peace in Piccadilly, Lady Birkenhead, Hamish Hamilton, London 1958.

Letters of Horace Walpole, Clarendon Press, Oxford 1903.

Lord Melbourne, L G Mitchell, Oxford University Press, Oxford 1997.

Melbourne: A Biography, Philip Zeigler, Random House, London 1976.

Manuscript Sources

Lady Melbourne's correspondence, Lamb papers, British Library.

Chatsworth Archive of correspondence between Lady Melbourne and the two Duchesses of Devonshire, Georgiana and Bess.

Lamb papers, Hertfordshire County Council Archives and Local Studies (HALS), Hertford.

Lovelace Collection for Lady Byron correspondence with Annabella, Lady Byron, Bodleian Library, Oxford.

Melbourne Hall Archives, Melbourne Hall, Lamb and Milbanke records.

Murray Archives for Byron letters, John Murray Publishers, London.

Chatsworth, Melbourne correspondence with Georgiana, Duchess of Devonshire.

Maidstone Libraries and Archives, correspondence regarding Cox Heath.

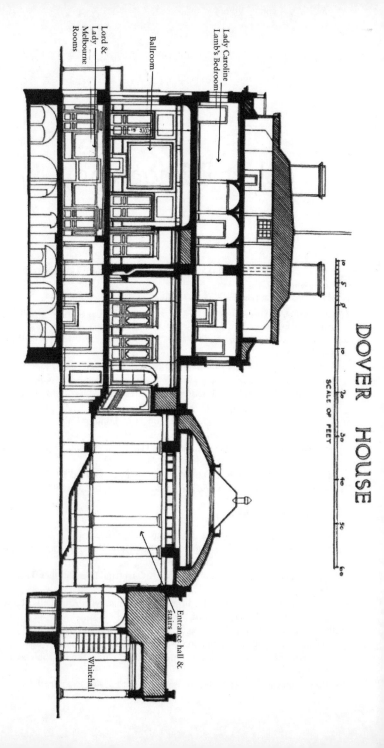

DOVER HOUSE

SCALE OF FEET

SECTION THROUGH CENTRE LOOKING NORTH

Lord &
Lady
Melbourne
Rooms

Ballroom

Lady Caroline
Lamb's Bedroom

Entrance hall &
stairs

Whitehall

Notes

Introduction

1 *Whitehall the Street that Shaped a Nation*, Colin Brown, Simon and Schuster, London 2009.

2 p24 *The Young Melbourne*, David Cecil, Constable, London 1939.

3 f46-47 Add MSS 45547 Lamb Papers British Library

4 p150 *Byron's Corbeau Blanc*, Jonathan David Gross, Liverpool University Press, Liverpool 1997.

5 p275 *Life of Lord Byron*, Thomas Moore, John Murray, London 1854.

6 *Records of a Girlhood*, Frances Ann Kemble, Chapter III Volume One, Henry Holt and Co, New York 1880.

1 A Marriage of Convenience

1 p1 *Fatal Females*, Howard Usher, Melbourne Hall Publications, Melbourne Derbyshire 1990.

2 Comparative prices are complex. I've used the online calculator at Measuringworth.com

3 p19 *Memoirs of William, second Viscount Melbourne*, edited by W. M. Torrens, Macmillan and Co, London 1878.

4 'Breeders and Breeding', David Wilkinson, *Early Horse Racing in Yorkshire*, Old Bald Peg Publications, York 2003.

5 Yorkshire Parish Registers and Bishop's Transcripts.

6 The Gay Delavals, Seaton Delaval, National Trust online https://www.nationaltrust.org.uk/seaton-delaval-hall/features/the-gay-delavals)

7 Baptism register 1751 Croft-on-Tees PR/CRO North Yorkshire County Record Office.

8 p41 *The Buildings of England – Yorkshire: the North Riding* by Nikolaus Pevsner, Yale University Press, New Haven and London 1966.

9 p36 J. Charles Fox, *Bench-ends in English Churches*, Oxford University Press, London 1916)

10 According to the school's archives he arrived in 1761 when he was only nine, but that may be a mistake. Eton College archives register of boys from 1441.

11 'Letter from a Gentleman at Hexham Monday night March 9', *Leeds Intelligencer* 24 March 1761.

12 The house was saved in 2016 by a £7 million government grant. 'Wentworth Woodhouse – why the government saved Britain's greatest and least known historic house', *Daily Telegraph*, 23 November 2016.

13 Milbanke, Vol II, *Pedigree of Yorkshire families*, Wilfred Head, London 1874.

2 Peniston

1 p150 Vol V *The Memoirs of Sophia Baddeley*, published by Mrs Elizabeth Steele, London 1787.

2 p2 *Fatal Females*, Howard Usher, Melbourne Hall Publications, Melbourne Derbyshire 1990.

3 X94 Lothian Box 1 Bundle 2 No 5, Lamb Archive, Melbourne Hall.

4 p3 Vol I *Lady Palmerston and Her Times*, Mabell Countess of Airlie, Hodder and Stoughton, London 1922.

5 p318 *George Stubbs Painter*, Judy Egerton, catalogue for Stubbs exhibition, Yale University Press, London 2007.

6 p55 ibid.

7 p52 *Lord Byron's Wife*, Malcolm Elwin, Macdonald and Co, London 1962.

8 T70/1507 'Company of Royal Adventurers of England trading with Africa', National Archive.

9 p10 Torrens.

10 Matthew Lamb MP, Eveline Cruickshanks, historyofparliament.com.

11 ibid

12 p8 Torrens

13 *The Complete Peerage of England*, Alan Sutton Publishing, Gloucester 2000.

14 X94/234/3/11 Melbourne Archive, Melbourne Hall, Melbourne Derbsyhire.

15 In the 1930s, the Lambs' house became the Sackville Gallery, which pioneered modernist painting; it survived the war but not the developers and was remodelled as offices. It is now the London office of Pakistan International Airlines.

3 'He Must and Would See Her'

1 p50 *Harris's List of Covent-Garden Ladies*, British Library PC 22a12-15.

2 p398 *The English, A Social History 1066-1945*, Christopher Hibbert, HarperCollins, London 1988.

3 Olive Baldwin, Thelma Wilson, 'Baddeley, Sophia' (bap. 1744, d. 1786)', *Oxford Dictionary of National Biography*, Oxford University Press, 2004; online edn, January 2015. http://www.oxforddnb.com/view/article/1017.

4 William Hanger, Mary M Drummond, historyofparliamentonline.com

5 p31 vol 1 *The Memoirs of Sophia Baddeley*.

6 *Restituta, Titles, Extracts and Characters of Old Books Revived* by Sir Egerton Brydges, Longman London 1814

7 Will of Dr Robert Lamb, Bishop of Peterborough, Prob 11_952_350, National Archives, Kew.

8 Sophia Baddeley mezzotint, Sir Joshua Reynolds National Portrait Gallery NPG D578

9 Sophia Baddeley engraving after Sir Joshua Reynolds, British Museum.

10 p144 *The Memoirs of Sophia Baddeley*.

11 p212 *George Selwyn his Letters and His Life*, T. Fisher Unwin, London 1899.

12 p4 *In Whig Society*, Lady Airlie, Hodder and Stoughton, London 1921.

13 p79 *The Memoirs of Sophia Baddeley*.

14 'The Way up was Horizontal', Selina Hastings, *Daily Telegraph* 18 August 2003.

15 p18 Torrens

16 p201, *The Memoirs of Sophia Baddeley*.

4 Maternal Affection and How to Create a Salon

1 p152, *Stubbs, The British School catalogue, National Gallery,* by Judy Egerton, Yale University Press, London, 1998.

2 Letter from Byron to Lady Melbourne 7 May 1813, British Library 1813.

3 p16 Torrens.

4 p142 Vol 3 *The Memoirs of Sophia Baddeley*.

5 p99 *Recollections of Society in France and England*, Lady Clementina Davies, Hurst and Blackett, 1872.

6 *Annals of Almacks*, E Beresford Chancellor, Grant Richards, London 1922.

7 p262 *The Life and Letters of Lady Sarah Lennox*, John Murray, London 1902.

8 Letter from Walpole to the Countess of Upper Ossory, 27 March 1773, *Letters of Horace Walpole* Volume Eight, Clarendon Press, Oxford 1903.

9 p263 ibid

10 p29 *George Stubbs, Painter*, by Judy Egerton, Catalogue Raisonné, published for the Paul Mellon Centre by Yale University Press, London 2007.

11 Vol I *Life and Times of C J Fox*, Earl Russell, London 1859-67.

12 p241 *The Art of Ceramics, European Ceramic Designs 1500-1830*, Howard Coutts, Yale University Press, London 2001.

13 p367-389 Albany, *Survey of London*, London County Council, London 1963

14 p91 *Sir William Chambers Architect to George III* edited by John Harris and Michael Snodin, Courtauld Institute of Art, published by Yale University Press, London 1996.

15 Chambers plan for Melbourne House, SM 43/3/45 John Soane Museum.

16 p93 *Sir William Chambers, Architect to George III* by John Harris, Michael Snodin, Courtauld Institute of Art, Yale University Press, London 1996.

17 f107 Add MSS 41133, Lamb Papers British Library.

18 The Panshanger Cabinets in Context, James Lomax, Firle Place website, www.firle.com/panshanger-cabinets-context/

19 f51 Add MSS 41135, Lamb Papers British Library.

20 p53 Torrens.

5 Halcyon Days at Melbourne House – and an Unmasking

1 p48 *Georgiana, Duchess of Devonshire*, Amanda Foreman, HarperCollins, London 1998.

2 p32 *Memoirs of Viscount Melbourne*, Torrens.

3 p3 *Clouds, The Biography of a Country House*, Caroline Dakers, Yale University Press, London 1993.

4 p474 Letter Lady Bessborough to Lord Granville Leveson Gower, 31 August 1813, *Private Correspondence of Lord Granville* Vol II, John Murray, London 1916.

5 p205 *The Home of the Hollands* by the Earl of Ilchester, John Murray, London 1937.

6 p15 *Peace in Piccadilly*, Lady Birkenhead, Hamish Hamilton, London 1958.

7 CS5/MSS 165, Letter from the Duchess of Devonshire to Countess Spencer 1 November 1776, Chatsworth Archive.

8 p4 *Fatal Females*, Howard Usher, Melbourne Hall Publications, Melbourne Derbyshire 1990.

9 p16 Torrens.

10 p143, Vol 5 *Memoirs of Sophia Baddeley*.

11 f114v Add MSS 41133, British Museum

12 Melbourne to Chambers letter, 13 November 1774 R.I.B.A. library.

13 ibid
14 p24 *The Young Melbourne*, Lord David Cecil, Constable, London 1939.

6 Georgiana

1 p22 *Georgiana, The Duchess of Devonshire*, Foreman.
2 13 October 1775, *The Letters and Journals of Lady Mary Coke*, published David Douglas, Edinburgh 1889-96.
3 p105-106 Vol II *Memoirs of Lady Hester Stanhope*, Henry Colburn, London 1845.
4 Horace Walpole letter to Countess of Upper Ossory, 1 February 1775, *Letters of Horace Walpole*, Clarendon Press, Oxford 1903.
5 f14 Add MSS 45548, Letter from Duchess of Devonshire to Lady Melbourne, Lamb Papers, British Library.
6 f92 ibid
7 CS5/MSS 37, 27 October 1774 Countess Spencer to Georgiana, Chatsworth Archive.
8 p48 *Georgiana, Duchess of Devonshire*, Foreman.
9 14 July 1775, *Letters and Journals* Lady Mary Coke
10 p275 *Life and Letters of Lady Sarah Lennox*.
11 On American Taxation, speech on a motion to repeal tea duty by Edmund Burke, published in January 1775
12 Bedfordshire Record Office L/30/9/97/36.
13 Hertfordshire election of 1774, historyofparliamentonline.org.
14 p5 Vol I *Lady Palmerston and Her Times*, Mabell Countess of Airlie, Hodder and Stoughton, London 1922.
15 CS5/MSS 94, Letter from Georgiana to Countess Spencer, 13 September 1775, Chatsworth Archive.
16 CS5/MSS 96, Letter from Georgiana Duchess of Devonshire to Countess Spencer from Chatsworth 21 September 1775, Chatsworth Archive.
17 *The Sylph, a Novel in two volumes*, Duchess of Devonshire, Lowndes, London 1779.
18 p24 *Byron's Corbeau Blanc*, Jonathan David Gross, Liverpool University Press, Liverpool, 1997.
19 p16 *Peace in Piccadilly*, Birkenhead.
20 6 July 1776 Letters, Lady Coke.
21 p261 Letter from Sarah Lennox to Susan O'Brien 20 November 1777 *Life and Letters of Lady Sarah Lennox*.
22 p139 *Memoirs of George Selwyn and his Contemporaries*, L C Page and Company, London 1902.

23 p241 *Georgiana*, Foreman.

24 6 July 1776, *Letters* Lady Mary Coke.

25 *Letters Horace Walpole* Vol 6 to Horace Mann 20 August 1776.

26 21 September 1776, *Letters* Lady Mary Coke.

27 p130 *Lesbian Dames, Sapphism in the Long Eighteenth Century*, Caroline Gonda, Routledge, London 2016.

28 Lady Sarah Lennox to Lady Susan O'Brien Goodwood 23 November 1778, *Life and Letters of Lady Sarah Lennox*.

29 p251-2 ibid

30 p174 *Life of Anne Damer, portrait of a Georgian artist*, Jonathan David Gross, Lexington Books, Plymouth UK 2014.

31 CS5/MSS 136.1, Letter Lady Melbourne to the Duchess of Devonshire August 1776, Chatsworth Archive.

32 p21 *Peace in Piccadilly*, Birkenhead.

33 p52 *Lord Byron's Wife*, Malcolm Elwin, Macdonald and Co, London 1962.

7 Cocks Heath

1 p114 *The Devonshire House Circle*, Hugh Stokes, Herbert Jenkins, London 1917.

2 *London Chronicle* 20-23 June 1778.

3 Colonel Lord Cranborne's Orderly Book, Hatfield House Archive.

4 CS5/MSS 213, Letter from Georgiana, Duchess of Devonshire to Lady Spencer 11 July 1778, Chatsworth Archive.

5 Field officers' short-tailed coatee Derbyshire militia, National Army Museum NAM 1960-07-198-1

6 *London Chronicle* 13-16 June 1778.

7 p117 *The Devonshire House Circle*, Hugh Stokes, published by Herbert Jenkins, London 1917.

8 CS5/MSS 213B, Letter from Georgiana to Lady Spencer, 13 July 1778, Chatsworth Archive.

9 CS5/MSS 212 ibid, Chatsworth Archive.

10 Cox-Heath Intelligence *Morning Chronicle* 18 July 1778.

11 CS5/MSS 233, Letter from Georgiana to Countess Spencer 26 October 1778 Chatsworth Archive.

12 p1 *The Countess, the Scandalous Life of Frances, Lady Jersey*, Tim Clarke, Amberley 2016.

13 p36 Vol 5 *Historical Memoirs of My Own Time*, Sir N William Wraxall, Kegan Paul Trench Trubner, London 1904.

14 p75 *The Devonshire House Circle*, Stokes.

15 CS5/MSS 233, Letter from Georgiana to Lady Spencer 26 October 1778, Chatsworth Archive.

16 p151 *Lady Worsley's Whim*, Hallie Rubenhold, Chatto and Windus, London 2008.

17 p147 ibid.

18 'A trip to Cock's Heath', etching by John Hamilton Mortimer, 1851.0901.9 British Museum.

19 CS5/MSS 217E, Letter from Georgiana to Countess Spencer 29 July-3 August 1778, Chatsworth Archive.

20 CS5/MSS 310, ibid August 6 1778 Chatsworth Archive.

21 CS5/MSS 227, ibid, 18 October 1778, Chatsworth Archive.

22 p169 *Observations on the Means of preserving the Health of Soldiers*, Vol I, Donald Monro, John Murray, London 1780.

23 CS5/MSS 237, Letter from Countess Spencer to Georgiana, 5 December 1778, Chatsworth Archive.

24 CS5/MSS 256 ibid, 30 October 1779 Chatsworth Archive.

8 William

1 The register for baptisms shows William was baptised at St James, Westminster but not exactly where. It may have been the Chapel Royal but I have assumed it was at St James Piccadilly, the same church the Melbournes used for Pen's christening.

2 p63 *In Whig Society*, Airlie.

3 Greville Memoirs part two of three, *A Journal of the Reign of Queen Victoria*, 29 November 1848, Longmans and Green and Co, London 1899.

4 p53 *Lord Byron's Wife*, Elwin.

5 p17 *Melbourne*, Philip Ziegler, Random House, London 1976.

6 p23 *Memoirs of the Rt Hon William Second Viscount Melbourne*, W M Torrens.

7 p320 *Biographical Catalogue of the Portraits at Panshanger the seat of Earl Cowper*, M. Boyle 1885.

8 Journal, William Lamb DE/Lb F2 Hertfordshire Archives and Local Studies, Hertford.

9 f3 Add MSS 45911, Letter from Peniston Lamb to Lady Melbourne 5 March 1780, Lamb Papers, British Library.

10 *The Turf Register and Sportsman Breeder's Stud-book*, W Pick and R Johnson, published by Sampson, York 1822.

11 p252 Vol XI, *Letters of Horace Walpole*, Clarendon Press, Oxford 1904.

12 CS5/ MSS 401.1, Letter from Lady Melbourne to the Duchess of Devonshire, Chatsworth Archive.

13 Amanda Foreman interview, 'Secrets of Chatsworth', PBS TV America.

14 CS5/MSS 401.1, Letter from Lady Melbourne to Duchess of Devonshire, Chatsworth Archive.

15 p416 *Georgiana, the Duchess of Devonshire*, Foreman.

16 p46 *George IV*, Christopher Hibbert, Penguin Books, London 1976.

17 8 August 1782 p23 Vol II Letters, *Lady Sarah Lennox*.

18 p32 *George IV*, Christopher Hibbert, Penguin Books, London 1988.

19 p356 Vol V Wraxall.

20 p45 *George IV* Hibbert.

21 William Pitt, HistoryofParliament online.

22 Lady Sarah Lennox to Lady Susan O'Brien 25 March 1783 p33 *The Life and Letters of Lady Sarah Lennox*.

23 The king's notes, royal recipe books, and the Prince of Wales's bills are available for the first time online thanks to the imaginative Georgian Papers Programme by Windsor Archives. RA, GEO/MAIN/5346 www.georgianpapersprogramme.com

24 p36 Vol II 25 March 1783 *Letters, Lady Sarah Lennox*.

9 The Affectionate Brothers

1 p29 *Memoirs of Lord Melbourne*, W. M. Torrens.

2 RCIN 810060, 12 April 1784 Thomas Rowlandson, Royal Collection.

3 1784 election www.historyofparliamentonline.com

4 Chapter VIII, *Carlton House*, British History Online, first published by Cassell Petter and Galpin, London, 1878.

5 ibid

6 p95 *High Society in the Regency Period*, Venetia Murray, Penguin Books, London 1999.

7 Georgian Papers Programme, gpp.royalcollection.org.uk

8 p199 Queen Victoria's Journals online www.queenvictoriasjournals.org

9 p3 *Fatal Females*, Howard Usher Melbourne Hall Publications, Melbourne Derbyshire 1990.

10 Lamb, Hon. George of Whitehall Yard Westminster, historyofparliamentonline.org 1820-32 ed D R Fisher Cambridge University press, Cambridge, 2009.

11 p427 Volume I, Letters of Sydney Smith/George Lamb MP www.historyofparliamentonline.org

12 p20 Greville Memoirs, Longmans Green and Co, London 1899.

13 p11 *Fatal Females*, Howard Usher, Melbourne Hall Publications, Melbourne Derbyshire 1990.

14 p27 *Memoirs of Viscount Melbourne*, Torrens.

15 p318 *George Stubbs Painter*, Judy Egerton, Yale University Press, 2007.

16 Friday 30 July 1841 Queen Victoria's Journals, online http://www.queenvictoriasjournals.org/home.do

17 22 December 1837 Queen Victoria's Journals, Windsor Castle online archive www.queenvictoriasjournals.org.

18 Melbourne papers, Hatfield House Archive, and p99 *In Whig Society*, Mabell Lady Airlie, Hodder and Stoughton, London 1922.

19 13 June 1816, *The Times* archive.

10 Emily

1 p9 *Fatal Females* Howard Usher Melbourne Hall Publications 1990.

2 *The Times*, 19 October 1786.

3 *The Times*, 17 August 1787.

4 DE/Lb F2, William Lamb's autobiographical journal, Hertfordshire Archives.

5 15 October 1838 Queen Victoria's Journals, queenvictoriasjournals.org

6 'The Genius of the Mad King' BBC 2017.

7 p127 *George IV*, Hibbert.

8 p51 *The Debate on the Subject of a Regency, House of Commons 16 December 1788*, published by John Stockdale, Piccadilly, London 1788.

9 What was the truth about the madness of George III? 15 April 2013, *BBC Magazine*.

10 Covent Garden, 3 December 1789, *The Times*.

11 The House Swap

1 p176 Vol V *Byron Letters and Journals* ed Rowland E. Prothero, John Murray, London, 1833.

2 f10 Add MS 45548 Lamb Papers, British Library.

3 p34 Vol I Torrens.

4 Correspondence of Sir William Chambers at the Royal Institute of British Architects archive.

5 Public Breakfast, 10 December 1791 *The Times* archive.

6 p30 *Peace in Piccadilly, the Story of Albany*, Lady Birkenhead.

7 p89-92 Obituary of Lord Egremont *The Gentleman's Magazine* 9,1 new series, 1838.

8 p20 *In Whig Society*, Airlie.

9 CS5/MSS 310, Letter Georgiana to Countess Spencer 6 August 1778, Chatsworth Archive.

10 p20 *The Young Melbourne and Lord M*, David Cecil Phoenix Press, London 2001.

11 p51 *Peace in Piccadilly*, Birkenhead.

12 p 248 Byron letter to Lady Melbourne 30 March 1814, *Lord Byron's Correspondence*, edited by John Murray, re-issue Cambridge University Press, Cambridge 2011.

13 1 April 1814 Letter Lady Melbourne to Lord Byron, John Murray archive.

12 Tragedy

1 Lady Melbourne to Prince of Wales, 10 July 1795 p82 *Byron's Corbeau Blanc*, Jonathan David Gross, Liverpool University Press, Liverpool 1998.

2 p169 *Prince of Pleasure*, David Saul, Little Brown, London, 1998.

3 p87 Vol III *History of Britain*, Simon Schama, BBC Worldwide, London 2002.

4 p61 Volume I Torrens.

5 10 March 1802 House of Commons report C J Fox motion on the Character of Francis, Duke of Bedford.

6 Commonplace Book, Panshanger f28 MSS D/ELb Hertfordshire Archives and Local Studies, Hertford.

7 Hon Peniston Lamb, R G Thorne, historyofparliamentonline.org

8 p56 Vol I Torrens.

9 p48 *Lord Melbourne*, L G Mitchell, Oxford University Press, Oxford 1997.

10 p525 *Melbourne: A Biography*, Philip Zeigler.

11 p32 *Lord Melbourne's papers*, Longmans, London 1889.

12 p79 *The Young Melbourne*, Lord David Cecil, Constable, London 1939.

13 p41 Torrens.

14 p66 *The Young Melbourne*, Cecil.

15 p47 *Lord Melbourne*, L G Mitchell.

16 p71 *In Whig Society*, Airlie.

17 f23 Add MS 45548 Lamb Papers, British Library. Lady Airlie p33 *In Whig Society* has transcribed 'recede' from Georgiana's handwriting but I think this is misread. By 'secede' Georgiana is referring to 'Loo' leaving the Whig party for the Tories.

18 f26 Add MS 45548 Lamb Papers, British Library.

19 f24 Add MS 45548 Lamb Papers, British Library.

20 p50 *In Whig Society*, Airlie.

21 Pic Nic Fete, 28 June 1802 *The Times*.

22 p40 *Byron's Corbeau Blanc*, Gross.

23 Journal William Lamb DE/Lb F2 Hertfordshire Archives and Local Studies, Hertford.

13 Two Weddings and a Funeral

1 p61 Vol II *Private Correspondence of first Earl Granville 1781-1821* John Murray, London 1916.

2 p80 *In Whig Society*, Airlie.

3 p222 *The Two Duchesses, family correspondence relating to Georgiana Duchess of Devonshire and Elizabeth, Duchess of Devonshire*, Blackie and Son, London 1898.

4 p8 *Lady Caroline Lamb, A Biography*, Paul Douglass, Palgrave Macmillan, London 2004.

5 p24 *Lady Caroline Lamb*, Douglass.

6 p211 Vol II, *Lady Morgan's Memoirs*, W H Allen, London 1862.

7 p43 *The Byron Women*, Margot Strickland, Peter Owen Limited, London 1974.

8 Lady Bessborough had devised code names for all the principal characters in her correspondence with Lord Granville when he became British ambassador to Russia. Canning was the Pope, Pitt – My Uncle, Fox – Anne, Grey – Eliza: p465 Vol I *Private Correspondence of Earl Granville 1781-1821* John Murray, London 1916.

9 p5 *Fatal Females*, Howard Usher, Melbourne Hall Publications, Melbourne Derbyshire 1990.

10 p223 *The Two Duchesses, family correspondence relating to Georgiana Duchess of Devonshire and Elizabeth, Duchess of Devonshire*, Blackie and Son, London 1898.

11 p51 *Lady Caroline Lamb*, Paul Douglass, Palgrave Macmillan, London 2004.

12 p232 *The Two Duchesses, Georgiana Duchess of Devonshire and Elizabeth, Duchess of Devonshire, correspondence*, Blackie and Son, London 1898.

13 p52 *Lady Caroline Lamb*, Douglass.

14 p31 *Lady Caroline Lamb*, Elizabeth Jenkins, Sphere Books, London 1974.

15 f81 Add MSS 45546 note by Caroline Lamb to Lady Melbourne, Lamb Papers, British Library. It is undated but was written probably in 1810 when her relations with Lady Melbourne broke down.

16 p236 *Whitehall, the Street that Shaped a Nation*, Colin Brown, Simon and Schuster, London 2009.

17 Letter Lady Bessborough to Lord Granville Leveson-Gower, 12 June 1805, p81 Vol II Private Correspondence of Earl Granville 1781-1821 John Murray, London 1916.

18 p6 *Fatal Females*, Howard Usher, Melbourne Hall Publications 1900.

19 p155 Vol II *Private Correspondence Lord Granville* Leveson Gower, John Murray, London 1916.

20 p265 *The Two Duchesses, family correspondence relating to Georgiana Duchess of Devonshire and Elizabeth, Duchess of Devonshire*, Blackie and Son, London 1898.

21 Making Decent, ie Broad-bottomites getting into the Grand Costume, James Gillray, J397 British Museum.

22 p30 *In Whig Society*, Airlie

23 p203 Vol II *Private Correspondence, Lord Granville*

24 p94 *In Whig Society*, Airlie.

25 Letter Lady Melbourne to Lady Byron, 14 August 1816; 92 f100 Lovelace collection, Bodleian Library, Oxford.

14 Scandal

1 William Lamb speech, House of Commons, 19 November 1806, Hansard.

2 p154 *Dearest Bess, the Life and Times of Lady Elizabeth Foster*, Dorothy Margaret Stuart, Fonthill Media, UK 2012.

3 Letter Lady Bessborough to Lord Granville 29 August 1807, p277 Vol II *Private Correspondence Lord Granville* Leveson Gower, John Murray, London 1916

4 p292 ibid

5 p292 ibid

6 p29 Vol I *Lady Palmerston and Her Times*, Mabell Countess of Airlie, Hodder and Stoughton, London 1922.

7 p157 *Dearest Bess, the Life and Times of Lady Elizabeth Foster*, Dorothy Margaret Stuart, Fonthill Media, London 2012.

8 p309 Vol II, *Private Correspondence, Lord Granville* Leveson Gower, John Murray, London 1916.

9 p346 Vol II, *journals and correspondence of Miss Berry*, Longmans, London 1865.

10 p134 *Lady Caroline Lamb*, Elizabeth Jenkins, Sphere Books, London 1974.

11 f93 Add MSS 45546, Letter from Lady Caroline Lamb to Lady Melbourne, 28 September 1816, British Library.

12 p60 Vol I *Lady Palmerston and Her Times*, Mabell Countess of Airlie, Hodder and Stoughton, London 1922.

13 p62 *The Byron Women*, Margot Strickland, Peter Owen, London 1974.

14 Sir Godfrey Webster Fifth Baronet, History of Parliament Online, www.historyofparliamentonline.org.

15 p237 Vol I, *The Journal of Elizabeth Lady Holland*, Longmans Green and Co, London 1908.

16 p100 *Holland House*, Princes Marie Liechtenstein, Macmillan and Co, London 1875.

17 1 April 1838 Queen Victoria Journal, www.queenvictoriasjournals.org

18 f15 MSS 45546, Letter Lady Caroline Lamb to Lady Melbourne, 14 March 1810, Lamb Papers, British Library.

19 f16 MSS 45546, Letter Lady Melbourne to Lady Caroline Lamb, 12 April 1810, Lamb Papers, British Library.

20 f20 MSS 45546 Lamb Papers, British Library.

21 f 21 MSS 45546 Lamb Papers, British Library.

22 p155 *Two Duchesses, family correspondence relating to Georgiana Duchess of Devonshire and Elizabeth, Duchess of Devonshire*, Blackie and Son, London 1898.

23 p416, ibid

15 Byron

1 p8 *Byron: the Last Phase*, Richard Edgcumbe, Charles Scribner's Sons, New York, 1909.

2 p36 *Conversations of Lord Byron*, Thomas Medwin, printed for Henry Colburn, London 1824.

3 p105 *Lord Byron's Wife*, Elwin.

4 p114 *Lady Morgan's Memoirs*, W H Allen, London 1862.

5 p105 Vol I *Melbourne*, Torrens.

6 p451 annexe to Vol II *Lord Byron's Works and Journals*, John Murray, London 1900.

7 p372 *George IV*, Hibbert.

8 p33 *Social England under the Regency*, John Ashton, Chatto and Windus, London 1899.

9 Xl Childe Harold's Pilgrimage, *Complete Poetical Works of Lord Byron*, Routledge and Sons London 1887.

10 p104 *Melbourne*, Torrens.

11 p169 *The Young Melbourne* Lord David Cecil Pan Books, London 1948.

12 p115 *Lady Caroline Lamb*, Paul Douglass, Palgrave Macmillan, New York, 2004.

13 p199, ibid

14 William Lamb, *History of Parliament 1790-1820* published by the History of Parliament Trust, London, 2017.

15 f3 Add MSS 45546, Letter William Lamb to Lady Melbourne 29 September 1812, Lamb Papers, British Library.

16 Lady M's Unlikely Lover

1. p446 Vol II Letter from Lady Bessborough to Lord Granville Leveson Gower 12 August 1812, *private correspondence of Lord Granville 1781-1821* John Murray, London 1916.
2. p129 *In Whig Society*, Airlie.
3. Letter Byron to Lady Melbourne Cheltenham 13 September 1812, NLS MSS 43469, p71 *Lord Byron's Correspondence*, John Murray London 1922.
4. Add MSS 45547, Letter Lady Melbourne to Lord Byron, 29 September 1812, Lamb Papers, British Library.
5. f43-45 MSS 45547, Letters Lady Melbourne to Lord Byron, 29 September 1812, Lamb Papers, British Library.
6. p151 *Lord Byron's Wife*, Elwin.
7. Add MSS 43469, Letter Byron to Lady Melbourne, 6 November 1812, British Library.
8. Letter, 9 December 1812, ibid.
9. Letter Lady Caroline Lamb to Lord Byron 3 June 1814, John Murray Archive.
10. p121 *Lord Byron's Correspondence*, John Murray, London 1922.
11. Letter from Lord Byron to Lady Melbourne, 12 December 1812, John Murray.
12. Letter from Lady Caroline Lamb to Captain Thomas Medwin, annexe to *Works and Journals of Lord Byron*, Vol II John Murrary, London 1900.
13. Add MSS 43470, Letter Byron to Lady Melbourne, 6 July 1813, British Library.
14. Add MSS 45547, Letter from Lady Melbourne to Byron, 7 July 1813, British Library.

17 Honeymoon in Hell

1. p251 *Lord Byron's Wife*, Elwin.
2. p109 ibid
3. Add MS 43469, Letter from Byron to Lady Melbourne 13 September 1812, British Library.
4. p70 Lord Byron's Wife, Elwin.
5. f43-45 Add MSS 45547, Letter from Lady Melbourne to Lord Byron, Lamb Papers, British Library.
6. p134 *In Whig Society*, Airlie.
7. p111 *The Byron Women*, Margot Strickland, Peter Owen, London 1974.
8. f44/92, Letter from Lady Melbourne to Annabella Milbanke, Lovelace Collection, Bodleian Library, Oxford.

9 f82-83 Add MSS 45547 Letter from Annabella Milbanke to Lady Melbourne, Lamb Papers, British Library.

10 p70 *Byron's Wife*, Elwin.

11 Milbanke family documents, North Yorkshire County Record Office.

12 p53 *Byron's Wife*, Elwin.

13 f102/92, Letter from Lady Melbourne to Annabella Milbanke, Lovelace Collection, Bodleian Library, Oxford.

14 f84 Add MSS 45547, Letter from Annabella Milbanke to Lady Melbourne, Lamb Papers, British Library.

15 Letter from Lady Melbourne to Lord Byron, 30 April 1814, John Murray archive.

16 p235 *Vindication of Lady Byron*, Harriet Beecher Stowe, R Bentley and Son, London 1871.

17 p336 *Byron's Wife*, Elwin.

18 *Halnaby People – A History of Halnaby Hall, the estate and the people who have lived there*, published privately by Eva Banner.

18 The Monster and the Weasel

1 f73-75/92 Letter from Lady Melbourne to Lady Byron, 12 March 1815, Lovelace Archive, Bodleian Library, Oxford.

2 p173 *In Whig Society*, Airlie.

3 Wellington was so concerned for her safety he wrote personal notes to Charlotte Wedderburn-Webster before and after the battle: *The Scum of the Earth*, Colin Brown, History Press, Stroud 2015.

4 Frederick never actually got to the ball. He intended to go, but decided to stay at his post after receiving a report of a sharp skirmish on his regiment's front with a warning the enemy was advancing. At about three am, he was ordered to move to Enghien, which he reached at six am. P240 *Lady Bessborough and her Family Circle*, edited by the Earl of Bessborough and A. Aspinall, John Murray, London 1940.

5 p171 *In Whig Society*, Airlie.

6 xvii, Canto the Third, Childe Harold's Pilgrimage, *The Complete Poetical Works of Lord Byron*, Routledge and Sons, London 1887.

7 *Records of a Girlhood*, Frances Ann Kemble, Chapter III, Vol I, Henry Holt and Company, New York 1880.

8 p339 note 33, *Byron's Corbeau Blanc*, Gross.

9 p542 Vol II *Lord Granville private correspondence*, John Murray, London 1916.

10 f141 Add MSS 82963 Letter from Caroline Lamb to Lady Melbourne, undated but thought to be circa April/May 1816, Lamb papers, British Library.

11 f33 D/ELB Papers of the Lamb family of Brocket Hall, Hertfordshire Archives, Hertford.

12 p3 *Miss Eden's Letters*, Macmillan, London 1919.

13 f91 Add MSS 45546 note from Lady Caroline Lamb to Lady Melbourne, 1816, Lamb Papers, British Library.

14 p56 *The Byron Women*, Margot Strickland, Peter Owen, London 1974.

15 Letter from Lord Egremont to Lady Melbourne, Melbourne Correspondence Box, Hatfield House Archive.

16 p92 *In Whig Society*, Airlie.

17 f119 Add MSS 45546 Caroline Lamb to Lady Melbourne, undated 1817, British Library.

18 f130 Add MSS 45548 Lady Caroline Lamb to Lady Melbourne 1816, British Library.

19 Letter from Lady Caroline Lamb to Captain Thomas Medwin, annexe *Byron's Letters and Journals* Vol II, John Murray, London, 1833.

20 p456 *Byron's Wife*, Elwin.

21 p14 *Vindication of Lady Byron*, Harriet Beecher Stowe, R Bentley and Son, London 1871.

22 p5-10 Journal of Queen Victoria, 30 March 1838 www.queenvictoriasjournals.org

23 p6 *Fatal Females*, Howard Usher, Melbourne Hall Publications 1990.

19 The Last Word

1 Letter from Lady Melbourne to Lord Byron, 31 January 1815, 377 Lovelace archive.

2 p352 *Byron's Corbeau Blanc*, Jonathan David Gross, Liverpool University Press, Liverpool, 1998.

3 De/LB f85/1 Lamb Papers, Hertfordshire Archives, Hertford.

4 d/Elb F85/5 ibid

5 Dec 31 1837-Jan 1 1838, Queen Victoria's Journal, www.queenvictoriasjournals.org.

6 p7 *Fatal Females*, Usher.

7 p463 *George IV* Christopher Hibbert, Penguin Books, London 1976.

8 DP46/1/60 Hatfield burial register.

9 p163 *The Works of Lord Byron, Letters and Journals* Vol II John Murray, London 1833.

Acknowledgements

In common with many writers, I owe a debt of gratitude to the many institutions that have uploaded rare and out-of-print volumes of letters and journals, papers and books to the internet for the first time; they include HM Queen Elizabeth II's Archives at Windsor, which have made available a vast quantity of material online, from Queen Victoria's journals, George III's essays and menus for royal banquets to the Prince Regent's household bills, through the imaginative Georgian Papers Programme. It is to be hoped the National Archives at Kew and the British Library get the funding they need to put more manuscripts and papers online. My thanks are due to the staff of the archives departments listed in my sources for their unfailing courtesy; Lord Ralph Kerr for access to the archives at his private home, Melbourne Hall Derbyshire and Gill Weston for the fascinating tour of the hall; Mrs R Lister for hospitality at Halnaby Hall Stables guest house and use of *Halnaby People*, the Milbanke family history; the staff at Brocket Hall for a personal tour of the house and its contents; Duncan Jeffrey and the library staff at Westminster Abbey; Robin Harcourt Williams and Malcolm Caie for help on the whereabouts of the Melbourne vault at Hatfield Church; the staff at Maidstone Libraries and Archives for access to the Cocks Heath archives; the staff at the Bodleian Library, Oxford, for access to the Lovelace papers; the staff at the Hertfordshire County Council Archives and Local Studies (HALS) at Hertford for the files of Brocket Hall and the Melbournes; Dr Gwyneth Endersby and the archives team at the North Yorkshire Record Office, Northallerton; Aidan Haley, assistant archivist at the Chatsworth Archive, for correspondence between Lady Melbourne and Georgiana, Duchess of Devonshire; Leela Meinertas of the Victoria and Albert Museum and Patrick Baty for their expert help on Dover House; Max Egremont and Alison McCann, archivist, for assistance with the Egremont archive at the Leconfield estate; Dr Frances Sands, Curator of Drawings and Books Sir John Soane's Museum, Martine Baines and Barbara Edwards for help with French translations of Georgiana's letters, and Shaun Barrington, my editor at Amberley Publishing, for having the vision.

Index